BEYOND THE MULTIPLEX

The publisher gratefully acknowledges the generous contribution to this book provided by the Humanities Endowment Fund of the University of California Press Foundation.

Beyond the Multiplex

Cinema, New Technologies, and the Home

BARBARA KLINGER

UNIVERSITY OF CALIFORNIA PRESS

Berkeley   Los Angeles   London

University of California Press, one of the most distinguished university presses in the United States, enriches lives around the world by advancing scholarship in the humanities, social sciences, and natural sciences. Its activities are supported by the UC Press Foundation and by philanthropic contributions from individuals and institutions. For more information, visit www.ucpress.edu.

University of California Press
Berkeley and Los Angeles, California

University of California Press, Ltd.
London, England

Library of Congress Cataloging-in-Publication Data
Klinger, Barbara, 1951–
    Beyond the multiplex : cinema, new technologies, and the home / Barbara Klinger.
        p.   cm.
    Includes bibliographical references and index.
    ISBN 0-520-22315-2 (cloth : alk. paper)—ISBN 0-520-24586-5 (pbk. : alk. paper)
        1. Television—Social aspects.   2. Television—Technological innovations.   3. Motion pictures and television.   4. Home theaters. I. Title.
PN1992.6.K55   2006
302.23'45—dc22   2005005751

Manufactured in the United States of America
15   14   13   12   11   10   09   08   07   06
10   9   8   7   6   5   4   3   2   1

This book is printed on New Leaf EcoBook 50, a 100% recycled fiber of which 50% is de-inked post-consumer waste, processed chlorine free. EcoBook 50 is acid-free and meets the minimum requirements of ANSI/ASTM D5634-01 (Permanence of Paper). ∞

For Matt, Richard, and Cosmo,
my favorite fellow home theater denizens

Contents

Illustrations

TABLE

Acknowledgments

In the course of my writing this book, the multiple media and technologies that serve as its subject continued to evolve, sometimes quite dramatically. The immensity and changeability of this media landscape added challenges to the typical rigors of completing a manuscript. I am thus especially grateful to the colleagues and students who were a part of this process and to my department and university for furnishing the support necessary to finish it.

Kathleen McHugh and Chon Noriega provided invaluable suggestions about the shape of this project in its earliest and most uncertain phases. Jim Naremore, Mark Jancovich, Steve Cohan, and Matthew Solomon read parts of the manuscript and offered characteristically insightful critiques. Bob Rehak helped me rethink some of my propositions about Internet technologies and Web films. Bob, Lori Hitchcock, and Jim Kendrick served as research assistants during different stages of the book's development, and Lauren Bryant helped clarify my writing and tame my penchant for intricate Germanic sentences. The anonymous readers for the University of California Press encountered a longer draft of the manuscript and were extremely helpful in proposing ways to sharpen its concepts and tighten its structure. Special thanks to my editor Mary Francis, who provided wise counsel and unflagging support throughout the process.

Two events were particularly important in helping me to conceptualize certain parts of the book. The 2003 Annual Commonwealth Fund Conference on American History, "American Cinema and Everyday Life," convened by Melvyn Stokes, Richard Maltby, and Robert C. Allen at the University College London, greatly expanded my sense of the significance of nontheatrical cinema. My work on the impact of globalization on American cinema was similarly enhanced by one of the best intellectual experiences of my career, the Flinders Humanities Symposium, "Hollywood as World

Cinema," held at Flinders University in Adelaide, Australia, in 2002. Warmest thanks to fellow colleagues who were involved in the stimulating conversations that took place and to the people who made this event happen, Richard Maltby, Ruth Vasey, and Mike Walsh.

My research was generously supported by the Department of Communication and Culture, the Office of the Vice Chancellor for Academic Affairs and Dean of the Faculties, Research and the University Graduate School, and the Office of International Programs. In addition, Jim Naremore, Joan Hawkins, Chris Anderson, Lori Hitchcock, Bjorn Ingvoldstad, Kristin Sorensen, Michela Ardizzoni, Sherra Schick, Courtney Bailey, and Mary O'Shea allowed me to conduct the empirical component of my research in their classrooms, giving me access to hundreds of students. I'm very grateful to them and to the students who participated in the survey, providing many insights into the mysteries and pleasures of re-viewing.

Last, but certainly not least, I want to thank my family, Richard and Matt, for their patience and understanding during the years I spent writing and, most of all, for vividly reminding me on a daily basis that there is life outside the book.

As I turned in the final version of the manuscript, my colleague Jim Naremore was retiring. I have long admired his dedication to the university, his consummate professionalism, and his incredible knowledge of and passion for cinema. I hope he knows how much he will be missed.

Introduction
What Is Cinema Today?

In America there are many Fortresses of Solitude, with their
wax statues, their automata, their collections of inconsequential
wonders. You have only to go beyond the Museum of Modern
Art and the art galleries, and you enter another universe, the
preserve of the average family, the tourist, the politician.

Umberto Eco, *Travels in Hyperreality*

Introducing DishPVR. You're never going to want to leave
your house again or see your friends. Unless they come over
to watch your TV, that is.

Advertisement, *New York Times,* 2001

One of the major controversies surrounding the 1999 Academy Awards
centered on the question of how Miramax's *Shakespeare in Love,* a romantic comedy about the Bard, could have possibly won the Oscar for Best Picture over Steven Spielberg's *Saving Private Ryan,* a World War II film acclaimed for its realistic depiction of combat. Moments before the Best
Picture winner was announced, Spielberg was awarded the Oscar for Best
Director, building anticipation that, like many other directors before him,
he would sweep both prizes. When *Shakespeare in Love* won, consternation
was visible on many faces in the Dorothy Chandler Pavilion. The shock continued long after the ceremony was over, with commentators trying to figure out how such a fanciful art film had managed to triumph over a serious
historical epic with patriotic themes. Theories customarily employed on the
occasion of such Academy upsets were evoked: Was it that the war film was
a summer release and thus suffered from Academy voter forgetfulness?
Was it the subject matter, with voters preferring Elizabethan-era comedy

over the grimmer fare of a combat film? Or was this a battle of industry titans, wherein Miramax head Harvey Weinstein had simply outmuscled
Spielberg and Dreamworks SKG with an expensive promotional campaign?
Although each of these factors may have contributed to the success of
Shakespeare in Love, observers also offered a less familiar but perhaps more
vexing explanation for this palace coup. Since studios sent Academy members video copies of contending films to ensure that they were seen by as
many members as possible, voting often proceeded without benefit of the
big-screen experience. As one industry insider argued, "'Saving Private
Ryan' suffers on [video]cassette. If you see it at home, you are by no means
as impressed with it as you were in the movie theater. And 'Shakespeare in
Love' is a more intimate picture, it plays well on cassette. It may actually be
enhanced by watching it at home." In response, Dreamworks' marketing
chief, Terry Press, countered: "That goes to a larger issue. You're a member
of the Motion Picture Academy, not the television video academy. These
movies are meant to be seen in movie theaters, all of them. They're not
meant to be stopped and started and paused when the phone rings or to feed
the dog."[1]

Rather than trying to determine the real reasons for the upset, I am intrigued by what this last dispute suggests about the state of cinema today.
Press's rebuttal is based on the seamless identification of cinema with celluloid and theatrical presentation. Meanwhile, the anonymous industry insider is operating within a certain realpolitik that often governs how members of the Academy of Motion Picture Arts and Sciences—people, Press
suggests, who should presumably know better—actually watch and evaluate the contending films. Like millions of other viewers, they encountered
these movies in the comfort of their own homes through VCRs and TV sets.
Taken together, these perspectives present a kind of schizophrenic identity
for cinema, derived from its shifting material bases and exhibition contexts:
it exists both as a theatrical medium projected on celluloid and as a nontheatrical medium presented, in this case, in a video format on television. In the
uproar after the Oscar ceremony, this double identity assumes an immediate comparative aesthetic and experiential value. The big-screen performance is marked as authentic, as representing bona fide cinema. By contrast,
video is characterized not only as inauthentic and ersatz but also as a re-
grettable triumph of convenience over art that disturbs the communion between viewer and film and interferes with judgments of quality.

If this dichotomy seems familiar, it is because it long ago achieved the
status of a truism. Television in particular has often come under fire for
compromising the integrity of the cinematic text. Film scholars have amply

chronicled television's shortcomings as a showcase for cinema, pointing to its inferior image as well as to the broadcast industry's substantial alteration of films through "panning and scanning," editing for length or content, and commercial interruption. Further, since the televised film is watched amid the distractions of domestic space, home exhibition dispels the supposed rapture of theatrical viewing.[2] With such infringements in mind, Susan Sontag may express the sentiments of the film aesthete most bluntly in stating, "To see a great film only on television isn't to have really seen that film."[3] Although cable movie channels, videocassette, home theater, and DVD resolve some of these shortcomings in various ways, film exhibition via television in the casual setting of the home still appears to constitute a break with the quality and mesmerizing power of cinema in the motion picture theater.

While differences certainly exist between theatrical and nontheatrical cinemas, my book rejects the value-laden dichotomy that has continually regarded home film exhibition through a comparative lens. On the one hand, the dichotomy presumes a kind of superior stability in theatrical exhibition. The darkened establishments illuminated by projector beams and dedicated to film screenings appear to provide an ideal space for viewers, an ideal difficult for other settings characterized by diverse activities and circumstances of viewing—say, the home or the airplane—to replicate. This perspective, however, minimizes the impact of historical variability on motion picture theaters. Which kind of theater exactly represents the optimum cinematic experience: the converted storefront nickelodeon, the luxurious motion picture palace, the dilapidated dollar cinema, the shopping mall theater with paper-thin walls, the modern multiplex with stadium seating and digital sound, or the fully digital theater that lacks altogether a celluloid dimension? This flux in the nature of theaters and the experiences they provide is only exacerbated when we enter the global stage, where the type and cultural prominence of theaters vary greatly from nation to nation.

On the other hand, home exhibition does not simply constitute a parallel history that exists separately from its theatrical counterpart. The public and private incarnations of cinema are financially and experientially connected. The theatrical motion picture business has long relied on the small screen to generate profits that help to support the production of its extravaganzas, a reliance that has only grown with the enormous success of DVD. Conversely, home exhibition venues often depend on movies for programming, while also cashing in on the ability of blockbusters and other noted films to attract viewers. As for contemporary viewers, they observe and fully anticipate a continuum between public and private cinemas. They can partake of the big-screen experience if they so choose, as well as watch, own, and perhaps ceaselessly replay films in their TV rooms. Moreover, although critics have complained that the allegedly sloppy aesthetics of television watching, in which viewers talk and engage in otherwise distracting behavior, have invaded movie theaters, scholars such as Roy Rosenzweig and Janet Staiger have shown that theaters have always been the site of such "misbehavior."[4] Even if we grant the presence of codes of viewing associated with other media in movie theaters, influences are surely reciprocal. Research on video consumption at home has demonstrated that viewing dynamics commonly linked to the motion picture theater—that is, attentive watching from beginning to end without interruption—have also affected domestic spectatorship.[5] Although the provinces of movie theater and home have unique characteristics as exhibition venues, they are not radically discontinuous; their relationship is richly and unavoidably interdependent.

Most important, the dichotomy has restrained a more fulsome critical and cultural study of nontheatrical exhibition contexts and modes of viewing. From the outset, films have been shown in numerous public places, including street carnivals, amusement parks, opera houses, tents, ocean liners, airplanes, schools, prisons, churches, and museums. Cinema has similarly enjoyed a thriving existence in private places, certainly in the form of "home movies," amateur productions shot by and featuring family members, but, to an even greater extent, in the form of commercial films that have pervaded the nation's households.[6] Thinking about the reception of films in such "nondedicated" locales is key to grasping the depth and breadth of cinema's social circulation and cultural function. Among nontheatrical exhibition venues, the home is particularly noteworthy for its persistent historical role as an ancillary forum for studio pictures and for its substantial contemporary economic significance to the industry.

Regarding the home as a crucial exhibition site for cinema, I examine how, from the 1980s to the present, new entertainment technologies designed to deliver films to household audiences in the United States—including home theater, cable TV, VHS, DVD, and the Internet—have influenced Hollywood cinema's presentation and reception in daily life. More than at any other time in history, today these technologies have not only made Hollywood cinema an intimate part of home entertainment but have also greatly enhanced its status as an American pastime. For approximately two decades, more U.S. viewers have been watching Hollywood films at home than at the theater, and the revenues generated from the distribution of feature films in the nation's households have surpassed big-screen box office takes.[7] As theatrical exhibition amounts to just one-quarter of Hollywood's global revenues, the home's centrality as an exhibition venue is even more pronounced in foreign markets.[8] In some countries where movie theaters are sparse and pirated videocassettes, VCDs, and DVDs proliferate, cinema is much more closely associated with television than it is with public screening venues.

Because my book explores film exhibition in relation to the immense territories of the home, new technologies, and media consumption, I cannot hope to address all of the issues and variables involved. Although, in order to grasp the multifaceted nature of home film exhibition, my analysis engages audience research, industry history, textual analysis, and critical and cultural theory, I approach my subject primarily through reception studies. This method of inquiry investigates the discourses that shape the environment in which viewing takes place—in this case, the forces that "invade" the house to mediate the encounter between films and viewers. I am particularly interested in how an active intersection of social developments, media industry practices, press coverage, and spectators' tastes helps to create viewing modalities in the home. Although I analyze specific audience data, I do not pursue actual viewers' responses beyond the framework of film exhibition discourses and related cultural contexts. My book thus differs from ethnographic research in the field based on face-to-face encounters between researchers and audience members that result in sustained analyses of how family dynamics or other aspects of domestic life affect media consumption.[9] My desire is not to challenge this valuable work but to contribute to an understanding of reception in the home from a different angle. By examining movie exhibition, I map the contours of a discursive field that forms an important and underresearched part of the social architecture of home viewing. Central to the circulation of films in the home, this field represents the presence of the public in the private, a context that helps to negotiate the relationships between viewers and films.

Granting that the contemporary home is flush with new entertainment technologies and media, I concentrate here on a range of representative venues that have had a major impact on domestic film viewing in the late twentieth and early twenty-first centuries. Some—cable television and VHS—have functioned as powerhouses of ancillary film exhibition since the 1980s. Others—home theater, DVD, and the Internet—have emerged more recently as significant film venues. Whether established or more recent, these outlets have more than just a pervasive presence in today's home media universe; they have shaped viewing sensibilities and activities that are central to understanding the use, meaning, and value of domesticated movies. As we shall see, the technologized home is, in fact, a site of bountiful taste distinctions, generating not only popular film canons but also notions of appropriate modes of film viewing.

Thus far I have emphasized the contemporary moment as key to analyzing the home as a forum for movie viewing. However, this locale has a long history as an exhibition site for Hollywood movies that gives it a cultural continuity to rival its big-screen relative. A brief look at this history clarifies the home's enduring importance to the media business and to the study of cinema itself. This history also provides a foundation for thinking in more detail about the home as an environment of exhibition and reception—its relation to the public sphere, its role in film culture, and its impact on the viewers, media technologies, and films that inhabit domestic space.

The Home Front

According to Ben Singer, films have been shown in domestic space since the medium's invention in the late 1800s. Only two years after Edison's Kinetoscope appeared in 1894, manufacturers began producing projectors intended for use in the home and in other off-theater sites. Regional brick-and-mortar outlets as well as mail order systems for renting or purchasing films quickly followed.[10] At the time, entrepreneurs saw cinema as another medium that could be successfully identified with and exploited for home leisure, along with other audiovisual phenomena such as phonographs, magic lanterns, and slide projectors. They hoped that defining a place for cinema in the parlor would compound the medium's popularity by appealing to families, for whom the concept of home entertainment was becoming increasingly important.[11]

The appearance of parlor cinema distinguishes the medium's domestic exhibition as an intimate part of its total history. At the moment of cinema's birth, media businesses grasped the economic incentives for developing this and other viewing contexts for the medium—signaling that cinema's invention was inextricable from its dissemination in other venues. While the sensational growth of movies as a cultural phenomenon would be initially realized in the nickelodeon and, later, the motion picture palace, studios and other enterprises suspected that part of building cinema's fortunes lay beyond the silver screen, in outfitting the home for exhibition, thereby stirring interest in the experience of cinema in the consumer's surroundings. These early experiments suggest that efforts to "domesticate" cinema were necessary moves toward the new medium's manifest destiny—its expansion into the household conceived as a means of additionally securing its place in American life.

After this inaugural moment, cinema's presence in the home was maintained through a series of technological developments and new media. In terms of the home exhibition of films on celluloid, the 1920s and early 1930s saw immense advances, including the introduction and standardization of 16mm and 8mm film gauges, color film stock, and sound projectors. Studio titles would be available in both gauges to home audiences for decades to come. But, beginning in the late 1930s, viewers could also enjoy films via their radios. Programs such as *Lux Radio Theatre* brought hundreds of radio adaptations of Hollywood films performed by Hollywood actors to millions of listeners. As the era of radio adaptations of Hollywood films drew to a close in the early 1950s, films were already being broadcast on independent and network television stations. In 1975, both cable television and analog video were introduced to the consumer market, later proving to be more profitable than network television as exhibition formats for Hollywood. More recently, other methods of home cinema delivery have included satellite television, pay-per-view, DVD, video on demand, and the Internet. If nothing more, this history reveals the film industry's tireless efforts to situate cinema within an arsenal of new, competitive entertainment technologies designed for home use. These efforts managed not only to increase industry revenues through ever-growing opportunities for ancillary distribution but also to weave movies firmly into the audience's routines, rituals, and experiences.

Although the Internet is developing as a place to screen films, television remains at the center of the domestic film universe. Presently, TV is not only the most important posttheatrical exhibition site for films; it also constitutes a fundamental screen experience for film viewers. Further, as TV provides a site around which many other entertainment technologies (such as DVD and home theater systems) are organized, it involves cinema and its reception in a broad intermedia context. Situating cinema in relation to different home media demonstrates both its affiliations with other domesticated entertainment technologies and its particular contributions to the dynamics of the media-saturated household.

The home's contemporary economic and cultural importance as a sphere of moviegoing seems to bear out the visions of the earliest entrepreneurs. Today, the home functions as a showcase par excellence for a definitive practice of the film business: repurposing. Providing a way to offset the high production costs of blockbusters, *repurposing* refers generally to the media industry's attempt to gain as much revenue as possible from a given property. For film, this may mean marketing tie-ins across a range of businesses and media, from fast-food franchise promotions and T-shirts to cartoon series spin-offs based on a film's original characters. It may also mean "taking a given property developed in one media form and repackaging it for sale in all the other forms possible."[12] This latter sense of repurposing is especially relevant here because it describes the systematic reissue of films in ancillary venues of exhibition. After its theatrical run, a recent film will reappear according to a "windowing" sequence that staggers its rerelease in multiple venues across a number of months, often beginning with VHS and DVD, then pay-per-view channels and direct satellite broadcasts, premium cable movie channels, basic cable, network television, and local television syndication.[13] This order is subject to variation and change, but each of these windows provides studios with valuable additional income from a single film. The rerelease sequencing of classic Hollywood and other older titles is not as intricate. At times, these films rematerialize on the big screen (such as the restored version of Alfred Hitchcock's *Vertigo* [1958] that appeared in 1996). More often, they are reissued on VHS and DVD or on cable channels that have amassed a large library of old studio titles (such as TBS).

In its ability to resell established properties, whether classic or contemporary, repurposing is an essential economic strategy for the studios that is, at the same time, enormously suggestive for the historical and cultural study of cinema. When a film is repurposed it enters into a different social and historical milieu, as well as a different context of reception—whether it be the new design of motion picture theaters forty years after the film's initial release or the TV monitor and the home. Accordingly, a film's original release period is potentially dwarfed by its extensive "afterlife." With Hollywood's economic engine behind it and the proliferation of forms of posttheatrical exhibition, textual afterlife has become inevitable. In fact, the most vigorous existence for many films lies in their revival by various institutions, from media industries to academe, long after they originally circulated. These are the moments in which films often literally become memorable; treated to mixed reviews in the 1950s, *Vertigo*, for example, went on to be acclaimed as a "classic" in its 1980s reissue and then as a "masterpiece" in its 1996 restoration. Research into the reissue expands the parameters of historical inquiry by reframing questions about a film's historical meaning through analysis of its afterlife. Focusing on such a "textual diachronics" allows us to track transfigurations in film meaning and in audiences as well as to examine procedures of canon formation in mass culture. A study of ancillary exhibition venues thus reveals the shifting identities that films assume in later circumstances of their revival and consumption.

In assuming a key role as an economic and cultural locus of movie watching, the home becomes a site of negotiation and tension between the public and the private. Here I want to invoke the image of the "Fortress of Solitude" to capture the ambiguities between public and private that characterize the home as an arena of media consumption. In common parlance, a fortress conjures up a vision of a staunchly insular and protected environment; such an association is only amplified in the explicit origins of the Fortress of Solitude as an important location in the Superman sagas. In the comic books and movies, the Fortress designates a place to which the superhero periodically flees to find solace. The Fortress is far removed from civilization, located deep inside a mountain range and further protected from the world by a massive steel door. In this majestic stronghold, with its screening room and archive of artifacts, Superman calls up and contemplates representations from his past, immersing himself in an environment that is safe and at the same time a personal museum. As the first of this introduction's epigraphs suggests, such a realm does not belong solely to the imaginary, aristocratic mise-en-scène of superhero stories. It is typical of far more quotidian and mortal settings, from the roadside museum to the home. Eco points out that, like many other American locales, the home functions as a type of private gallery, brimming with reproductions and supporting technologies.[14] But more than any public location, today's U.S. home approximates the Fortress's representation of a getaway. Stocked with an array of devices for audiovisual entertainment, the home is a place where individuals can withdraw to engage in private shows and reveries via the playback of cinematic and other images. While often not solitary, viewers are increasingly armored by technology, controlling the ebb and flow of media within the comforts of a self-defined refuge.

However, the sense of insularity elicited by fortress imagery disguises a more complex state of affairs. The media-rich home's sense of safety, solitude, and pleasure is intimately linked to an arsenal of goods produced by social, industrial, and economic forces. As scholars have long observed, despite the home's presumed status as a sanctuary from the working, public world, developments in private space are deeply connected to larger cultural developments, such as industrialization and modernization. David Morley points out that communications technologies of all kinds, including radio and television, exemplify this interdependent relationship, as they necessarily breach the boundaries between public and private by opening the home to the outside.[15] This interdependency does not invalidate the fortress as a suitable image for today's home; indeed, it helps to distinguish the relevance of this image within contemporary accounts of the home. Like many other advertisements for new media technologies, the second epigraph, by producing an appealing vision of the home as a cocoon, uses the idea of the fortress to ward off recognition of its permeability. In the process, the ad subtly defines private space as possible only through the acquisition of the appropriate goods.

The interrelationship of sanctuary and hardware is part of consumer consciousness, detected in architectural plans that wire every room in the house for multimedia as well as in the colloquial way that individuals express their desire to retreat into their homes to immerse themselves in media environments, complete with home theaters and remote controls. In fact, we can further characterize the home as a site of a potentially infinite regression of minifortresses enabled by personal technologies (e.g., the Walkman, the PlayStation, and the Game Boy) that allow individuals to sequester themselves additionally within the household. The vision of the fortress, then, presents the home as a conundrum—an apparent retreat from public space that is dependent on technologies of visual and audio reproduction not only for its mise-en-scène and sound track but also for its very sense of privacy.

In this intricate relationship between public and private, social discourses enter the home and surround the experience of media consumption. But just as surely, when they become household objects or, in Eco's terms, artifacts within the home's gallery of "inconsequential wonders," media texts are domesticated. Roger Silverstone observes that this process of domestication involves "the transition, which is also a translation, of objects across the boundary that separates public and private spaces." Domestication begins with "bringing objects in from the wild"—that is, from public spaces. As they are incorporated into the structure of everyday life, these "wild" things are tamed, brought under personal control and subordinated to individual subjectivities. However, public objects are not simply appropriated into personal universes; their transition and translation into private space entail a reciprocal relationship between producing and consuming cultures.[16]

Home film exhibition and reception necessarily involve the domestication of films and the interaction between producing and consuming cultures. Producing cultures such as media industries help to shape the nontheatrical identities of films. Directors' commentaries on DVD, for example, are clearly designed to sell films in the ancillary market, but they also play a powerful role in negotiating film meaning for home viewers. If we understand exhibition as engaging a broad range of discourses surrounding a film's circulation, it becomes more than a set of industry practices; it also includes the activities of consuming cultures. Web sites, newspaper articles, and other sources provide accounts of viewers' tastes and viewing strategies, making public different ways in which films are appropriated in the home. In this way, the sphere of exhibition provides insight into the multiple interests at work as films circulate in domestic space.

I consider the viewers who appear in these pages as both "active" and "implicated." All viewers—including couch potatoes—are implicitly active. Even if their strategies defy an academic sense of aesthetics or politics, viewers' daily encounters with the cinema and other media in their homes entail decoding and evaluation as well as, at times, a passionate attachment to domesticated media objects. However, activity does not necessarily translate into a progressive political position. Rather, it often involves the juggling of various meaning-making agendas. My study of exhibition aims to uncover a variety of meaning-making agendas that accompany a film in its repurposed materialization in the home—agendas that disclose much about the home as an aesthetically and ideologically charged environment of reception. While this approach cannot comprehensively grasp the diverse ways in which people use the media in the home, it does identify areas of synergy between viewers' activities and larger networks of meaning at play in this sphere, demonstrating the deeply social nature of media consumption. Thus, viewers are active, insofar as they eagerly and devotedly decode films in the home, and implicated, insofar as their modes of viewing occur in relation to existing frames of reference, from industry practices to their own socialized experiences. Far from generating static modes of viewing, the prolific discourses that flow through the home inspire responses to films that are diverse, multifaceted, and changeable.

To address more specifically the dynamics involved in domestic viewing, I introduce the notion of film culture as relevant to a discussion of movies in the private sphere. I define the home as host to an array of film cultures, each characterized by an elaborate set of aesthetics, viewing modalities, and pleasures. More specifically, each chapter focuses on a film culture that has developed in domestic space within the last twenty-five years in relation to technologies responsible for making cinema into an indispensable part of home entertainment. By linking the concept of film culture, normally associated with the public sphere, to the private sphere, I want not only to suggest the concept's applicability to this new terrain but also to continue to qualify any sense of the home's insularity.

Home Film Cultures

Tom Ryall provides a particularly useful definition of a public film culture. Initially quoting Siegfried Kracauer, he writes that it is "'an intermingling of ideas and institutions into recognisable formations' . . . constituted by the ideologies of film that circulate and compete in a given historical period and the forms in which such ideologies are institutionalised." These cultures emerge from "the immediate contexts in which films are made and circulated such as studios, cinemas and film journals, and those contexts which have to be constructed from the material network of the culture, the philosophies and ideologies of film." Film cultures coalesce into recognizable formations, composed of diverse ideas and discourses that circulate both in specialized locales and across the social spectrum. In this sense, a film culture should be considered not as uniform or homogeneous but as a "complex non-monolithic entity containing within itself a set of practices and institutions, some of which interact in a mutually supportive fashion, some of which provide alternatives to each other, and some of which operate in a self-consciously oppositional fashion." As an "ensemble of practices," a film culture thus provides an influential framework for film exhibition and consumption.[17]

Far from being a barren site for the experience of films, the home is similarly characterized by a series of formations, influenced by various institutions and ideologies, that exert pressure on how viewers see Hollywood films in domestic space. Despite their private setting, these formations—or what I refer to as home film cultures—do not operate in isolation from the larger culture. As we shall see, they are intimately connected to society, as it shapes tastes and conventions of movie watching; identities pertaining to family, age, gender, race, and class; and ideas about consumerism, nationalism, and globalization. Moreover, as home film cultures are acted on, they in turn act back on society, making any hard-and-fast divisions between private and public difficult to draw and maintain.

Yet, even with such intricate affiliations, home film cultures have characteristics that distinguish them from theatrical counterparts. For instance, the activities of both media businesses and consumers affect the identity and circulation of genres in domestic space. Each creates and popularizes new ways of grouping films that lie outside of established formal genres, introducing "local" genres that flourish within ancillary markets. Classic Hollywood cinema, a site of many genres, has become a genre itself, categorized as such in video stores where "old" movies are now united under the banner of "classic" films. Similarly, within home film cultures, bygone categories have been resurrected (e.g., the short film), and existing genres (e.g., "chick flicks" and parodies) have achieved special prominence. Alternately, while some viewers return ritually to see blockbusters on the big screen, repeated viewing has become a cornerstone of movie playback in the home. On videocassette or DVD, viewers can watch the same title over and over again in their own environments and under their own control. Although repeat viewing is possible in both public and private screening venues, home film culture's strong affiliation with repetition raises the question of how this dynamic transforms the movie experience in a particularly striking way.

Certain groups of viewers emerge as particularly significant in the home film cultures I discuss, including the most important demographic for theatrical films, a body of viewers that media industries also recognize as significant for the small screen: adolescent and young adult males. Older audience members often associated with home viewing, such as adults in middle- and upper-class families, are also represented in this book. Since men within these two groups tend to embrace new media and technologies with particular enthusiasm, *Beyond the Multiplex* explores the central place in the universe of contemporary home viewing of what Shaun Moores has called "gadgeteers," men preoccupied with the acquisition and operation of technology.[18] Mainstream discussions of cinema and new technologies address young women and the elderly less frequently than these "specialists"; however, these groups, too, figure in my case studies. Although I often treat viewers who are especially committed media enthusiasts, it is important to note that I do not consider fandom as a manifestation of a spectacular subculture.[19] Rather, I regard fans as fixtures of the mass cultural landscape. Both cultivated by media industries and constituting an active and heterogeneous cadre of devoted viewers, fans represent a crucial, but normative, part of the circuit of exchange between producing and consuming cultures. As a standard rather than an exceptional class of viewers, they are central to my investigation of the material, quotidian aspects of home viewing.

The majority of viewers represented in mainstream commentary on home film exhibition are white. This indicates that, thus far, this "revolution" in entertainment is being depicted and conceived along racial lines. But this focus on white consumers in exhibition discourse has deeper implications as well. Representations of certain new media technologies often operate implicitly as discourses of whiteness. As Hazel Carby argues, whiteness tends to appear as invisible, attaining the unspoken status of a norm against which all other differences must be measured. Its invisibility, coupled with its pictorial and discursive ubiquity, functions to erase it as a category of racial identity, so that whites appear as "just people."[20] The sphere of home film exhibition often perpetuates such assumptions, particularly as it portrays the connection between whiteness and new technologies as natural. Positioning certain consumers as ideal, the arena of exhibition generates notions of race, gender, class, and age that help to constitute the ideological dimensions of home film cultures.

The concept of home film cultures thus embodies several central themes and concerns of the book: the significance of nontheatrical exhibition venues, repurposed forms of movies, and the "textual afterlife" to research in film and media studies; the consideration of the home as a discursively charged forum that generates taste formations and shapes film meaning; the importance of cinema's relation to new technologies and media that act as home delivery systems; and the vicissitudes of ordinary active viewing, particularly as it involves the negotiation of industrial and social discourses that attempt to influence the private consumption of films and the identities of viewers. The chapters are not scripted in exactly the same way with respect to these concerns; rather, the central thematics are differently balanced and foregrounded, depending on a chapter's subject matter and emphasis.

Each chapter examines one or more of five technologies involved in ancillary exhibition (home theater, VHS, DVD, cable television, and the Internet), the viewing strategies with which each technology is associated, and the discourses that accompany each into the home. I am particularly interested in the threshold periods in which these technologies flourished in the home and the vanguard groups of viewers associated with their initial success. It is in these moments that we can see with special clarity the factors that coalesced to produce the home film culture and its particular impact on viewing modalities.

In the first chapter, I discuss home theater, one of the most important trends in entertainment in the 1990s and early 2000s. Home theater represents a "high-tech" upgrade of the household, often requiring architectural renovation or other transformations of domestic space. As such, it offers an opportunity to investigate how new entertainment technologies have reshaped conceptions of the family, gender roles, and the home while creating taste cultures that redefine the activity of sitting in front of the "tube." Continuing this focus on gender and the high-tech redrawing of taste cultures, chapter 2 examines the growth of film collecting since the advent of the VCR. I trace how film collecting on VHS, laser disc, and, more recently, DVD has become an integral part of the viewer's media landscape in the United States. I explore in particular the procedures of selection and evaluation that characterize the archival aesthetics of male, high-tech collectors. Once a film becomes a collectible within a gadgeteering ethos, how do its identity, value, and meaning change?

While a focus on technological innovation tends to privilege the new, developments in home film exhibition have always found a significant place for the old. Cable television and, before it, network television have given Hollywood's vintage products a robust afterlife. In chapter 3, I focus on cable movie channels, especially those dedicated to airing films from the silent and classic Hollywood eras for primarily middle-aged and elderly subscribers. My case study concerns one of the chief self-defined custodians of U.S. film culture that rose to prominence in the 1980s and 1990s: AMC (American Movie Classics). As it consecrates films from the past, this forum creates a kind of archival aesthetic different from film collecting, using classic films as material for a revisionist history that celebrates the state of the nation in the face of complex contemporary times.

Chapter 4 addresses another ubiquitous dimension of home film recycling: viewers watching the same films over and over again. To investigate why audiences choose to repeat certain titles, I survey the home viewing habits of contemporary university students. Since many of these students were among the first generation to begin rewatching films on VHS and cable television as children, their strategies of viewing provide especially fertile territory to address motivations for re-viewing and the everyday pleasures provided by this ritual. Moreover, their viewing activities reveal stratifications in taste influenced by gender and other social identities within their particular corner of youth culture.

Although the first four chapters concentrate on the exhibition of commercial feature films on TV, the last chapter discusses new developments on a different small screen. Since the late 1990s, the Internet has functioned as an important emerging exhibition site for cinema, making the computer an alternative viewing venue. While feature films are streamed on the Web, the short has risen to particular prominence in this world. For this reason, I investigate the business and art of the film short, exploring the operations of one of the largest short film exhibitors—AtomFilms.com—and a type of short, often made by fans of Hollywood blockbusters, that has seen tremendous online popularity, the film parody. As it directs our attention to avid viewers who have become filmmakers, this genre brings the relation of producing and consuming cultures full circle. Further, while many film parodies are made by amateurs and independents, they paradoxically make the very idea of Hollywood into a powerful presence on the Internet. As we shall see, the shift to the Internet short does not remove Hollywood from the picture; it reveals Tinseltown's influence from a different angle.

By considering cinema's relation to a series of new entertainment technologies in the home, I aim to shed light on forces that define home film cultures, examining how the flurry of discourses that penetrate domestic space operate to make meaning for cinema. Of course, the home is a complex sphere distinguished by an extensive network of relations, so my work provides only a partial account of the discourses at play in this realm. At the same time, my focus allows a detailed study of core exhibition forums, industries, technologies, films, and viewing sensibilities involved in domestic reception over the last twenty years. Ultimately, I hope to demonstrate the importance not just of home screens as sites for further inquiry but of nontheatrical film exhibition more generally for what it can contribute to a cultural and historical analysis of cinema and its viewers beyond the darkened aisles and brightly lit exit signs of the multiplex.

1 The New Media Aristocrats

Home Theater and the Film Experience

Home theater is an enduring concept in the annals of new entertainment technologies designed for domestic use. Contemporary home theater resurrects a notion of media synergy that historians have traced back as far as the late nineteenth century, when entrepreneurs and visionaries speculated about the possibility of showing moving pictures, complete with sound, in living rooms on a mass scale. Early formulations depicted phonographs and motion picture projectors as conveying sounds and images to patrons, with the telegraph and telephone transmitting the signals long-distance, so that the effects could be experienced nationwide. Writing in 1912 in an article entitled "The Future of Home Theater," S. C. Gilfillan discussed how two machines would enable one to "go to the theater without leaving the sitting room." One machine would combine Thomas Edison's phonograph and Kinetoscope to show movies rented from libraries. In a prefiguration of television, the other would be an "electric vision apparatus with a telephone." Here telephone and telegraph wires would, with "the throw of a switch," send picture and audio from "a central stage to millions of homes."[1] Predictions like this regarded home theater as the culmination of a flurry of nineteenth-century innovations in communications and media that demonstrated the ability of North American know-how to bring "the whole world into the home."[2] The conception of media technologies as capable of collapsing the boundaries between private and public space defined the home as a media hub that synthesized grand technical achievements.

Later incarnations of home theater in the post–World War II era continued to portray the home as a crossroads between public and private that could, by adopting media technologies, admit the world's wonders. As Lynn Spigel has pointed out, the invention of television allowed the 1950s home theater to advance beyond its forebears in realizing certain key features of the original vision.[3] Television accomplished the instantaneous transmission of images and sounds "from a central stage," which had formed such an important part of turn-of-the-century ideas. This new entertainment center featured a TV set, radio, phonograph, movie projector, movie screen, loudspeaker, and (in a nod to suburban lifestyles) barbecue pit. Given the rivalry with the more established medium of film, broadcast industry ads promoted home theater as able to reproduce the theatrical experience for viewers in their family rooms, promising an image competitive with that of the big screen in terms of quality (a promise difficult to keep in an era of widescreen, Technicolor cinema).

Although technologies have been in continual flux, the rhetoric that has accompanied these early and the more recent versions of home theater has maintained a visionary character. In fact, as we consider how persistently inventors have pursued the notion of integrating the home and media technologies, we are reminded of another insistent dream underwriting film history—what André Bazin has called "the myth of total cinema." Bazin argues that, more than any other factor, the idea that cinema could faithfully re-create the world and achieve perfect verisimilitude drove inventions, such as sound and color.[4] Similarly, in the case of home theater, the concept of a total domestic entertainment universe that could synthesize and embody public mass media has propelled developments in the field of entertainment. Because such ideas are difficult to realize to absolute perfection, they continue to push and animate technological innovations, which, in turn, strive to come closer to attaining the complete vision. Unlike Bazin's formulation, however, myths that inform technological innovations don't simply exist in the minds and imaginations of men, waiting for implementation; they are motivated by economic imperatives and forces that have broad cultural implications and effects. The long-term pursuit of the invention and advancement of home theater testifies to how central this concept has been both to certain ideals of technological progress (in which the fusion of inventions and the ensuing modernization of the home represent the successful state of society) and to the canny expansionistic tendencies of business enterprise (for which the home signifies a potentially boundless new frontier).

Through the quality imprimatur of digital technology, contemporary home theater reaches further than its predecessors toward this fusion of public entertainment media for the purposes of domestic amusement. In the process it involves multiple industries bent on redefining the home as a site par excellence for media consumption. As home theater has become almost synonymous with watching movies in private, it is essential to an understanding of film exhibition in the contemporary household. At the same time, the home theater movement is part of a larger-scale reimagining of domestic space through digital technology. For instance, the concept of "home audio-video interoperability" describes a household with interfaces among home video, audio, and computer equipment, while the "smart home" represents a more global reconfiguration of domestic space, wherein lighting, security, phones, temperature control, computers, home entertainment, and even pet care are automated and networked, enabling the realization of a "fully computerized dream house."[5]

To approach the dynamics of film viewing in the home theater habitat, I focus on how this habitat has been publicly constituted as what Raymond Williams would call a "signal system." A signal system is a "deep cultural form" that marks the "practical social organization" of the arts by defining the manner in which they are presented to the public.[6] This system makes up an environment of exhibition that, through various institutional cues, shapes the audience's disposition toward the artifact it is about to behold. For example, whether paintings are exhibited in a museum, on an urban street, or in the foyer of the Ramada Inn affects how they will be perceived; each situation carries with it a loaded cultural charge that orients the beholder's roving eye. Institutional signal systems have exactly this function in relation to the cinema as well. If the same film were to be shown at an art house and a drive-in theater, the patterns of consumption already associated with each venue would influence the audience's viewing attitudes and behaviors. Art houses, for instance, recommend an observant and deferential mode of viewing associated with overt aesthetic experience, while drive-ins include a host of "unaesthetic" distractions associated with family life and courtship, from squalling infants to backseat romances. The film is materially the same, but the experience of it changes dramatically.

Just as motion picture theaters provide integral settings that influence reception, the home and its various signal systems create an influential domestic environment that affects how films will be consumed. To characterize home theater as representing one such environment of exhibition, I examine how media industries, consumer magazines, and other sources have circulated the idea of home theater to the public. How have these sources characterized the relationships among television, film, and audio—the component parts of the contemporary entertainment center—to situate cinema in a multimedia framework? How have they offered certain concepts of domestic space, leisure, and lifestyle to consumers? And, finally, how do the appeals of home theater discourse define viewers and viewing in a private context?

As we shall see, one of this new technology's most powerful interventions into domestic space has been the creation of an "aristocracy of culture," to use Pierre Bourdieu's term.[7] That is, public discourses on home theater define its machines of reproduction as possessing special qualities that bestow "titles of cultural nobility" on the viewers who use them. The aesthetic associated with these machines relies on privilege as a key term of its appeal: it is defined by particularly attentive viewing sensibilities and heightened sensory experiences, by domestic surroundings that exude class and "good taste," and by pervasive equations of technology itself with art. Like promotions for other media innovations before it, home theater discourse attempts to establish a competitive place for these new machines by distinguishing between their capabilities and those of already established media—in particular, between the "highbrow" adventures apparently offered by recent technologies and the "lowbrow" experiences of traditional TV.[8] According to longstanding strategies of advertising, such distinctions give consumers a sense of class mobility through acquisition and the exercise of taste, in the process ordaining a new domestic aristocracy permeated with certain notions of masculinity, race, and a gendered reconfiguration of family space.

Ultimately, the home theater aesthetic aims to produce an image of a commodity necessary for revitalizing viewing and the domestic sphere itself. In its interrelationships with the domestic sphere, home theater participates in a long and tangled history that has seen the domestic increasingly dependent on "outside connections" for its very definition. Since the late eighteenth century, private space has often been idealized as a refuge from the difficulties and demands of public life. However, as Eric Hirsch argues, it has been in fact "sustainable only through an ever-widening and interrelated set of connections with the public, the world of work, and 'society,' from which it was self-consciously separated." Technologies, including electronic and digital technologies, have been instrumental in facilitating these connections. As the example of today's smart home illustrates, the concept of domestic self-sufficiency itself and the fortress mentality that sustains it exist in a strong "mutually constitutive" relationship with new technologies. The home can be self-sufficient only if it is furnished with goods "imported" from public commerce, from surround sound to security systems; the more the home appears to be sequestered from the hurly-burly of the outside world, the more it is saturated with commodities that enable its apparent isolation. As Hirsch explains, "The creation of the private sphere has been central to the elaboration of consumer demand, so essential to the expansion and accumulation process which characterizes modern societies."⁹ The notion of domestic self-sufficiency thus serves the requirements of industries within a growing consumer culture. Further, as these industries seek to feather the homeowner's nest, they circulate discourses that strive to define the domestic environment as a context for the employment and enjoyment of various new technologies.

As a self-proclaimed "total" entertainment system, home theater embodies this contradictory sense of domestic self-sufficiency. It proposes itself as a superior stay-at-home alternative to theatrical moviegoing, while opening the home up not only to high-tech audio-visual machines and paraphernalia but also to multifarious discourses that identify the household as both a private media paradise and a harbor from the perceived dangers of public life. However, before I address these issues in more detail, we should consider exactly what home theater is, examining its place in the media industry and the world of home entertainment.

Home Is Where the Hardware Is

The equipment and accessories marketed for home theater are diverse, changeable, and seemingly without limit. Although specifics can vary widely, then, the basic elements of home theater are a controller, usually an A/V receiver with audio and video switching; an AM/FM tuner; a power amplifier; a surround-sound processor (such as Dolby Pro Logic, Dolby Digital [DD], or Digital Theater Systems [DTS]) to separate sound into multiple channels; at least five loudspeakers situated strategically in a room (front center, left, and right; rear left and right) and possibly a subwoofer to deepen bass; a large-screen television set of at least twenty-seven inches or a projection-TV system with screen; and a DVD player or Hi-Fi VCR. Gadgets and features that are often added to the basic home theater include HDTV tuners and George Lucas's THX sound, a controller enhancement that helps home systems to better approximate movie theater sound quality. The market also encompasses numerous auxiliary items, including audio cables, universal remote controls, lighting systems, CD and DVD storage units, and furniture especially made for home theaters (such as entertainment center cabinets and an assortment of specially designed "cinema chairs"). Since the home theater can house many other components, including a cassette deck, a CD player, and a Sony PlayStation, a Microsoft Xbox, or other gaming system, it literally represents an entertainment mecca in domestic space.

Like other new technologies, when it first appeared on the market in the mid-1980s, home theater was expensive and largely reserved for the rich.

Through the growing affordability and diversification of components, home theater has since become widely available to the middle class. By 1997, approximately thirteen million households in the United States were equipped with the multichannel audio-video systems characteristic of home theater. By 2000, this figure rose to twenty-two million, or more than 20 percent of homes; early 2004 saw home theater's penetration grow to 30 percent.[10] Displays for entertainment centers of this nature have become a central feature of electronics showrooms (such as Circuit City), chain department stores (such as Sears), and online sources (such as BestBuy.com), and an abundance of consumer magazines selling the necessary hardware populate the shelves of Barnes and Noble, Borders Books and Music, and other mainstream booksellers. In the current climate, a wealthy cinephile or audiophile can still spend tens to hundreds of thousands of dollars on high-tech equipment to create, as the trade refers to it, an "extreme home theater" system. However, at the opposite end of the spectrum, the consumer can purchase the enormously popular "home-theater-in-a-box" for as little as ninety-nine dollars.

A by-now generic feature of entertainment culture, home theater has helped to redefine and revivify the media industries associated with it. In 1999, sales of both audio and video components related to home theater amounted to $4.3 billion, an 11 percent increase over the previous year. In 2000, revenues for the entertainment center's audio equipment alone rose 32 percent over 1999 figures.[11] As Lee Goehring, senior buyer of home audio components for Best Buy states, "Home theater is our whole reason for being." These sentiments are echoed by a reporter for the *New York Times*, who succinctly comments on directions in the audio industry: "If you aren't in the home theater business, you aren't going to be in business long."[12] Similarly, the big screen television set, so important to the home theater system, "represents not only the essence of home theater but also the fastest growing segment of the television industry"; in 2002, 37 percent of U.S. households owned a thirty-inch or larger TV set.[13]

Generally speaking, we can understand the current "home theater craze" as a result of a successful positioning of home theater as the apotheosis of digital entertainment technologies. As an umbrella term that encompasses several machines devoted to audio and visual reproduction, *home theater* appears to embody the advantages and vast potentials of this technology within domestic space. It visibly and successfully trades off the enormous cachet that the term *digital* carries as a measure of technological advancement and quality (a cachet advertisers have been quick to exploit by attaching the digital label to almost any contemporary home entertainment device, even when its properties are still technically analog). Further, digital capabilities bring home-based media closer to their Holy Grail—the achievement of the quality of their public counterparts. For visual technologies, that achievement is the replication of theatrical cinema, while for audio it is "closing the gap between performed music and reproduced music at home."[14] Collateral developments in entertainment technologies that contribute to this quest, such as DVD, have bolstered the digital credentials and growth of home theater. Rising from a 2 percent to a 30 percent penetration of U.S. homes from 1999 to 2002, DVD players have inspired owners to upgrade their entertainment equipment so that the superiority of DVD picture and sound can be fully realized (Hafner D1, D7).

In its aspirations to the standards of motion picture theaters and in the intricate relationships its digital universe forges among four of the most potent home entertainment machines to date—television, the stereo system, the VCR, and the DVD player—home theater presents films within a complex multimedia framework. This framework negotiates between public and private, at the same time situating cinema within diverse technological and aesthetic economies that create a kind of *Gesamtkunstwerk* of the possibilities of fusing sound and image in the household with the utmost veracity and impact. As individual media enterprises involved in home theater trumpet their wares, they engage in intermedia competition, suggesting the superiority of their presentation of image and sound to other venues or technologies, particularly motion picture theaters and old-fashioned television sets. Marketing campaigns establish such competitions to demonstrate home theater's ability both to capitalize on the advantages and to remedy the deficiencies associated with established public exhibition forums and "outdated" home entertainment equipment.

Home theater businesses and audio companies contend that this media center not only compares favorably with but actually surpasses the conditions of watching films in motion picture theaters. Technical advances, such as Dolby Digital surround sound, THX sound, sophisticated A/V receivers, and powerful subwoofers available for the home provide the springboards for such claims. Thus, McIntosh advertisements state: "Not only are movie soundtracks reproduced with unsurpassed precision and accuracy; the overall fidelity is among the best you will hear in *any* theatrical venue." Increasing the stakes, a promotion for Sound by Singer boasts, "Today's home theater systems can actually surpass the excitement and sound of a movie theater—right in your own home! Movies, sports, the news . . . everything looks and sounds incredibly real! And, without the hassle of going out."[15] Sound, the component of the film experience long ignored by developers of technology and audiences alike, is now the ultimate commodity. Parasound Products is typical in insisting that "a truly moving theater experience is built around sound even more than picture."[16]

Along with impressive technical capabilities in the reproduction of sound, businesses and public commentators often cite the familiar conveniences of the domestic setting for entertainment as providing another edge over theatrical moviegoing. As a newspaper reporter points out, "The advantages over commercial theaters are obvious. Watch a film from within the confines of your own domestic fortress and you are spared the annoyance of being seated directly behind tall hair or directly in front of someone with a dangerously contagious-sounding cough. You needn't listen to others crinkle their candy wrappers. And blessedly absent is the know-it-all offering a running commentary for all those nearby" (Hafner D7). The "hassle of going out" also includes paying a babysitter, finding a parking place, and standing in line to buy tickets. Such inconveniences, along with noisy, obstructive, even germ-ridden audience members, can further compromise public moviegoing.

Interestingly, this comparative logic reverses common wisdom about the theater and the home as exhibition venues. Critics often presume that the behaviors that characterize television viewing (particularly those having to do with distraction and talking) have had a deleterious effect on audiences in movie theaters, corrupting a once-civilized milieu and its attentive viewers. Certainly such assumptions are simplistic and ignore a longer history of talking at the movies and a series of causes for it. But home theater discourse adopts conceptions of "proper" theatrical filmgoing to portray a transformed domestic domain for viewing. In fact, as this discourse insists on the home's ability to compete with the theatrical experience, it presents the movie house as the uncontrolled environment riven with distractions; the entertainment center comes to epitomize the possibility of a stress-free, quiet, and unimpeded rapport with the screen. The motion picture theater even appears as a site of possible contagion and thus of some danger. Buoyed by the growth in sales of home theater systems after September 11, entrepreneurs tout home theater as embodying not only a viable practical and aesthetic alternative to the cineplex but also a safer locale, a private domain able to protect viewers from public exposure to unknown threats. As I mentioned, the home has often represented a haven from the pressures of work and other aspects of public life. After September 11, when travel and attendance at public events declined and a stay-at-home mentality gained ground, the fortress imagery of the home assumed a more literal meaning; indeed, industry executives have referred to the act of installing a home theater system as "bunkering the house" or "post-9/11 cocooning."[17] Already claiming home theater's parity with or superiority to the theatrical experience, the industry presents it as providing self-sufficiency and refuge from the hazards of the public sphere at a time of national crisis.

However, the home theater industry compares cinema and the motion picture theater more favorably when it comes to the discussion of traditional television. Ads often define the viewing of a film as a major event, a "memorable occasion for both you and your guests."[18] This kind of promotion marks another moment in the evolution of the relationship between these two media in which producers attempt to present feature films as exceptional, as special programs that stand out from television's regular broadcast flow; building an "event status" for televised films has been central since the 1950s and 1960s, when the networks ran such series as ABC's *Hollywood Film Theater* and NBC's *Saturday Night at the Movies*. This strategy customarily attempts to lend the prestige associated with motion pictures to television, while showing television's ability to accommodate diverse aesthetic forms. Within promotions for home theater, however, film's touted superiority is used as a means of illustrating not the capaciousness but the insufficiency of television. As an ad for audio company Kenwood argues, "The sound quality of most televisions is almost enough to keep people from watching them altogether. . . . Watching ice fishermen scratch themselves. Watching buttermilk coagulate. Watching mimes debate economic theory. Anything is preferable to enduring TV with inferior sound. And so we created Kenwood home theater systems with surround sound. Systems that give you true movie sound reproduction at home."[19] Particularly through improvements in sound, home theater companies promise cinematic quality, with which the "puny" capabilities of television technology cannot compete. Thus, by reproducing the big picture and big sound associated with cinema's conditions of exhibition, home theater "rescues" the family television from what promoters depict as its lack of spectacle and technological refinement.

An ad for Runco projectors (figure 1) in *Home Theater* underscores the "then and now" claims of contemporary entertainment centers. In a small black-and-white inset photo, the ad pictures a 1950s vintage home theater— a nondescript cabinet with a very small television set, which happens to be showing a feature with a dinosaur. A family of four sits squeezed uncomfortably onto a sofa; a doll lies haphazardly on the floor. The Runco home theater of today takes place in a much different setting. The decor is tasteful and upscale. Although the room is empty of people, the seating— stepped, spacious, and comfortable—indicates its ability to accommodate

This was home
theater...

Figure 1. Old versus new home theaters. (Advertisement courtesy of Runco International.)

numerous film viewers. Two full wine glasses and a plate with grapes, cheese, and crackers indicate that an adult couple will soon be enjoying the system. Most important, one wall of the room is dedicated to a large screen onto which a scene of predatory dinosaurs attacking their prey is projected. At the very top of the room, the Runco projector is barely noticeable. The copy for the ad makes the standard claim ("Runco brings the excitement of Hollywood's big screen entertainment into the home") while reminding readers that Runco is prepared to bring them HDTV when it becomes widely available on the consumer market (HDTV, with its improved resolution, being another technology that promises to collapse the boundaries between television and cinema). Ads for plasma TVs define them in similar terms. According to a Marantz plug, "Plasma TV is like a painting on your wall. But with a high resolution, 42" widescreen picture, it's more like a theater in your living room. The letterbox, 16.9 viewing area brings the quality of cinema into the comfort of your home."[20]

Promotions thus strive to reform television by associating it with cinematic and digital standards for picture and sound reproduction. Far from giving the traditional family television any quarter, home theater discourse simply exacerbates social suspicions about the deficiencies of this medium. That is, by revamping television through an aristocratic techno-aesthetic, the discourse acts upon the legacy of television's negative reputation as a form of "low" mass culture that attracts mindless consumers. Connected to sophisticated audio systems and further "upgraded" through an association with cinema-quality picture and sound, television can be better reconciled with the demands of the digital era and hence more effectively marketed to consumers. As television manufacture shifts to embrace digital capabilities, the set itself becomes part of the futuristic landscape mapped out by new technologies; meanwhile, the "old-fashioned" small-screen TV is on its way to becoming the Rodney Dangerfield of the media, unable to get any respect. The contemporary media center thus vividly represents the efforts of a new signal system to replace an old through the language of deficiency. This language is an intimate part of the hierarchy that market forces continually attempt to establish between old and new technologies as a means of "educating" audiences about the new sensory experiences that await, once they update their machines.

As William Boddy notes of recent electronic imaging technologies, there is a remarkable consistency in the way these technologies have been pitted against television. Advocates see one of their chief virtues as a "promise to remake or destroy conventional television: to transform the scorned and degraded domestic TV set into a good cultural object."[21] Home theater promotions participate avidly in this intermedia competition posed as a cultural war. The pictures of technologically updated televisions, whether they be large- or flat-screen sets, projection systems, or HDTV, present them as incarnations of performance excellence, beautiful purveyors of high-quality images and sounds. Interweaving the standards of film theaters with the reputation of digital technology, TV is removed from its associations with the plebeian and transformed into an integral part of a high-tech domestic universe. At the same time, the remade set continues to deliver the convenient viewing situation associated with television. However, as the Runco ad suggests, even this viewing situation has been transfigured to provide a more suitable habitat for the technological riches represented by the home theater system.

As the public discourse surrounding home theater defines its place and value within the intermedia universe of home entertainment, it also describes this new technology's intimate relation to decor and lifestyle. Echoing the broadcasting industry's introduction of television in the 1950s, home theater companies make it clear that home theater is not just a technology but part of an overall concept of domestic design and leisure. It is particularly in this refashioning of the home via technology that the class-based nature of the media industry's appeals becomes evident.

The Motion Picture Palace Redux

The motion picture theater business experienced a building boom in the 1990s, continuing the renaissance in the number and design of theaters that had commenced in the 1980s, when the swankier cineplex superseded the shopping mall theater—with its dreary architecture, sticky floors, and un-adorned presentation of films—as the norm. In the mid-1990s, when the most recent building boom began, there were approximately twenty-seven thousand movie screens. By 2000, according to the National Association of Theater Owners, there were almost thirty-eight thousand screens, a number that nearly tripled the expansion that characterized the previous five-year period.[22] Although some theater owners quickly ran into financial difficulties because the market could not sustain the plethora of new screens, this expansion otherwise resulted in the birth of a new, influential theater design.[23] Construction in the 1990s tended to focus on producing theaters with stadium seating, rocking chairs with cup holders, and improved digital sound systems. Stadium seating created the sense of a public event of some magnitude, chairs and cup holders provided audiences with comfort and convenience, and big screens and booming sound systems heightened immersion in the spectacle. The new theater thus offered an ideal forum for Hollywood fare, especially the blockbuster.

On the one hand, we can see these renovations partly as a response to the popularity of home theater. Although these shifts cannot resolve some of the perceived deficits of public moviegoing, they strive in design to preserve theatrical primacy and the special character of the motion picture theater and big-screen experience in the face of competition from home entertainment: expansive stadium seating cannot be easily duplicated in the home, yet comfortable chairs with places to put drinks replicate or better some of the comforts and conveniences of domestic space. As home venues attempt to approximate motion picture theaters, these theaters in turn must seek ways of demonstrating their unique prowess in attracting mass audiences. On the other hand, while this competition is real for theater owners, the stakes for some businesses may not be so high. As the case of George Lucas's THX sound demonstrates, many companies involved in developing technologies for the big screen or designing aspects of motion picture theaters also produce equipment and other accessories for home theater. As fast as public theaters develop new concepts, whether technological or architectural, home theater quickly follows suit. For example, at the high end, products such as Acoustic Innovation's Cinema Chairs and Theatre Design Associates' Dream Lounger duplicate the plush seating of the multiplex and offer spatial designs similar to stadium seating. Reciprocity occurs, then, between public and private theaters as each borrows the perceived advantages of the other.

The similarities between public and private theaters are sometimes quite literal. Home theater designer Theo Kalomirakis built a facsimile of New York's famous Roxy Theater in his home and has since made a career of creating downsized replicas of old movie palaces for rich clients.[24] The close relationship between public and private is also manifested in the reigning vision of the home presented by consumer magazines: to be a suitable place for a quality experience of motion pictures, the home must be transformed into a motion picture theater. In this spirit, numerous ads in home theater magazines show the family domicile converted literally into a movie house. For example, Zenith advertises its home theater system with a picture of a home at night, lit from behind by spotlights and from the front by a neon movie marquee affixed over a two-car garage (figure 2). The parking spaces are sufficient for a small crowd, and a red aisle rope leads up to the front walk. On the marquee, the family name, Kimble, serves as the name of the theater. The show *(Summer Vacation)* is rated PG and hyped as all digital.[25] Of course, the producers of this ad intend it as a humorous exaggeration of the possibilities of remaking the home in the image of the movie theater. Nonetheless, the ad projects the promise that media can vividly transfigure the home, making it an important social site in the neighborhood. Since home theater installation requires modifications of the household, these discourses suggest not only how those changes might be conceived but also which vision of the home best accords with the introduction of new entertainment technologies.

For most home theater owners, a family room or other already established space doubles as a home theater. Wealthier consumers often create a dedicated room or buy or build houses with the idea of a home theater foremost in their plans. In addition, some gravitate toward "multiroom home entertainment" systems, which provide images and music in every room as well as in exterior places, making media inextricable from living space. Whatever the extent of the renovation, home theater companies emphasize the architectural integration of entertainment technologies with

Figure 2. Home theater makes any home into a movie theater. (2002 advertisement courtesy of Zenith Electronics Corporation.)

home design, thus advancing a notion of interface. Sometimes this interface requires buying new furniture to ensure a union between technology and decor. For instance, in an ad for Sanus Euro Furniture, we see a drawing of a TV set and stereo system mounted on boards supported by cinderblocks, with speakers resting on books or cartons. Shown in comparison with this lopsided, ramshackle arrangement, Sanus's black-lacquered, modular equipment stands are stylish, sturdy, and orderly. The ad reads, "You've invested thousands in a high-end system . . . don't sell yourself short by displaying it on old, under-sized furniture. Match the quality of your system with Sanus Euro Furniture . . . it'll enhance the appearance of every system."[26] At other times, home theater discourse emphasizes how certain equipment can merge easily with existing arrangements. For example, a business advertising in-wall speakers claims that its products offer the discerning homeowner an "ultimate sound landscape" destined to become part of the "living environment of the home." Here, at last, is "seamless decor integration and reference-quality performance."[27] An ad for AudioEase systems continues to promulgate an effortless synergy between the household and technology while espousing the restorative powers of the latter: "Re-discover the wonder of your home. There is a place beyond the limits of the ordinary home control system. Where the promises of technology are realized. Where comfort and control come together. A place called home."[28]

Enjoy Mozart in the Garden
The Rolling Stones by the Pool
Jurassic Park in the Home Theater
and Whitney Houston in the Hot Tub

Who would ever have thought that high-fidelity sound could look so good?

Figure 3. Invisible entertainment systems. (Advertisement courtesy of Stereostone, Inc., North Hollywood, CA.)

Disguising the presence of technologies materializes as an ideal within this aesthetic of integration. Like in-wall speakers, large screens are often hidden from sight within the home's decor—not unlike a secret panel in the old mansion of a mystery story—until the fateful switch is flicked. Multi-room home entertainment systems further dramatize the importance of seamlessness. For example, promotions for Stereostone audio (a company that houses its components in artful-looking rocks; figure 3) propose that we can "enjoy Mozart in the garden, the Rolling Stones by the pool, *Jurassic Park* in the home theater, and Whitney Houston in the hot tub" without being aware of the presence of technology.[29]

In designs coordinating home and home theater, the option of the invisibility of the equipment exists at one end of the spectrum. At the other end is a full display of the apparatus, which then visually dominates the room in question. The technology may be integrated into the overall decor, but, rather than quietly fusing with the mise-en-scène, it strongly shapes the living space. For example, AudioVisions displays its home theater in a dedicated room replete with huge speakers and screen. The image shown on the screen is that of the *Titanic,* a fitting visual for a technological arrangement that strives toward spectacle. Discussions of the flat-screen TV also often recommend overt exhibition of the technology. Such televisions are already less bulky than their forebears and so are less intrusive in domestic space. But they are also expressly designed for display, opening up "whole new avenues for people to integrate television into their homes." As one interior designer comments, "These screens are so futuristic, so stunning . . . TVs are no longer pieces of equipment that one wants to conceal." Whether the set is on or off, the "flashy screen" is capable of giving "a contemporary gleam to the gilded master bedroom." As a sign of how the flat screen itself is regarded as an objet d'art, one designer "surrounded a Sony flat screen with more than a dozen framed, matted photographs on the living room wall," an act that transparently lends "aesthetic legitimacy to what's on television, as well as to the television itself."[30] There is no reason to conceal the television; the technology (as well as what it exhibits) accedes to the realm of the artistic while its grandeur testifies to the owner's wealth and commitment to quality.

The aesthetic of integration thus offers various possibilities for the relationship of technology to interior design: homeowners can display or disguise the machines; they can also retool the home to meet the quality standards of the technology or purchase equipment designed to blend invisibly with the domestic setting. The issue of the invisibility of technology resonates with 1950s design suggestions that attempted to accommodate the new presence of television in the home by effacing it. Lynn Spigel describes how magazines often recommended camouflaging the TV set. She contends that this advice complicates arguments about how television functioned as a sign of status in middle- and lower-class homes, since it characterizes the apparatus as an intrusive machine that signified "bad taste." Charlotte Brunsdon's work on satellite dish installations in Britain shows how "taste wars" continue to develop in relation to television when it appears to be alien to an architectural environment.[31] Interior decorating tips that advocate invisibility as the best standard of home theater installation today similarly attempt to negotiate the equipment's place in the home with respect to issues of taste.

However, the strategy of disguising the presence of the machines so as not to imperil the good taste of one's home with displays of wealth or signs of mass culture inevitably invokes class status. That is, the home theater may be hidden within the decor, but this gesture on the part of the homeowner ultimately testifies to his or her refined sensibilities. The camouflaged home theater still manages to signify the aestheticization of the home, because the homeowners have shown discernment, even ingenuity, in hiding the equipment. Such an exercise of "restraint" is a pervasive feature of bourgeois aesthetics. Thus, whether home theater equipment is highly visible or invisible within interior space, it can be mobilized as a sign of good taste that reflects favorably on the mise-en-scène of the home and the dispositions of the homeowner.

The revisualization of the home touts the ability of the media center to convert the U.S. household into an elite setting. The home becomes a domestic version of the motion picture palace that presents entertainment to its consumers in luxurious surroundings. Even if the domicile lacks opulence, the machinery appears to secure an improved class status for the viewer. Through its associations with quality and sophistication, digital technology represents a "trophy of consumerism" that testifies to the homeowner's discerning powers while adding splendor to the domestic realm.[32] In this technologically assisted milieu, the viewer can imagine him- or herself as a king or queen, just as patrons of motion picture palaces were encouraged to do by theater owners in the 1920s.[33] In this way, private residences become visions of the good life.

The basic vocabulary used in ads and articles about home theater—"home theater chic," "artful living," and "lifestyles of the rich and home theatrous"—equates ownership of these systems with upper-class status. As one advertiser reports, "Meridian Audio is part of living well. . . . Now you too can enjoy the convenience and luxury found in the most prestigious home theater systems in the world."[34] Consumer magazines depict the preferred environments for home theaters with a range of viewers in a range of styles, from mansions to more humble accommodations. The decor itself is sometimes drawn from modernism or postmodernism, styles that are meant to communicate the visionary, futuristic qualities associated with home theater as a "revolutionary" new technology. The tactic of associating technologies with "hip" aesthetic movements dates back at least to the early mass marketing of radio.[35] As with such previous home entertainment novelties, advertisers employ these styles to show how purchase of the new hardware revitalizes the domestic environment, not only through its association with the futuristic, but also through its links to the artistic and up-to-date.

Settings may feature well-heeled families, couples, neighbors, or other guests, but the rooms depicted are often free of viewers. This absence both invites the reader to imagine him- or herself in these surroundings and enables the decor and the machinery to be on unimpeded display. Further, the empty rooms seem indirectly to signal the dispersed nature of television watching in today's home. Most U.S. homes contain more than one television—an average of 2.43, according to Nielsen research—allowing individuals to watch the shows they prefer in separate rooms; since cable television and VHS alone have multiplied and diversified offerings along demographic lines, the image of the family gathered in front of the sole television set has possibly lost the currency it once had.[36] Whether adults are actually present in the ads or whether two wine glasses perched on a counter in a dedicated room suggest that this is their habitat, multiple television sets and viewing options may encourage the depiction of high-end home theaters as adult territory. In any case, ads often align the sophistication of the machinery with adult tastes, tending to marginalize children as appropriate viewers for this new (and expensive) wonder.

The sense of privilege connected with home theater is additionally manifested through discussions of lifestyle and leisure, particularly in relation to entertaining and food. Home theater provides the "multiplex experience . . . with better food." Within this framework, "old-style" television is comparable to a forgettable fast-food restaurant meal, whereas home theater represents the more memorable "candlelit dinner."[37] One writer sets the scene for enjoying home media in a quite elaborate way: "It's 9 o'clock on a Saturday night and you've just topped off a sumptuous meal of braised lamb chops and roasted garlic potatoes with a perfect praline souffle. Your well-sated guests are waving no to a third cup of cappuccino. . . . As you glide toward the soft-upholstered sofa that beckons your guests, you tap the discreet keypad marked ENTERTAIN on the wall to your left. The dining room chandelier fades to darkness . . . the gas fire ignites, and your audio system delivers Joshua Redman's brilliant tenor sax."[38] In this well-sated world, the host glides, sofas beckon, and buttons are discreet, suggesting a "civilized" upper-class leisure setting. The consumption of music, like the consumption of food and drink, occurs in an environment of distinction, of aesthetic perfection.

A regular feature of *Home Theater Technology* called "Snacks, Wine, and Videotape" demonstrates explicitly the links between food and film aesthetics. In one installment the author declares, "Fire up the grills, pop the corks, and celebrate the launch of summer with a great selection of films, food, and beverages." The object of this column is to pair food and drink with particular films, in the thin guise of a film review. *The Shawshank Redemption* (1994), for example, "shows us not only the extreme brutality of incarceration, but also the strange, comfortable resignation that it can foster. . . . The combination of brilliant performances and skilled production bring this story to the screen in a most remarkable way." The author recommends "two brilliant wines from contrasting price ranges" as "suitable companions to this film" (the 1991 Caymus Special Selection Napa Valley Cabernet Sauvignon and the 1992 Caymus Napa Valley Cabernet Sauvignon). He also suggests the appropriate snack to further accompany the film: "Barbequed filet mignon marinated in Dijon peppercorn mustard, cognac, and lemon zest, served with skewers of mushrooms and quartered Maui and red onions, brushed with sesame oil and soy sauce."

By contrast, *Ed Wood* (1994) is "the story of one man's crusade to direct an eclectic batch of eccentrics in what turned out to be some of the most wonderfully horrible films of the 1950s." It is "an extraordinarily crafted film in which cross-dressing, drug addiction, confused sexual identity, debatable talent, and passion all come together in a journey through Hollywood's dream factory." The author here recommends "two Technicolor Zinfandels . . . to fill out the color spectrum a bit . . . barbequed hamburgers on grilled buns with lettuce, tomatoes, and red onions . . . Dijon mustard . . . Worchester sauce [and] Thousand Island dressing. Serve potato salad and chilled grapes on the side."[39]

Judging by the menu selections for each film, *The Shawshank Redemption* has a closer relation to art cinema, signaled by its pairing with filet mignon and exotic marinade (the equivalents of high culture in the food world). Certainly, the focus of the film on the effects of prison deprivation serves here only to signify "serious" cinema rather than to dictate a more thematically appropriate menu (i.e., soggy vegetables and mystery meat). By contrast, the choice of hamburger to accompany *Ed Wood* suggests that the film's concerns (i.e., cross-dressing, drug addiction, and bad filmmaking) give it a more questionable, campy status that detracts from its consumption as "serious." However, even here, hamburger is made more respectable by associating it with Dijon mustard, Thousand Island Dressing, and chilled grapes. Thus, the hamburger is rescued from ordinariness by accompanying relishes and food items, allowing the dinner to attain some degree of refinement. For both films, the presence of wine on the menu helps finesse the snack's genteel character. This sense of upward mobility represented by food and drink continues in such regular columns as *Home Theater*'s "Libations," where home theater is defined as the right habitat for microbrewed U.S. beer (as opposed to a keg of Budweiser, for example) and home-delivered porterhouse steaks or gourmet meals.[40]

While columns such as "Snacks, Wine, and Videotape" and "Libations" may seem laughable, they simply revive an association between movies and food as old as the nickelodeon in the early 1900s. At this time working-class patrons used theaters as lunch rooms or bars, eating and drinking as they watched films, a tradition that continued as patrons bought their treats from confectionery stores near their neighborhood theaters before buying tickets.[41] In the 1930s, the movie house concession stand became a fixture, institutionalizing the intimate relationship among cinema, beverages, and food that had already become a customary aspect of moviegoing. Watching TV shows or movies in the home has similarly included a long association between food and visual entertainment, as audiences consume everything from snacks to dinner in front of their sets. Banking on this association, *Dinner & a Movie*, a TBS show that began in the 1997/98 season, features hosts who prepare dishes strategically matched with the featured films. In the first installment of *Dinner & a Movie*, hosts Annabelle Gurwitch and Paul Gilmartin prepared a dish called "Man-Eating Shark . . . and Loving It" while offering "a three-course cinematic seafood special." Promotions for this show gave the viewer suggestions: "You should whet your appetite with Steven Spielberg's 1975 thriller *Jaws* . . . gorge yourself . . . with *Piranha* (1978) . . . then wash them both down with . . . *Orca* (1977)."[42] In this case, the film-food partnership is used for more campy effects to exploit the cult value and low-brow status of these films (including *Jaws* once it is associated with take-offs *Piranha* and *Orca*). Whatever the class affiliation, the pairing of media and food continues to be highly visible and consistent—to wit, the publication of *The Sopranos Family Cookbook*, which enables viewers to concoct the same kinds of Italian cuisine so prominently featured on the HBO series.

Although motion picture theaters sometimes offer upscale concessions to their customers and viewers consume junk food as they watch television or DVDs, home theater discourse presents the domestic "palace" as surpassing the typical offerings of popcorn, candy, and soft drinks at the cinema or chips in front of the TV with full-scale gourmet delights (figure 4). Defining films in terms of upscale food selections heightens their signification of a refined lifestyle. Certainly such variables do not completely define the viewing experience, but they nonetheless play a subtle role in creating the setting in which media are viewed—that is, within the rituals of domestic space and the priorities of the home (e.g., buying, eating, entertaining).

In addition, as Bourdieu points out, the word *taste* has a dual meaning: it pertains to judgments of preference and value in both the aesthetic and the culinary worlds. These two worlds are normally kept in a state of artificial separation, with the aesthetic classified as part of a lofty culture of refinement and the "flavours of food" considered as more elemental and broadly cultural. But Bourdieu argues that these two senses of culture are in fact

What if you could go to the movies...

and bring your own snacks?

Figure 4. Upscale snacks in the domestic motion picture palace. (1999 advertisement courtesy of Zenith Electronics Corporation.)

deeply interrelated. As he writes, "One has only to remove the magical barrier which makes legitimate culture into a separate universe, in order to see intelligible relationships between choices as seemingly incommensurable as preferences in music or cooking, sport or politics, literature or hairstyle" (99). These choices are additionally revealing in that their correspondences show how the exercise of taste across various cultural practices helps to establish and maintain class relations (and, in the case of *The Sopranos Family Cookbook*, certain notions of ethnic identity) within a society.

As media industries and consumer magazines depict in glittering detail the seamless alliances among home theater, decor, and lifestyle (down to the dinner menu) within an "elite" class vocabulary, advertising breaks down the magical barrier that separates apparently different cultural strata to establish and exploit profitable homologies among them. The result is a unified vision of the "good life" that perpetuates existing images of class while also continuing to characterize refined class sensibilities as the most desirable. Home theaters may be installed in diverse economic settings. But the point is that the semiotic freight of this technology encourages consumers to idolize high-end products and to project how their ownership of such technology will enhance their cultural capital within a highly stratified society. Thus, visions of economic mobility are articulated through the selection of commodities, effectively redefining social change through the principles and goals of consumer culture.

By claiming a revolutionary impact on lifestyles, home theater advocates participate in the kind of discourse that has been used to celebrate diverse media developments from radio to cable television to new electronic imaging systems such as virtual reality.[43] As part of a historical continuum, home theater discourse stresses how its machinery redefines watching and listening, particularly through enhanced sensory experience. Operating as a signal system, home theater proposes a new film culture in domestic space, a culture that requires not only specific pieces of equipment and an elevated sense of decor and lifestyle but a change in viewing habits as well.

Exiling the Couch Potato

Home theater advertisers attempt to create a TV-watching elite out of the once notoriously democratic television audience. The figure of the couch potato, the familiar icon of the media-addicted, indolent television viewer who indiscriminately watches whatever television's flow offers, is nowhere to be found in the pages of home theater magazines, except as a foil to the new awakening that awaits the purchaser of a home theater system. Home theater owners imagine themselves as worlds apart from "Joe Six-Pack"—the lazy, beer-guzzling, regular-guy television viewer. In home theater discourse, the substitution of an image of aristocratic engagement for slothful consumption is concurrent with such other trends as "quality" television programming (e.g., *ER* and *West Wing*) and what James Naremore has referred to as "boutique cinema" (e.g., festival and art films)—trends aimed at "up-market" audiences.[44] In general, attempts to cultivate or claim such audiences have long been a part of discourses around both television and cinema as they have sought respectability and richer demographics. To reach more rarified heights, promotions for contemporary home theater seek to cultivate a sense of the improved status of the televised film and the television viewer.

As I mentioned earlier in the chapter, home theater technology is often defined as redressing the limitations of "old-fashioned TV" through large-screen or projection television sets, sophisticated surround-sound systems, and quality playback components such as Hi-Fi VCRs and DVD players. However, this technological edge over previous modes of home film exhibition is not sufficient for a more complete rewriting of film in domestic space; again, the rhetoric of high art pervades the promotion of home theaters. Hence, a call for subscriptions to *Home Theater Technology* asks of its readers, "Put a masterpiece in your living room. . . . Whether it's a Michelangelo or Marilyn, a great home theater makes every picture a work of art."[45] Advertisements frequently show the television screen in close proximity to paintings, making their intentions clear: to define television and televised feature films (no matter what they are) as sublime, or, more accurately, to define the new entertainment technologies as inherently aesthetic, able to reconstitute any media text as a "masterpiece." This association situates cinema in an encompassing aesthetic environment, where home theater components, film, and decor are all perfectly integrated to suit discriminating tastes. When an ad for Pioneer Special Editions tells us "to invest in classic entertainment that only gets better with age," we can see that, like the work of the Old Masters, cinema is being defined simultaneously as art and commodity.[46] And it is not just films from Hollywood's classic period that are defined in this way. Advertisements often prominently feature images from blockbusters on home theater screens. With its pronounced technological character, the blockbuster testifies vividly to the power of the audio-visual system to deliver the film industry's prize product to home viewers, just as the system is able to elevate the most commercial of Hollywood's fare beyond sheer spectacle into the realm of art.

This slippage between film and exhibition machinery is additionally manifested in the appearance of the home theater "auteur." Advertisements subtly create a pantheon of directors in their promotions. Through film images shown on home theater screens, such directors as Steven Spielberg and James Cameron—both associated with science fiction, blockbusters, and the mastery of special effects—signify technological excellence and spectacle, particularly in relation to digital special effects. The same is true of George Lucas, creator of the *Star Wars* series and innovator of THX sound, whose name appears prominently in promotions for THX. Also acting as a key reference point for home theater discourse, Martin Scorsese brings a different valence to this technology. Featured in ads for Vidikron's projection system, Scorsese's association with serious cinema, coupled with his championing of film preservation efforts, brings an enhanced prestige factor to home theater. Pictured in an artfully lit black-and-white photograph, Scorsese is quoted as saying, "As a filmmaker, I want to duplicate the motion picture theater experience as closely as possible in the home. Vidikron is the best projection system I've ever seen. You actually believe you're watching film." Playing off Scorsese's reputation, the text of the ad argues, "Compromise is *not* what the great movie directors are all about. They simply will not settle for second best in their movies. . . . Nor is there compromise built into their personal Home Theater. That's why they demand Vidikron video projectors. In fact, the people who create Vidikron equipment are just as uncompromising. . . . Vidikron: the Director's Choice."[47] While Spielberg, Cameron, and Lucas help signify the cutting-edge digital technologies so important to the idea of home theater—as well as the ability of these technologies to provide more realistic, bigger, and better visual and audio reproduction—Scorsese brings the aura of art and high-brow aesthetics to the system. The Vidikron ad deploys the vision of Scorsese's artistic integrity to support a corresponding vision of its technology as able to reproduce authentically the theatrical experience.

Home theater promotions thus draw from the celebrity of contemporary filmmakers to create their own set of auteurs. Aligned with state-of-the-art spectacle or higher-brow art cinema, these auteurs help to signify the performance quality of home theater products at the same time as they help to provide a sense of authenticity that renovates the often disparaged domesticated film for consumption. Linked to both the convincing delivery of spectacle and art, this sense of authenticity also informs the construction of the ideal home theater spectator; to experience fully the splendors of home theater and renovated media, ideas about home viewing must undergo a sympathetic revolution.

One of the ideal audiences for home theater is akin to the legendary original audiences of the Lumiere films at the moment of cinema's invention: home theater viewers react to the screen as if its images were real, testifying to this new technology's vivid powers of reproduction. In the mid-1990s, because of *Jurassic Park*'s (1993) popularity, the image was not of a train arriving at the station but of a roaring tyrannosaur or a crafty raptor approaching the viewer. Home theater discourse further elaborates the dimensions of this active form of spectatorship by emphasizing the intense sensory experience that the technology can deliver. As AV Architecture, a firm specializing in media furniture, states in one of its ads, "We're not just building state of the art home entertainment furnishings, we're building to pervade your senses."[48] This pervasion can take the form of an adrenaline rush, one of the "wilder" pleasures associated with film, music, and the other arts. A promotion for Toshiba DVD, for example, says: "Sound hits you at a speed of 760 mph. Light hits you at a speed of 671,000,000 mph. Toshiba DVD makes it actually feel like it. . . . Your pulse races. Your gut quivers. That little vein in your forehead is throbbing. Senses—meet Toshiba DVD. . . . You've got senses. Use them . . . your senses will thank you for this complete and total assault. As soon as they're out of traction."[49]

But, as home theater technologies have developed, companies also have addressed more nuanced reaches of sensory experience, the more subtle sensations characterized by reflective immersion. Martin Logan Limited advertises its systems by pointing out the differences between "old" home theater sound aesthetics and those with more delicate dimensions, particularly in the delivery of sound effects and music: "T-Rex *chomps* the utility vehicle as if it were tin-foil with a *roar* throwing you back into your seat. . . . *Yaaaawwwn,* 'pass the popcorn, any home theatre system can do that.' *Listen.* What was that? It's beginning to rain! You almost *feel* it. You hear the saxophone player on the street subtly breathing in between each musical phrase . . . *you are there!"*[50] Sound still transports the listener-viewer and immerses him or her in the experience, but it does so through a more apparently cultivated use of the senses.

As an expression of just how exalted the sensory experience of home theater can be, hardware magazines often depict sound systems as providing private, quasi-religious experiences. Against the backdrop of a palatial cathedral, a Parasound ad tells readers: "Music is the universal religion. Be sure to build the proper altar." With a tastefully nude Asian woman in the background, an ad for Energy Loudspeakers sells its "connoisseur-series speakers" as "musical truth . . . resonant with expanded meaning . . . you sink deeper and deeper into a private experience."[51] Music and sound have the potential to transport the listener into a private spiritual realm (signified in these two cases, respectively, by the cathedral and the stereotypical association between Asians and a Zen-like transcendence, in this instance underwritten by an erotic component). This is at once an aesthetic realm (signified, again, by the grand architecture of the cathedral and the art historical resonance of the tasteful nude). Rather than provoking a frenzy of the senses, then, sound systems can elevate them by calling on music's associations with spirituality, inwardness, beauty, and truth. In either case, the effects are not confined to the visuals; they are also monumentally auditory in nature.

Home theater advocates thus press into service music's legendary oppositional functions, its powers to incite or to exalt. Untroubled by this opposition, they promote both functions as they redefine television viewing. Whether characterizing a Lumiere-like or a Zen-like audience, home theater discourse champions an active, fully engaged viewer as necessary to the "proper" consumption of televised films and music. Activity here is not equivalent, however, to critical engagement. Rather, it represents an increased involvement in the verisimilitude and other pleasures provided by home theater.

In fact, media industry discourses tend to equate technology with experience, so much so that it becomes difficult to conceive of one without the other. A writer for a magazine editorial entitled "Are You Experienced?" illustrates this slippage between encounters with the world and with technological reproductions. Home theater is about

> clean, sharp images with accurate colors and soundtracks that sound like real life . . . it's about the experience. Living vicariously through the genius of Spielberg and Scorsese, Wilder and Huston, Cameron, Bertolucci, and Merchant-Ivory. Watching the tears dry on Michelle Pfeiffer's face. Racing headlong on the knife's edge with Harrison Ford during a Blade Runner's last assignment. Sprinting low to the ground through primeval woods with Daniel Day-Lewis at your side. Feeling the Enterprise's engines straining all around you. Gasping in wonder at dinosaurs, aliens, or the spark in Ingrid Bergman's eyes. You need hardware to enjoy these experiences to the fullness of their potential.[52]

Here we find ourselves in the familiar arena of hyperreality, a sphere of simulation, which, according to Jean Baudrillard, "begins with a liquidation of all referentials—worse: by their artificial resurrection in systems of signs."[53] Home theater enables consumers to surround themselves with a star-studded environment of experience that vividly outstrips the quotidian. The élan of celebrity mingles with the sensory impact of image and sound, supplanting the ordinary with the simulated. The simulated in turn becomes a self-enclosed system of meaning in which pathos, action, romance, spectacle, and other cinematic illusions are synonymous with participation in "real" events or events that are deemed better than real. The equation of technology with experience in the home theater aesthetic ("You need hardware to enjoy these experiences to the fullness of their potential") sells mediated sensations as *the* sensations to have. Mediation thus becomes the ultimate arbiter of experience. In this way, the affective power of image and sound is displaced onto the machinery that delivers it. As technology achieves authority, the spectacle of images and sounds is once again underwritten by another spectacle—the grand proficiency of the machines of reproduction themselves.

Moreover, one can *control* this magisterial array. New entertainment technologies are notorious for frustrating homeowners who attempt to assemble connections and operate the various components. Once the mysteries are solved, however, the homeowner becomes the master of technology, the owner and operator of a complex, sophisticated, state-of-the-art system. Certainly, media industries have taken note of the appeal of control as a selling point of these technologies. In 1980 Sony advertised its VCR with the slogan "Experience the freedom of total control." The company promised the viewer the ability to "master time, memory, and circumstance" through time-shifting.[54] In 1997, Universal Remote Control, a home theater business, similarly invoked the appeal of its device with "Take Complete Control with Home Theater Master . . . the only universal remote control you will ever need for your home theater."[55]

But who is actually in control of home theater technologies? Statistics suggest that, although women are often considered the main purchasers of items for the home, men are the primary consumers of media center hardware (for example, 85 percent of Pioneer's home theater products are purchased by men). Another indication of this bond between men and media centers is that they post the majority of messages on Web sites such as hometheaterforum.com. It comes as no surprise, then, that commentators have regarded home theater as the equivalent of a "car fixation" for these consumers (Hafner D7). Making this association explicit, German home theater company Loewe pictures a shiny chrome-colored car on the first page of its ad, captioned with "It's said the Germans know a thing or two about performance and design." On the next page, there is a matching, high-tech chrome-colored television, shot with the same lighting, captioned with "Introducing the sports car of television. Digital television is about to shift into high gear [with] a whole new dimension in sight and sound. . . . Your test drive is waiting" (figures 5 and 6).[56] Fast cars and home theater components appear analogous, then, through language intended to appeal to the male shopper, who apparently has the knowledge and the bank account to make the serious economic commitment to excellence demanded by these technological objects.

Companies attempt to lure male consumers through such "manly" iconography, while their emphasis on decor intends to reconcile women with the changes in their homes that inevitably follow home theater installation. This is true despite indications that men tend to choose the furniture for the home theater environment as well, particularly when it involves "'home theater looking style' furnishings," such as Berkline Tempur-Pedic cushioned stadium seating, which women find "more acceptable" than the ad hoc placement of a sofa sleeper in front of the entertainment center.[57] The taste of the decor in home theater promotions, then, is meant not only to reflect the sophistication of the equipment itself but also to connect with women, who otherwise might be alienated by the sight

Figures 5 and 6. Combining cars and TVs: the implicit appeal to the male home theater buyer. (Advertisement courtesy of Loewe.)

of unadorned, improperly integrated machinery in their homes. Nice home theater seating and entertainment cabinets, as well as sleeker, less obtrusive televisions such as plasma TVs, soften the blow of a room heavily defined by technology and overcome obstacles to purchase presented by what the industry refers to as the WAF (wife acceptance factor). Part of the selling of new technologies thus attempts to address the variables of gender through traditional means—by emphasizing the wizardry of the machine's capabilities for men and by demonstrating the principles of home beautification that surround the machine for women—while also subtly providing a role for men as purchasers of furnishings destined to complete the family's entertainment space.

Public accounts acknowledge that the entry of home theater systems into the household does not always proceed without conflict or resistance from women, especially since installation can involve a major remapping of family needs and expenditures. As one woman remarked, "We've just moved into the house. . . . We have no furniture yet except the media room. You can see where my husband's priorities are."[58] The lexicon section of the Web site DVD Journal spells out the perils of this situation; it defines A/V as an "acronym for Audio-Video, a general term for home theater, e.g., I have spent so much on home theater equipment my wife moved out." Yet, newspaper and magazine stories suggest that a wife's skepticism can be overcome not just by plush cinema chairs but also by the charms of the high-tech equipment itself. In the best-case scenario, these stories depict the husband as a pioneer who "tames" the technology and then offers it to his family. Initially reluctant, the wife becomes a convert who cannot imagine watching films without home theater (Hafner D7). Such conversion narratives enhance the sense of the husband's stewardship of the home and his ability to make domestic space his technological domain. By demonstrating family unanimity, these narratives also strategically attempt to suppress anxieties about the husband's willfulness or irresponsibility in regard to his technological priorities as well as their potential to disrupt the family unit.

Unlike some scenarios of television in the 1950s in which the father's place was challenged by the dominance of television in the household (as well as by displays of fatherly foibles in situation comedies), the public construction of contemporary home theater defines a central role for the authoritative exercise of the paternal function—even in relation to men who, because of their overinvestment in home entertainment technologies, may otherwise seem "nerdy" or eccentric.[59] Accounts often depict the husband as a forward-thinking, savvy master builder, responsible for the modernization of the home in a time when its digitalization (through the smart home concept and other developments) is an especially prized achievement.[60]

Home theater specialists thus join the ranks of Moores's gadgeteers—men devoted to purchasing, mastering, and tinkering with technology, including electronics of all kinds. Whether their commitment is to audio systems, computers, satellite television, or other devices, the "specific configuration of technology and masculinity" that produces and sustains the technophile creates a form of male pleasure and male culture central to understanding the social function of certain kinds of technological innovations.[61] Given his affiliation with high-tech mastery, this technophile suggests that the presence of a new technology does not revolutionize as much as subtly reinforce traditional gender roles and power relations in the home. As Ann Gray has argued in her work on the VCR, technologies are neither innately feminine nor masculine; they attain certain gendered values as part of their social use and circulation.[62] With this in mind, home theater (particularly with its high quotient of audiophilia, an area typically associated with men) appears as a male preserve.

As we have seen, home theater discourse involves an important inclusive dimension that further enhances the centrality of the technophile. With gadgeteers' recruitment of women as devotees of new entertainment systems and the modernizing effects they have on the home, male dominion has extended beyond any merely technological realm designated for the husband's use (i.e., a garage or den) into the design and function of the home itself. Although not a totalizing operation, home theater installation amplifies the sense of masculine jurisdiction, modifying the home's traditional association with the feminine sphere. At the same time, the manner in which high-end technologies are presented to and adopted by well-to-do white male publics helps to perpetuate the status quo in terms of race as well as gender and class. This state of affairs is in the process of changing; however, mainstream ads heralding the desirability of home theater have been filled with Caucasian faces, signifying an upper- and middle-class whiteness and an exclusion of people of color as vividly as they display male mastery.

Discussions of new technologies often depict mastery as a significant virtue. Scholars such as Sean Cubitt and Henry Jenkins have argued that technological developments offer viewers potentially unprecedented degrees of power over the image. The VCR's ability to time-shift, for example, allows audience members to tailor their viewing time to suit their own desires rather than be held captive to network programming schedules; similarly, the remote control's fast-forward and rewind buttons enable substantial manipulation of the image. This impact of new technologies cannot be denied, but media industries' promise of the experiences of freedom and mastery to consumers as a mainstay of their sales campaigns should give us some pause. *Freedom* and *mastery* are loaded terms that do not apply solely to small victories over equipment manuals or the capacity to operate on images. Rather, these terms often refer to "the ability of each person to emulate or aspire to emulate the tastes of the upper classes . . . [through] consumption."[63] In the case of high-end products such as home theater, the consumer is invited to participate in the rarefied leisure world of the upper class. As Bourdieu writes of the sales of other kinds of luxury goods to consumers, "Technical competence is less important than familiarity with the culture of the dominant class and a mastery of the signs and emblems of distinction and taste" (141). The consumer's gratification, then, relies not just on mastery understood as a concrete exercise of skill but also on a sense of symbolic superiority constituted by his or her conversancy with the exalted class status of the goods in question. In this sense, the command of technology should not be understood as a purely masculine capability. Bourdieu's passage encourages us to see that, beyond the "nuts and bolts" knowledge of new entertainment technologies, another kind of mastery exists—a mastery of the symbolic capital of high-tech machines as they reside in the home, among the owner's other possessions. Thus, as much as home theater perpetuates certain classic distinctions between genders in terms of technological initiative and competence, the discourse portrays both white men and women as ultimately unified in their access to this kind of capital.

This is not to say that viewers are entirely coopted by such strategies or that the industry's vision of consumer control exhausts the possible exercises of freedom. Neither entirely an occupied territory nor a utopian island free from constraints, the home is a fully contested space, caught between media industry significations and individual deployments of the technology. Mastery is, however, a potent feature of the way that new entertainment technologies are written into the private sphere. This discourse accompanies the penetration of corporate enterprise and consumer culture into the home as it is refashioned into an entertainment zone. At the very least, as an intimate part of the techno-aesthetic offered to home audiences, this promoted feature complicates celebrations of viewer freedom by raising questions of how commercial representations of technology affect the viewer's domestic media encounters and how, in turn, these representations signify inclusion and exclusion in terms of race, gender, and class.

Home theater may offer individuals flexibility in their use of cinema, then, but its presence in the home is underwritten by mediating forces—here, public enterprises that attempt to define how this technology is to be perceived and implemented. Despite the continual description of digital technology as revolutionary, the manner in which media industries promote the idea of home theater abides by conventions in advertising, particularly as those conventions promise the revitalization of the home, film, television, and the viewing experience through associations with upper- and middle-class white sensibilities and the traditional distribution of gender roles. In this way, home theater's example strongly suggests how old values can become encoded in new technologies, how the new is likely to be articulated within preexisting languages.[64]

The male subculture of technophiles will likely persist as home theater use continues to grow. However, home theater's broader promotion and dissemination mean that other discourses will become increasingly visible, forecasting a potentially different public face and signal system for this newest addition to the concept of the entertainment center.

Home Theater as Film Culture

As we have seen, the public image of home theater that enters domestic space is unambiguous in distinguishing it as a commodity that confers privilege, even nobility, upon its users. Characterizing home theater as superior to preexisting entertainment technologies—a modernizing force that yields heightened sensory experiences to engaged, discerning viewers—media industries and consumer magazines attempt to create an aristocratic domain in the much-maligned domestic zone with its "antiquated" television set and passive viewers. This revision of the viewer's relation to media in the home depends on aestheticizing digital technologies designed for domestic use, a development that parallels the contemporary rebirth of the motion picture theater through the promotion of digital advances in visual and audio representation and the accompanying upgrading of theater facilities. As such a "charged" exhibition venue for movies and other media, home theater aims physically and ideologically to redesign the home as a suitable environment for these new goods.

In defining movie presentation in domestic space, home theater acts to displace the specificity of the film being screened. The array of machines and their capabilities operate as environmental cues that filter the film experience through a class-based, culinary, "high-art" aesthetic that ultimately reflects the magnificence of the system itself. Just as in the case of the motion picture palace with its unparalleled glamour and upper-class trappings, the specific film may matter less to viewers than the accompanying milieu. However, ads' preoccupation with action sequences or special effects films suggests that the blockbuster is the cinematic ideal that best realizes the system's grandeur. Home theater and the blockbuster enter into a tangle of mutually beneficial effects: the former is depicted as sure to deliver the full impact of the latter, and cinematic extravaganzas are just as sure to demonstrate the media center's technical prowess. Even more modest films may be given a semiotic boost toward epic status under the auspices of home theater.

Insofar as it reintroduces sound as a crucial factor in exhibition, home theater, like the contemporary public theater, represents an intervention in film reception that parallels the coming of sound to motion picture theaters. Certainly, the size of the image signifies the media center's ambitiousness and is integral to claims that it rivals the public motion picture theater. But the delivery of impressive sound effects and film music are just as, if not more, important in the domestic experience of films. Although ads emphasize the subtleties of sound in these systems, like those in motion picture theaters, home theaters embrace digital technologies that provide "bigger" audio delivered in a separate-channel surround format. This feature continues to serve the blockbuster particularly well. Big sound graphically realizes the impact of awe-inspiring special effects that involve explosions, rampaging dinosaurs, and intergalactic battles. Digital sound also greatly enhances the hallmark moments of action films—for example, the gunfire, screeching tires, and general chaos of chase and battle scenes. Pumped-up music further underscores the intensity of moments that showcase such generic spectacles. Again, any film may benefit from audio enhancements of the narrative, but home theater's technological capabilities seem especially designed to bring the blockbuster experience to home audiences, acting as one more means of increasing the blockbuster's dominion beyond the big screen.[65]

Theorists such as John Ellis have argued that a primary distinction between cinema and television can be found in each medium's association with image and sound. According to Ellis, the image dominates the experience of cinema, and sound dominates the experience of television (a medium he finds less detailed and refined in its visual capabilities).[66] If we try to update this dichotomy to apply to home theater, we could say that, despite its reliance on television, home theater strives to deliver the theatrical screen's visual fascinations; conversely, as an audio powerhouse, it maximizes TV's reliance on sound as a fundamental means of gaining viewers' attention. However, this opposition between film/image and TV/sound is surely outdated. HDTV alone powerfully aligns television with quality image-making. Well before this development, though, as John Caldwell has persuasively argued in his work on televisuality in the 1980s and 1990s, television practices emphasized excessive displays of visual style.[67] Similarly, it is impossible to think of contemporary cinema without realizing its profound reliance on sound.

Home theater makes media boundary crossings strikingly visible. Its synthesis of multiple technologies forces reconsideration of traditional estimations of medium specificity. For many, viewing films at home is unthinkable without the combined effects of audio, cinematic, televisual, and digital texts and technologies. At the very least, in this world, image and sound attain parity. This intermedia context makes sound as mesmerizing as image, potentially directing viewers to significant dramatic moments and relegating audibly quieter moments to a less important narrative status—acting, then, as a kind of sound "italics" devoted to an overall ideology of the spectacular.[68] This ideology continues to serve the blockbuster's hegemony while shaping viewers' expectations about what is valuable in their film experience. As the commodification of audio in both public and private exhibition venues circles back into production practices, affecting the design of motion picture soundtracks, the cycle reinforces the centrality of sound across a spectrum of movie practices.

Home theater then emphasizes spectacle—the spectacle of its own machines and of the images and sounds they reproduce. Rather than regard this forum as compromising the experience of the total film, we should view it as another in a long line of media industry strategies to sell movies through the language of spectacle, whether it be the twin displays of sex and violence in film content or the technological displays of special effects and digital capabilities. As a signal system, home theater not only defines movie watching through a class-based aesthetic bound up with refined tastes; it also finds myriad ways of promoting the sensory dimensions of image and sound as central to the household consumption of motion pictures.

Beyond its shaping of movies in the home, the contemporary media center is linked to conceptions of the home in the late twentieth and early twenty-first centuries. On the one hand, the example of home theater permits us to reflect on how technological progress operates through social categories designed to reinvent continually the home as the site where class relations can be forever articulated and understood as strategies of consumption and use. On the other hand, it allows us a glimpse of the home within a broader national context. As we have seen, early home theater entrepreneurs, inspired by industrialization, envisioned the home as a site wherein the magnificence of American technological achievements could be further realized. Following the invention of television, another significant articulation of home theater in the 1950s regarded the home as a synthetic place for entertainment technologies. Within this Cold War setting, as Elaine Tyler May has shown, household technologies in general became particularly important to U.S. ideologies: they testified to capitalism's superiority to communism, while defining the family (with appropriate gender roles) and the home as fortresses against the subversiveness of communism and the threat of a nuclear war.[69]

As the phenomenal growth of contemporary home theater dovetailed with millennial anxieties and with 9/11, coverage of potential disasters that made the public sphere look unstable and dangerous (e.g., Y2K, computer viruses, global warming, terrorist threats, and apocalyptic movies such as *Independence Day* [1996] and *Armageddon* [1998]) echoed Cold War fears about the end of the world. With their reassuring depictions of the good life surrounding exquisite media experiences that do not oblige circulation in the public sphere, home theater ads promote the view that technological prowess is a signifier of American superiority on the world stage (a view that counters the frequently expressed idea in disaster discourses that technologies are at the root of global destruction). Moreover, the idea of home theater suggests that private space, supervised by the expert consumer father, can be made into a self-sufficient zone, complete with the advantages offered by public entertainment. As one of the key ingredients of survivalism, self-sufficiency promises its adherents a relatively safe harbor from the risks outside, as well as the ability to prevail over those risks should the occasion arise.[70]

Figure 7. Imagery that suggests the home theater as a kind of fortress. (Ad design by Machado Design. Advertisement courtesy of Runco International.)

Sometimes literally pictured in ads as a castle keep surrounded by a moat (figure 7), home theater helps to provide the cocooning effects of the fortress that are, in turn, part of the contemporary response to images of disaster. Equipped to bring the world to the home viewer, it implies that it can provide all of the pleasures of mass entertainment without any of the attendant potential perils of public life. As a far less stark, self-sustaining inner sanctum where homeowners can seek shelter from dangerous, invasive forces, home theater represents a utopian version of the Cold War–era bomb shelter and of the more contemporary "panic room" (vividly depicted in the film *Panic Room* [2002]). As always, this interiorized vision of the home partakes of the full ironies of the fortress image in which one attains a sense of insularity only by duplicating the technologies and experiences of the outside world, exposing domestic space fully to industries and interests located in the commercial public sphere.

Linked to a series of contexts, this film culture, then, is shaped by certain definitions of entertainment media, the home, lifestyles, the viewer, and the public sphere. Through traditional advertising tactics used to sell new technologies, it promotes a white, upper- and middle-class vision of taste, masculine mastery, and media consumption. It also more subtly portrays the United States as a thriving economy and the home as a retreat from the anxieties that characterize the political and social realm. There may be an occasional outcry about the social isolation associated with home theater (a protest that accompanied the introduction of the Sony Walkman and other technologies designed for personal use) or the Orwellian dimensions of technology's engulfment of private space (crystallized in the reality show *Big Brother*, in which a group of people live for months in a house under surveillance by video cameras). Similarly, as we have seen, the impact of male home theater obsessions on family unity raises some concern. Perhaps seeking to quell such concerns, mainstream commentary tends to treat home theater as a ringing tribute to the latest developments in new entertainment technologies.

It is important to point out, as Raymond Williams does, that such signal systems do not operate in isolation; they occur within a complex sociology of signal systems. The activities of media industries and consumer culture need to be weighed alongside other factors, including the uses of media centers by families and individuals within existing household dynamics. We should view the distinctions cultivated by media industries, then, as part of an intricate series of factors that bear on domestic viewing. These distinctions help to describe what David Morley has called the "social architecture" of the home viewing experience, the impact that multiple contexts in the household have on how media are consumed.[71] With this in mind, we see that the public construction of home theater as aristocratic is an integral piece of the puzzle, helping us to understand the multifaceted and changing cultural rituals that occur around home entertainment.

The high-tech accoutrement related to film exhibition in domestic space extends, of course, beyond home theater, having embraced such technologies as Hi-Fi VCRs, laser disc players, and DVD players. Although these components have all been associated with home theater, they are also responsible for generating other home film cultures. As an enterprise that has grown exponentially since the advent of these devices, film collecting is especially prominent among these cultures. In the next chapter, I consider this dimension of the high-tech aesthetic and gadgeteering ethos, focusing on the growth of a collecting mentality in the home and its role in negotiating film meaning.

2 The Contemporary Cinephile
Film Collecting after the VCR

> Let us grant that our everyday objects are in fact objects
> of a passion—the passion for private property, emotional
> investment in which is every bit as intense as investment in
> the "human" passions. Indeed, the everyday passion for
> private property is often stronger than all the others, and
> sometimes even reigns supreme, all other passions being
> absent.
>
> **Jean Baudrillard,** *The System of Objects,* 1996

Since the 1970s the term *cinephile* has conjured definite meanings and associations for film scholars. Christian Metz and other psychoanalytic theorists have characterized the cinephile as an extreme but logical extension of
the regular filmgoer who loves the cinema with a "passion for seeing" that
is tied inextricably to the movie hall's "theatre of shadows" and the technology that makes it possible (i.e., the camera, projector, and screen). Ultimately "enchanted at what the machine is capable of," the film devotee enters the theater not just to encounter a particular film but to take ardent,
fetishistic pleasure in the viewing conditions themselves.[1] The cinephile
thus vividly realizes the capacity of the cinematic apparatus to transfix its
spectators through the darkness of the theater, the brilliantly lit screen, and
other conditions that constitute cinema's spellbinding nature and array of
visual fascinations.

Given these characterizations, it is not surprising that scholars have since
regarded cinephilia as essentially and exclusively a big-screen experience,
absolutely dependent on the projection of celluloid within the public space
of the motion picture theater. Assuming that film pleasure arises expressly
from being "submerged in the darkness of the theater," Roland Barthes once
argued that the televised film elicits "the opposite experience," that is,

"nothing, no fascination; the darkness is dissolved, the anonymity repressed, the space is familiar, organized (by furniture and familiar objects), tamed."[2] Particularly because of its domestic setting, then, television appears as the antithesis of the movie theater as an exhibition site for films, a prime example of the "death" of rapture caused by removing film viewing from its proper context. In the wasteland of affect defining the home and its subdued, private entertainment space, the exercise of cinephilia would be unimaginable.

While claims about the utter impoverishment of television as a screening venue for films are often based on cinematic or cultural elitism, developments in entertainment technologies designed for home use have made it harder to ignore television's connections to diverse, sometimes intensely invested, film cultures. Although the dynamics of household viewing may not replicate the psychic parameters of spectatorship in the motion picture theater, certain home film cultures suggest that passion for the cinema is not anomalous within domestic space. In fact, as we saw in the case of home theater, the home has been equipped and acculturated to produce its own kind of connoisseurship, its own brand of fascinations.

In this chapter, I explore a type of home film culture based on playback technologies, a culture that, in a particularly telling fashion, provokes reconsideration of the image of the domestic viewer bereft of viewing pleasure. One of the most avid viewers to emerge from this culture has been the film collector, the consumer who purchases films on VHS, laser disc (before it was superseded by DVD), and DVD to create an extensive media library. Seated in front of the television set, today's collector is a member of a corps of impassioned film devotees who are, like Metz's cinephile, "enchanted at what the machine is capable of," that is, mesmerized by the machines of reproduction that deliver the cinematic illusion. However, the mesmerizing apparatuses in this case are not the camera, projector, and screen related to the exhibition of celluloid, but the accoutrement associated with cinema playback in the home. The contemporary film collector's romance with various technological aspects of the films and machines that make up the experience of cinema in domestic space suggests that cinephilia has been broadened to encompass the "forbidden" territories of television and the home. Film's domestication has not obliterated cinephilia; rather, the conditions fueling this kind of zealotry have been relocated and rearticulated within the complex interactions among media industries, commodity culture, and the private sphere. Although media industries do not control the activity of collecting, they have played a significant role in inspiring its growth as a routine activity, a commonplace aspect of the viewer's relation to film. In league with other social forces, these industries have had a dramatic impact on defining films as collectibles in the marketplace and on shaping their reception in the home.

My consideration of the phenomenon of film collecting in the home begins by addressing several preliminary questions. How has collecting become an integral part of the viewer's media landscape in the United States? Who, exactly, collects? How do we situate this pastime, often regarded as personal and idiosyncratic, within a cultural frame? To examine in more detail the implications of contemporary film collecting for reception, I focus on a figure who vividly incarnates the domestic cinephile: the high-end collector committed to the best technological standards in playback equipment and films. As we shall see, there are different kinds of collectors, yet this subculture reflects with particular clarity the substantial effects new technologies have had on film consumption in the home. Like the home theater enthusiast, this collector helps to shed light on the relationship of gender and home film cultures, demonstrating a persistent equation of men and machines. Collecting enables us to see from a different angle the importance and function of the male technophile or gadgeteer to home film cultures, as well as the special "exclusionary discursive practices" that animate and define this world.[3] As contemporary cinephilia is associated with audio-visual technophilia, a range of discourses persistently address this collector as an "insider," an individual with highly specialized industry knowledge. At the same time, as films become possessions within this world, technophilic systems of value generate an influential aesthetic that assesses Hollywood film reissues of old and new films alike according to digital standards, shifting their identities and meanings for a new echelon of consumer.

Although this collecting enterprise foregrounds technology in a way that affects both collectors and films, cinema's very status as private property also helps to define this home film culture. Since film collecting is definitively characterized by a desire for ownership, I consider how the establishment of a home archive—the arena in which the possession of films is most vividly realized and displayed—affects reception. Appearing at first glance as simply a utilitarian procedure, the organization of films within the personal library is a significant activity. As the collector assumes control over his or her videocassettes and DVDs, classifying titles within the order and logic of the collection itself, the personal archive appears as an inner sanctum. Here, the archivist gains a sense of mastery over a private universe, while the historical identities of films undergo yet more changes. As it creates an apparently self-regulated space, the archive can obscure the substantial pressures exerted by public discourse on this area of consumer life—a masking central to the pleasures of ownership and to the dialectic between public and private that characterizes home film cultures.

Why Rent When You Can Own?

According to Anthony Slide, the 1970s and 1980s marked a period of abundant activity for those who collected films in 8mm and 16mm formats. During this time, numerous companies devoted to film distribution in these formats sold titles to individuals at reasonable prices.[4] The early history of film collecting in 8mm, 16mm, and 35mm formats by individual collectors (including well-known collectors such as David Bradley, David Shepard, and William K. Everson) predates this particular high point, as does the acquisition of film libraries by various archives around the country.[5] Although films in the libraries of individuals and organizations were frequently screened in public and of course enjoyed in private, film collecting was still a relatively specialized activity until the advent of the video player, most avidly pursued by dedicated film lovers, museum curators, and archivists. Film collecting on celluloid continues today. However, the contemporary collector is no longer only a cinema specialist living in the Hollywood hills surrounded by hundreds of prints or an academic screening films on a 16mm projector in the basement. As movie ownership has become more pervasively defined by VHS and DVD, it has become dramatically democratized.

Part of the reason for this shift is that the videocassette and DVD have provided viewers of all types—from the most to the least cinephilic—with unparalleled physical access to the cinema. Viewers can now own and operate what once was an unapproachable medium, hovering in the distance on the silver screen or subject to broadcast flow, its transient appearance guaranteed by the end of its theatrical run or the beginning of the next television program. Today cinema can be contained in small boxes and placed on a shelf in a room, left on the coffee table, or thrown onto the floor. Viewers can pause, fast-forward, rewind, or mangle images through the VCR; they can select scenes precisely through the chapter-search feature on the DVD remote. On VHS or DVD, films can be screened repeatedly at an individual's whim and achieve an indelible place in everyday routines. As Timothy Corrigan remarks, within home economies of viewing, people often "adopt movies," transforming public objects into home furnishings that respond to the concerns and rituals of domestic space.[6] This previously physically remote and transitory medium has thus attained the solidity and semipermanent status of a household object, intimately and infinitely subject to manipulation in the private sphere.

The 1975 introduction of VHS to the consumer market, the 1978 entrance of laser disc, and the more recent appearance in 1997 of DVD have provided venues that are more "user friendly" and less expensive than celluloid, inspiring cinema's contemporary cultural omnipresence. Although laser disc was unable to penetrate the U.S. market beyond a few million homes and hence maintained a boutique identity, VHS and DVD have experienced different fortunes. In 2002, VCRs were in approximately 90 percent of U.S. households (with home video bringing in more than double the revenue of theatrical sales, constituting 58 percent of Hollywood's total income). Considered "the hottest selling consumer electronics product in history," as mentioned in chapter 1, DVD players were in 30 percent of U.S. homes five years after their commercial introduction. Although estimates vary, the Consumer Electronics Manufacturers Association found that DVD's penetration rate a year later, in 2003, had increased dramatically to 57 percent of homes. Forecasters predict that this number will rise to 80 percent by the end of 2005.[7]

As these statistics suggest, cinema's domestic presence has become an almost inextricable component of leisure and life that has, in turn, broadened the horizons of public and private film cultures. As a *New York Times* reporter comments in a 1997 article entitled "Land of the Cineplex, Home of the Cassette," "Americans are watching movies any way they can . . . watching movies has become something of a national pastime."[8] Within the national pastime of watching movies, a marked trend toward purchasing videocassettes and DVDs has helped redefine film collecting as a more democratic art. Many consumers are not satisfied with renting certain titles for one-night stands; to embrace their favorites truly, they want to possess them, organize them into personal libraries, and view them repeatedly.

Along with the sheer availability and accessibility of cinema in the home, certain economic factors, such as the falling prices of VCRs and DVD players and the development of a strong sell-through market for videocassettes and DVDs, have played an important role in the growth of the home "movie habit." In addition, marketing campaigns that promote films as collectibles and address certain kinds of collectors have been central to enhancing the attractiveness of ownership.

According to Robert C. Allen, a different pricing structure for films on video gained momentum between 1983 and 1992, when feature films "priced for sell-through increased at an average annual rate of 52 percent, from 59 million copies to 264 million."[9] In sell-through, studios offer their films on VHS or DVD at a low enough price that the consumer is encouraged to buy rather than to rent the film in question. Whereas once consumers had to spend about a hundred dollars to purchase a videocassette, with some exceptions, a sell-through market meant they could obtain it for approximately twenty dollars (or less).[10] This arrangement not only helped to spur a movement toward film acquisition; it also proved financially advantageous for the studios. By 1989, the sell-through market already made up a three-billion-dollar industry.[11]

The last ten years have seen the increasing importance of the sell-through market to Hollywood while also witnessing the ascendancy of DVD. In 1992, VHS sales alone surpassed the theatrical take for the first time and continued to gain ground through the decade. In 1996, when revenue from the domestic box office totaled about $5.9 billion, patrons rented $8.7 billion worth of videocassettes and spent $7.6 billion on prerecorded tapes.[12] Since then DVD has made significant advances. For the first time in 2001, DVD sales revenues superseded those of VHS, constituting 52 percent of the $10.3 billion U.S. consumers spent on purchasing films. By mid-2003, Video Business reported that $4.8 billion worth of DVDs were sold, whereas the sales of videocassettes amounted to only $1.05 billion. In the same year, DVD rentals also surpassed video rentals. As the cases of *Training Day* (2001), *The Fast and the Furious* (2001), and many other titles show, revenue from DVD releases can easily exceed that of first-run theatrical box office releases.[13] In any case, with consumers spending $15.5 billion on DVD purchases in 2004 (and $5.7 billion on DVD rentals), the home continues to represent not only a formidable market but also a site of rising populations of DVD aficionados.[14]

Multiple factors have contributed to DVD's success and its growth as a sell-through market. Its use not restricted to the stand-alone DVD player, DVD has been featured on or associated with other massively popular digital technologies identified with high quality and personal use, such as CDs, PCs, laptops, and gaming systems. The presence of DVD has contributed to a sense of the versatility of these other machines while allowing DVD itself to attain a diffuse presence in the household. Moreover, given its superior image and sound, DVD seems a more logical counterpart to another significant home entertainment form—the home theater system—than the Hi-Fi VCR. In fact, purchasing a home theater system often provides a strong incentive for building a DVD collection. At the same time, DVD's cost and quality have given it a comparative advantage over VHS in the market. Certainly, lower prices for DVD players and the inexpensiveness of disc manufacture in comparison with VHS—a boon to both vendors and studios—

have figured into its rapid growth.[15] Like the face-off between the LP and the CD in the music business, VHS, an analog-based medium with limited image resolution and a proclivity for deterioration, has all but been displaced by DVD, a digitally based technology boasting better reproduction and less susceptibility to degeneration (as well as the practical advantage of taking up less shelf space). Because DVDs can be watched repeatedly without substantial alteration in image and sound quality, this format appears to be a better preservation medium, making it especially attractive to film buyers and collectors. Moreover, DVR machines give this technology the recording capabilities lacking in other earlier would-be competitors of VHS, such as laser disc.

While VHS has been outmatched by DVD—seen by the falling stature of VHS as a revenue source as well as by its absence or dwindling presence in video rental stores and in the minimal shelf space devoted to VCRs in electronics showrooms—it is important to remember that DVD is a relative of VHS in its playback capacities and concentration on Hollywood films. In this respect, as we shall see, DVD raises similar kinds of issues about home film cultures. However, because of its superior technical capabilities, DVD also refines and redefines what VHS has been able to offer viewers, significantly transforming certain characteristics of these cultures.

Within the rerelease market, irrespective of format, any film is potentially a collectible. But certain films are also explicitly designated as such through a host of labels, including special collector's editions, widescreen editions, director's cuts, restored or remastered classics, anniversary editions, and gold, silver, or platinum editions. Each of these labels suggests that the rereleased film is a privileged form that stands outside of the normal avalanche of videocassettes and DVDs. Packaging of these editions can be quite elaborate, underscoring their elite position in the flow of movie goods. The Criterion Collection, a film distributor co-owned by Janus Films, was influential in propagating this marketing strategy. Beginning in 1984 as part of its efforts to sell and popularize laser discs, this company sold special collector's editions of films. These editions might feature digitally remastered versions of films in their original widescreen formats (if appropriate) and provide extras such as the director's commentary and accompanying background material, including trailers, outtakes, and "making of" documentaries. Criterion has been especially associated with film as "high art," promoting the work of renowned directors and classic films. Thus, the company announced its 1997 collection by telling its patrons, "The cornerstone of any movie collection is the work of a few great filmmakers," adding that its list of "popular favorites, lost treasures, and landmark films from around the world [will provide] the closest thing we know to a perfect shelf of movies."

Although the special collector's edition began as a niche market for film buffs and academics interested in buying films on laser disc or widescreen VHS, the extras it boasts have become an intimate part of DVD release—so much so that consumers expect to get behind-the-scenes information with their rentals or purchases. Studios have made extras such a fixture that it would be hard for fans of *The Matrix* (1999), for example, to imagine the film's home version without facts about the accomplishment of its special effects (especially "bullet time") or the choreography of its martial arts fight scenes by Hong Kong master Yuen Wo Ping. DVD extras and a sense of a DVD aesthetic have already become a prime feature of film culture. This is especially visible in the case of younger generations of viewers attracted to both blockbusters and technology and for newspaper and magazine columnists covering home releases who routinely refer to certain films (particularly those heavy on special effects) as "perfect" DVD movies.

The broad acceptance of this new technology reflects the perception that the digital era in theatrical cinema has finally found its aesthetic equivalent on the domestic front in DVD. Since DVD offers film images with good resolution in widescreen formats and sound that performs well through surround systems, it approximates the theatrical experience, thereby altering a film less dramatically than previous distribution venues. DVD thus provides an interesting twist to discussions of the inferior status of nontheatrical exhibition and the debased forms of film presentation often thought to be characteristic of the nontheatrical. Moreover, although specialized markets in film collectibles still thrive, at once high-tech and popular, apparently exclusive and omnipresent, DVD is in the process of expanding the notion of the aesthete beyond the laser-phile addressed in Criterion's pioneering days to include more mainstream consumers. At the same time, given the proliferation of industry discourses that accompany the feature film on DVD, this technology has enabled media companies to extend their reach into the home, shaping the patron's relationship to specific films as well as to Hollywood itself.

With the progressive development of the sell-through market and the special edition, film and other media industries have explicitly targeted collectors in their packaging and selling of titles. In its broadest configuration, collecting is undertaken by the consumer who purchases just a few favorite titles to put on a shelf as well as by the rabid devotee who pursues hundreds or thousands of titles systematically in order to create a model library of films. Film production companies, electronics firms specializing in home theater, VHS and DVD vendors, and other businesses avidly pursue the spectrum of possible collectors, attempting to ignite and feed their desires. In fact, there appears to be a strong link between the purchase of DVD players and starter collections,[16] a link the industry has nurtured by releasing "completist" boxed sets of the works of specific directors, actors, genres, and TV series. Generally, the goal of media industries in relation to collectors is to tap into a middle-class consciousness about the superiority of ownership. As an ad for the VHS edition of *Star Trek: First Contact* (1996), priced at $14.95, puts it, "Why Rent Space When You Can Own It?"[17] But the industry also issues specific appeals to various demographic and taste groups associated with collecting. As a sign of its mainstream presence, youth, men, women, and families are all recognized as potential collectors.

One ad, for example, asks the reader to "Accessorize Your Evening" by buying *The First Wives Club* (1996), *Clueless* (1995), *Sabrina* (1995), and *Harriet the Spy* (1996) as "the perfect additions to your home video collection."[18] Against a backdrop consisting of personal accessories of clothing, jewelry, and roses, the ad attempts to sell a package of chick flicks (that is, films conceived for and marketed to female viewers) to younger and older women. While women are thus "targeted," sales charts for VHS have long indicated that families provide a major market for sell-through, because they consistently purchase titles for their children and grandchildren—a group likely to want to see the same films repeatedly. As Robert Allen points out of the pre-DVD era, "The core markets for both video rentals and sales are families with children under the age of seventeen. Households with children are more than twice as likely to be frequent renters and heavy buyers of films on video." As he continues to note, "Sixty percent of all U.S. households own feature films on video, with an average number of titles in family collections standing at forty-one."[19] Thus, the majority of the ten best-selling videocassettes of all time by the mid-1990s (such as *E.T.* [1982] and *The Little Mermaid* [1989]) were children's films or films oriented toward youth. Today, families are in the process of moving strongly into the DVD market, reflected by the presence of children's films such as *Finding Nemo* (2003) and *Shrek 2* (2004) at the top of DVD sales charts.

The way in which film collectors can be identified as more truly composing a niche audience lies in the distinction between "high-end" and "low-end" practices. Typically, high-end collectors buy expensive entertainment equipment and concentrate on the acquisition of DVDs, good-quality videocassettes, or, during their heyday in the 1980s and early 1990s, laser discs. Low-end fans are less focused on glamorous machines and images, preferring often obscure titles that may be several or more generations removed from original video versions (available, for example, from vendors such as Sinister Cinema or Something Weird Video). For this group, the less pristine the image, the more authentic it seems.[20] The growth of legitimate film purchases coexists with this "shadow" culture of collectors who pursue fringe titles and frequently engage in "illicit" practices, such as dubbing films illegally from prerecorded tapes or buying bootleg titles, to form their libraries.

Film collectors, then, do not constitute a homogeneous community. As I have mentioned, my analysis primarily concerns the media industries' pursuit of high-end collectors—typically, white males intent on building a film archive within an upscale entertainment environment. In many ways, these individuals overtly display the kind of dedication and specialized knowledge associated with the activity of collecting. Moreover, as they are enchanted with what the machine is capable of in a domestic setting, they enable the most vivid connections to be drawn among cinema, new technologies, and home exhibition. In addition to its passion for the cinema, this group has been particularly invested in developments such as home theater (as it promises "theater-quality" image and sound), laser disc, and DVD. As in the case of home theater discourse, the high-end collector is approached through class-based appeals that define not only the entertainment equipment but also certain videocassettes, laser discs, and DVDs as designed for the "serious" film viewer, the "discriminating movie fan" who insists on quality in the film viewing experience as well as in the selection of films for purchase.[21] As the direct legatees of the so-called digital revolution, these collectors are very much a part of high-tech home film cultures that have recently emerged.

Media industries often refer to this type of collector as a "-phile" of some sort—for example, an audiophile, cinephile, or videophile. These various -philes are hailed as serious viewers and media specialists who exhibit a zealous preoccupation with picture and sound reproduction that can be satisfied only through the purchase of the most refined electronic systems. For this group, the desire for cinema is inextricably linked to the desire for the newest and best technology, aligning a passion for cinema with the gadgeteer's passion for hardware. As we shall see, film collectors often discuss issues that have more to do with technology than with other aspects of the cinema, giving technophilia an authoritative role in this brand of cinephilia.

This predilection for the shiniest new machines on the part of the high-end -phile precipitated, in the early years of DVD, a skewing of playback technologies in terms of gender. Demographic analysis comparing DVD and VHS households showed that adults in homes with DVD players tended to be male, whereas adults in homes that had only VCRs tended to be female. Further, research suggested that DVD buyers focused on genres traditionally identified with male audiences, such as action and science fiction blockbusters, with those who bought videos gravitating toward fare associated with women viewers and children, such as comedy and animation. In terms of other variables, such as age and class, DVD owners were younger and had higher-than-average incomes.[22] What the industry observed, then, is that "DVDs are a man's world." Because younger, well-to-do white men continue to be important purchasers of DVD players, their tastes, which lean toward such high-octane fare as *Terminator 2: Judgment Day* (1991) and *The Fast and the Furious,* continue to exercise strong influence on the ancillary market.[23] Given that DVD sales are the "biggest, most profitable, and fastest-growing component" of the already lucrative income earned from home video, this influential male demographic is expected to gain additional sway over which films are approved for production.[24] Thus, DVD has attracted the kind of consumer who customarily makes up the first wave of patrons for new entertainment technologies, forging along the way a strong link to certain types of cinema.

However, since increasing numbers of films are being released on DVD, and DVD players are more common in households, women as well as families are becoming more substantial DVD viewers. Evidence also exists that the extra features present on many DVDs do not appeal just to film buffs but are also embraced by older viewers and "average Joes" who buy films at Wal-Mart, intrigued by the supplemental information and the sense that they are getting more for their money.[25] Thus, because of the gender, racial, generational, and class mobility implied by the successful dissemination of this technology, the niche audience of prosperous male film collectors has company that will further increase the mainstream status of DVD collecting. Yet, though more diverse groups of collectors have emerged, white men occupy a dominant place in discussions of film collecting online or in other forums and are most often hailed as committed collectors by consumer magazines.

The zealotry of these -philes is undoubtedly characterized by individual whims and obsessions. However, this kind of consumption is also affiliated with the practices and ideologies of an array of social contexts.

Unpacking the Film Library

Walter Benjamin's essay "Unpacking My Library" speaks eloquently about the private pleasures of collecting. In Benjamin's meditation on his own fas cinations with book collecting, he admits that amassing a library has very little to do with actually reading the purchased texts. He writes, "The most profound enchantment for the collector is the locking of individual items within a magic circle in which they are fixed as the final thrill, the thrill of acquisition, passes over them." Ownership, "the most intimate relationship that one can have to objects," enables an intensely personal relationship to develop between collector and collectibles. The books do not, as we might expect, "come alive" in the collector; rather, it is "he who lives in them." For the book conjures memories of its own past, from its original period and region to its former ownership. It also invokes memories of when the collector purchased the book—the time, the city, the store. Ultimately, the possession of a book produces a host of recollections that mingle personal autobiography with the book's history. As Benjamin asserts, "To renew the old world—that is the collector's deepest desire when he is driven to acquire new things." The collector "disappear[s] inside" his collection, at once his possession, his intimate terrain, and his connection to the past.[26] Book collecting, then, becomes a form of personal reverie, a means to reexperience the past through an event of acquisition.

Benjamin's account clearly presents the passionate, subjective nature of collecting. Yet, his essay also suggests strong associations between collecting and external considerations, between what appear to be strictly private practices and broader cultural systems. While Benjamin does not explore some central issues, such as why certain objects in this world of connoisseurship acquire value in the first place, he highlights the linkage of collectibles and collecting subjectivities to commodity culture (the thrill of acquisition), to the private sphere (as the collector disappears inside the collection), and to memory and history (to renew the old world). Benjamin's essay, then, invites us to entertain questions left unraised in his meditation about the book collector and to pursue provocative allusions to the social forces latent within the act of collecting. Despite its inescapable personal dimension, collecting cannot be entirely removed from broader dynamics in the public sphere. Like other aspects of the private, it is infused with the concerns of the external culture in which the individual dwells.

As James Clifford notes of personal collections in general, "The collection and preservation of an authentic domain of identity cannot be natural or innocent . . . inclusions in all collections reflect wider cultural rules—of rational taxonomy, of gender, of aesthetics . . . the self that must possess but cannot have it all learns to select, order, classify in hierarchies—to make 'good' collections."[27] Any kind of collecting—stamps, war souvenirs, art, books, toys, and so forth—is affected at the very least by notions of value, systems of classification, and other frameworks utilized by larger cultural provinces and institutions. In the case of post-VCR-era film collecting, classification systems from academia, media industries, and vendors of VHS, laser disc, and DVD intervene in the collecting process. Thus, a collector might arrange films by period, genre, nation, director, studio, actor, or simply alphabetically, demonstrating familiarity with procedures of arrangement employed by other institutions. To assist the collector, software and online sources (such as DVDaficionado.com and Guzzlefish.com) are similarly available to "catalog, search and sort your collection by title, director, genre and other categories."[28]

Similarly, a collector's selection of particular artifacts may be shaped by the perceived value those artifacts have acquired as classics, rarities, oddities, and other marketable categories of collectibles. For instance, media industries define most of what they sell in special editions as "classics." The Goldwyn Classics Library advertised a series of Eddie Cantor films under the slogan "These classics just got more classical";[29] *Vertigo*, available from MCA/Universal Home Video, is Alfred Hitchcock's "masterpiece" and *Alien* (1979) became an "instant classic" upon its original release, as the copy for both of their collector's editions tells us. Special-edition marketing in particular provides an opportunity to elevate film to the status of high art, either by cashing in on an existing canon or by attempting to create one by affixing the "classic" label. In addition, through the often extensive background materials that accompany it, a special edition appears to furnish the authenticity and history so important to establishing the value of an archival object.

Since videocassettes, laser discs (in their prime), and DVDs are mass-produced and hence widely available, this type of collecting would seem to hold little potential for pursuing the ultimate collector's commodity—the rare artifact. Scarcity of the precious collectible—an elusive first edition of a book or a 35mm print of a forgotten work by a noted director, for example—is a condition that appears to be sorely lacking in this context. Nonetheless, the language of scarcity permeates the discourses around film rereleases. When Pioneer Entertainment reissued the seven *Star Trek* feature films on laser disc, its ad stated that these "deluxe box sets are numbered and *limited to just 8000* to satisfy the true collector." This type of *limited* special edition, which offers relatively few copies to the consumer, seeks to define itself as outside of the excesses of contemporary mass reproduction and therefore more rare. It thus attempts to carve out an aesthetic place by appealing to the conditions of scarcity, conditions so important to constituting an aura of value for collectibles. Further, the box that contains the discs for *Star Trek: Generations* (designed as a "space dock") is "deluxe." The discs themselves are "encoded with Dolby Surround AC-3 Digital" and "utilize THX technologies for the ultimate audiovisual experience at home."[30] The rare item, then, is complemented by a showcase package and the highest standards (at the time) in audiovisual reproduction, finessing the associations among collecting, value, and aesthetic experience.

However, there is a rarer market than that represented by promotional efforts. Various newsletters (such as the *DVD–Laser Disc Newsletter*) and online sites (such as MoviesUnlimited.com, which promotes itself as having thousands of titles that are impossible to find in local video stores or other mail-order operations) regularly list music and film titles imported from overseas. These include such items as concert albums (e.g., *Sex Pistols: Winterland*), boxed sets of U.S. television series (e.g., *Lost in Space*), and foreign films often not readily available in the United States (e.g., Hong Kong releases before their reissue "boom" in the late 1990s). Crossing high- and low-end tastes, these sources also advertise "rare out-of-print" films for the home market and the "serious film collector." Thus, for example, Movies Unlimited features on DVD or VHS the Western *Red Sun* (1971), directed by Terence Young and starring Charles Bronson and Toshiro Mifune, an animated version of *Great Expectations* (1983), *Rebel* (1970), an early Sylvester Stallone movie, and *Group Marriage* (1972), a soft-core "classic" directed by Stephanie Rothman. Companies dealing in rare titles also focus both on films not released in commercial ancillary formats and on imported widescreen reissues available only in pan-and-scan versions in the United States.

Hence, forgotten, out-of-print, cult, exploitation, noncommercial, widescreen, foreign, and other types of offerings that fall outside of the exhibition mainstream help to constitute the uncommon, sought-after media object, suggesting that the collector's trade has found a way to construct the categories of authenticity and rarity for mass-produced film artifacts. The existence of these artifacts also helps to stimulate the competitive gamesmanship and "sport" characteristic of this enterprise in general (i.e., to see who can procure the rarity). As avid film collector Charles Tashiro points out, it is particularly in the acquisition of items without broad circulation "where we can locate the bravado in video collecting."[31]

We can begin to see, then, how contemporary film collecting is situated within already charged systems of classification, selection, and value, engaged in a pas de deux with market forces. To "unpack" the film library more fully, however, we must explore further how collecting passes through the filter of culture. I am particularly interested in how the discourses of new media technologies help to cultivate a sense of membership in this world of film connoisseurs and to renegotiate established values for films. At the very least, contemporary cinephilia is shaped by an insider identity for the devotee and a hardware aesthetic that affects the way films are seen and discussed. Because individual collecting is a form of consumption enacted in the home, both of these dimensions of domestic cinephilia are additionally related to dynamics within consumer culture and the private sphere.

The Insider

Media industries attempt to appeal to the collector as a film industry insider, privy to a secret world of information about filmmaking. Insiders have obtained apparently special knowledge possessed by relatively few others. This special knowledge may take several different forms, influenced by the educational efforts of hardware and software magazines, industry reports, reviews, film reissues, online community postings, and so on. Having done the research, individuals may carefully choose and install the best audio-visual components of home theater in their entertainment spaces. Similarly, they may be caught up in debates about the comparative virtues of emerging technologies that reproduce the cinema—for instance, whether laser disc is superior in quality to DVD or whether Digital Theater Systems (DTS) surpasses Dolby Digital (DD) in audio quality. Those "in the know" are also aware of when certain films will be reissued on VHS or DVD and amass information about the strengths and weaknesses of their transfers to ancillary formats. Culling data from the various sources that cater to the cinephile-collector, these viewers can also recite the facts of cinema, which include behind-the-scenes stories about the making of particular films, gossip about stars and directors, and myriad other historical, technological, and biographical details.

Concentrating on one of these sources—the special collector's edition—for a moment, we can see how such reissues school the viewer in just this type of information, helping to create a cognoscenti among collectors. Special collector's editions can be quite intricate affairs. Beyond presenting widescreen feature films in their original aspect ratio, they may also offer the director's cut with bountiful additional footage that ended up on the cutting-room floor or was reserved for DVD release. In addition, commentary about the feature film provided by its directors, writers, producers, and/or stars is de rigueur. While other items may find their way into these reissues, special editions showcase what they refer to as the "collector's supplement." The supplement often provides extensive preproduction, production, and postproduction information about the film, including storyboards, different versions of the script, information about how special effects were done, trailers, and documentaries about the film's production.

As I mentioned, laser discs preceded DVDs in offering viewers the opportunity to become steeped in a plethora of seemingly exclusive behind-the-scenes facts. For example, in Criterion's special edition of *Citizen Kane* (1941) (along with *King Kong* [1933], the first of the company's laser disc releases in 1984), the viewer learns that Orson Welles had to wear a prosthetic nose designed by the makeup artist extraordinaire of that film, Maurice Seiderman. Apparently, Welles's nose was deemed unphotogenic because of an "underdeveloped" bridge and "unusually large" nostrils. Delighted with the change in his appearance, Welles went on to wear the "Seiderman nose," as it was referred to, in later films, including *Journey into Fear* (1942), *Touch of Evil* (1958), and *Compulsion* (1959). Similar disclosures occur in the commentary on *The Graduate* (1967) laser disc. We are informed that it was not Anne Bancroft/Mrs. Robinson's leg that graced the famous cover of the sound-track album for *The Graduate* (an image that came to stand for the perverse links between the generations in the late 1960s), but Linda Gray's, an actress who later played Sue Ellen Ewing in the prime-time television soap opera *Dallas*. In the special edition of *Alien*, we discover that director Ridley Scott's children took the place of the principal actors in the extreme long shots of the astronauts' first encounter with the "Space Jockey" aboard the derelict spaceship, so as to make the creature and entire chamber seem larger. Since the replicas of space helmets were not fully operational as efficient oxygen-pumping devices, the children were overcome by carbon monoxide fumes and passed out on at least one occasion. Similarly, we find out that the person playing the monster in *Alien* was a Nigerian graphic arts student living in London, Bolaji Badejo, whose six-foot-ten height and slim build suited designer H. R. Giger's requirements for the alien.

Voted the best laser disc of all time from 1992 to 1997 by readers of a specialty laser disc magazine, and also the disc with the best supplement, *Terminator 2: Judgment Day* vividly represents how detailed and extensive special edition supplements can be.[32] The director, James Cameron, invites viewers to look "behind the curtains of *T2*'s creative process," revealing elements involved in every stage of the film's production. Viewers gain insight into the film's planning process, including the original screenplay, storyboards, casting decisions, location scouting, set design and building, actor training, and decisions about costume, makeup, weapons, and stunts. They are also privy to information on the film's postproduction, as it involves sound design, musical scoring, editing, trailers, posters and ads, the music video (by Guns N' Roses), and responses of critics, the public, and international markets, as well as details of the video transfer. But in the sea of images and data, the capstone element of the supplement is unquestionably the section devoted to visual effects. T2 was considered a breakthrough in special effects technologies, and the supplement demonstrates in great detail the different processes used to create various elements and scenes. Chapters in this section of the supplement are organized according to each company that designed effects for the film, from Industrial Light and Magic's computer-generated imagery for the T-1000 (the advanced, morphing terminator) and 4-Ward Production's simulation of a nuclear blast to Stan Winston's prosthetics, mechanized effects, and stunt puppets (figure 8). The exhaustiveness of T2's supplementary materials, as they have been preserved and expanded in the film's release on DVD, has managed to maintain its place near the top of "Best DVD" lists, even fifteen years after its original reissue on laser disc.

These earlier efforts on laser disc were apparently not in vain. Trade association DVD Entertainment Group reports that after the superior quality of its picture and sound, DVD extras are now a major drawing card for consumers.[33] Moreover, DVD viewers appear willing to buy multiple copies of the same film, as long as they are offered different, expanded attractions. The original 1999 widescreen reissue of The Matrix on VHS, for example, featured key extras such as a "making-of" documentary with behind-the-scenes explanations of bullet time and kung fu sequences. The DVD release the same year contained the "making-of" documentary, commentary by cast and crew, and a music-only track discussed by composer Don Davis. In addition, it included several concealed elements, or "Easter eggs." No longer available through an obvious spot on the menu, the bullet-time piece was accessible through a hidden image of a red pill in the supplement's "Dream World" segment (figure 9). The same segment featured another Easter egg, a "Follow the White Rabbit" sign that was hidden behind a "continue" command. To follow the white rabbit—a reference to the Alice in Wonderland allusions in The Matrix—the viewer must press "enter" on the DVD remote or mouse click when the rabbit periodically appears on screen to get an in-depth look at how a particular stunt and/or special effect was done. If the viewer does not act quickly, the rabbit disappears. This same DVD contains interactive DVD-ROM elements for PCs that continue this kind of gamesmanship and puzzle solving. Yet another DVD spin-off from The Matrix, "The Matrix Revisited" (2001), is advertised as "A Mind-Expanding Look at 'The Matrix' from Conception to Phenomenon." It includes an

Figure 8. Special effects master Stan Winston and two of his stunt puppets for *Terminator 2: Judgment Day,* as featured on *T2*'s supplemental disk.

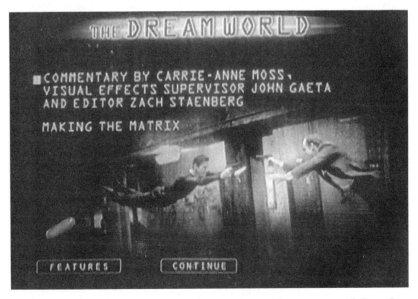

Figure 9. *The Matrix* supplement: "The Dream World" segment and the red pill Easter egg (in the lower left-hand corner), which leads to a short documentary on bullet time.

"in-depth exploration of the filmmaking process, a sneak peek on location of the upcoming sequel, a first look at 'The Matrix' anime, never-before-seen footage, hidden features, and more." Thus, not only do the supplemental features serve to differentiate one version of *The Matrix* from another, they also promote associated media products, including the anime and an upcoming sequel.

Such is the health of this market that ancillary variations do not necessarily require a staggered time line. Initially released in both full screen and widescreen versions in August 2002, Peter Jackson's *The Lord of the Rings: The Fellowship of the Ring* saw a holiday release a few months later in two special editions—the first, a "platinum edition" of the film (priced at $39.99), with thirty minutes of extra footage restored and thirty hours of additional attractions; and the second, a "collector's DVD gift set," with more extras and deluxe packaging (priced at $79.92). Rereleases of *The Two Towers* and *The Return of the King* (2003) have followed a similar multiple-version strategy.

In their ability to "remake" a film, successive special editions enable the kind of product differentiation so important to repurposing, that is, to the strategy of repeatedly reselling the same titles. In the process, through shifting supplemental materials, the feature film has an instant built-in and changeable intertextual surround that enters into its meaning and significance for viewers. Special collector's editions are as suggestive for textual study as they are for theories of reception. As feature films appear in new cuts with added footage, their definition as texts becomes unstable. Which is the authentic film—the version initially theatrically released or the DVD director's cut? Given that films today are often shot with the idea of saving certain footage for DVD release, the notion of the expandable text has become an intimate part of the production process, at the very least making it necessary to reframe the issue of authenticity with respect to the home market.

The details of how these intertexts shape and reshape film meaning through kaleidoscopic perspectives are important. Here, however, I want to focus on a presumption that oversees the encounter between edition and viewer more generally: the media industry address of the specialized consumer as an "insider." The special edition trades off the revelation as a key ingredient of its appeal. Each of the above examples exposes an assumption (e.g., that it is Welles's actual nose) or provides answers to questions (e.g., how did the filmmakers create bullet time or a morphing Terminator?) by dispensing behind-the-scenes information that reveals the cinematic tricks behind appearances. Revelations about the execution of special effects are particularly important to collector's editions. Because many of these effects deploy digital technologies, the viewer gains admission to a relatively new, highly specialized, and complex sector of the motion picture industry. This aspect of the address is especially evident in the hidden features of *The Matrix* DVDs, where viewers are invited to use skills derived from playing video games or surfing the Web to "crack" the puzzles offered them by the DVD designers. Let in on industry "secrets" and capable of mastering further enigmas if need be, the viewer enters the world of filmmaking to reside in the privileged position of the director and other production personnel—the puppet masters—who are responsible for such effective illusionism.

Far from demystifying the production process, these revelations produce a sense of the film industry's magisterial control of appearances. Rather than inciting critical attitudes toward the industry, then, behind-the-scenes "exposés" vividly confirm Hollywood as a place of marvels brought to the public by talented film professionals. As viewers are invited to assume the position of an expert, they are further drawn into an identification with the industry and its wonders. But this identification, like any identification viewers may have had with the apparently seamless diegetic universe of the film itself, is based on an illusion. Viewers do not get the unvarnished truth about the production; they are instead presented with the "promotable" facts, behind-the-scenes information that supports and enhances a sense of the "movie magic" associated with Hollywood production.

This kind of appeal to viewers suggests that one of the major foundations of fandom—the accumulation and dissemination of the smallest details involved in the production of media objects—is substantially informed (though not wholly determined) by industry discourse. Whether the media industries or fans first introduced the importance of trivia to mass cultural pleasures is unimportant; trivia has become a significant part of the feedback loop between industry and fan, with the industry recognizing the importance of the mastery of obscure details to enthusiasts and dutifully producing massive amounts of this kind of information.

Thus, while trivia is, as Henry Jenkins argues in his study of television fandom, "a source of popular expertise for the fans and a basis for critical reworkings of textual materials," it is doubtful whether it can be considered a transgressive brand of "unauthorized and unpoliced knowledge."[34] In comparison to academe and other official cultures of taste, trivia may seem at first glance to produce a culturally disenfranchised kind of knowledge. But, for many viewers, trivia often appears as a source of vital information that is more important and authentic than the "stuffy" intellectual accounts issuing from official sources. Ultimately, however, the types of knowledge generated and embraced by academe may not always be clearly distinct from those of the industry—as, for example, the information gleaned from DVD commentary and supplements increasingly becomes part of both faculty and student discussions.

More important, special editions remind us that trivia has a substantial presence in popular culture, which is materially influenced by the media industries. From the earliest days of the film industry to the present, entertainment facts have achieved a particular visibility and viability as a type of knowledge and discourse in mass culture. Crossword puzzles, board games such as Trivial Pursuit, television game shows, and online movie Web sites are just a few of the public forums that ask participants to marshal their knowledge of Hollywood. A traffic in trivia created by various culture industries, both authorized and policed, plays a strong role in negotiating the audience's relationship to the media. As purveyors par excellence of such microdata, special collector's editions give viewers a still-mystified account of the cinema as a part of the cultural capital they possess as "masters" of the cinematic fact. The identity of trivia as a kind of sub-rosa knowledge possessed by the privileged few only enhances the effects of this mystification. In online and other forums, viewers are encouraged to become disseminators of trivia, a process that inevitably helps to secure the place and importance of the media industries in culture.[35] Hence, while film trivia may lack respect as a form of knowledge in certain circles, it is not genuinely marginalized or unsanctioned; it is a major form of currency that helps to build relationships not simply among fans but also between fans and media producers and promoters.

Beyond the appeal to the viewer as insider, the collector's culture is also shaped by the various machines designed to reproduce films in the home. As we have seen, technology already figures as a major component of the insider identity, since various technologies involved in filmmaking are responsible for creating the illusionism so enthusiastically elaborated by the special edition's supplemental sections. But technology also plays an important role in the collector's culture as a series of commodities to be purchased. The "secret" world of the collector is enhanced additionally by the primacy that machines and their capabilities of reproduction have as purveyors of quality and indicators of cinematic value. The machines involved in the high-tech collector's world help to create a film aesthetic that can transform a film's previous value (created through film reviews or academic criticism, for example) for domestic consumption.

The Hardware Aesthetic

As they circulate in mainstream magazines as well as within the community of collectors themselves, discourses on home entertainment technologies tend to evaluate films through the lens of hardware priorities, through what I refer to as a "hardware aesthetic." The hardware aesthetic conceives of value according to imperatives drawn from technological considerations. The prominence of these imperatives in assessment results in a number of different effects, including the enshrinement of the action and/or special effects film, a reversal in aesthetic fortune for titles regarded as either classics or failures, a rereading of films through the ideology of the spectacular, and the triumph of a particular notion of form over content.

In his essay "The Contradictions of Video Collecting," Tashiro reveals the critical importance of technology in the mentality of the collector. Inspired by Benjamin, Tashiro is primarily interested in elaborating Benjamin's "lyrical approach" to collecting, which he argues is "the only legitimate [approach] to what remains a highly private process." Nonetheless, Tashiro's discussion of his own collecting habits demonstrates a telling shift from Benjamin's reverence for books as gateways to the past to a reverence for technological excellence and the presentism this standard embraces. For example, like many film collectors in the mid-1990s, Tashiro preferred laser discs over videos; videotapes are "second-class citizens" because they degenerate. Unlike books or videocassettes, laser discs (as well as their successor DVDs) do not embody their own histories by showing age. It is in fact the physical appearance of the disc that forms a large part of the appeal: "Discs fascinate as objects, their clear, cool surfaces promising technical perfection . . . discs promise modernism at its sleekest, the reduction to pristine forms and reflective surfaces." Rather than being a signifier of worth, age signals that a replacement disc should be ordered.[36]

Tashiro contends that this preference for new versions of the old—a distinct departure from other collecting aesthetics—is partly driven by a faith in "the potentially perfect copy . . . expressed in the exploitation of ever-newer technologies, striving always to get closer to the film's original. . . . As a result, change is valued for itself, and with each new technical capability, both collectors and producers feel compelled to improve on what has come before." Further, progress is defined not so much in terms of the films themselves as in terms of "the technical capabilities of the disc medium." Thus, quality is judged according to "the number of dropouts, the amount of hiss, the degree of fidelity in digital reproduction. The logic of the surface of the disc spills over into its production and consumption: the cleaner,

sleeker, shinier the image, the purer, richer, clearer the sound track, the better the disc." As Tashiro continues, "This technical 'reason' serves as a perfect rationalization [for staking] an emphatic claim to the importance of picture and sound over story and character, to those *technical* aspects of film
best served by laser disc reproduction. . . . That claim . . . lay[s] the ground-
work for the overall structure of the collection, its bias toward those films
that favor visual style."[37]

Though striving to depict collecting as irrational and subjective, Tashiro's
perspective is exemplary in expressing the technocentric nature of contemporary film collecting. A film's worth is judged by the quality of the transfer, the aura of the digital reproduction of sound and image, and even the
pristine surface of the disc itself. These priorities in turn lead to a preference
for certain kinds of films over others—that is, films that have visual surfaces
and technical features that appear to highlight and reinforce the capabilities
of digital technology. Hence, when Michael Grossman, a Canadian school-
teacher with a collection of more than seven hundred DVDs, chooses to buy
a DVD, it is typically an action-adventure film distinguished by copious special effects that will optimize his large screen and powerful speakers.[38] This
kind of material pleasure also characterizes other technophiles whose film
collections are based on the mutually reinforcing ability of their equipment
and films to provide compelling audio-visual experiences.[39] As the rise of
DVD has seen the preference for quality in sound and picture "main-
streamed" beyond the niche audience of laser disc collectors, issues of film
reproduction have assumed an unparalleled centrality in home film consumption.

Along with collectors and consumer magazines, producers of entertainment hardware put a premium on obtaining the newest and best technological rendition of a film. Typical ads for home theater components mix
technical details with promises of spectacular effects. For example,
Faroudja's Laboratories' TV enhancer offers adaptive color processing, edge
detail processing, and color alignment correction to "make images from big
screen TVs jump off the screen!" Polk Audio's LS f/x high-performance
surround speakers "can transform the surround channel from a typically
flat monochromatic noise to a detached, spacious, and coherent soundfield"
and "are excellent for space-ships flying overhead or the growls of moving
tanks and cranes, just the stuff of which impressive home cinema is made."[40]
The technical considerations that dominate promotions for home theater
systems or playback components make reproduction itself into the prime
aesthetic criterion while privileging a type of reproduction that favors
verisimilitude mingled with spectacle. In this context, the film experience is

composed of spectacular visuals and sound that bring seemingly authentic sensory perceptions to the forefront. Thus, collectors and producers of home entertainment equipment tend to discuss film and the film experience in similar ways, contributing to and reinforcing a hardware aesthetic. The evaluation of films in a variety of forums that address collectors, from consumer magazines to online chat groups, illuminates how this kind of aesthetic more specifically affects film reception. As I have mentioned, newspaper accounts and consumer magazines characteristically refer to certain films as "perfect DVD movies." This moniker has at least two meanings. When it refers to blockbusters such as *The Matrix* and *The Lord of the Rings*, it indicates the achievement of a perfect harmony between cinema and the quality expectations of the digital era as they are incarnated in DVD technology and home theater. That is, when action blockbusters with a high quotient of CGI (computer-generated imagery) meet DVD, the thundering sound and magisterial illusionism of the film in its theatrical presentation are able to be captured by the superior sound and image quality of digital playback, particularly when it is part of a surround-sound system. Although blockbusters are not the only kinds of films that translate well into DVD, public commentary depicts them as best able to realize the sheer capacities and capabilities of the digital. Thus, film appreciation is based on the appearance of a seamless marriage between certain feature films and home formats through a mutual articulation of digital standards of excellence.

The importance of this union is already forecast in evaluations of films on laser disc. In a review of the laser disc reissue of Walter Hill's *Last Man Standing* (1996), a remake of Kurosawa's *Yojimbo* (1961), the writer explains that he hadn't cared for the film in the theater. But listening to the reissue "in our home, with the sound turned way up, made it a lot more appealing, regardless of the ridiculous plot." The new digital soundtrack makes the difference: Ry Cooder's score "takes on more detail and omnipresent vibrancy, while the gunfights on the DTS disc make the Dolby Digital gunfights on the earlier disc sound monophonic." The reviewer continues, "Throughout the film, subtle touches of sound—the wind seeping through a crack or a creaking door down the street—are given more clarity, stimulating your senses and making the tough questions, like what is a sheriff doing in a town that doesn't have any people in it, not matter."[41] The convergence of film and home technology can inspire reappraisals, then, even of films considered to be "duds" in their initial runs.

Conversely, when there is a "disconnect" between film and digital standards, the aesthetic axe falls. Such is the fate for the DVD release of Woody Allen's *Annie Hall* (1977), a film by a director whose oeuvre is inimical to

Hollywood's sonorous, eye-popping spectaculars. Assessing the soundtrack, the reviewer for consumer magazine *Total DVD* writes, "There's a great bit where a fleet of helicopter gun ships attacks the Martian invasion party with missiles, and another where the nuclear silo explodes just as Woody escapes on a jetski. No, just kidding. As we have come to expect from Allen movies, you just get mono sound, with perfectly clear dialogue and the usual smooth jazz soundtrack, but there's really nothing here to get excited about."[42] Since Allen's film does not measure up in a world of multichannel sound reproduction, it is vulnerable to send-up through the hardware aesthetic and its implicit association with action genres.

The second meaning of the "perfect DVD movie" lies in the greater storage capacity of digital technology—its ability to contain the feature film and some supplementary material on one disc (although special editions often run to several discs). Films on DVD are rated on the number and quality of the extras they provide. Because *Annie Hall*'s DVD offers only a trailer and a choice of subtitle and soundtrack languages, it is judged as "pretty poor, though much what we've come to expect from Allen films."[43] On the other end of the spectrum lies what *Entertainment Weekly* judges as the "50 Essential DVDs" (among them *Fight Club*, *A Bug's Life* [1998], *Brazil* [1985], and *Terminator 2*). The magazine makes it clear that these are not "the greatest movies ever or the coolest vintage-TV collections." Rather, the list is a "celebration of unique-to-disc extravaganzas that best exploit DVD's massive storage capacity and multiple-choice, chapter-surfing flexibility to somehow radically enhance whatever the main event is."[44] We have already seen how extensive these extras can be. While the film itself is the "main event," these other features represent DVD's extraordinary inclusive capabilities. In addition, given the greater, more precise kinds of manipulation afforded by this technology, viewers attain a level of control they are accustomed to having with the computer mouse and the selection of menus and features available on the Internet.

However, along with the breadth of behind-the-scenes elements, the complexity and imaginativeness of supplemental features are substantial indicators of the reissue's worth. Thus, of *A Bug's Life*, the reviewer writes:

> The computer-animation maestros at Pixar take the multi-gigabyte-supplement idea seriously and send it up at the same time. Thus you get golly-gee director John Lasseter and snarky Stanton [the co-director] making gag-me faces behind editor Lee Unkrich as he explains the wonders of storyboarding. . . . And nifty extra features just keep marching by, from effects-only audio to concept art to jokey interviews with the insect stars. The retina-rattling transfer of the main event comes directly from

Figure 10. The all-digital *A Bug's Life.*

digital computer files, so it doesn't just outdazzle VHS—it stomps theatrical prints, too. . . . The whole package makes the DVD-movie interface
feel totally, digitally organic.[45]

Not only does this disc present extras, it also strikes a self-reflexive, parodic
relationship to the genre of DVD supplements, marking it as a knowing and
clever addition to DVD releases. Moreover, as a Pixar animation, *A Bug's
Life* (figure 10) is totally digital. The reviewer thus depicts it as able to fuse
with DVD more seamlessly than films based on live-action with CGI components; in this way, *A Bug's Life* achieves the oxymoronic ideal of organic
digitality. In the process, the film on DVD represents the great digital hope
of home theater: it surpasses older format VHS, and, better still, it results
in film reproduction that outstrips theatrical presentation.

Supplements sport other features that testify to the filmmaker's or DVD
designer's creativity. As we saw in the case of *The Matrix* with the red pill
and the white rabbit, some DVDs feature Easter eggs, a term named after a
practice in computer programming wherein the designer plants hidden features for ingenious users to discover. On DVD, such features, once uncov-
ered, provide ambitious viewers with more behind-the-scenes secrets or
other special information to which those less ambitious or less familiar with

computer gaming will not be privy. Although the list is long, some other DVDs that contain Easter eggs include *The Phantom Menace* (1999), *X-Men* (2000), *Gladiator* (2000), *Terminator 2* (The Ultimate Edition), *Magnolia* (2000), and *Boogie Nights* (1997). With the exception of the last two titles, which are Paul Michael Anderson films with an independent flair, each is a blockbuster dependent on special effects. In the case of the blockbuster, Easter eggs simply reinforce what is already enunciated by the theatrical film—that it is a masterful display of Hollywood's digital pyrotechnics. With both blockbusters and independent films, these features also testify to the creativeness of the filmmakers—their savviness about digital technology and the gamesmanship its complexity can so ably accommodate (even when others may actually be responsible for executing the DVD design).

Thus, the hardware aesthetic makes several interventions in aesthetics and reception in relation to contemporary cinema. Films are rated not only for how they fulfill digital standards of sound and picture but also for how their reissues realize to the fullest extent the physical capacity of the disc itself, especially when this capacity is deployed to render DVD as an autonomous art form. Thus, it is not surprising that with the arrival of laser disc and DVD, a canon of "reissue" auteurs has been established. When James Cameron and George Lucas are enshrined as kings of laser disc and DVD release, this canon often acts to confirm and extend existing technocentric systems of value in popular culture. But new LD and DVD auteurs have also been born; for example, collectors consider Terry Gilliam's science fiction film *Brazil*—not a great success in theatrical release—as among the most interesting and sophisticated of all "behind-the-scenes" reissues featuring multiple cuts of a film. Similarly, the reputations of auteurs such as Woody Allen may suffer if their work appears as increasingly less salient because of a lack of attention to digital expectations. In relation to its impact on authorship, DVD also enhances the public standing of action films, science fiction, independent films, and a few other genres, because they have been translated so effectively for this new ancillary market. At the same time, viewers continue to be addressed as insiders; their ability to unlock the mysteries of the Easter egg or navigate successfully the sometimes intricate menus on DVDs testifies to their special access to industry or technological secrets.

Since a studio's back catalogs have such importance for repurposing, the hardware aesthetic is also mobilized in relation to classic Hollywood and foreign films. In the case of these collectibles, the hardware aesthetic might entirely displace the canonical status of the legendary film (as it did with *Annie Hall*) or reify it to suit the demand for spectacle.

For instance, the 1995 laser disc reissue of Akira Kurosawa's *Sanjuro* (1962) occasions this comment from a critic for *Widescreen Review:* "The Tohoscope framing has been recomposed at 2.11:1, although the transfer credits proclaim 'its original aspect ratio of 2.35:1.' The picture lacks detail and sharpness, shadow detail is poor, and generally negative dirt artifacts are prevalent throughout." In addition, "the original soundtrack theatrically was Perspecta Stereophonic Sound . . . but this edition has been dubbed from a mono optical track which is undistinguished and characteristically noisy."[46] A review of another classic film, *The Fly* (1958), reissued to the home market in 1996, similarly addresses the fine points of its digital reproduction. The film is "framed at 2.35:1, exhibits inconsistencies in color fidelity with mostly dated and subdued colors and fleshtones. Overall the picture is out of focus, except for the occasional close up shots of a fly. Noise and artifacts are apparent. . . . The overall sound is on the bright side and never sounds quite right."[47]

Such unfavorable criticism is not, of course, the fate of all classics. If the transfer is good or the supplemental features intriguing, the "old" film more successfully negotiates the requirements of the aesthetic. Thus, a reviewer judges *Judy Garland: The Golden Years at MGM*, a "lavish" box set of three Judy Garland films—*The Harvey Girls* (1946), *The Pirate* (1948), and *Summer Stock* (1950)—as looking "absolutely gorgeous. This is especially true of *The Pirate*, which accents director Vincente Minnelli's exotic use of color in lighting, sets, and costumes, greatly intensifying the mood of scenes like the fiery 'Pirate Ballet.'" But, the reviewer notes, "it's a shame . . . that the audio track for *The Pirate* was often marred by a harsh, scraping, practically vibrating tone."[48] The excess and grandeur of Minnelli's trademark style of mise-en-scène, preserved and perhaps even heightened in the transfer process, coordinate felicitously with the superior, vivid visual experience associated with digital entertainment technologies. But in this case the experience is qualified because of the flawed reproduction of the musical's soundtrack.

Perhaps even more than for contemporary films, supplemental features can be a distinctive signifier of worth for the classic film. At times, it is possible for the classic film to be deemed as less important than the extra features. Thus, in one reviewer's estimation, the DVD version of *The Sound of Music* (1965) is "awesome," although he or she admits to never having seen the film. The rating is based not on the film but on the difficulty and ingenuity of the games on the disc, which the reviewer was unable to beat.[49] More often, the classic film is further authenticated by its accompanying materials. Although opening to mixed reviews in 1939, *The Wizard of Oz,* for example, has since gained renown as a family classic and star vehicle for Judy Garland. As a sign of its continuing status, it has appeared in multiple special collector's editions in deluxe packaging that offers the viewer an extensive array of extras. Thus, supplemental features for the 1999 DVD gift set (priced at $43.99) include the theatrical trailer, original script, rare still photos, color theatrical poster reproductions, a behind-the-scenes documentary ("The Wonderful Wizard of Oz: The Making of a Movie Classic") hosted by Angela Lansbury, outtakes (including the rarely seen "Jitterbug" dance), interviews with secondary stars, special effects stills, stills from the Hollywood premiere, original sketches and storyboards, costume designs and makeup tests, excerpts from previous film versions of the L. Frank Baum novel (such as the 1914 and 1925 silent films, as well as a 1933 cartoon), five rarely seen trailers, newsreel excerpts, and a series of audio supplements (such as hours of recording-session material and the first public performance of "Over the Rainbow" on a 1939 radio broadcast). From this list, one can see the significance of the all-inclusive nature of the supplement to the film's value as a collectible, especially when materials are defined as rare or never before seen or heard. The collector has a sense that he or she owns not only the film but also its history; further, the more arcane the history, the more the film appears as a worthy archival object, deserving of a place in the personal library.

In the land of new technologies, the past is reborn to exacting standards that demand pristine visuals in original aspect ratios and crystalline soundtracks. It is not enough for a film to be made by Kurosawa; the terms of the transfer must reproduce the correct aspect ratio, picture resolution, and sound quality of the celluloid version. Furthermore, the classic film must live up to another set of standards that are an integral part of the home theater experience with its large-screen TVs and surround-sound components. Ideally, films from the past should have lively, vigorous visuals and a bold (or subtle and nuanced) soundtrack amenable to digital enhancement and/or astonishing supplemental materials that amplify their historical importance. In some cases, technical updating proves to be difficult, since, aside from the practice of sloppy transfers, the original internegatives may have deteriorated or be possessed by "dirt artifacts" and other demons involved in the improper storage or aging process of celluloid. As we have seen in the reviews of *Sanjuro* and *The Fly*, the hardware aesthetic has little room for the cinematic equivalent of the dusty, dog-eared volume. Thus, while recapturing the standards of the original remains important to collectors, their sense of authenticity is more compellingly influenced by the nature of the upgrades performed on a film to render it suitable to the digital eye and ear.

In these estimations of films, sound and image may displace other tried-and-true priorities in critical criteria, such as auteurism and existing canons. This not to say that such traditional critical criteria are unimportant in the world of collecting. Auteurism and the canon carry enormous weight as a means of marketing reissues and as factors that enter into a collector's decision about which films to select for the archive. In fact, the film industry routinely produces boxed sets of the works of specific directors, one sign among many of the continuing influence of authorship on the constitution of archival value. At the same time, quality is not always a deciding factor in collecting. Collectors may buy videocassettes or DVDs that are inferior in quality just to own a coveted title or complete a sector of their media libraries. But the clarity of the transfer and the film's delivery of the kind of audio-visual spectacle that best exhibits the prowess of the playback equipment are pervasive and potent aspects of the hardware aesthetic shared and propagated by collectors.

As the reviewer's minimization of the incoherent plot of *Last Man Standing* suggests, this aesthetic often harbors a certain disregard for content. Thus, a writer for *Video Magazine* acknowledges that *Forrest Gump* (1994) is "a certified phenomenon" but suggests that we "not fret over 'What It Says About Us' and get right down to the chocolate, er, heart of the matter." The heart of the matter is that "*Gump* . . . boasts a wide-screen transfer of about 2.1:1, and though it is done up to THX standards (the image is quite good, if not exceptional), it displays a tendency toward soft colors. *Gump* isn't much of a surround-sound showcase, either, since the intimacy of the story line dictates that most of the dialogue, musical score, and ambient sounds must be positioned front and center.[50] Similarly, Pioneer Entertainment's special edition of *Platoon* (1986) presents "a motion picture that defined for many Americans the inhuman, hostile and futile act of the Vietnam War" as an "impossible-to-resist hardbound, display-quality volume designed with the look and feel of a Vietnam Veteran's scrapbook, complete with embossed silver images of 'dog tags' hanging from the top edge of the cover." Further, the film is "matted at 1.85:1. Detail and sharpness are exemplary. . . . Fleshtones are accurate and blacks are deep and solid for an exceptionally natural rendering. The soundtrack also is impressive over that of the theatrical mix . . . the original discrete six-track elements have been re-mixed and encoded for a more potent surround effect and greater dynamics."[51]

As we have seen, films and their transfers must ultimately meet the standards of home theater excellence. Thus, *Forrest Gump* "isn't much of a surround-sound showcase," while *Platoon*'s soundtrack "is impressive over that of the theatrical mix." Within this orientation, the issue of content is swept aside as secondary by more pressing concerns: the quality of the transfer, the film's suitability for maximizing the capabilities of home theater, and the opportunity the reissue presents for commodification—in the case of *Platoon*, deluxe packaging.

Such modes of evaluation differ significantly from those characteristic of Anglo-American moral criticism. This tradition, personified in the 1950s by such critics as Bosley Crowther of the *New York Times* and Arthur Knight of the *Saturday Review* and still pervasive in contemporary writing on film in the popular press today, judges films on the basis of the relevance and worth of their social messages. In the above reviews, the collecting sensibility clearly sees such messages as a mere backdrop or even as a potential distraction to what is really noteworthy about the films—accurate fleshtones and resonant multitrack sound. Despite both *Forrest Gump*'s and *Platoon*'s concern with the 1960s, one of the most hotly debated eras in U.S. history, and the protracted discussions both experienced in the press about their depictions of this era, reviewers of their digital rereleases produce a detailed technical vision of these films, describing them in an alternative language seen as vital to their consumption by the cinephile.

It is important to point out that the reviews in consumer electronics magazines and other sources do not just echo the industry's unqualified hype about its rereleases; they exist as guides to buyers and collectors. Internet groups devoted to collecting take this role of consumer watchdog seriously, spreading the word about superior or deficient discs, debating the comparative merits of playback equipment, and generally soliciting advice from fellow subscribers. As one participant writes, "I remember renting *The Silence of the Lambs* Criterion/THX CAV version and the rolling dropouts were the worst I have ever seen. I want the new CLV Criterion version. Does anybody know if this disc suffers from the same HORROR?" Another writes, "I have just purchased the new THX *Apocalypse Now* and I am VERY impressed with the EXCELLENT transfer[;] video and audio wise it is beautiful, but I am concerned with the 1.9:1 ratio. I always thought the film was 2.35:1. It does not state anywhere on the disc why the director of photography recomposed the film to the ratio it is at on this transfer." Another subscriber answers the question: "The transfer is presumably the same as the older version. Storaro (the DP) felt that the 2.35:1 ratio would shrink the image too much, resulting in loss of detail. . . . Incidentally, the film wasn't necessarily 2.35:1. The 70mm version would have been 2.2:1."[52]

The detailed interrogations of industry products by online groups and other consumer guides provide an alternative source of information for consumers. Yet, industry promotions, consumer magazines, and Internet groups tend to embrace the technology involved. Debates among consumers in the second half of the 1990s often concerned aspect ratios, transfers, and home theater technologies—the pros and cons of laser disc versus DVD, the superiority of AC3 sound systems to Dolby Pro Logic, and so forth. Films become vehicles for the performance and assessment of these technologies (as one online commentator succinctly puts it: "You want to test your THX and AC3 hardwares? Watch *Strange Days*").[53] What is noticed, valued, and appraised about films in this part of their afterlife is how their characteristics—mise-en-scène, special effects, sound, supplemental features—either exploit or fail to realize the capabilities of the machines of reproduction. This aesthetic mechanism allows the generic horror of *The Silence of the Lambs* (1991) to become the technological horror of the rolling dropout.

The Thrill of Acquisition

The fact that cinema can be acquired and taken home opens up vast possibilities for its use and its meaning in the post-VCR era. As one example of these possibilities, collecting represents a distinct instance of the impact that new technologies have had on film reception in the home. In the constitution of the "insider" identity and the coordinates of the hardware aesthetic, we glimpse part of the elaborate world inhabited by the high-end and, increasingly, mainstream film collector. Positioned by the industry as a privileged subject and captivated by the machines of reproduction, the collector is the new film connoisseur, the cinephile existing outside of the motion picture theater. Recent technological developments have helped this film culture to flourish, providing bountiful films for sale and shaping the terms of their consumption within a domestic environment in which both the television set (via home theater and HDTV) and the films themselves have been reinvented to meet the expectations of digital quality. Within the high-end collecting sensibility, films from different national traditions, canons, and eras are transformed into signs of the technical proficiency and potential of the contemporary arts of electronic and digital reproduction. Particularly in this sense, this kind of cinephilia is inextricable from technophilia in home film cultures. In turn, technophilia is made possible by acts of consumption that enable collectors to experience such rapport with machines and mass cultural artifacts.

In an exemplary instance of the bond between producing and consuming cultures, the domestic world of the cinephile is constructed from a series of purchases: tapes, VCRs, DVD players, DVDs, AV receivers, surround-sound speakers, large-screen television sets, monster cables, and so forth, each purchase justifying the others. These are not simply instrumental acts; as we have seen, the goods that enter the home are saturated with meaning and significance that enter into the field of reception. As they always have, media industries attempt to shape the consumption of cinema—in this case, by catering to collectors and attempting to define them as industry insiders who gaze upon the cinema through high-tech eyes and ears. While these industries have not invented film collecting or these elements of suasion, they capitalize on existing trends, striving to educate viewers and organize their consuming desires in certain ways. Although high-end collectors may indeed domesticate their machines and films through personal means, a strong component of this home film culture responds with the same language and same modes of evaluation that characterize producing cultures.

Patrons not only watch films, then; they also own them and situate them in relation to their entertainment centers and other less luminous household items. Owners who are collectors intensify this sense of possession by selecting films on the basis of their technical quality, among other criteria, and then by organizing individual titles according to systems of classification. An excitement about both of these processes signifies the thrill of acquisition and the accompanying pleasure involved in creating a homemade universe out of such cinematic trophies. In this way the collection is a sterling example of what Baudrillard refers to as the peculiar "passion for private property" that marks our relationship to the objects populating our home environments, a passion that can be every bit as intense as that more commonly associated with relationships that humans have with one another.

This sort of possession imposes a certain abstractness on collected media objects. Within this abstracted state, the collected object undergoes a kind of surgery with respect to its historical origins. As the case of *The Wizard of Oz* suggests, the historical context in which a film initially appeared can be partly resurrected in the reissue; in fact, this context is a prized commodity. Materials used to historicize a title invite the viewer to reexperience the past, selling the film through appeals to authenticity and revelation (e.g., the inclusion of a rarely heard 1939 radio broadcast of the first performance of "Over the Rainbow" in the film's gift set). This information, in turn, bestows upon the collector the special, obscure knowledge so valued in the trade. In the process, rather than focusing on the sociohistorical or political dimensions of the bygone era, this mode of historicization emphasizes the entertainment past; tinged with an aura of nostalgia, it tends to romanticize that past. At the same time, such a reified history obscures the power of the contemporaneous context to affect perceptions of the object. As in the remastering of analog musical recordings for CD, digital technology resurrects old media and gives them to audiences, ostensibly in new, improved forms that realize their full potential for vivid reproduction of sound and/or image.

Thus, part of the process of abstraction involves a selective, nostalgic historicization of the film that is embedded ultimately in the presentism of the digital aesthetic. In a fascinating mix of the antiquated and the new, collector's editions of silent or classic-era films are remade according to sellable high points of their past and an overall modernizing visual and aural facelift. In contradistinction to Benjamin, renewing the old world in film collecting today involves a complex interplay of nostalgia and presentism that glories in the past and its acquisition only if the past has been renovated through the newest technological standards. Presentism and nostalgia both vigorously repackage the past, demonstrating the force that the diachronic positioning of a text has on its public reappearance and estimations of value.

Scholars addressing the phenomenon of collecting are often deeply concerned—and divided—about the effects it has on time and history. Susan Stewart argues that collecting represents a loss of origins for an object as it is repositioned within the logic of the museum or personal collection. By contrast, Maurice Rheims claims that the "passion for collecting is joined to a loss of any sense of the present time"; that is, the collector, in seeking immersion in the past through the historical references offered by an artifact, is of necessity disconnected from the present. Still another view is offered by Baudrillard, who contends that the collection "abolishes time" altogether; that is, *"the organization of the collection itself replaces time."* Because the collection reduces "time to a fixed set of terms navigable in either direction," it represents an opportunity for the owner to travel anywhere historically with complete control.[54] Thus, the collection's temporal dimension points neither to the present nor to the past but ultimately to the internal logic and order of the collection. Like Stewart, I argue that the dynamics of film collecting operate ultimately in the "presentist" mode, especially given the nature of evaluation within the high-end film-collecting world. In this world, contra Rheims, the viewer's access to the past is filtered through a shiny new machine ethos, and, contra Baudrillard, the high-end collection itself, although it mixes and matches texts from different historical moments, is still muscularly underwritten by the priorities of the digital aesthetic.

Another substantial level of abstraction worth discussing takes place as films join private collections. The shift in exhibition contexts removes them from the public sphere, inserting them into a private totality. Most obviously, this means that films will enter certain systems of classification that affect their identities. In the clearest markings of organization, films within private collections can be faithfully assigned places that accord with their histories, echoing the blend of nostalgia, presentism, and mass media expertise embodied by the formula of the collector's edition. Thus, *The Wizard of Oz* might be classified under "MGM musicals" or, alternately, "the films of Judy Garland." Films can also, à la the video store, be regrouped in private collections under more "consumer-friendly" categories; thus, along with films of every other generic stripe and time period, *The Wizard of Oz* might be shelved with "Hollywood classics" or "family and children's films." Conversely, little organizational logic may be in evidence; the collector may simply collect favorite films, meaning that individual titles become part of a potpourri. While these cases of organizing personal collections seem to present a spectrum of possibilities that range from affiliations with "official" systems of organization to more haphazard and personal methods, each signals a meaningful adoption of the film into the household, an adoption that displaces the film's original historical context, either through an enthusiastic crystallizing of that context into a number of elements (e.g., the studio, the star) or through a purposeful remotivating of its generic identity through alternative labels. Whatever the particular system of organization or disorganization, a film is given a particular resonance and identity that makes it useful within the collector's universe and alters whatever affiliations it may have had when it appeared initially to the public.

As the owner-collector becomes the maestro of his or her film library, this role comes to have an importance that surpasses and obscures the person's function as a consumer in the marketplace. As Stewart remarks, the collecting self "generates a fantasy in which it becomes producer of those objects, a producer by arrangement and manipulation." In "subsuming the environment to a scenario of the personal," the collection thus "acquires an aura of transcendence and independence" in relation to larger economies of value that it actually mirrors.[55] The joys of collecting, then, are bound up not merely with acts of consumption but also with the powerful sense the collector has of being the source, the origin of the objects purchased and organized into a system. This is a psychology that clearly recalls Metz's theatergoing cinephile. The enchantment with machines, the false sense of mastery that indulges a fantasy of control, and the recognition of "I" as the origin of the show are characteristics of contemporary film collecting that resemble theatrical cinephilia. The possibility of analogous fascinations is enhanced by the ultimate inseparability of theater and home: the experience of cinema at home is not isolated from public moviegoing; nor, conversely, is the multiplex divorced from the household encounter with films. The same viewers inhabit both spheres, meaning that reciprocity, rather than discontinuity, better defines the relation between the fascinations found in public and private movie consumption.

As the theater-home analogy suggests, self-reference is a key ingredient in the individual's relationship to and pleasure in commodities.[56] In the case of cinema, collected objects ultimately refer to the collector as a kind of auteur, a producer of an intelligible, meaningful, private cosmos—a dynamic that occludes the relations the collection has to the outside world, particularly to the social and material conditions of mass production. A chain of logic among property, passion, and self-referentiality helps to explain the collector's zeal and also the significant place films have attained in the home as personal possessions. Subject both to the collection's particular organization and to the collector's apparently self-contained world, the collectible thus offers the radiant pleasure that an investment in one's domestic space can bring.

Relying as it does on a slippage in the collector's identity from consumer to producer, cinema's domestication within this particular film culture tends to minimize awareness of the alliances between cinema and public institutions, between home film cultures and broader spheres of influence. As we have seen, while the world of the collector seems exclusive and personal, it is strongly influenced by discourses of media industries and their technologies. As media industries offer consumers the rhetoric of intimacy (i.e., "secrets" of the cinema) and mastery (i.e., technological expertise or media knowledge), they enhance the sense of owning a personalized product. Owning and organizing films into a library further emphasize the private dimensions of the experience by giving the collector the sense that he or she repossesses, transforms, and remakes in some way the industry product. Solipsism is central to the pleasures and the paradoxes of collecting: considered a most private, even eccentric, activity, collecting is unavoidably tethered to public enterprises and discourses.

Contemporary high-end film collecting gravitates, then, toward apolitical modes of evaluation. Further, it upholds standards forwarded by a white male technocentric ethos, functioning, as does home theater discourse, to support technocratic visions of media and consumption and, by implication, the "good life" in U.S. society. In the process, this taste culture inspires a certain clublike identity, from which women, people of color, and individuals without the means to "digitize" their homes are excluded. However, by pointing to these characteristics, my intention is not to define collecting as a demonic Other to some pristine set of ethics or ideals. All aesthetics are influenced by cultural forces and operate through a dynamic of inclusion and exclusion. As but one mode of evaluation, high-end collecting represents a set of interpretive priorities that enter into the inevitable war of aesthetics that takes place publicly and privately every day. Through these priorities, contemporary high-tech cinephilia embodies a particular means of constructing subjectivity and history and of maintaining an association between masculinity and technology that signals the role new technologies subtly play in perpetuating the cultural status quo. However, as high-end collecting becomes democratized through the continuing dissemination of DVD, the cultural implications of this manner of textual appropriation will change; the variables of technology, cinema, ownership, and the personal archive are bound to interact differently in relation to increasingly diverse audiences.

In the next chapter, I address in more detail the ramifications that the home recycling of Hollywood films has for the public construction of history. I examine cable television as a venue that is especially revealing in this regard. All manner of cable channels, from premium channels and superstations to basic cable channels, have long been central to the ancillary exhibition of Hollywood titles, substantially enhancing the sense that movies lie easily within the home viewer's reach. Some channels, such as American Movie Classics (AMC) and Turner Classic Movies (TCM), have attained distinctive identities as showcases for the cinema of yesteryear. In resurrecting "old" films in large numbers, the dedicated classic movie channel provides a particularly intriguing case for studying how the Hollywood past is presented and remembered within the context of today's media industries. Lacking the solemnity and architectural grandeur of other sites dedicated to the preservation of the past, this kind of channel nonetheless functions as a museum, incarnating a space in which the past is both commemorated and rewritten in accordance with contemporary national values and concerns.

Remembrance of Films Past

Cable Television and Classic Hollywood Cinema

> The procedure which today relegates every work of art to
> the museum . . . is irreversible. It is not solely reprehensible,
> however, for it presages a situation in which art, having
> completed its estrangement from human ends, returns . . .
> to life. . . . [Museums] have actually transformed works of
> art into the hieroglyphics of history and brought them a
> new content while the old one shrivelled up. No conception
> of pure art, borrowed from the past and yet inadequate to it,
> can be offered to offset this fact.
>
> **Theodor W. Adorno,** "Valery Proust Museum," 1967

> As we enter the second century of great American
> filmmaking, AMC will, through its commitment to
> preserving this unique portion of our cultural heritage,
> continue to be the Museum of Classic Hollywood.
>
> **American Movie Classics promotion,** 1994

Deanna Durbin smiles an impossibly sweet smile as she convinces the famous Leopold Stokowski to conduct an orchestra of down-on-their-luck
musicians in *One Hundred Men and a Girl* (1937). Lupe Velez prevails,
through sheer charisma, over a society matron trying to break up Velez's
marriage to the matron's nephew in *Mexican Spitfire* (1939). The Ritz
Brothers get hopelessly drunk toasting all of the French kings named Louis
in their version of *The Three Musketeers* (1939). Cornell Wilde, square jaw
firmly set in place, flees through the African bush from a tribe bent on
killing him in *The Naked Prey* (1966). These scenes may not have the
mythic resonance of the burning of Atlanta from *Gone with the Wind*
(1939) or Kane's utterance of the word *Rosebud* at the beginning of *Citizen*

Kane, but they are, nonetheless, part of the legion of classic-era Hollywood films shown every day in the United States.

While vintage films appear periodically in various high-profile venues, especially when they are rereleased on the big screen or materialize on network television during the holidays, they have become a staple of cable television. Venues that once acted as primary recycling centers for Hollywood features in the post–World War II era, such as network television and retrospective movie houses, either no longer regularly program this fare or, in the case of retrospective houses, have largely gone out of business. Beginning in the 1980s, VHS and cable TV displaced the networks as providers of all manner of Hollywood films, making old films, including the most obscure and forgotten titles, an even more intimate part of everyday life. With its round-the-clock programming, cable has become a repository for what is popularly referred to as "classic Hollywood cinema," that is, studio films made between the 1920s and 1960s. From A&E (Arts and Entertainment) to USA, cable stations have made classic films and television series a significant part of their offerings. In the process, they have become major purveyors of the media past. As they persistently re-present classic films to contemporary home viewers, cable stations help to create a home film culture devoted to the commemoration of vintage American cinema.

The resurrection of artifacts is, of course, an integral activity of all institutions associated with the arts. Indeed, it would be hard to imagine the U.S. cultural landscape without museum exhibitions of the Old Masters, performances of classical music, bookstores featuring canonical novels, DVD reissues, TV reruns, and "golden oldie" radio stations. We expect and even rely on the ready availability of forms from the past long after their original appearance. Since both media industries and audiences are substantially invested in reestablishing contact with past forms, it is worth examining the cultural forces that influence how we remember and value these artifacts.

Memory studies devoted to film typically analyze either the emotionally potent connection between visual media and individual histories or how certain texts (e.g., *Schindler's List* [1993]) attempt to construct the past and its public memory.[1] Each of these approaches provides valuable information about film's relationship to memory; however, far less attention has been paid to the practices of media companies committed to showcasing the media past. Yet, the visibility and centrality of Hollywood studios and media conglomerates, coupled with their immense capacity to revive bygone texts, suggest that they should be considered, along with museums and government memorials, as institutions of memory par excellence. Like museums and memorials, Hollywood acts as a custodian of the past, orchestrating meaningful and influential confrontations with its archive for viewers. And like these other sites, Hollywood has its share of aesthetic treasures and historic monuments; in a sense, *Gone with the Wind, Casablanca* (1942), and *Citizen Kane* have become as much markers of the nation's cultural heritage as Plymouth Rock is. How, then, do media companies repackage reissues for public consumption? In the process of reinventing "old" products for contemporary audiences, how do they reconstruct the past? What implications do their strategies of display have for understanding the connections between media industries and the social production of memory?

To pursue these questions, I examine the home presentation of classic films by one of the chief self-defined custodians of U.S. film culture today: cable movie channels devoted to the exhibition of vintage cinema. In this chapter, I concentrate on American Movie Classics (AMC), the oldest and most successful of these dedicated channels.

In a 1997 *New York Times* article, "Teaching New Generations the Joys of Old Movies," Stephen Henderson commends AMC, Turner Classic Movies (TCM), and Movies from Fox (FXM) for playing "a huge role in keeping the nation's film history alive." He writes that because they are "just about the only places movie fans can find their old favorites . . . the movies these networks choose to show will become the ones known by generations to come. . . . Without channels showing 30's hits and John Wayne westerns, millions might grow up film-illiterate." Henderson suggests that, while profit-motivated, AMC, TCM, and FXM have achieved the status of central archives of the past, promoting the viewer's awareness of film history, selecting films that will be remembered by future generations, and helping to prevent film illiteracy. The executives of these channels have taken it upon themselves to "simultaneously entertain and educate . . . citing a need for raising awareness of America's film heritage."[2] AMC's role as a showcase for the Hollywood past has been especially widely recognized. Cable executives and audiences alike have referred to AMC as the "the Metropolitan Museum" and "the Masterpiece Theater" of classic movies.[3]

As a part of mass culture that is zealously commemorative, AMC is an instructive example of how America's film past is preserved in the realm of domestic leisure. As we shall see, the channel is very much a part of what Michael Bommes and Patrick Wright define as "national heritage culture." National heritage culture involves a "public articulation or staging of the past . . . of immense extent, variety, and ubiquity."[4] In its public presentation of the past, national heritage culture selects aspects of the past for commemoration, supplying historical context to explain their significance to audiences. Heritage culture often also involves the care, preservation, and management of the selected past, ensuring that it will continue to represent the nation's achievements across generations. The acts of selection, contextualization, and preservation are necessarily ideological. Whether these acts seek to promote and maintain one vision of the past over possible others or to present diverse viewpoints, they enter into the cultural fray about the meaning of the nation's history.[5]

Typically, we tend to regard civic, state, government, and other official organizations as being responsible for preserving the physical aspects of the nation's past (e.g., its buildings and landscapes) as well as the memories of the persons, events, and rituals that compose its history (e.g., through monuments and public pageantry such as reenactments and parades). Bommes and Wright provide an important revision to such assumptions. They argue that reminders of a nation's heritage occur through a "whole battery of discourses and images" that echo throughout the culture's representations, including such things as advertisements and other mass cultural ephemera (253). National heritage culture, then, is not only the preserve of the museum or government memorial; it can also be vividly expressed and maintained in even the most quotidian forms of representation. Aspects of nationalism become part of the language of mass culture through strategies designed to heighten a product's visibility, legibility to its audiences, and resonance as a specifically American good.

With their elaborate exhibition strategies and consciousness of preserving and promoting the nation's film heritage, cable movie channel "cinemuseums" provide an opportunity to examine the specifics of the traffic in classic film titles as well as the larger cultural and historical implications of resurrecting vintage texts. To begin, these cine-museums allow us to examine the classic label itself. Classic films are not born; they are made by various media, educational, and other agencies interested in revitalizing old properties within contemporary taste markets. Further, as a means of locating Hollywood relics within these markets, exhibition venues forcefully rehistoricize them, giving them new sellable, historical identities. Not surprisingly, the classic film is surrounded by discourses that emphasize a nostalgic view of the past, particularly through a lavish attention to "old" stars. Not only do stars act as agents of nostalgia; classic movie channels also define them as potent representatives of gender and race capable of supplying verities about America, past and present. Thus, the recycling of movies on cable involves a juggling of aesthetic and historical values that provide insight into the place of the classic within mass cultural hierarchies and its function as a platform for the popular writing and rewriting of U.S. history.

Certainly, the classic movie channel's historical revisionism is part of a public articulation or staging of the past, as Bommes and Wright say. But its participation in a national heritage culture devoted to film is also more explicitly realized. The rise of classic movie channels took place within a highly charged cultural moment in which saving the film past was freighted with concerns about the health of the nation. AMC and other such channels that have featured "preservation festivals" of various kinds in their programming are part of a larger film preservation movement, fueled in the late 1980s by government legislation and the support of certain social agencies and organizations. In addition to having significant ecological value and virtue, historical preservation is also a political mission, subject to perceived national concerns and crises. As I will argue, the contemporary film preservation movement was articulated in relation to multiple challenges to the sovereignty and identity of America at the end of the twentieth century. Within the politics and ideologies of this time, the classic cable movie channel participated in a discursive reconstruction of the nation spurred by a variety of perceived internal and external economic threats.

By studying this home film culture's aesthetic and historical "makeover" of the classic film and its prizing of film heritage, we can consider which memories of the cinematic and American past enter the highly valued market of the home, literally reaching viewers where they live. Given this film culture's preoccupation with history, we can also grasp far-reaching connections between the province of the home and institutions involved in the management and circulation of the past, while meditating on the nature of mass-produced memory itself. Before we engage with these issues, however, it is necessary to provide some background on AMC's history as the first cable station to program exclusively and without commercial interruption feature films from Hollywood's classic era.

About AMC

Launched in 1984 as a pay service to 250,000 subscribers, AMC gained a more solid footing in the industry three years later when it became part of basic cable, an arrangement that allowed subscribers to have the channel as part of a flat monthly fee. In 1991, Rainbow Media Holdings, Inc. (a subsidiary of Cablevision Systems Corporation and NBC) and TCI (Tele-Communications, Inc.) each owned half of AMC.[6] TCI and Cablevision were ranked, respectively, first and sixth among U.S. multisystem operators (or MSOs, companies that own more than one cable system), associating AMC with two top cable providers early in its history. At the time, TCI was also one of the largest media companies in the United States, just behind such other giants as Time

Warner Inc., the Disney Company, and the Sony Corporation.[7] Presently, AMC is fully owned and operated by Rainbow Media Holdings.

Given its auspicious beginnings, by the early 1990s AMC was well situated in terms of two integral components of cable success: number of subscribers and programming rights acquisition. In the years following the channel's introduction, subscribers rose from 3.2 million in 1985 to 24 million by decade's end to 39 million in 1991.[8] By the mid-1990s, 61 million subscribed to the channel, making AMC sixteenth among the top twenty cable networks, just below CNN Headline News (at 62,619,000) and MTV (at 65,900,000). In 2004, AMC reached 84 million homes. As Douglas Gomery remarks, for both cable operators and viewers alike, AMC represents "one of the great success stories in the development of cable TV."[9]

Certainly, AMC's early part ownership by TCI was influential in its growth; this connection alone substantially enhanced AMC's audience, because, by 1991, TCI possessed nearly one-quarter of all cable subscribers. More subtly, Ted Turner's purchase of MGM/UA in the mid-1980s had considerable impact on AMC's success. When Turner bought MGM/UA Studios and its library of films, he found to his dismay that many of the films were under contract with AMC and other organizations. Taking legal action, Turner challenged AMC's cable rights to the films, but he eventually paid the channel fifty million dollars in order to reclaim older Warner Bros. and MGM titles. AMC used some of this money to secure new movie rights to enhance its own library of films, helping to build a solid and diverse foundation for programming.[10] By 2000, AMC had more than five thousand films in its library as well as licensing agreements with, among others, Samuel Goldwyn, RKO, 20th Century Fox, Paramount, Warner Bros., Universal, Columbia/Tristar Television Distribution, MGM/UA Domestic Television Distribution, and several independent distributors.[11] It should be noted that, despite a reputation for showing uncut versions of films, AMC often shows "TV-ready" prints edited for content such as nudity and offensive language.

At its inception, AMC's programming was aimed at a category of viewers long considered to be "cable resisters" by the industry. By showing older films—uninterrupted and uncolorized—AMC attracted the "gray demographic," the middle-aged and elderly audience.[12] AMC's early choice of hosts reflects this priority. The main host of the show, Bob Dorian, was part of the older demographic himself, as were many of the celebrity guest hosts who appeared on the channel in the 1980s and 1990s, including such stars of Hollywood's golden years as Debbie Reynolds, Shirley Jones, and Douglas Fairbanks Jr. The end of the 1990s found AMC trying to broaden its appeal to include younger, "hipper" viewers. At this point, AMC began to hire slightly more youthful hosts (such as John Burke and Neal Gabler) and to showcase guest celebrity hosts from contemporary films (such as Dennis Quaid, Darryl Hannah, and Samuel L. Jackson). AMC also featured original programming designed to put "a new spin on classic movies," to render them "more palatable to a wider audience."[13] These original programs, such as *Knockout: Hollywood's Love Affair with Boxing* and *Hollywood Goes to Court,* attempted to revitalize the classics by showing clips that trace the relevance of old films to fundamental aspects of American culture—in these cases, sports and the judicial system, respectively. In 2002, AMC modernized its offerings yet again in a stronger bid for the youth market. Along with some older fare, the channel regularly screens more contemporary films and has launched special programming in tune with the times, including reality-based shows and DVD-TV, a series that exhibits films with accompanying supplemental features, directors' commentaries, and other extras associated with DVD. To generate more revenue, AMC's film showings are now interrupted by commercials. As part of these most recent changes, AMC's Web site (www.amctv.com) features images of twenty-somethings, ads for upcoming movie releases, and information about the AMC Movie Academy, a filmmaking program aimed at youth.

Through most of its history, AMC has organized its programming through "branded blocks," groupings of films according to certain themes, a concept that has long been a popular way for television networks and other programmers to repackage and promote classic Hollywood fare. These blocks have been thematized according to stars, directors, genres, historical periods, and special topics (such as the femme fatale and movies showcasing the Big Band sound). The channel's original programming has often taken the form of documentaries tied to the thematic festivals of the month (e.g., "Stars and Stripes: Hollywood and World War II" and "Between Heaven and Hell: Hollywood Looks at the Bible"). Further, since 1993 AMC has run a series of film preservation festivals in association with major nationwide organizations devoted to film preservation and restoration. In addition to its on-air strategies of presenting the past, beginning in 1988 AMC published a monthly magazine, *American Movie Classics,* which contained articles about Hollywood along with the channel's monthly screening schedule. AMC no longer publishes the magazine, but the magazine's content is available free of charge on the channel's Web site and in its newsletter.

AMC's 2002 transformations are interesting for what they indicate about changing strategies of classic film exhibition in a shifting and increasingly competitive multichannel cable universe. AMC appears to be leaving most of the market for pre-1950s Hollywood films to TCM, a cable channel that continues to court older viewers and die-hard classic movie fans. However, this chapter focuses on AMC in the 1980s and 1990s, when the channel's commitment to older Hollywood classics was key to its phenomenal success and to the role it played in American culture. During this era's political ferment, especially with respect to anxieties about globalization, establishing the concept of film heritage became an urgent and widespread national preoccupation. Cinema's past, perhaps, had never mattered more to so many.

Among the different facets of the classic cable movie channel, one of its most important operations is to assert the value of the aged artifact. An obvious goal perhaps, but the heritage industry's way of achieving it involves a vigorous reassessment of the relationship between past and present, forging an intimate link between the attribution of aesthetic worth and historical revisionism. With this in mind, we can examine three interrelated strategies AMC has used to affect the value of classic Hollywood films: the expansion of the classic film canon to make it more inclusive; the definition of film classics as vital historical documents; and the establishment of a crisis in our cinematic heritage accompanied by the need to rescue it from the ravages of time. While AMC's practices do not apply to all institutions that resurrect Hollywood's "Golden Era," its case presents an instructive view of the internal dynamics involved in contemporary film heritage discourse and the economic and political forces that interact with this discourse as it enters the viewer's domain.

What's in a Name?

We might expect that only those films that have been ranked in "best of cinema" lists, such as *Citizen Kane* and *Casablanca,* or, at the very least, those that were made during Hollywood's classic era (roughly from the 1920s through the 1950s) would be labeled as classics. However, AMC's use of this term is not so selective. Like many other media companies in the business of selling Hollywood films, AMC refers to nearly all of its properties as classics, no matter when they were made or how humble their reputation. Revealing the broad usage of the term, the channel has shown films as part of categories such as "Early Morning Classics," "Matinee Classics," "Saturday Classics," and "Classics Collection." In this context, it is entirely possible to see *The Ghost and Mr. Chicken* (1966), starring Don Knotts, hailed as a "comedy classic" and Bo Derek touted as a "legendary screen star."[14] Thus, AMC's use of the classic designation is inflated, a rhetorical gambit designed to canonize all Hollywood products, even those that have long flown under the aesthetic radar, in the hope that their instant value will translate into instant profit.

Although it may be driven by the most basic commercial motives, the attribution of classic status has substantial cultural implications. It represents a bid by what Pierre Bourdieu calls "agents of consecration" to create or enhance the legitimacy of works—an effort that circulates in culture as part of the identity of these works. Such agents are interested in conserving "the capital of symbolic goods," that is, in producing or maintaining the prestige value of artifacts within a system of cultural relations.[15] This act of conservation serves commercial interests but also attempts to secure status for the agents and their goods in the social hierarchy. Certain social institutions, such as museums and the educational system, as well as more informal groups, such as reading circles and fan clubs, routinely strive to establish or confirm the value of certain artists and their works. No matter whether their acts of consecration take place in what are traditionally considered high or low cultural arenas, these entities become tastemakers. They acquire the sheen of discerning readers or viewers within their particular territories. Such activities are omnipresent in the media, with the industry, critics, talk show hosts, fan clubs, and other groups generating lists of top books, CDs, films, television shows, and so on.

In Bourdieu's schema, additional agents—"agents of reproduction"—educate consumers to attain competency, to become "good" readers or viewers, thus enlisting them to support and to continue to reproduce the status of these works (121). Like a museum, AMC engages in both of these activities. The channel asserts the value of its artifacts as timeless classics and, through various means such as the commentary of hosts and the monthly magazine (which often featured articles by film academics), guides viewers in the art of classic film appreciation. Educators who appear on the channel give its films the respectability associated with literate, academic tastes.

In the process of manufacturing an aesthetic preserve for old Hollywood movies, media companies demonstrate the permeability of boundaries between high and low culture. Bourdieu writes that certain institutions operate in relation to a "field of restricted production," an aesthetic sphere primarily identified with high art. This sphere is tightly knit in terms of producers and audiences—for example, classical musicians and avant-garde artists performing for an edified cognoscenti. It also does not overtly identify itself as concerned with economics; rather, its concern appears to be with notions of art. Such fields are, at first glance, utterly opposed to what Bourdieu refers to as "large-scale production," or what is commonly called mass culture. Commercial productions in TV, film, radio, and literature are driven by the bottom line and aimed at the "average" consumer. Because of its obsession with profit and with reaching general audiences, large-scale production is, by definition, middle-brow. It is this middle-brow audience that "producers of this type of art and culture *explicitly* assign themselves, and which determines their technical and aesthetic choices" (125–26). Even when large-scale producers seek a targeted audience (e.g., women, men, teenagers), they still participate in an overall industry strategy of reaching increasing numbers of consumers.

However, because both the restricted and the large-scale spheres of production strive for crossover appeal, they are not as diametrically opposed as they seem. For example, art museums demonstrate their desire for the financial success associated with mass commercial enterprises by screening Hollywood films, embracing blockbuster exhibits, and devoting ever-increasing floor space to museum shops, where art-related paraphernalia is sold. Similarly, the producers of mass culture often aspire to escape their perceived debased status by defining themselves in relation to so-called legitimate culture. Media industries have long struggled to achieve the kind of symbolic capital or accumulated prestige that characterizes high art. Hollywood's history is marked by repeated efforts to align itself with respectability, whether through the European-inspired architecture of the silent era's motion picture palace, the adaptation of "serious" literary works, or the ceremonial bestowing of Oscar nominations and awards.

The classic designation becomes one means among many, then, of associating film producers and consumers with the symbolic capital of refined culture. Further, as such a marker of value, the classic label serves strategically to defend the status of the old product in the contemporary world of media consumption. When media companies define vintage films as classics, they help to create a cultural orthodoxy around Hollywood cinema of yore, protecting it from forces that could detract from or obliterate its significance. In a time that rabidly privileges new media products and technologies, the classic label wards off the appearance of obsolescence for the reissued film, allowing it to find a place in the market. To this end, AMC frequently characterizes classic-era movie stars as surpassing any subsequent achievements by contemporary celebrities who might appear to be more accomplished. Thus, Bing Crosby's casual, crooning singing style—the rage during the 1940s and 1950s—"changed the sound of popular music forever," while his song "White Christmas," which has sold thirty million to forty million copies, is "by far the best-selling single of all time. . . . Nobody has sold more records. Not the Beatles. Not Michael Jackson. Nobody." Similarly, an AMC magazine writer reports that it is "all but impossible to find an actor today who can match Cary Grant." In an article entitled "The Complete Cary: It Takes Five Modern Leading Men to Make

Figure 11. It takes five modern leading men to equal one classic movie star—Cary Grant as T. R. Devlin in *Notorious* (1946).

One Classic Grant," the writer finds that Grant's versatility as an actor could be matched only by building him, à la the Frankenstein monster, out of five contemporary actors, each of whom represents one part of Grant's multifaceted persona. Thus, we would need Hugh Grant, Pierce Brosnan, George Clooney, Harrison Ford, and Sean Connery to be able to re-create Cary Grant's talents (figure 11).[16]

Insisting on the superiority of Hollywood's Golden Era to the present, this kind of discourse shows the continuing relevance of old films to today's mass culture. As we shall later see, the classic label's defensive function also includes a cultural dimension: it helps to deflect criticisms that the vintage film could be subject to in the present, especially regarding dated, stereotypical portraits of gender and race.

In sum, although the classic label may not be a reliable indicator of aesthetic value (indeed, it demonstrates the term's slipperiness), it nonetheless strives to give an important status to aged forms as well as to their exhibitors and viewers, to create responsive audiences in a highly competitive media world, and to avoid the threat of devaluation. Situated squarely within large-scale production, AMC is an enterprise that nonetheless uses the language of so-called legitimate culture to bless the resurrection of old

Hollywood, transforming the profane into the sacred. Once considered by some critics to be the home of mammon (just as contemporary Hollywood often is now), the Golden Era, with its crusty studio moguls and corporate backing, appears as more artistic, more innocent of the bottom line, than today's multinational media conglomerates. Removed from the taint of late capitalism, all kinds of old films—the noted, the forgotten, and the critically decried—can achieve aesthetic status by virtue of their historical vintage.

As AMC portrays the value of old Hollywood, it seeks to affect the home viewer's film literacy in order to sustain and reproduce the aesthetic and entertainment worth of the classic label. Often involving a comparison between past and present, the channel's exhibition strategies and appeals to its audiences are underwritten by a strong component of nostalgia. AMC presents Hollywood's stars, directors, and films as either evidence of a better past or a vital reminder of the best tendencies of the present. Because the baby boomers and their parents, who once constituted AMC's sole demographic, grew up watching many of these films in theaters or on network television, the audience is primed for reminiscence. As the classic is extolled as an emblem of the good old days, the viewer is treated not only to fond recollections of Tinseltown but also to pointed reassessments of the American past and present.

Seeing Stars

Some of AMC's invitations to experience classic cinema nostalgically are overt. For example, advertisements for its Big Band–era festival, which included *The Glenn Miller Story* (1954) and *The Benny Goodman Story* (1955), asked viewers to take "a sentimental journey down musical memory lane . . . put on your dancing shoes, roll up the rugs, turn up the volume and enjoy the sights and sounds of the Big Band Era." Similarly, in a series entitled "America's Movie Palace Memories," AMC let its audience participate in "the magic of a Saturday matinee." This series re-created the matinee experience by showing a block of cartoons, shorts, serials, newsreels, coming attractions, and feature films to take viewers "back to the glory days of Hollywood." The cablecasts were also set in "landmark movie theaters across the nation. . . . 'Great American Cinemas' [that] . . . serve as opulent reminders of the part neighborhood theaters played in our film heritage."[17]

Invariably historical in nature, these kinds of celebrations of the past are filled with a wistful yearning for yesteryear that is tinged with a view of bygone eras as superior to the present day. Nostalgia tends to arise at times of social change as a means of lamenting progress; thus, nostalgic presentations often show the past as a simpler, more harmonious time that can serve as an antidote to what is perceived as the messy complexity of the modern. Anxieties about the direction in which progress will take the country result, then, in indulgences in reveries meant to deny or offset the impact of change.[18] Certainly, through its "America's Movie Palace Memories" and other series, AMC defines itself as a place where such reveries can occur. However, the brand of Hollywood nostalgia on display is not simply concerned with the depiction of an earlier, rosier time as a means of reacting against change. Nostalgic enterprises also construct the relationship between the past and the present in a way that stress continuities rather than ruptures in a nation's history—a different means of dealing with perceptions of historical discontinuity. By showing a linear, rational progression in the nation's narrative, such enterprises reassure citizens that certain traditions and values that have always held the nation together will continue to do so. In the process, the backward gaze produces historical accounts that enter the field of public memory.

The problem with nostalgia in either its reactive or its inclusive variations is that, once empowered to tell the nation's story, it operates through what historiographers call "selective memory"—a pointedly partial retelling that often results, as Fredric Jameson argues, in a "chronological laundering" and neutralization of the past.[19] Nostalgic discourses tend to whitewash the past, repressing or minimizing conflicts that marked the nation so as to provide an affirmative picture of its political order and way of life. This is especially true of organizations that, like AMC, are commercially invested in resurrecting the past. As Michael Kammen argues, because it seeks to sell history to tourists and consumers, to make history into a "feel good" entertainment experience, this type of "entrepreneurial mode of selective memory" is as interested in forgetting unseemly aspects of the past as it is in commemorating its high points (535). While we can agree that nostalgia often produces unreliable narratives, nostalgic accounts are nonetheless significant because they represent popularizations of the past that vie for dominance in mass culture, circulating specific conceptions of history to citizens in public and private space.

AMC's particular mode of popularizing the past relies on establishing parallels between Hollywood and the nation. For Hollywood films to be able to signify the national story, they must first be intimately and transparently identified with U.S. history. AMC's strategies of display strive to deepen the value of old Hollywood products by repeatedly emphasizing their significance as unmediated documents of American life. As an AMC staff writer matter-of-factly comments, "AMC's commitment to classic movies runs deep, because classic movies are deeply rooted in American culture." Similarly, on the occasion of one of the channel's film preservation festivals, Martin Scorsese states, "Film is history. With every foot of film that is lost, we lose a link to our culture, to the world around us, to each other, and to ourselves."[20]

This sense of Hollywood's historical status informs the presentation of various film series on the channel. For example, in 1993 AMC programmed "Shots Seen 'round the World," a series designed to "celebrate the heights of motion picture achievement." The title of the series plays off one of the founding moments of the American Revolution, when, in 1775, farmers in Concord, Massachusetts, fired upon British soldiers who were going to destroy their guns and other means of waging resistance, an event commemorated as the "shot heard 'round the world." In its version of shots *seen* 'round the world, AMC presents film stills that have become a familiar part of the public's recognition of Hollywood. These shots are "moments audiences will cherish always. They've had an effect on our shared culture." The moments included in the first installment of the series are King Kong's battle with navy biplanes from the top of the Empire State Building (figure 12); the scene from *Citizen Kane* in which Kane (Orson Welles) expires, uttering the word *Rosebud*; the foggy airport runway in *Casablanca* with Humphrey Bogart and Ingrid Bergman; Will Kane's (Gary Cooper) climactic walk alone down the deserted street in *High Noon* (1952); the beach scene with Deborah Kerr and Burt Lancaster's embrace in the surf in *From Here to Eternity* (1953); and Roger Thornhill's (Cary Grant) attempt to escape the crop-dusting assassins in *North by Northwest* (1959).[21] Through its presentation of these iconic images, this promotion accomplishes several rhetorical feats: it equates cinema and U.S. history, distinguishes the importance of cinematic imagery to the nation, and uses the language of heritage ("they've had an effect on our shared culture") to further stress cinema's historical significance. While few would deny film's close relationship to society or the need to preserve it as part of a culture's heritage, we should not overlook the significance of the way in which these issues are explained. The explanation allows the historical enterprise not only to stake certain claims about the importance of classic cinema but also to create a specific narrative of the nation's history.

In another kind of parallelism that relates cinema seamlessly to American life, AMC's film festivals are routinely aligned with holidays and special occasions, including Thanksgiving, Christmas, Black History Month, Memorial Day, and the Fourth of July. In addition, these festivals often coordinate a particular star with a holiday or event. Classic-era stars, the most

Figure 12. One of the "Shots Seen 'round the World": King Kong atop the Empire State Building, fighting off biplanes in the final sequence of *King Kong.*

visible, recognized, and promoted component of old Hollywood, become a central means of commemorating both the cinematic and the national past. Stars are everywhere in AMC's representations; besides appearing in films, they adorn advertisements for memorabilia in AMC's various venues, grace every cover of *American Movie Classics Magazine,* and are prominently featured on the Web site. They promote AMC's programming and act as co-hosts as well as interviewees in on-air programming. Even more than film directors or the films themselves, stars are the major subject of the channel's discourse. Their omnipresence allows the channel to draw from the cultural authority that celebrities have as representatives of the media industry while banking on them as a currency that has long driven the market in Hollywood memorabilia. Without stars, the world of film nostalgia would be a wasteland. Their familiar presence alone enables them to act as gateways to the American past for home viewers who grew up with them. Their gateway function, in turn, gives them a measure of historical authority that can be deployed within histories focused both on celebrating the grandeur of the past and on elaborating continuities between past and present that affirm contemporary life as well.

John Wayne, for example, who as late as 2001 ranked in the Gallup Poll as America's all-time favorite movie star (ahead of Julia Roberts, Tom Hanks, and Al Pacino), has also been a tremendously popular actor with AMC's viewers. On Memorial Day in 1992, one of AMC's many film festivals dedicated to his work featured some of his war films and Westerns. On this occasion, AMC magazine writer Nat Segaloff observes, "If there is one individual who symbolizes America to the rest of the world, it is John Wayne. 'The Duke' . . . portrayed such a range of heroes throughout his 50-year career that his face, voice, gait, and ethics may say more about this country than any scholar, industrialist or elected official." Segaloff acknowledges that in the 1960s Wayne became a controversial figure because of his right-wing politics, specifically his support of the Vietnam War. Any controversy was put to rest, however, during Wayne's illness and eventual death from cancer in 1979. This led "his fans, young and old, liberal and conservative" to send him "an outpouring of love and support. Few of them knew John Wayne the man; they were responding, instead, to Nathan Brittles, Ethan Edwards, Rooster Cogburn, the Ringo Kid, and an unequaled screen legacy that not only enriched our lives but helped to define them as well" (figure 13).[22] Wayne's symbolic power and screen legacy are so influential, Segaloff suggests, that his passing caused generational and political differences to collapse. In this case, cinema appears as more real than reality, capable of displacing and perhaps even resolving historical conflicts because of the audience's emotional attachment to characters and actors who represent American identity. Further evidence that Wayne, once referred to as "an Extra Star on the American Flag," is still considered a "true American hero" is amply provided by fan Web sites dedicated to the actor's accomplishments and memory.[23]

AMC's programming strategies underscore this identification of actor, role, and history. By staging a festival of an actor's films in association with a holiday, a double action occurs: the star comes to represent a ceremonial moment in American history, and that moment is observed in relation to the actor and the films in which he or she appears. In this case, Memorial Day is an occasion when war dead are remembered by loved ones and honored by the nation for sacrifices made to maintain the American way of life. Wayne films shown during the AMC commemoration include *Tall in the Saddle* (1944), *Flying Leathernecks* (1951), and *Fort Apache* (1948), in which he plays, respectively, a cowboy, a Marine, and a cavalry officer. These roles not only represent the classic U.S. masculine types of Westerner and soldier; they also portray episodes of national and global conflict that defined the nation's development and status in the world—the settling of the

Figure 13. American icon John Wayne as the Ringo Kid in *Stagecoach* (1939).

West and World War II. The synergy between film and occasion casts the actor as a player in American martial history and uses the classic film as the site of commemoration, reinforcing the sense that Hollywood is, as Scorsese insisted, history. Hollywood thus appears as a purveyor of the national narrative, telling stories that remember both the gains and losses of war, with Wayne personifying the struggles involved in building and maintaining the nation's security.

Henry Fonda is another AMC mainstay likewise associated with America, although to slightly different ends. To celebrate the Fourth of July in 1995, the channel programmed a festival of his films, including *Young Mr. Lincoln* (1939) and *The Grapes of Wrath* (1940). Writing for the channel's magazine, Gerald Peary remarks that Fonda is "an actor whose roles are so closely identified with the nation's history, he has become an American icon. . . . [His] movie legacy trailblazed an unforgettable path through our nation's history." Peary argues that Fonda, particularly in his roles as the title character in *Young Mr. Lincoln* and as Tom Joad in the adaptation of John Steinbeck's *The Grapes of Wrath*, "provided hallmarks of our national identity . . . [representing] the social conscience's unbending need that justice be served."[24]

This characterization of Fonda resonates suitably with Independence

Day. The Fourth of July recognizes the success of America's victory over British forces in the 1770s—that is, the ability of patriots to pursue the aims of democracy in the face of oppressive powers. Fonda's portrayals of Lincoln and Joad likewise represent moments in U.S. history when individuals had to fight against overwhelming odds to further the cause of democracy. In these cases, the inequities exist within the democratic system itself in the forms of slavery and poverty. Although critical of the system, Fonda's characterizations suggest that democracy can rectify these wrongs through the actions of heroic individuals who oppose injustice. Unlike Wayne, who in his AMC biographies represents a relatively untroubled nationalism, Fonda embodies a kind of patriotism that exhibits faith in America's ability to resolve crises through the spirit of social conscience—democracy's mechanism for righting social wrongs. Thus, each actor's persona depicts a different way to accomplish the same thing: confirming the essential rightness of the American way. The strong association of each with director John Ford, a filmmaker often regarded as the representative recorder of the American experience, only adds to the nationalistic meaning attached to their star personas.

AMC, then, makes little or no distinction between the actor's real and reel personas. Making actors and their roles seem indistinguishable suggests that actors are playing on the stage of American history rather than on a sound stage in Hollywood. To blur this distinction further, AMC's discussions of stars often emphasize their offstage contributions to the nation: for example, Jimmy Stewart's stint as a bomber pilot and Clark Gable's enlistment as an army private in World War II. Rarely in the discourse on classic stars is there any sense that these actors were involved in a fictional, fanciful, or misleading rendition of American history. Yet films, like all texts, maintain complex, highly mediated relationships to historical developments that must be decoded.

Moreover, because stars' historical representativeness requires their idealization, this type of recollection generally avoids acknowledging aspects of a star's persona that might threaten his or her ability to radiate the resilient American character. Problems that characterize the industry or the star's life may be mentioned but only briefly. In this sense, the classic movie channel is the opposite of the "kiss-and-tell" celebrity biography or autobiography that revels in unsavory details (as does Kenneth Anger's *Hollywood Babylon,* for example). The scandalous exposé remains a bête noire among these more upbeat visions of the Hollywood past. The "clean" reromanticizing of stars far exceeds the world of AMC, defining other contemporary manifestations of celebrity worship, from A&E biographies to

Web sites for fans of classic film, even sites devoted to such legendarily troubled stars as Judy Garland.[25]

This is not to say that the process of commemorating classic cinema is entirely unequipped to handle issues more difficult to square with a celebratory narrative. In fact, part of nostalgic revisionism involves the selective confrontation and handling of just those issues. In this vein, while male celebrities such as Wayne and Fonda may serve as relatively easy props for nationalistic rhetoric, women and people of color present greater challenges to representations of the past.

On AMC, old Hollywood appears to be stocked with sturdy stars, both male and female, whose performances testify to the system's ingenuity. Like their male counterparts, some female stars are recognized as vital national symbols. Katharine Hepburn, for example, is subject to a particularly rhapsodic account of her national representativeness. She is "the Statue of Liberty, Eleanor Roosevelt, and Lady Luck. The American ideal personified: the image of discipline, drive, the Puritan ethic fulfilled. She has been liberated since birth. There is nobody like her. She's KATE." Hepburn's Americanness is tied to her individualism, which in turn is composed of strange bedfellows: Puritanism (linking her to the nation's origins but also to the austerity associated with the Puritans) and personal liberation with a tinge of feminism, as evoked through the analogy to Eleanor Roosevelt. Her strength and rebelliousness left "an indelible mark on the film world with a body of work that serves as a testament to her indomitability. How lucky for us that the strengths, weaknesses, spirit, humor, and conviction of this American original were captured on film."[26]

Rosalind Russell, too, appears as an "indomitable" Hollywood figure (figure 14). AMC held a festival of the actress's films on American Business Women's Day (September 22), including *Flight for Freedom* (1943) and *She Wouldn't Say Yes* (1945), in which Russell plays, respectively, an aviatrix and a psychiatrist. The actress is credited with giving "working women a tremendous boost." The festival's commentator remarks, "Long before *Working Women* magazine, sneakers with suits and flex time, there was Rosalind Russell, one of the career-minded leading ladies." Russell's "mastery of the female go-getter paved the way for strong professional women roles in the decades to follow, as working women gained equal footing at the office." Russell, it appears, was tough offstage as well, "a match for Tinseltown's most hard-boiled movie moguls."[27]

However, Russell's depictions were often compromised. The actress complained that the formula of her films began with business but ended with a "negligee and a desire for marriage." The AMC commentator ac-

Figure 14. Rosalind Russell, the screen incarnation of the career woman, as Hildy Johnson in *His Girl Friday* (1940).

knowledges the limitations imposed on actresses by the convention of compulsory marriage but insists that the films still presented women's success in professions usually closed to them at the time, showing that they could earn a living on their own. With less qualification, Hepburn, too, was tamed. Her strong individualism was "tempered by love in the nine films she and [Spencer] Tracy made together. Her acting style became more naturalistic and her aquiline features seemed to soften . . . the taming of the shrew was about to begin. [She] was tough, but conquerable."[28] Whether in the form of Hollywood conventions or real-life relationships, love manages to domesticate the independent actress and the characters she plays.

Although love stories typically tame female characters, commemorative discussions of "strong" female stars must negotiate the consequences of this taming for the stars' personas as well as for its impact on Hollywood's legacy. In Russell's case, AMC depicts her characters as transcending the romantic conventions of the industry. Therefore, Russell is still able to represent the resourceful American working woman and, by extension, Hollywood's ability to foster and feature such images. In Hepburn's case, romance saves the star from extremism. It mitigates her independent streak, resulting in an improvement in her acting style and a greater sense of approachability in her characters. Thus, the felicitous influence of the relationship with Spencer Tracy on- and offscreen preserves the already legendary dimensions of this pairing and saves Hepburn from a too-shrill independence.

By proposing that compromise via the love story either has a salutary effect or is superseded by the strength of a female star's persona, AMC updates its images of women to conform better to contemporary gender ideals in a postfeminist era. That is, classic Hollywood actresses appear as forerunners of feminism, feminists before the second-wave women's liberation movement took place. Through actresses such as Russell, who represented strong independent professionals, Hollywood appears as prescient, anticipating the later women's movement. The industry may have even helped to inspire the movement, as women could see their own lives and ambitions reflected on the screen. Certainly, this recollection of classic Hollywood acknowledges difficulties with stereotypes that militated against fully liberated representations. Ultimately, however, these accounts portray old Hollywood as not only relevant to understanding the course of events in American history but also, through its embodiment of progressive elements, able to anticipate the liberation movements of the 1960s.

Just as it has attended to postfeminist attitudes, the channel has also responded to more contemporary thinking about race. AMC runs stories on African American actors and actresses, often resurrecting little-seen examples of their work in Hollywood. A story on Bill "Mr. Bojangles" Robinson in a 1991 issue of the AMC magazine relates how he was not only the "first black solo dancer to star on the white vaudeville circuits" but also the "world's most famous tap-dancer." In fact, he was so popular by 1930 that he "could sell out the largest and most prestigious houses in the land." Similar praise for another artist accompanies the April 1999 centennial celebration of Duke Ellington's birth. On this occasion, AMC host Nick Clooney interviewed John Hasse, Ellington's biographer, who contended that Ellington was "the greatest all-around musician this country has produced . . . more brilliant and original than any other—including Gershwin, Copland or Bernstein." Hence, Ellington has been "a towering influence on our culture, transcending his time, the jazz form and, eventually, even race."[29]

Beyond extolling the talents and centrality of African Americans to show business, AMC exhibits their film work to situate it within U.S. race histories. Thus, although movies represented opportunities for "Mr. Bojangles," his first film for RKO, *Dixiana* (1930), ran into problems with southern censors who "cut his numbers . . . a common fate then for any scenes in which blacks appeared as anything but servants or African 'savages.'"[30] In 1935, however, Robinson appeared with Shirley Temple in *The Little Colonel*, assuring his place in movie legend. Race also made "Ellington's connection with Hollywood superficial for most of his life," but "that doesn't mean his film appearances don't please."[31] In April 1999, AMC presented two of his rarely seen filmed shorts, *Black and Tan* (1929) and *Symphony in Black: A Rhapsody of Negro Life* (1935), as well as a number of feature films for which he had composed the score, including *Cabin in the Sky* (1943), Vincente Minnelli's all African American musical (figure 15).

Similarly, for a celebration of Black History Month in February 1994, AMC unveiled such relatively unknown films as *Anna Lucasta* (1958), a race melodrama; *St. Louis Blues* (1958), a biography about father of the blues W. C. Handy (played by Nat King Cole); and *The Slender Thread* (1965), starring Sidney Poitier as a crisis line volunteer. As in the discussions of Robinson and Ellington, the festival's commentary acknowledges that "through Hollywood's lens, the image of African-Americans is distorted and disturbing." Writing for AMC, Thomas Doherty chronicles the stereotypes and limitations imposed on African American actors and actresses by racial prejudice, including southern censorship. At the same time, he points out that the past was not completely bankrupt in its depictions: "Even when the movies, like the nation, operated under a strict Jim Crow regime, an extraordinary assemblage of musicians, comedians, and actors surmounted the subservient status assigned by the scripts and lent dignity to roles designed to demean." With contemporary directors such as Robert Townsend and Spike Lee and actors such as Denzel Washington and Danny Glover, "successful filmmakers and stars have taken the reins of motion-picture production," allowing "the stories and talents of black artists [to enrich] the American cinema. . . . Today, the motion picture industry is experiencing a renaissance of African-American talent. No longer Hollywood's servant class, African-Americans now project their own images."[32]

In its celebration of African American contributions to entertainment and its presentations of rare or underplayed examples of race films, the channel depicts the integrity of African American stars as able to transcend social prejudice. Acknowledging that Hollywood itself was fraught with racial difficulties, the channel also insists that the industry nonetheless reg-

Figure 15. Duke Ellington performing with his orchestra in Vincente Minnelli's *Cabin in the Sky.*

istered and preserved the performances of a Robinson or an Ellington. In this way, AMC joins other organizations in numbering these celebrities among America's national treasures and in regarding their work as part of the nation's cultural heritage.[33] At the same time, the cable channel's admission of prejudice in its chronicle of American history allows it to maintain credibility with its audiences, many of whom experienced the liberation movements of the 1960s firsthand.

The passing acknowledgment of prejudice can serve, however, to inoculate against a more penetrating assessment of race relations in the industry's past. Heritage narratives that feature racial inclusion often substantially deemphasize the depth of racial prejudice and the extent of the challenges it presented to actors and actresses of color.[34] These narratives also tend to offer a vision of history in which the problems of the past are well on their way to being resolved, ignoring problems that continue to exist in the industry and in society by presenting an untroubled vision of present-day gender and race relations. The absence of reflection on contemporary debates about the relation of Hollywood, women, and people of color (including their lack of representation in executive industry professions and the continuing use of stereotypes in film) and the accompanying depiction of contemporary life as free of gender and racial tensions (excluding developments such as the backlash against affirmative action) enable such simple assertions of progress, even as they render these narratives seriously suspect. Certainly, such assertions should be tempered by the public record;[35] but to treat American history more fully would necessitate a substantive critique of the gender and racial politics of Hollywood and of the nation—then and now—thus disturbing the ultimately affirmative goals of the heritage narrative.

It is important to point out that the commemorative activities of AMC are not unique or extraordinary in this regard. In fact, just the opposite is true. AMC provides one example of the rampant utopian historicism characteristic of institutions involved in the commercial management of memory. In such histories, painful aspects of a nation's past must be recognized to a certain extent, so that audiences will not be alienated by outright sanitization. Nonetheless, the stories finally emphasize the triumph of progress, the righting of past wrongs. As Michael Wallace argues in relation to another corporately sponsored revisitation of the past (Epcot Center's "American Adventure" in Disney World), through a selective reconstruction of the past, history gets redeployed "within a vision of an imperfect but still inevitable progress."[36] In the process of recording such a history, accounts emphasize consensus and unity over radical dissent and difference. While acknowledging inequities, these accounts highlight significant moments of the past that demonstrate the presence of enlightened social attitudes. The inexorable movement of history toward justice resolves cultural problems, essentially affirming the political and social arrangements of the present. The inevitability of progress secures a sense of the self-correcting rightness of the democratic system and the humane clairvoyance of the national character. The nostalgic and utopian commemorations offered by AMC and other organizations provide a vision of the past that is, in Kammen's words, "essentially history without guilt" (688).

Within these remembrances, films and stars appear as national treasures, as vital parts of the past that allow immediate access to the nation's history. This memorializing of Hollywood cinema not only emphasizes the value of its films and personnel but also symbolizes the nation's greatness. As Dipesh Chakrabarty argues, history writing is best envisioned as a practice of monumentalizing objects, in which making a "'heritage' out of assorted objects is essential to the politics of both nationalism and the nation-state."

Through this process of monumentalizing, history becomes, "the business of the citizen, the subject of the grand narratives of Freedom and Progress that, ultimately, legitimize both the nation-state and the modern market."[37] Although only one voice in an immense sea of discourse devoted to defining the nation's history, the classic cable movie channel demonstrates how the promotion of recycled films and stars as indelible classics participates in the everyday confirmation of ideal notions of U.S. democracy. AMC's contribution to understanding the circulation of popular history, then, lies only partly in the traditional brand of nostalgia it offers. It also vividly illustrates the ability of neotraditional narratives of nation to continue to thrive, not only in the public space of theme parks, monuments, and museums, but on television and in the home, where such narratives are presented to millions of viewers.

Shouldering the weight of U.S. history, such entrepreneurial modes of selective memory are of course vulnerable to unintended revelations.[38] By raising past representations of women and African Americans to the surface and by resolving the issue of prejudice so expediently, AMC's stories risk revealing as much as they try to conceal about minority experience. We must grant the potential presence of such ideological instabilities in any memory project. At the same time, it is important to acknowledge the overt aspirations of heritage businesses and their place within larger cultural narratives devoted to memory. Built on an "artificially constructed past," tradition-driven nostalgia strives toward an "illusion of social consensus" that affirms the present order (Kammen, 4–5) and, consequently, attempts to quiet and displace views disruptive to the more agreeable history on offer. In the case of agencies involved in fostering film memories, these attempts are bolstered by affiliations between a single voice such as the classic cable movie channel and larger social forces that support and amplify its particular take on classic Hollywood.

Certainly, the channel's conflation of Hollywood and American history, in which history appears to be directly expressed in film narratives, presents the past in a way that resonates with other popular manifestations of history in late twentieth-century U.S. culture. As historians have chronicled, during his presidency in the 1980s, Ronald Reagan improvised revisions of history that rearranged the past for conservatives, who were bent on restoring a national identity impervious to radical self-doubt (hence, Reagan's transformation of the Vietnam War from stigma to a source of national pride). In his "reign of error" he uttered factually incorrect statements, misremembered historical events, and confused movie events (including those from his classic Hollywood days) with actual historical occurrences. Hollywood provided the ex-movie star president with a "major source of the mythic iconography" to be deployed in his presentations and policies.[39] Whether he used movie references to bolster his campaigns or programs, from "Win One for the Gipper" to "Make My Day," or actually substantiated a historical event through its cinematic representation, Reagan's presidency was suffused with Hollywoodiana. In the process, Hollywood became one instrument in a revisionist toolbox, helping to renew traditional patriotic feeling in the nation.

Granting the affinities between AMC's presentation of the Hollywood past and Reagan's brand of historicism, the national narrative available on the cable movie channel also has a significant relation with a less obvious historical coordinate: the film preservation movement of the late 1980s and 1990s. During this time, the view that classic films were an endangered species that the U.S. government, national media organizations, and the public should rally to preserve gained particular momentum. Conservation, not just commemoration, was necessary to prevent the loss of precious objects from the past and the subsequent impact their loss would have on the nation's identity. With this identity at stake, discussions of film preservation on AMC and in other venues continued to magnify the nation's progressive accomplishments. However, preservation discourse concentrated additionally on technology's impact on the relationship between past and present. This emphasis on technology ultimately reveals an association between commemorative efforts directed at preservation and government laws, policies, and debates in the 1980s and 1990s that centered around a perceived crisis in U.S. sovereignty and hegemony due to the growing multinational global economy.

Saving the Past

AMC is not alone in its interest in film preservation—a salvage operation aimed at locating films in peril, physically repairing them, and seeing to their proper storage. Other cable movie channels, notably TCM, share AMC's activism in relation to preservation, showing documentaries on the subject *(The Race to Save 100 Years)* and attempting to raise public awareness and money for the cause in other ways. Film preservation is also part of larger industry trends as well as efforts by U.S. film archives to lobby for national recognition of the importance of rescuing the film heritage. If we understand the relatively recent rise of concern about preservation to include a broad range of efforts to save or renovate old films, from explicit preservation activities to restorations and digital reconstructions, then maintenance of the cinematic past emerges as a central facet of contemporary film culture.[40]

The industry has not always had an archival consciousness. In the past, media industries often discarded or misplaced films and television shows or left them to disintegrate in poor storage conditions. Because these industries felt that many of their products were valuable only in their initial runs, an enormous number of films (particularly from the silent era) and TV programs have been lost forever.[41] Over the last two decades, however, the economic rationale of repurposing has helped change the attitude of media companies toward their warehoused products. As we have seen, as ancillary exhibition sites and new media technologies have developed, old films and TV series (many rejuvenated with digitally remastered sound and image) have provided valuable content for home venues from cable TV to DVD.

Consequently, studios have come to see the importance of having preservation facilities on site. For example, for most of its history Columbia Pictures had no preservation laboratory. This situation changed after the Sony Corporation purchased the studio in 1989. In the process of developing high-definition television, Sony saw the possibility of rereleasing films and television programs in Columbia's library in ancillary formats. They spent millions of dollars constructing a preservation laboratory. For these products to be sales worthy in a world of new technologies, especially digital technologies, they had to be preserved, repaired, and updated so that they could appear in good form to new audiences accustomed to quality images and sound. The cost of making preservation masters, creating computer inventories, and using cool and dry storage vaults thus came to be seen as a necessary expense for protecting valuable assets.

As this example suggests, while the cause of film preservation has an important ecological dimension, it is also deeply influenced by economic imperatives. Like many preservation movements, it is motivated by the double concerns of conservation and commerce—that is, by both the commitment to safeguard a resource and the desire to find a profitable use for it.[42] These concerns are often opposed to one another, but at times preservation efforts succeed only when commercial benefits can be foreseen. In the case of cinema, it is arguable whether ecological considerations alone could have prevailed if new technologies and the accompanying need for programming content had not persuaded media conglomerates that there was literally gold to be found in the old Hollywood hills.

To return to cable television, the dynamics of preservation and profit in AMC's coverage of the cinematic past become particularly clear through three examples: its coverage of motion picture palaces, documentaries on the subject of preservation, and preservation festivals, conducted in cooperation with major film archives across the country.

At one time, *American Movie Classics Magazine* ran a monthly feature story on motion picture palaces. These circa-1920s theaters represent an important moment in film exhibition history, when exhibitors built extravagant theaters to attract audiences to films by offering them luxurious surroundings. AMC provided information about the current state of many of these theaters, including the Wang Center in Boston, Massachusetts (formerly the Metropolitan Theater); the Stanley Performing Arts Center in Utica, New York (formerly known as the Stanley); and the Paramount Theater in Oakland, California. The stories of all these theaters are remarkably similar: they were saved from the wrecking ball (a fate for most motion picture palaces) by private interests, civic-minded citizens, and/or local governments; they were then renovated for contemporary use, usually as performing arts centers featuring ballet companies, symphony orchestras, classic film series, and/or Broadway theater.

As AMC tells us, each motion picture palace represents the glories of the past and the threat posed by urban modernization. But the resolution of this conflict is a happy one: once properly renovated for contemporary use, these theaters can serve as cultural centers for cities while still exuding the exceptional character of the past. Boston's Metropolitan Theater, for example, was a "sumptuous entertainment palace that extended for a full city block and five stories into the sky . . . adorned with gold and marble fit for royalty." When it was being refurbished as the Wang Center, the process revealed "a vision of grandeur and extravagance hardly imaginable in a day when movies mean television or tiny black-box theaters."[43]

The description of the renovation process constructs a view of the past as well as a relationship between past and present. As we saw in the case of classic movies, old Hollywood is depicted as glorious—so glorious, in fact, that the experiences of cinema it offered remain unparalleled in today's viewing venues. The sumptuous art and architecture of the motion picture palace, coupled with its frequent contemporary function as a city center, help such buildings to gain admittance to the National Register of Historic Places. Nostalgia, combined with a sense of civic purpose, underwrites this particular heritage narrative. At the same time, these monuments of the past require extensive overhaul to operate in the present.

Preservationists refer to this kind of overhaul as adaptive reuse. The term *adaptive reuse* refers to a recycling of the past that integrates it with the present, preferably for profit. Historically, this strategy has provided a way to satisfy both preservationists and developers. Neither left in "sterile isolation" as a historical artifact nor destroyed in the name of progress, the past is saved and renewed to serve a contemporary function (Wallace 177).[44] Adaptive reuse provides the means for the past, languishing in profit limbo, to be revived by various social agencies willing to gamble on its born-again marketability. In the case of motion picture palaces, renovation allows the theater to be transformed into an integral part of today's civic society. Contemporary resources are necessary to save the splendid past from the more savage impulses of capitalism (which would see it in ruins) and to realize its potential for continued contributions to commercial as well as aesthetic and civic arenas.

The principles and rhetoric of adaptive reuse are also visible in the restoration of specific classic films. Alfred Hitchcock's *Vertigo*, for example, was restored and rereleased on the big screen as a special event in 1996. In 1995, Robert Harris and James Katz, film preservation experts who had previously restored *Spartacus* (1960) and *My Fair Lady* (1964), went to work on *Vertigo* with more than one million dollars of support from Universal Pictures. While *Vertigo* had been a critical disappointment when it first came out, its theatrical reappearance in 1984 (along with other Hitchcock titles kept out of distribution for many years) changed its reputation; critics began to regard it as one of the director's masterpieces. Thus, Universal's financing of its restoration was a fairly safe investment. As it turned out, audiences lined up in urban areas to see the restored *Vertigo* on the big screen, and its widescreen VHS counterpart sold out its first 250,000 units in a few weeks.[45]

When Harris and Katz initially examined the negative and color separations of the film, they found them faded, scratched, and shrunken. How they proceeded after this discovery is the subject of an AMC original documentary, *Obsessed with "Vertigo": New Life for Hitchcock's Masterpiece* (figure 16). This documentary aired on the channel in the mid-1990s and is also available on the special collector's editions featuring the restored film on VHS, laser disc, and DVD. In *Obsessed with "Vertigo,"* the restorers agree that "time does things to movies . . . along the way *Vertigo* was almost lost to us forever . . . a film that looked nothing like what Hitchcock had created." But Universal, "at the forefront today of film preservation," stepped in to rescue the film "from the ravages of time."

Through researching such elements as the original colors of 1950s automobiles and the wardrobe for the film, designed by Edith Head, Harris and Katz sought to restore the film's original color schemes. They also worked on sound, digitizing the original orchestral recording sessions so that the

Figure 16. *Obsessed with "Vertigo": Vertigo's* negative during the restoration process.

film music would play well over today's theatrical and home sound systems and reinventing the foley and effects tracks, which Paramount Pictures had long ago discarded after it lost the rights to the film. In addition, the original version of *Vertigo*, shot in a widescreen process called VistaVision, was reduction-printed at 35mm in the 1950s because many theaters were not equipped to project this particular widescreen format. The film's restoration produced a true version of VistaVision in 70mm, regaining the quality that had been lost previously to reduction printing.[46]

Thus, the restored *Vertigo* reappeared to the public in theaters in 70mm VistaVision and DTS stereo sound, followed by widescreen special editions in THX sound for the home market. As Dave Kehr of the *New York Daily News* wrote, "For those who have never seen *Vertigo*, here is evidence that movies can occupy the highest plane of artistic expression. If you have seen it, you owe it to yourself to see it like this."[47] "To see it like this" intimates that there is something about the restored *Vertigo* that not only brings the film back from the dead but does so in style. Although discussions of the film's renovation emphasize how assiduously Harris and Katz aimed at reproducing Hitchcock's original, equal attention is paid to the role that technology and other contemporary variables played in delivering the "new, improved" version of the film. For example, *Vertigo's* 1996 trailer tells us that it is "presented for the first time in 70mm and DTS Digital Stereo . . . fully restored and remastered," in a "stunning . . . version featuring enhanced picture and sound." These enhancements are depicted, however, as maintaining the spirit of the original. The AMC documentary and other forums define technical progress as being able both to re-create "the precise visual texture Hitchcock intended for every shot" and to improve on his vision in ways he would endorse. *Vertigo* was "seen as Hitchcock could only have dreamed it would look and sound . . . now for the first time people can see *Vertigo* the way that it was intended to be seen."[48]

The discourse of restoration includes numerous appeals to originality and authenticity, while leaving no doubt that the present improves on the past.[49] Along with other innovative elements involved in the process, restored and digitally enhanced visuals and sound signify the superiority of contemporary resources. The commentary surrounding *Vertigo's* reissue reconciles whatever problems might arise concerning authenticity under these circumstances by assuring us that the new film can be re-viewed in a way that ultimately *realizes* the director's original intent. Because technology was inferior decades ago, Hitchcock could not achieve his full artistic vision. Now *Vertigo* can be seen in real VistaVision, remastered with improved image and sound. In this way, the aesthetic demand for the authenticity of the original is balanced with the marketability of technologically advanced effects.

Here, the principle of adaptive reuse meshes harmoniously with repurposing: the past is indeed saved, while being regenerated specifically in relation to the profit-conscious standards and demands of the present. Universal and the restorers rescue the past from the ravages of time as well as from any imperfections in its original design owing to dated technologies. Maintaining the cachet of the past as the repository for film classics, contemporary Hollywood provides a better past, inevitably underscoring the achievements of the present and the promise of the future. Again, as in AMC's star-driven historical accounts, these discussions of technology provide a progressive narrative, complete with the depiction of a slightly problematic past followed by a better today. Even a trace of heroic discourse is present in this commentary, particularly in relation to the ability that capital and technology have to triumph over the various limitations and liabilities of time. From this perspective, Hollywood and its personnel can be seen as protagonists in an epic historical drama, in which skill and powerhouse technological capabilities enable the preservation of the past in spite of what seem like insurmountable odds. In the visions of progress that accompany such preservation commentaries, the success of capital and technology in this mission ultimately testifies to the power of both the media industries and the nation.

Certainly part of the audience's excitement at re-viewing reissues is the anticipation that they have been "spruced up," restored, and/or digitally re-mastered to achieve a better-than-original status. In fact, a large part of the reissue market for "oldies," from CDs to DVDs, promotes these products under the banner of the "remaster." Nostalgic accounts may insist that the "good old days" are superior to the present, but the artifacts of those days must nevertheless be modernized. At the same time that audiences are daz-zled by enhanced visual and audio delights, the promotion of the remas-tered version encourages them to be impressed by the technical prowess of the film industry, by its virtuoso performance as an entity that has the abil-ity to ward off the effects of time while providing audiences with the latest in digital wizardry. Pleasures in re-viewing vintage cinema, then, are linked to an awe of the institution itself. The remembrance of films past is an ex-perience permeated by the spectacle of Hollywood as the embodiment of advanced technoculture and therefore as exemplary of the capital enterprise that helps to define the exceptional power of the nation. This spectacle is present, then, not only in Hollywood's special effects extravaganzas such as *Titanic* (1997), which was often seen worldwide as representing the ex-traordinary capabilities of U.S. capitalism and technological advancement; it is amply portrayed in the promotions for recycled Hollywood products as well.

In this sense, media industries attempt to channel our memories of old films so that we regard them as monuments to the accomplishments of Hol-lywood, much like the Parthenon testifies to the glories of ancient Greece. Such self-referential activities help to define Hollywood as an important cultural institution devoted to preserving the past. Further, the industry characterizes its vintage titles as landmarks of cinematic and cultural achievement not simply by declaring their classic status but by carefully framing them within a technocentric narrative that updates and elaborates their appeal as examples of the industry's technical ingenuity and, ulti-mately, the nation's grandness.

AMC's film preservation festivals help to clarify more explicitly what is at stake in these testimonials about the nation's achievements. Efforts by high-profile activists such as film director Martin Scorsese and film archives across the country, as well as economic and political factors associated with globalization, have helped to bring about congressional legislation designed to salvage remaining American films from neglect and to bring the cause of film preservation into greater public awareness.

Conducted as fund-raisers for the cause, AMC's annual film preservation festivals have occurred in partnership with the Film Foundation (which includes Martin Scorsese, Francis Ford Coppola, George Lucas, Sydney Pollack, Robert Redford, and Steven Spielberg) and the foundation's Archivists Council. The council's members include the International Museum of Photography at George Eastman House, the Library of Congress, the Museum of Modern Art, the American Film Institute's National Center for Film and Video Preservation, and the UCLA Film and Television Archive.[50]

In 1993, AMC's first preservation festival focused on *Citizen Kane* and other well-known classics, with subsequent festivals organized according to themes. For example, the second annual festival was devoted to "keeping alive America's Western movie heritage"; the third, to Buster Keaton and film comedy; and the fourth, to the musical.[51] AMC made arrangements with several of the above archives to show their preservation prints of such films as "The Great Train Robbery" (1903), *The General* (1927), *The Iron Horse* (1924), *His Girl Friday* (1940), and *My Darling Clementine* (1946). This is only a small sample of the more famous classics screened by AMC. The channel has also shown more obscure films and listed many lesser-known titles that are in the process of being preserved by various archives.

Commentary accompanying these festivals cites statistics that demonstrate the need for intervention to save the film heritage. These statistics are most likely drawn from a widely cited 1990s congressionally mandated report on the state of film preservation in the United States. Researchers found that less than half of U.S. films made between 1895 and 1950 survive. Specifically, fewer than 20 percent of feature films from the 1920s and only 10 percent of features from the 1910s exist in complete form. Films made after the 1950s on acetate stock are also endangered; they face deterioration from color fading, "vinegar syndrome" (an irreversible film base decay), and other factors of age. In addition, many American films survive precariously in foreign archives and need to be reclaimed. Meanwhile, funding for film preservation has fallen to less than half of its 1980 levels (when adjusted for inflation).[52]

Writing about the preservation festivals for AMC magazine, Robert Moses emphasizes the urgency of saving Hollywood's past: "Fred Astaire's flying feet, the frosty allure of Greta Garbo, Groucho's manic rambles . . . these are among the dreams in the dark that American moviemakers shared with the world. As the 1900s became the American century, our country gave form to the first medium that could capture the dynamics of a rapidly changing world, to an art in motion and light that became the literature of the common man." Because of the loss, disintegration, and fading quality of the old films, "our entire motion picture heritage . . . may not be available to enrich the lives of future generations." Web sites devoted to film preservation concur: "Over the last hundred years, America has been documented by a nation of filmmakers—professionals and amateurs alike—working in every corner of the country. These filmmakers have recorded our traditions, captured the events of the day, and expressed our ambitions. Their work is the collective memory of the twentieth century." With the film heritage at risk, the alliance between film industry leaders and cinema archives and museums will "turn back time's threat to movie history." Indeed, AMC's preservation festivals help to celebrate this "triumph of preservation technology over time."[53]

The threat of loss clearly elevates cinema's importance as an exceptional record of history: its unique modernity allowed it to tune in to the rhythms of the twentieth century. Further, preservation commentary claims cinema as a uniquely American art form connected to a uniquely "American century." Without cinema, it is argued, present and future generations would lack the keys to the twentieth century and hence lose a sense of historical continuity that helps to maintain the nation's identity. While there is no doubt that films should be preserved, the promotion of film preservation continues to show the substantial investment of some social and media institutions in defining classic films as unmediated signifiers of American history. Moreover, cinema comes to embody American exceptionalism—the sense of the nation's sovereignty and superiority, particularly as it rose to economic and political prominence during the 1900s.

As I mentioned, the growth of discourse about film preservation is linked to a flurry of activity that has taken place on this subject in Congress, especially since the 1980s. A series of legislative efforts, including the passage of the National Film Preservation Acts of 1988, 1992, and 1996, has formally recognized film as part of the nation's heritage. The language arguing for the protection and preservation of film varies from bill to bill, but generally Congress has found that "(1) motion pictures are an indigenous American art form that has been emulated throughout the world; (2) certain motion pictures represent an enduring part of our Nation's historical and cultural heritage; and (3) it is appropriate and necessary for the Federal Government to recognize motion pictures as a significant American art form deserving of protection."[54]

While it is beyond the bounds of this chapter to detail the complex nature of this legislative history, several major outcomes are relevant here. In 1988, along with other heritage bills concerning funding for such things as the American Revolution Bicentennial Administration, the National Film Preservation Act became law. The act established the National Film Registry and the National Film Preservation Board. Administered and overseen by the Library of Congress, the National Film Registry selects films "that are culturally, historically, or aesthetically significant." The librarian provides "a seal to indicate that the film has been included in the National Film Registry as an enduring part of our national cultural heritage." This seal may be used "in the promotion of any version of such film that has not been materially altered."[55] The National Film Preservation Board, consisting of members from many units, including the Academy of Motion Picture Arts and Sciences, the Director's Guild of America, the Writer's Guild of America, the National Society of Film Critics, the Society for Cinema and Media Studies, and the American Film Institute, selects films for the National Film Registry.[56] Each year the board chooses twenty-five films to add to the registry.[57]

The National Film Preservation Act of 1992 reauthorized the earlier law.[58] In addition, this act asked the Library of Congress to study the current state of film preservation in the United States. It also authorized the library to establish procedures for including films in the National Film Registry, to help to create public consciousness of film heritage and the importance of preservation, and to provide reasonable access to prints for scholarly and research purposes. The study of the current state of film preservation and restoration activities produced under the directives of this act was entitled "Film Preservation 1993." Cited previously in relation to AMC's preservation efforts, this study found that America's film heritage was at serious risk. The National Film Preservation Board went to work to develop a plan that addressed archivists' concerns about these issues. The resulting plan, published in 1994 under the title "Redefining Film Preservation," represents the consensus that emerged from this process.[59] The board's response was to propose the formation of the National Film Preservation Foundation to raise grant money for preservation projects and programs.

The National Film Preservation Act of 1996 authorized the National Film Preservation Board for another seven years and formally created the National Film Preservation Foundation.[60] Starting operations in November 1997 and awarding its first grants in 1998, the foundation is a federally chartered, independent private-sector, nonprofit organization "designed to save America's film heritage." The foundation regards its mission as part of "our shared national responsibility to guarantee that the broadest range of America's film heritage can be seen by future generations." It raises private monies, matched with federal funds, to provide grants to "nonprofit film archives, historical societies, and other nonprofit institutions with film collections throughout the nation." Specifically, grants are to focus on so-called orphan films—films that would not survive without public support because they lack "commercial protectors" or "preservation benefactors" such as Hollywood. Orphans include "public domain films, silent films, documentaries, independent films, films of historical and regional importance, and films by or documenting minorities."[61]

Contemporary preservation causes run the gamut, then, from orphan films to more commercial Hollywood ventures. The motives and issues involved in the politics of the film preservation movement are as extensive and varied as this spectrum implies. Certainly, the imprimatur of President Clinton and Congress, as it supported the creation of new organizations devoted to the study and funding of film preservation, has provided official public recognition of silent and classic cinema's importance to the national heritage. This recognition has given commercial venues such as AMC a dignified rationale for pursuing high-profile conservation activities.

However, Congress's actions also reflect a different set of concerns. As the history of preservation in the United States shows, preservation tends to become an important issue during times of crisis. Between 1850 and 1920, conservationists helped to develop the national park system (with the support of federal legislation) in response to a multitude of factors. Among them was a perceived crisis in American national identity and purpose, fostered in part by the popularity of the "Turner Thesis." Advanced by historian Frederick Turner, the thesis defined the pioneer encounter with the Western frontier as the defining characteristic of American identity. Turner concluded that, because of successful settlement and the encroachments of industrialization on nature, the frontier was "closed." Thus, preserving the wilderness became an important means of maintaining American identity at a time when radical shifts in American life helped to transform a pastoral, agrarian ideal into the reality of a "tamed" industrialized space.[62]

A similar reaction occurred in the post–World War II era. During this time, suburbanization, the dissolution of inner-city historic neighborhoods through acts of urban renewal, and the construction of vast interstate highway systems dramatically changed the nation's landscape. To conservationists, the geographical conformity promoted by these developments and the forces of unrestrained growth precipitated something of a national emergency. As these changes severed the country's connections to the past, they threatened the sense of historical continuity that underpinned national identity. Without history—without a sense of the rootedness of national traditions—conservationists feared that the citizenry would lose its social cohesiveness, its sense of what it means to be American. In documents such as *With Heritage So Rich* (1966), conservationists argued that the nation was in a precarious situation that it could not afford to tolerate during the Cold War—an era when democracy was being challenged worldwide by the Soviet Union and other communist governments.[63] At the same time, the 1950s and 1960s saw the tremendous growth of mass tourism to historic sites (due in part to the new highways), showing entrepreneurs that history could be a "cash crop" (Wallace 173–76). The combination of politics and profit resulted in the creation of the modern preservation movement.

During the last two decades of the twentieth century, national identity was again called into question by an array of powerful forces. The emergence of media conglomerates, global capitalism, the explosion of new technologies in the information age, and the piracy of American media products confused and challenged traditional notions about the status of U.S. commerce and subsequently the nation itself.

The 1980s and 1990s saw a succession of takeovers and mergers in the communications and media industries that blurred the identities of companies that have long been major players in American business. For example, Viacom's purchase of CBS in 1999 consolidated a host of television, cable, movie, home video, publishing, and other businesses to make Viacom the world's second largest media company after Time Warner, Inc., combining the identity of these businesses under the ever-expanding umbrellas of corporate ownership. For some, such fusions of business interests in the world of communications called into question the survival of a democratic system. When AOL purchased Time Warner in January 2000, marrying the interests of the world's largest Internet service provider with one of the titans of the media business, news commentators raised concerns about one conglomerate's control of information in so many forums (the Internet, magazines, newspapers, movies, etc.).[64] A huge corporation's potential to exercise so much power over public access to information suggests the possibility of a totalitarian-like monopoly. Since freedom of information is one of the foundations of American democracy, this kind of venture represents a possible threat to the nation's principles, self-image, and future.

That the activities of media companies figured strongly in debates about the state of the nation becomes clearer in the case of the foreign purchase of U.S. businesses and other concerns. When the Japanese-owned Sony Corporation bought Columbia Pictures, the Gubar-Peters Entertainment Company, and CBS Records (the largest record company in the world) in the 1980s and Matsushita bought MCA/Universal in 1990, these particularly visible deals caused substantial controversy and emotional debate about the loss of major U.S. media to foreign interests. The purchases occurred at a time when politicians and citizens were already alarmed about the inroads that international companies were making onto American soil. The 1980s saw a significant growth in the sales of American farmland, real estate, factories, and banks to foreign companies. Adding fuel to the fire was the Japanese purchase of U.S. landmarks, particularly Rockefeller Center (including its skating rink and Christmas tree) and Radio City Music Hall in New York City. As one commentator put it, "What's next? . . . Mickey Mouse, Mickey Mantle, and the N.Y. Yankees?"[65] Thus began what David Morley and Kevin Robins have called a "Japan Panic," hysteria rooted in long-established ideologies about the invasion of the West by forces of the Orient, bolstered further by Japan's technological proficiency and growing superiority to the United States in a prized area of "superpower" strength.[66]

The acquisition of well-known American businesses, particularly media concerns, and major American landmarks resulted in legislative activity that sought to limit foreign ownership of entertainment companies and landmarks. The fear, shared by citizens as well, was both that foreign interests would dominate the nation's culture industries—industries with tremendous influence over citizens' everyday lives—and that foreign ownership of landmarks would put the custodianship of the nation's past into alien hands.[67] In addition, economic success in the twenty-first century was seen as strongly linked to dominance in telecommunications and electronics.

Thus, in 1989 Congress held a hearing with politicians and media industry representatives to discuss the impact of the global economy—the massive flows of money and capital across political boundaries—on American media. In these proceedings, politicians marshaled evidence and rhetoric to demonstrate the threat of foreign influence, while media representatives tried to assure them that, despite foreign ownership, business operations would be conducted in autonomous and traditionally American ways. Nonetheless, these proceedings tended to prompt a panicked response to globalization that envisioned the foreign takeover of American hearts, minds, and pocketbooks.

A number of politicians at the hearing offered evidence of the decreasing American presence in the media and communications industries. Some mentioned that only two decades before, U.S. companies had held an influential position in consumer electronics and in the record industry, making electronics companies such as RCA, Magnavox, General Electric, and Motorola into household words and more than a dozen U.S. record companies into worldwide competitors. By 1989, only Zenith remained a name in consumer electronics, and only two U.S.–owned companies, Warner and MCA, were among the top record companies. In these and other industries (such as the auto industry), Japanese and other foreign investors had made huge gains in U.S. markets; conversely, U.S. companies had not been able to purchase controlling shares of foreign companies because of indigenous laws against such arrangements.

These kinds of circumstances helped to create a general ideological climate of protectionism about American business and underscored the sense that the media embody the spirit of America. Because the media industry generated a trade surplus of three billion dollars in 1988, legislators concerned about the U.S. trade deficit and deficit spending in general took special notice. In the course of the hearing, Majority Leader Richard A. Gephardt argued, "The current international media industry is very much a child of America. Film, for example, is a uniquely American art form: we brought it to life, we made it talk, we used it to address our deepest social concerns. Now, we see our media industry on the global auction block" (Congress, House, 1989, 3). This nationalistic take on the history of cinema is echoed in other political statements and, as we have seen, in preservation discourses that identify cinema as essentially American. At the same time, the communication industry in general is viewed as "most vital to our national well-being. The lifeblood of democracy is communications, because it gives our citizens access to the marketplace of ideas . . . in the age of 'media without frontiers,' it's even more important that Americans maintain their First Amendment rights in the electronic media free from outside influence" (Congress, House, 1989, 5).

This nationalizing of media goods is spurred by at least one other factor: the rise in piracy of American films. Technologies from video to the Internet have made the piracy of U.S. media at home and abroad an extremely lucrative enterprise. Annually, the major movie studios lose approximately $250 million to domestic piracy and more than $3 billion overseas.[68] The use of the Internet as a venue for pirated films has only exacerbated the studios' immense concern about the illegal traffic in Hollywood films. In particular, the loss of revenue to overseas pirates enforces the sense that the media are an important economic and symbolic battleground in an era when the global flow of goods and information defines world economies.

Besides obvious economic ramifications, the question of how globalization affects national sovereignty lies at the heart of congressional discussions—how, that is, the purchase or theft of U.S. goods by foreign interests impinges on the definition of America as an autonomous entity that can exercise supreme authority. This is, of course, a key question in larger debates on this topic. Certainly, many scholars view globalization as meaning the "Coca-colonization" or McDonaldization of the world—the rise, rather than the fall, of Western hegemony. Concerns about this hegemony have been additionally fueled by what the *New York Times* refers to as "Net Americana," the global reach of U.S. companies involved in the Internet business.[69] For other scholars, however, globalization promises the potential demise of *"Pax Americana,* of American hegemony" by dispersing and dismantling American business concerns via multinational corporate ownership, the economic rise of other international powers, and other forces.[70] Yet, as Robert Holton argues, the massive changes associated with globalization "dispose neither of the idea of sovereignty as state autonomy from external coercion nor that of sovereignty as a bargaining resource that political elites may use in negotiation with external interests."[71] One of the challenges globalization presents to a nation is exactly how to maintain the ideology of sovereignty in the face of conditions that could seriously undermine its existence. At the very least, this ideology serves to perpetuate the idea of the nation in order to project state power and economic viability in a rapidly changing world environment.

The views promulgated during the congressional hearing demonstrate the aggravated relationship that globalization has to concepts of sovereignty: in short, globalization makes defining America a problem. Part of this problem is addressed through the promotion of nationalism. The more American businesses become dispersed, dissolved, or unrecognizable through economic ventures, the more discourses turn urgently to the tasks of emphasizing self-determination, of clarifying principles that have traditionally defined the nation, of preserving aspects of the heritage that are threatened. Further, as the cases of films endangered by time and piracy show, maintaining the nation's hold on its own products is increasingly threatened by both lack of attention to film as heritage and illicit capitalists. Thus, as Congress put it, the nation must try to "repatriate 'lost' American films from international archives"; meanwhile, the Motion Picture Association of America's Internet piracy division works with the FBI to shut down piracy Web sites.[72]

Popular cultural artifacts have often served as insignias of the American character. The late twentieth century saw this association greatly amplified by concerns about the relationship between globalization and the self-determination of American businesses, between globalization and national identity. In the 1980s and 1990s, the impulses of nationalism materialized in claims made about objects from the past, whether they were the movies or the Rockettes. These objects were especially important insofar as they represented a time in the nation's history when American businesses appeared to be free from outside economic influences or threats. They thus could more easily embody the concept of America as a unified, hegemonic power.

With this in mind, one role that the film preservation movement played during this time was to protect the nation's heritage in the face of proliferating corporate mergers and other developments that increasingly complicated a product's identification as specifically American. Part of the rescue mission was to save a past that seemed to be clearly American—a past that appeared never to have experienced the complexities of the contemporary economy or to have been subject to compromise in the arena of national identity. In preservation discourse, Hollywood maintained its cachet as the site of distinctive American products, just as it helped to recall an era when the industry reigned supreme at both home and abroad. Retaining such an image of the past responded to threats against the sovereignty of American identity that some felt characterized the developing global economy. This is, then, part of the stake in saving classic Hollywood as part of the national heritage: holding on to artifacts that proclaim their American origins without apparent complication. In this way film preservation, driven by a spectrum of ecological and economic motives, gains an ideological dimension.

Postmodernist and other studies have suggested that global extension, international flows of capital and information, and the disintegrative forces of separatism, among other things, have deeply complicated any monolithic notions of nation. I have argued, conversely, that these very forces have helped to make nostalgia and other evidence of tradition more compelling. In times of crisis, social institutions work overtime to produce a historical "glue," often built on evocations of the past, with which to bind citizens to a reassuring sense of individual and collective identity.[73] In this vein, the recycling of classic Hollywood helps to demonstrate that master narratives of nation are alive and well in today's polymorphous cultural mix. They continue to be repackaged in highly visible ways by media conglomerates and dispersed to millions of viewers not only in public but also in the everyday environ of the home. The employment of such historical visions by key cultural institutions suggests that the confrontation with the cinematic past is often at the same time a confrontation with what Homi Bhabha has called that "prose of power that each nation can wield within its own sphere of influence."[74] Memories of old Hollywood appear to have far less stake in public memory debates than, say, memories of the Vietnam War or the U.S. bombing of Hiroshima and Nagasaki; in fact, the old film's quaintness and lack of apparent connection to contemporary politics make it seem quite distant from the agonistics of such debates. All the same, strolling down the cinematic memory lane involves encounters with highly charged images of America that are just as invested in placing indelible truths about the nation's history on the cultural stage.

Film and Memory: A Coda

Vintage artifacts may often be forgotten and doomed to decompose in a lonely corner of someone's basement, but when they are resurrected as events for public consumption, they can become, as Adorno suggests in the epigraph to this chapter, hieroglyphics of history. They appear as ciphers, characterized by an outdated system of writing set in a faraway past. To achieve sense in the present, they must be both decoded to make their past legible to contemporary audiences and recoded, that is, otherwise prepared for life in new circumstances of exhibition. Cine-museums and companies devoted to the commercial management of memory step in to perform this work of coding by recirculating meanings these artifacts once had for audiences and by inventing fresh meanings. This is part of the standard repackaging of "ancient relics" as they reappear to various audiences over time.

However, it is important to reiterate that the work of the cine-museum does not monopolize the social production of memory; memory is a contested terrain. Since old Hollywood films are bountifully recycled in culture, we can expect that their meanings are mobilized to support diverse, conflicting accounts of the past, depending on the contexts that reintroduce them to audiences. In addition, viewers will have differing relations to the historical visions produced by classic movie channels. Part of this different orientation arises from the special place films from the past may have in the recollections of individual viewers, bringing the personal strongly into the mix. As Annette Kuhn and Jackie Stacey have shown in their respective studies of individual memories of films, old features can have deep autobiographical resonances for audience members, shaping the manner in which these films signify history.[75] As we shall see in the next chapter, the potential for films to be repeated endlessly in the private space of the home makes them especially liable to the process of personalization. Further, as Lipsitz argues, viewers' responses, as they are informed by personal experience, may be at such strong variance with "hierarchically prepared and distributed mass culture" that oppositional interpretations of texts result. If these interpretations are sustained and integrated into a community—especially, for example, minority communities often left out of or misrepresented by grand historical narratives—they generate "counter memories," memories rooted in the local and immediate that force revision of totalizing dominant accounts.[76]

At the same time, a memory experienced locally or individually is not necessarily less problematic ideologically than one offered by a master narrative. Moreover, it is unlikely that private and public memories can be neatly separated. As Marita Sturken points out in her study of the impact of films and docudramas on Vietnam vets' memories of their own encounters with war, media representations of past moments can become extremely powerful, "weaving themselves into experiences and memories . . . [becoming] part of cultural memory." Her research finds that those who had participated in the war have difficulty at times in recalling their experiences *without* the mediations of film or television. Hence, the industries' historical revisions are not necessarily at odds with individual recollections; they can, in fact, gain a substantial foothold in the personal, the private, and ultimately within the collective memory of certain social groups. In other words, as the Popular Memory Group writes, "Private memories cannot . . . be readily unscrambled from the effects of dominant historical discourses. It is often these that supply the very terms by which a private history is thought through."[77] The home exhibition of media exemplifies this complex relationship between public and private memories. The images of classic Hollywood and television that enter the home on cable TV as part of each and every day's programming magnify the possibilities that individuals will construct personal relationships with the classics, just as these images enhance the presence of media companies in negotiating how that relationship will be formed or re-formed.

The classic movie channel cine-museum cannot unearth all of the elements that make up the "strangely composite constructions" of memory in such circumstances. But it does provide a concrete demonstration of how a particular vision of the past is produced and privileged in an attempt to construct an official account of the past within certain contemporary social contexts. While the complexities involved in creating public memories must be acknowledged, we should not minimize the salience and persistence of "processes of domination in the historical field" or these processes' ability to become a seamless part of private reveries.[78] Given the diffuse presence of Hollywood's commemorative activities, we should consider film memory as partly negotiated by agencies involved in the business of media recycling. Any Proustian model of memory, then, must be refracted through the lens of mass culture to capture how the remembrance of films past is shaped by the industries that revive the past as part of their capital enterprise.

4 Once Is Not Enough

The Functions and Pleasures of Repeat Viewings

> How often a child rejects a new story, preferring to hear one
> he has already been told a hundred times. And as he hears
> again the often-heard, his eyes glaze over with pleasure, his
> body relaxes, and the story ends in peaceful slumber. The
> recurrent outlines of a familiar experience have returned. In
> that well-known and controlled landscape of the imagination
> the tensions, ambiguities, and frustrations of ordinary
> experience are painted over by magic pigments of
> adventure, romance, and mystery. The world for a time
> takes on the shape of our heart's desire.
>
> **John Cawelti,** *Adventure, Mystery, and Romance,* 1976

When a film becomes a blockbuster, a large part of its success is generated
by audience members who return to see it again in theaters. Such megahits
as *Titanic, The Matrix,* and the *Lord of the Rings* trilogy attracted repeat
viewers in droves, benefiting handsomely from ticket sales to devoted fans.
While most films on the big screen are generally lucky to draw a 2 percent
repeat audience, blockbusters can entice as many as 20 percent of filmgoers
to see the films again during their original runs.[1] In the case of many phe-
nomenally successful films, the returning viewers often come from the
media industry's most coveted demographic: teenagers and young adults.
The industry has found that this group is most likely to repeat, in part because of their amount of free time and disposable income. Young men are
more likely to engage in multiple theatrical screenings of their favorite
films; however, the example of *Titanic* shows that young female audiences
are also a force with which to reckon. Many women under the age of
twenty-five saw the film at least twice, with some returning to theaters four
or five times, helping to propel *Titanic* to record-breaking grosses.[2] If recent

cinematic history is any indication, multiple viewings are not only a critical component of theatrical success but also, for some audiences, a vital part of the cinematic experience.

As significant as it may be, the phenomenon of repeated viewings on the big screen only begins to suggest how crucial repetition is to film exhibition and reception. Decades ago, the industry worried that rerunning films and television shows was not a workable strategy: viewers would not be able to screen a text more than once without losing interest or becoming hypercritical. This anxiety was put to rest rather emphatically in the 1950s, when industry experiments with re-airing syndicated TV shows and Hollywood films—a gambit aimed at cost-saving through repeat programming—met with surprising success.[3] Since then, TV reruns have become an institution, and cable television, VHS, DVD, and other developments have exponentially increased the presence of rereleased films and TV series on home screens. Audiences have more exposure to repeats, whether countless broadcasts of *Top Gun* (1986) or the syndicated daily appearances of *Seinfeld*, than industry insiders could have imagined years ago. Moreover, while repetition can breed aversive, even disgusted, reactions (e.g., "Not that same commercial again!"), it also can inspire great interest and loyalty (despite *Seinfeld*'s ubiquity in syndication, it was among the most requested titles for DVD release). Repetition, then, is a cornerstone of the consumer's experience of entertainment that has the potential to be as enjoyable as it is inescapable.

For decades, the VCR has been identified with the practice of repetition. Indeed, viewing the same films over and over again on VHS quickly became a routine household pastime.[4] The immediate physical and experiential access to movies provided by VHS has, in turn, deeply affected the medium's relationship to its audiences. As Uma Dinsmore-Tuli writes, "The domestication of the cinematic text through repeat video viewing may facilitate a level of engagement with, love for, and knowledge about movies that exceeds or extends that which it is possible to achieve during cinematic screenings."[5] Certainly the big screen fascinates, but it cannot compete with the potential control over and immersion in favorite titles that home-based playback technologies such as VHS and DVD afford. Yet little is known about why many viewers prize repetition as an integral and pleasurable component of their film experience. What brings viewers back to the same film repeatedly? Why is once not enough? Since private space is such a significant locus for repeated film encounters, these questions are key to understanding how individuals use and enjoy movies in their daily lives.

To pursue these questions, I want to examine repeat viewing in relation to a specific group of viewers known for their attraction to media repetition not only of films but also of TV shows, music, and video games: contemporary college-age youth in their late teens and early twenties. Although media repetition is not solely the province of this group—indeed, children and fans outside of this demographic avidly seek this experience—young adults provide a rich resource for study.[6] Not only do they constitute a significant audience for theatrical movies and the group most likely to return to see favorite titles on the big screen; they also represent the first "video generation" in the United States. Growing up in the 1980s and 1990s, when the videocassette had truly become a home entertainment staple, many of these viewers began watching their favorite films repeatedly in this form, becoming thoroughly accustomed to having domesticated versions of Hollywood films at their disposal. Studying this generation's home-viewing habits provides a crystalline example of film reception by an audience who has never known a time when movies weren't available in small boxes or couldn't be manipulated by VCR and, now, DVD remotes to suit personal needs and desires. Their repeat viewings thus allow insight into the quotidian appropriation of cinema in a space where film viewing is part of a home entertainment universe as well as daily rhythms and activities.

In previous chapters I have concentrated on the home's discursive construction as an exhibition venue for cinema, registering viewers' reactions indirectly through industry sources, newspaper and magazine articles, Web sites, and scholarly accounts. While still positioning viewers' reactions in relation to exhibition discourses, I take a step closer to the audience in this chapter. My discussion of repeat viewing is based on a survey I conducted in 2000 with students from a dozen largely introductory classes in the Department of Communication and Culture at Indiana University.[7] The survey was composed of nine open-ended questions (the full text of which can be found at the end of the chapter). Among other things, I asked students to list the titles of films they liked to watch repeatedly as children and now as young adults. They were also queried about why they are drawn to these films time and again—what pleasures they derive from multiple viewings. In order to concentrate on instances that demonstrate more of a commitment to repetition than would be required by an additional encounter or two with the same film, I requested that participants discuss only those films they have seen five or more times. In addition, I asked them to focus their attention on screenings that took place in homes or other domiciles such as dorm rooms.

Participation in the survey was voluntary and anonymous; students were asked to provide identifying information about gender, race, and age.

Three hundred fifty-four students responded, with response rates in each class varying from 75 percent to 95 percent.[8] A little over one-fifth of students were majors within the department, while others were affiliated with diverse departments, including English, theater, business, and physical education.[9] Of the total number participating, 184 were female and 170 were male. Thirty students of color responded (including African Americans, Asians, Hispanics, and Native Americans), composing just over 8 percent of participants.

Because it involves the viewing practices of a small group of predominately white young adults at a midwestern university, my sample is circumscribed by considerations of race, age, and the region in which the survey took place.[10] Moreover, although most participants were not majors within the department, the media class context and, more generally, the educational setting provide additional layers of specificity to this group.[11] As research in cultural and media studies has shown, reception is deeply affected by a host of variables, including the gender, race, and class of viewers, the sphere—national or local—in which viewing takes place, and the social structures that surround the interactions between people and media texts.[12] A shift in any one of these variables can produce a different vision of an audience and how it makes sense of the media. With the social nature of meaning production in mind, my study involves a localized sample that cannot be taken as representative of all audiences, including all youth audiences.[13]

This is not to say that the survey represents completely isolated or anomalous viewing behaviors and practices. As we shall see, film discussions on the Web and in other sources echo my survey participants' reactions, giving them relevance within broader spheres of film consumption. Further, research on motivations for film re-viewing among different demographics bears some resemblance to my findings, suggesting that, although important particulars vary, audiences may share some reasons for returning to favorite texts.[14] Hence, as an exploration of media repetition by a group of invested viewers, my study, while producing only a partial picture, helps to illuminate the phenomenon beyond immediate circumstances.

As in previous chapters, I focus on several issues central to understanding contemporary film exhibition and reception in the home. First, the phenomenon of repeat viewing on the small screen arises directly from the impact of recent entertainment technologies on home film cultures. Playback devices that enable film repetition exercise dramatic effects on text and viewer, shaping the narrative experience and its place within the viewer's imagination. Armed with a remote control, any home viewer can manipulate a film with glee, fast-forwarding, rewinding, or otherwise interrupting narrative chronology to refashion the film according to his or her desires. Since repetition makes a film particularly well-known, it inspires the viewer to travel through the text selectively via the remote control, performing surgical strikes to locate favorite bits. Although use of the remote control doesn't lead all viewers to fragment films, survey responses help us to understand the role this kind of textual familiarity plays in the appropriation of narrative and genre in the home.

Through testimonials about the significance certain films have for viewers, the survey also provides a detailed view of the effects of film domestication. As Roger Silverstone argues in *Television and Everyday Life*, studying the phenomenon of domestication reveals the "effort and activity which people bring into their consumption of objects and their incorporation into the structure of their everyday lives."[15] Repetition amplifies any domestic medium's ability to become part of viewers' daily lives, even part of their autobiographies, resulting in an intense process of personalization. Like other objects, films experienced repeatedly in the home can attain an intimate, quasi-familial status that affects their meaning and influences individuals' perceptions of themselves and the world. As it brings viewers back to a familiar experience, repetition may operate subtly to confirm individual identities. However, as it juxtaposes past and present (the experience of the film *then* with its experience *now*), the ritual of return may introduce more volatile dynamics into the mix, inciting reassessments of the viewer's self or worldview.

Second, media repetition provokes further consideration of the construction of taste and taste hierarchies in the home. Survey respondents' relationship to cinema in private space entails various modes of aesthetic discrimination; films, after all, have to be deemed worthy of replay to become part of this viewing ritual. Yet, as Ellen Seiter has pointed out in the case of children, intellectuals and other arbiters of culture often define the consuming habits of those associated with "lower" social registers as driven by hedonism and devoid of value.[16] Often publicly associated with robotic consumption, the teen–young adult audience has been similarly disparaged. The fact that they might watch the same texts over and over again on television—a medium some critics already associate with passive viewing—exacerbates the notion of mindless activity.

However, such concerns are often based on an untenable presumption of passivity and a monolithic critique of taste. As Silverstone and others contend, there is no such thing as passive viewing; all viewing involves "some form of more or less meaningful action (even in its most habitual or ritual mode)."[17] At the same time, teen tastes are more heterogeneous and varied in their social function than many critics would suppose. I approach the viewing practices of young adults, then, as multifaceted instances of film consumption performed by active and discriminating individuals who make meaning of, evaluate, and sometimes substantially transform the media they watch. Rather than pose correspondences between viewers and ideological positions (in which active viewers are resistant and passive viewers are dupes), I regard engagement as a part of "regular" media consumption that reveals both the diversity and the social nature of viewing.

Third, I continue to explore the situated nature of viewing—that is, the relationship between domestic viewing practices and larger industrial and social forces. The survey invites us to consider links between forms of avid film engagement and more extensive worlds of textual decoding, including those represented by peer groups, media industries, mass cultural sources of criticism, and academe. An individual's response, even when it personalizes a text or abrogates its authority, is informed by other spheres of media consumption that, while offering alternative ways of appropriating texts, may still fall within the mainstream. Like the love of one's film collection, the replay and emotional adoption of a favorite title involve reciprocity between viewers and public discourses that circulate through domestic space as a prime site of film repurposing.

As the empirical dimension of my research provides a closer look at the connections between viewers and films in the home, it also reveals certain aspects of the surveyed group's shared culture. A limited method of inquiry into reception, the questionnaire cannot provide expansive information about shared audience cultures.[18] Media studies scholars generally prefer more intensive and immersive methods, such as interviews, to produce ethnographic studies.[19] However, according to S. Elizabeth Bird, anthropologists have often deployed different kinds of texts to launch ethnographies, including nonfieldwork sources such as autobiographies, diaries, and surveys. Under certain circumstances, particularly when findings are placed within larger cultural contexts and the researcher is familiar with the culture in question, some ethnographic observations can reasonably be offered.[20] Balancing my data's limitations against my acquaintanceship with students' media tastes and assessment of their responses within broader frameworks, I provide a modest view of this group's shared culture.

I am especially interested in examining how teens and young adults use media to create or to confirm what Sarah Thornton has identified as "systems of social and cultural distinction that divide and demarcate contemporary culture." According to Thornton, youth audiences "seek out and accu-

mulate cultural goods and experiences for strategic use within their own social worlds," a process that produces internal stratifications within youth
culture and affects the dynamics of popular culture more generally.[21] The
transactions between social groups and mass culture thus provide a means
for investigating the hierarchies and principles that inform group identities
as well as their function in society. With respect to repeat film viewing, participants' responses suggest that making distinctions is a pervasive characteristic of how young adults explain their film preferences, which in turn
conveys a sense of self and a sense of status within peer communities. Gender acts as an especially important determinant of taste, influencing what
films certain students deem repeatable and why.

Since film repetition is not a universal practice among my survey participants, I want to begin by more carefully considering its place within the
group's media habits. I then turn to an overview of the survey's findings, in
which certain genres and films emerge as particularly significant to respondents. Following this, my discussion addresses the central question of why
these individuals returned repeatedly to favorite films—what functions and
pleasures this ritual offered them—within the context of larger cultures of
film consumption related to repetition. Although my study is not all-
encompassing, I hope to produce a view of what repetition as a pervasive,
even definitive, part of media experience means to audiences and to the appropriation of films in the home.

To See or Not to See

A Welsh woman named Myra Franklin earned a place in *The Guinness Book
of World Records* for having seen *The Sound of Music* 940 times. While this
is a special case, it illustrates the fascination films can hold for some viewers, as well as cinema's sheer iterability. Students in the survey have not
tended to scale such spectacular record-breaking heights; they reported
watching their favorite titles on average between five and thirty times.
However, some have viewed their favorites more than a hundred times, approaching what might be considered "extreme" repetition. But not everyone in the survey has been drawn to repeat.

Overall, about 10 percent of participants did not indulge in repetitious
film watching in their childhoods (some had no television sets, others preferred watching TV shows). This figure dropped to 2 percent by the time
participants reached adolescence, meaning that film repetition has become
a fixture in almost everyone's later experience. A slightly higher number (4
percent of respondents) said they do not engage in significant repetition of

other media, including television, music, and video games. Generally, students who avoid repetition prefer to hear or see new things, finding familiar texts boring. Some even try to avoid listening to the same music—the medium others pursue most passionately for the pleasures it brings via repetition.

These figures provide a sense of the extent of repeat viewings, but they do not reveal its relative value to this audience. When asked whether returning to favorite films has been a nonexistent, marginal, or central desire, thirty students (roughly 8 percent of the respondents) answered that it has been nonexistent. Either they watch in order to have background noise while relaxing or simply don't partake at all. As one woman put it, "There are better things to do out there besides watch movies." Even students who have found themselves viewing the same films over again defined this pastime as marginal. About 30 percent of respondents fell into this category, watching familiar films for want of anything else to do. For many of these, repeated encounters with films seem an almost inevitable part of life, given the omnipresence of VCRs and cable TV—an experience that is not special, simply hard to avoid. This penetration of film into everyday life caused one student to remark of repeat viewing, "I never make time for it, it always just seems to happen."

The rest of the sample, or just over half of the students, defined repetition as a significant desire. One female participant said, "This is something that I LOVE to do!" while another admitted that she rewatches her favorite films on a daily basis if possible. A male student wrote, "Movies are my life. Watching movies multiple times is a testimony to my love for that movie." Another assessed this habit as a "heavy desire—right up there with writing, reading, and painting as a central and important activity." For some, a film's worth increases, like that of a music CD, if it has "replay value," that is, if it stands the test of time in bringing pleasure again and again. Repeat movies are also sometimes seen as a more attractive choice than other entertainment, including recent movies or TV. As one student observed, "I can't trust the movies of today, so I turn to my favorites for something more reliable." Defining himself as a film lover, another participant wrote that he depends on "video as an alternative to TV programs."

For many of these young adults, then—whether by happenstance or by design, whether out of ennui or out of desire—rewatching films at home is a routine and sometimes ritual part of their leisure activities. It becomes only more so by the communal social climates that characterize the dormitories, apartments, fraternities, and sororities in which these viewers often live. But whether marginal or central, both valuations are instructive, providing a sense of the presence and status of this mode of film consumption in the home. The casual and the serious re-viewer alike are thus important for a full-bodied analysis of this phenomenon. Whatever the individual's attitude, the film preferences of this group display some consistencies, congealing into a canon of repeatable titles.

Canons on the Loose

Altogether, students mentioned 676 different films that they have re-watched regularly as children and adolescents. Since many remarked that time or space on the survey wasn't sufficient to mention all of their favorites, this figure only begins to suggest the group's repertoire. With this in mind, if we break the groupings down according to student designations, the hundreds of films mentioned fall into the following genres or categories: dramas (140); comedies (135); chick flicks (70); classic Hollywood cinema (60); independent cinema (50); action/special effects films (45); foreign films (45); New Hollywood cinema (35); animation and fantasy films (30); horror films (25); musicals and concert films (20); the films of Steven Spielberg and George Lucas (11); martial arts films (7); and documentaries (3). These groupings are not rigorous in a critical sense, nor are they always internally coherent. They are, rather, colloquial (informal, conversational) identifications of films that spring from the consuming modalities of viewers. For example, many Spielberg and Lucas titles could be classified as action or special effects films, but because the work of these filmmakers looms so large within repeat movie practices, participants regard them as constituting their own brand of films. Similarly, although Warner Bros. produced *GoodFellas* (1990), students regard it as an independent work by Martin Scorsese, a filmmaker with a reputation for producing movies that challenge Hollywood norms. In both cases, classifications stem from viewers' desires to mark their repeated returns to certain titles as acts of taste (to present themselves, respectively, as either aficionados of Lucas and Spielberg blockbusters or of more unconventional fare). Hence, as James Naremore and others have argued, genre definition often results from discursive strategies that characterize film consumption rather than from the internal essence of the film itself.[22]

Given the spread of titles within each category, it is significant when a substantial number of participants listed the same titles as favorites. The recurrence of titles suggests a critical mass of films, an implicit canon of works important to this audience. This critical mass represents a "popular" canon, created outside the bounds of institutions officially sanctioned as granters of textual value (such as academe). Despite the academic milieu, a significant number of the films that students regarded as most repeatable would not be found in academic canons. Rather, these films have been selected from commercial youth culture, attaining a status as "classics" for this cohort.

Many titles in each category were named only once or twice; hence, some categories contain no or few films that drew more than one repeat viewer. These categories include animation and fantasy, documentaries, foreign-language cinema, concert films, martial arts films, and, despite their big-screen popularity with this demographic, horror films.[23] In table 1, I focus on the categories and titles that have attracted a critical mass of followers. Specifically, twenty to sixty students, or roughly 5 to 15 percent of respondents, regarded these films as favorites, sometimes watching them more than thirty times. I list the total number of students who named a title, breaking that number down into female and male respondents. The left-hand side of the chart features the most popular films. To provide a more comprehensive view of the clusters of favored titles, the right-hand side of the chart mentions a second tier of films that have generated less, but still conspicuous, enthusiasm.

For now, we will consider what the survey students prefer to re-view and how their choices help to shed light on the idea of popular canons. Although subcommunal variations in taste are evident (especially in relation to gender), I will examine the implications of these variations in more detail later. We should keep in mind that in time, like all tastes rooted in generational identity, these youth film preferences will no longer be as relevant. Nonetheless, they help to identify certain trends in popular culture at the turn of the century, when, through rites of generational succession, *The Breakfast Club* (1985) superseded *The Graduate* as a saga of the alienation of youth.

As these titles suggest, those surveyed gravitate toward Hollywood films of the 1980s and 1990s—the period that corresponds to their childhood and adolescence. Not surprisingly, they tend to prefer films aimed at the youth market, meaning that industry efforts have met with some success not only in theaters but in home venues as well. Although young men are often identified as the preeminent repeat viewers for theatrical films, on the home front it is clear that young women are also significantly involved with repetition. The most rewatched films in descending order are the original *Star Wars* trilogy (1977, 1980, 1983), *Pulp Fiction* (1994), *Pretty Woman* (1990), *The Breakfast Club*, *The Matrix*, *Austin Powers: International Man of Mystery* (1997), *Sixteen Candles* (1984), and *Titanic*. The table reveals that five of these films are strongly identified with female tastes, with three of them falling explicitly into the chick flick category. All but *Star Wars*, *The Matrix*, and *Pulp Fiction* have a preponderance of female re-viewers. Overall, chick flicks rank third in the number of titles mentioned for any category (seventy)—a not so insignificant standing when one considers the more general, capacious categories represented by comedy and drama.

Given its prominence in this canon and uncertain generic status, the chick flick deserves further commentary. Certainly, the term *chick flick* is an intimate part of contemporary film lingo, used readily not only by young women in the survey but also by film guides and Web sites. It also has a strong counterpart in "chick lit," represented by successful novels such as Terry McMillan's *Waiting to Exhale* (1992) and Helen Fielding's *Bridget Jones's Diary* (1999), both of which have been adapted into films. Although chick lit and flicks are often considered the bastion of white artists, characters, and audiences, McMillan's success paved the way for a rising number of African American women to pen novels in the genre, depicting black worlds and attracting black female fans.[24] The genre has thus found success with diverse female audiences in multiple media.

Although culturally salient, many films in the chick flick category are often critically marginalized. Part of the reason for this may lie with the term itself: it depends on disparaging language—*chick* being a slang expression for a girl or woman; and *flick*, a popular coinage for movies. Neither term flatters; indeed, each is often used as a form of belittlement. Another part of the reason may lie with the chick flick's affiliation with the woman's film. Indeed, we can regard the chick flick as a contemporary manifestation of the woman's film (itself a popular variation of melodrama in the 1930s and 1940s and during the women's movement in the 1970s). Like its forebear, the chick flick focuses on a female protagonist who struggles with the difficulties of relationships. Also like its forebear, it is marketed to female audiences and identified with female tastes, desires, and emotions. Both genres, in addition, have been accused of delivering indulgent romantic fantasies and cheap emotional thrills. Their various associations with things feminine, from protagonists and plots to viewers, have often wrongly consigned them to a low aesthetic status. The chick flick's particular connection to young female audiences makes it even more prone to critical devaluation.[25]

Further, chick flicks seem a hodge-podge, an indefinite heterogeneous mix of films. Unlike the woman's film, which critics identify with melodrama, chick flicks cross generic boundaries. In the survey, repeatable chick flicks are often romantic comedies, such as films starring Julia Roberts (an important

Table 1   A Teen Canon

First Tier				Second Tier			
Titles	Total	Female	Male	Titles	Total	Female	Male
ACTION/SPECIAL EFFECTS							
The Matrix	32	7	25	Armageddon	10	7	3
Titanic	30	24	6	Die Hard	10	2	8
Top Gun	24	15	9				
CHICK FLICKS							
Pretty Woman	40	38	2	The Princess Bride	16	12	4
The Breakfast Club	37	32	5	Clueless	15	15	0
Sixteen Candles	30	27	3	Grease	14	14	0
Dirty Dancing	21	21	0	Reality Bites	12	12	0
				My Best Friend's Wedding	12	12	0
				Empire Records	12	12	0
				Pretty in Pink	11	10	1
				Say Anything	11	10	1
				Beaches	11	10	1
				Heathers	10	10	0
NEW AMERICAN CINEMA							
The Godfather	20	15	5	Apocalypse Now	12	1	11
				A Clockwork Orange	11	1	10
COMEDY							
Austin Powers	30	21	9	Back to the Future	11	7	4
American Pie	24	4	20	National Lampoon's Christmas Vacation	11	7	4

Title			
Friday	24	12	12
Billy Madison	22	12	10
Dumb and Dumber	21	8	13
Ferris Bueller's Day Off	21	10	11
Happy Gilmore	20	6	14
Tommy Boy	20	10	10
Half-Baked	10	3	7
Goonies	10	8	2
Jerry Maguire	10	5	5
Liar Liar	10	2	8
The Wedding Singer	10	5	5

DRAMA

Title			
Braveheart	26	4	22
The Shawshank Redemption	23	9	14
Boyz N the Hood	10	3	7
Field of Dreams	10	4	6
Forrest Gump	10	3	7
Good Will Hunting	10	7	3

INDEPENDENTS

Title			
Pulp Fiction	44	17	27
Dazed and Confused	24	12	12
Mall Rats	20	11	9
The Usual Suspects	16	6	10
Clerks	13	6	7
The Big Lebowski	12	3	9
Swingers	12	5	7
GoodFellas	12	4	8
Chasing Amy	10	4	6
Boogie Nights	10	4	6

SPIELBERG/LUCAS

Title			
Star Wars first trilogy	52	11	41
Indiana Jones trilogy	22	4	18
Jurassic Park	10	2	8

icon for this group), Sandra Bullock, Meg Ryan, or John Hughes's "Brat Pack" luminary Molly Ringwald. However, along with fantasy and adventure films, the chick flick canon includes dramas, such as *Romeo and Juliet* (1996), musicals, such as *Grease* (1978) and *Dirty Dancing* (1987), and the occasional blockbuster, namely, *Titanic* (the action version of *Romeo and Juliet*). While African American students in the survey named some of these films as well, they also embraced romances with African American casts, such as *Waiting to Exhale* (1995) and *love jones* (1997), reminding us of the social specificity of any canon.

Academics have long since rescued the woman's film from critical neglect. By contrast, the chick flick continues to fly under the aesthetic radar. Yet, its colloquial appearance should not prevent us from recognizing its interesting novelty as a genre. Because romances materialize in diverse forms, chick flicks represent not a disorganized grouping but a supergenre that transcends the boundaries of a specific category. If they feature female protagonists, foreground relationships, and are primarily marketed to and viewed by female audiences, different kinds of films become allied under the chick flick banner. As a master genre of this sort, chick flicks achieve a cultural visibility that provides insight into contemporary female tastes and the social forces that avidly seek to address them.

As highly gender-specific, the films of Julia Roberts and Molly Ringwald rarely, if ever, appear among male re-viewers' preferences in the survey. The films most identified with this group include Spielberg's *Indiana Jones* series (1981, 1984, 1989) and Lucas's *Star Wars* series. As in the case of some chick flicks, these films attract enthusiasts and watch-alongs (those who see a film because someone else wants to) from the other gender.[26] However, male students produced the strongest testimonials about the importance of these films, especially *Star Wars*. Similarly, several dramas are also distinctly preferred by men (although also appreciated by some female viewers), particularly *Braveheart* (1995), Mel Gibson's historical epic about Scotsman William Wallace's fight against British rule, and *The Shawshank Redemption*, based on a Stephen King story about two men's triumph over a brutal prison system. Drawn to its narrative mysteries and special effects, men are also the major re-viewers of *The Matrix*. Quite different in other respects, each of these films features male protagonists involved in violent quests that may have a romantic component but otherwise concern issues often regarded as having more gravitas than those treated in women's films—for example, fighting social injustice and/or saving the world. These preferences form a counterpart to the chick flick; they represent the "testosterone flick" designed for male audiences and characterized by indomitable heroes, violent action, and/or special effects. Testosterone flicks can, similarly, cross generic borders. However, since films oriented toward male viewers tend to represent the Hollywood norm, they appear more as a production mainstay than as a demographically exceptional class of film.

The film selections that drew the most exclusive responses from female and male viewers in the survey thus break down along familiar gender lines, with women preferring romances centered on relationships and men attracted to tales of action. However, not all preferences were strongly polarized according to gender. For example, both women and men consider comedies and independent films worthy of replay. Survey responses show that re-viewers are most often attracted to comedies, not only because of the opportunity to revisit the laughs, but also because these films fit particularly well into peer settings. Already flexible in their attractiveness across tastes and genders, comedies can also be more readily shared among friends than, for instance, complex or unsettling dramas, which might fail to entertain. In any case, favorite titles in the genre either focus on teen sexual antics, such as *American Pie* (1999), or feature comics, such as Adam Sandler *(Billy Madison* [1995]), Mike Myers *(Austin Powers)*, and Jim Carrey *(Dumb and Dumber* [1994]). In addition, comedy fans in this group regard John Hughes's *Ferris Bueller's Day Off* (1986) as a teen standard—a must-see film for youth—while also expressing copious enthusiasm for *Friday* (1995), a crossover cult hit starring rapper Ice Cube.

Many films that students named in the independent category were directed by the contemporary "who's who" of hip filmmaking: Quentin Tarantino, Paul Michael Anderson, Kevin Smith, the Coen brothers, and Richard Linklater. As I have mentioned, what is most important about this category is that it *appears* to students as an alternative to Hollywood, whether or not the films in question were actually independently produced. The attraction stems from the sense that these films are outlaw texts, able to deliver either entertainment or aesthetic experience that exceeds what mainstream films can offer. The films range from titles that students see as representative of their lives, such as Linklater's high-school film *Dazed and Confused* (1993), to titles they regard as narratively and aesthetically exciting, especially Tarantino's *Pulp Fiction.*

Whether the top films and genres are gender specific or relatively gender neutral, we can see that those most important to, even cherished by, this group—especially chick flicks and comedies—often depart from standards of "good taste." This departure helps to define several aspects of the relationship between the tastes of these young adults and those of the parent culture. First, the students' selections do not challenge the traditional notion of canon on political grounds; that is, they do not represent minority voices striving to be heard within the competition for textual value and legacy. Predominately white and middle-class, this cohort may be set apart from adult culture by aggregates of values shared by its members; however, these individuals are avidly pursued by consumer culture as part of a desirable and significant market.[27] Thus, a sense of "generational cohesion" is maintained through both self-definition and the support of social institutions that constantly hail youth (via advertising, for example).[28] In this way, these students' tastes represent part of a mainstream subculture—that is, a cohesive group recognizably different from the parent culture but nonetheless occupying a visible, influential place within society.

Repeatable classics for this demographic offer, then, a different contribution to the concept of canon. As Ava Preacher Collins points out, academe has often cast itself as the arbiter of timeless, transcendental textual value, characterizing the bids of other institutions as suspect. As a result, the busy construction of classics and canons by all manner of mass cultural institutions, agencies, groups, and individuals has often been ignored or defamed.[29] As I have argued in previous chapters, mass culture is a critical and endless site for the evaluation and ranking of aesthetic objects. But little is known about value formation in reaches of culture outside the academy or the museum and, hence, about the lively way that traditions are established throughout American society. Examining the creation of a teen film canon directs attention to a region of taste often maligned by media academics (who may lament their students' lack of interest in anything at variance with contemporary standards) and by newspaper critics (who may see teen tastes as the rule of the mob intent on "dumbing down" American culture).

Negative attitudes toward youth and mass culture also appear in scholarship that specifically concerns rereading and re-viewing. Mike Budd, for example, argues that formulaic commercial texts are exhausted after the first viewing, while innovative, complex modernist fare such as *The Cabinet of Dr. Caligari* (1919) demands critical reengagement. He suggests that because modernist films involve a sizable labor of interpretation, they reward repeated contact with greater edification and pleasure. Similarly privileging refined texts over the "poor and mediocre" in his book on rereading, Matei Calinescu additionally champions the "mature rediscovery of texts" over youthful rereading in the former's ability to inspire full involvement with the text.[30] Thus rereading and re-viewing are associated with "serious" works and older, erudite consumers. By comparison, when performed by youth in a mass cultural context, these activities are linked to compulsive behavior or the desire for mindless entertainment.

In this way teen tastes are marginalized; lacking respect, they fall outside the pale of aesthetic credibility and legitimacy. With this in mind, analyzing a body of repeatable classics not only provides a practical lesson in canon formation; it also helps to redress the outright critical dismissal of youthful viewing habits and preferences. By shaking up official canons, we can investigate how value is constructed during routine film viewing and how even viewers whose aesthetics are disparaged create worlds of meaning through the taste hierarchies they embrace and perpetuate.

What remains to us now is to take a closer look at how film choices illuminate the lived aesthetics, pleasures, and viewing strategies of the teen audience. Mass cultural texts are hardly exhausted upon their first screening; they often inspire multilayered responses from their viewers upon successive viewing. Far from compulsively and mindlessly pursuing repetition for its own sake, youths in the survey approached their favorite titles with different agendas and desires.

Why Repeat?

At the end of an episode of the WB's *Dawson's Creek* (May 4, 2000), Joey climbs up the ladder to Dawson's room, as she has been doing ever since they were children, bringing with her a video of Steven Spielberg's *E.T.: The Extra-Terrestrial*. Dawson is a bit surprised to see her, because she has been in the midst of turmoil about which man to choose—him or his rival, Pacey. Their conversation goes as follows:

DAWSON: *E.T.?* After everything that's happened, this is what you rented?

JOEY: I thought it was time to see it again.

DAWSON: You said this movie was sad and depressing, remember?

JOEY: I just feel like watching something tonight with an ending I know like the back of my hand.

DAWSON: E.T. turns to Eliot and says, "I'll be right here."

JOEY: Right now, those are some of the most comforting words in the world.

Coming from a network TV series designed for young audiences, this example of returning to an old favorite at a critical time in a relationship suggests why repeat films can achieve such relevance for these viewers. As the exchange between Joey and Dawson implies, film can be used as therapy as well as a nostalgic means of comfort that helps viewers to escape, forget, or remember. Joey's decision to revisit *E.T.* attempts both to restore childhood ties to Dawson through a shared rite and to put her mind at rest by re-watching a beloved film. She remarks that the very familiarity of the film itself is valuable; the fact that she has seen it countless times does not diminish, but rather heightens, her pleasure. Rewatching *E.T.* provides an occasion in which autobiography, nostalgia, and comfort mix within the safe zone provided by a familiar text in domestic surroundings.

Many of the reasons survey participants gave for repeating films echo this moment in *Dawson's Creek* while offering other possible motivations for returning to certain titles. In my survey, the range of motives for re-viewing films include: aesthetic appreciation; boredom; familiarity; genre; getting high; identification; memorization of dialogue; nostalgia; preprofessional training; family or peer ritual; stars and directors; and therapy. Many of these motivations apply to theatrical moviegoing as well; for instance, one may go to a film on the big screen because of the star or genre. That said, being able to repeat on demand the same film on VHS or DVD in private space gives a particularly potent value, import, and affect to certain rationales for re-viewing that cannot be matched in the theatrical situation. Although I will touch upon other categories, I concentrate here on those motivations that were both most discussed by students and most indebted to repetition in the home for the full achievement of effects and pleasures: familiarity, aesthetic appreciation, therapy, nostalgia, and dialogue memorization.

Since familiarity itself is an inherent by-product of repeat viewing, it frames other reasons for engaging in this habit. In fact, it is at once a central arena of satisfaction and the root of other functions and pleasures. Yet critics have often regarded it as a degraded component of textual and other experience. By weighing the foundational role that familiarity plays in re-viewing, we can revisit the term with an eye toward reconsidering its value.

Play It Again, Neo

It is a commonplace that familiarity breeds contempt. Translated into narrative terms, this commonplace often leads critics to assume that once a story has been consumed, it has been "used up." Knowing the narrative already—its critical moments and how they are resolved—makes further encounters unnecessary, even potentially displeasing. This sentiment was clearly expressed by some viewers in the survey who find that they are easily bored with movies they have already seen or that they anticipate story moves too much while watching. Once the story's secrets are known, the viewer loses the thrill of deciphering the chain of narrative causes and effects.

In certain discussions of mass culture, the issue of familiarity is treated to an even stronger critique. As mass culture generates homogeneous offerings, the audience's subsequent reliance on formulas in their aesthetic experience gives way to "easy" textual encounters that are passive and co-opted by the dominant ideology. This mode of consumption stands in stark contrast to the formal and ideological challenges offered by more difficult texts. In Theodor Adorno's work on popular music, for example, mass culture redefines the listener as a child "who demands the one dish they've been served" over and over again. This standardized familiarity projects the listener into a regressive, inattentive state and becomes the "surrogate for the quality ascribed" to a piece. Liking a piece becomes simply an act of recognition, devoid of genuine aesthetic discrimination. Adorno's abhorrence of repetition has a moral dimension: repetition is a wrong, an evil to be redressed if freer, more genuine aesthetic and social experiences are to be salvaged.[31]

Adorno's condemnation of standardized experiences is valuable insofar as it exposes the constraints that commercial interests exercise upon textual production and reception. Indeed, people are attracted to the same films, the same television shows, or the same music because these media demand little of their attention or give them "the one dish they've been served." But as one of the most sought-after experiences in mass culture, familiarity plays multiple roles in the process of reception. As the variable that most compellingly drew viewers in my survey back to the same films, it emerges as a more complex dynamic in reception than detractors have assumed.

Survey participants counter the idea that once a narrative is consumed, it is spent. Repeating the same movie multiple times provides a foreknowledge of the narrative that is the source of a series of pleasures. For instance, a male student who likes to re-view the *Star Wars* trilogy, *The Big Lebowski* (1998), and *The Matrix* wrote, "I enjoy watching them over and over again, because they instill a sense of familiarity. It makes me feel relaxed. I know what's going to happen and when it's going to happen. This works for jokes in a comedy or action sequences in an action film." Similarly, a female student, whose favorite films include *Beauty and the Beast* (1991), *Clueless*, and *Ever After* (1998), commented that repeating a favorite film makes her feel good: "I like to know how it is going to end. I don't really like surprise movies. . . . It's a question of how you're getting there that makes the movies repeat-worthy. There is a certain pleasure for me knowing exactly what comes next or to be able to say a line at the same time as the actor." This sense of gratification extends even to a film's ending—the moment when most narrative enigmas are usually resolved. As one male student remarked of *Braveheart* and *The Shawshank Redemption*, "The emotional impact is so deep that even though I know the outcome of the film, it still gets me." Another male student whose preferences include *The Good, the Bad, and the Ugly* (1966), *Rear Window* (1954), and *Pulp Fiction* identified an aesthetic dimension to re-viewing: "I thrill in sitting through these films, knowing how they're going to end, watching each piece of the puzzle come into play. . . . There's always the 'I never noticed that before' element. But more enjoyable to me is the element of 'I've noticed that every time—and I still love it.'"

Familiarity enables viewers to experience both comfort and mastery. Foreknowledge of the story alters the narrative experience by lessening the tension associated with suspense. Viewers can be more relaxed, shifting their priorities to a knowing anticipation of events to come. Rather than deadening anticipation, foreknowledge enhances it; once viewers are conversant with a comedy's jokes, for example, they look forward to the laughs they know these jokes will bring. The viewer also finds delight in the repeated recognition of patterns and the delivery of expected emotions. Further, once the story's uncertainties are resolved, re-viewing brings a "sense of one's own skill level" to the fore, allowing the viewer to experience his or her conversancy with the text as a form of pleasure.[32]

Knowing a text like the back of one's hand also enhances another area of reception. The narrative comfort some viewers experience when watching an old favorite can mutate into a more general kind of comfort as the film becomes part of their world. Movies become "friends," akin to other everyday elements associated with solace and contentment. One woman fan of *Sense and Sensibility* (1995), *Aliens* (1986), and *Labyrinth* (1986) wrote, "The stories are familiar. It's like spending time with old friends I care about, the characters, what's happening. By watching a movie multiple times it becomes almost a part of you." Another likes the "consistency of viewing the same movie" because "seeing it in a new place" makes her feel "more at home." Watching chick flicks and other films such as *Top Gun* and *Happy Gilmore* (1996) is like "putting on an old pair of sneakers, you just feel comfortable. . . . I like to curl up with a blanket on the sofa and watch my favorite movies." Respondents frequently mentioned the substantial sense of security and satisfaction they gain from favorite films—how the presence of these films alone is reassuring in new surroundings or in the face of outside difficulties.

Familiar material, then, brings enjoyment via a combination of both mastery and solace: mastery of the narrative and one's own world; solace in the sense of control that predictability brings and in the way the screening of the same narratives can transform a space into a secure environment. But does familiarity still invoke a sense of an oversimplified and debased manner of engaging texts? Once placed within the continuum of human experience, familiarity appears less sinister. As Ed S. Tan argues, "People's desire for variety and new experiences is more or less balanced by the fact that they enjoy what they know. In psychological studies . . . the hedonic value of a stimulus is said to be based on the extent to which it agrees with a prototypical instance of the class to which the stimulus belongs."[33] Choosing the same coffee shop or restaurant to frequent, the same sneakers or T-shirt to wear, or the same family stories to retell is a commonplace of life. Like such choices, watching the same film or TV show acts as a guarantee of pleasure or satisfaction as well as a way to give a controllable shape to everyday existence. In this way, an inevitable daily dance takes place between the known and the new. Too much of either would be unsettling or displeasing. Thus, familiarity is just as key to experience as novelty. To deny the pleasures that one finds within the precincts of the familiar text is to ignore the intrinsic and necessary place that the known occupies in broader social circumstances. As a student said of the CDs, TV shows, and movies he likes to replay, "When something is that good and means that much to you, you never want to lose it and want to utilize it as much as possible."

At the same time, it is questionable whether no work is involved in the consumption of the formulaic for pleasure. Critics of the familiar in aesthetic experience rely to varying degrees on the Protestant ethic, wherein enjoyment has to be earned by hard work and "the deepest pleasure is consequent upon suffering."[34] From this perspective, things that appear easy or simply gratifying are suspect. But some scholars have argued that this dichotomy cannot be sustained when studying reading for pleasure. In *Lost in a Book*, Victor Nell finds that "the simpler passages fill cognitive capability more completely than the difficult ones. Indeed, the richness of the structure the . . . reader creates in his head may be inversely proportional to the literary power and originality of the reading material and vice versa." Thus, while reading James Joyce may "require frequent pauses and regressions," reading pulp fiction "may impose a heavier continuous load on attention" given the "well-practiced ease with which the reader can image his stereotyped characters and settings" (77). Surely, reading can be used to dull consciousness. However, Nell's study suggests, contra Budd and Calinescu, that formulaic texts inspire an attentiveness and a resourcefulness that sur-pass what occurs with modernist texts, which, because of difficult structures and indecipherable moments, may impede the reader's deployment of imag-ination.

Here, we might recall Roland Barthes's paradoxical description of reread-ing as saving "the text from repetition." As it delivers the reader from com-mitment to narrative chronology and simple consumption of the story, rereading indulges in a kind of play that remakes the text into a plural text—"the same and new."[35] This play opens the text to a potentially intense refashioning, which, while perhaps frustrating for the aesthete invested in a concept of textual self-determination, nonetheless represents an active process of appropriation. For survey participants drawn to a film's familiar-ity, such activities as rearranging narrative priorities, altering the rhythms of anticipation to deemphasize tension and heighten pleasure through fore-knowledge, and using cinema for comfort reflect a series of operations that convert the old into the new. Along the way, the repeated text becomes a launching pad for experiences of mastery, solace, and observant engage-ment. In this sense, rereading is work without suffering.

By thus reconsidering the familiar, rereading and re-viewing gain a po-tential aesthetic dimension. Successive reencounters with a favorite title re-sult in different experiences of it, inspiring recognition of its multifaceted nature—a recognition of richness intimately linked to aesthetic apprecia-tion. Within their embrace of the familiar, survey participants mentioned aesthetic curiosity and the pursuit of aesthetic pleasure most frequently as reasons for re-viewing a variety of films.

Aesthetic Appreciation: Discovery and Decoding

While students expressed multiple reasons for returning to films, aesthetic evaluations, from the formal to the more casual, are found everywhere in the survey. Often, students articulated this pleasure in re-viewing in rela-tion to films they see as substantially different from contemporary Holly-wood. As we might expect, foreign and art films elicit an aesthetic response from some viewers. A freshman double-majoring in English and history watched his "all-time favorite" movie *The Seven Samurai* (1954) thirteen times because it "is so condensed with information and realism that it takes time to analyze and catch all [Kurosawa] put into it. I focus mainly on the background actions which are just as wonderfully directed as those that are in the foreground." For a theater major, Peter Weir's *Dead Poet's Society* (1989) is "brilliant, inspirational, thoughtful, powerful, poetic and witty";

another student finds Ang Lee's *Sense and Sensibility* "excellent for all aspects of filmmaking—acting first, then lighting, cinematography, mise-en-scene, sound, etc."

The idea that a film cannot be adequately consumed on the first viewing is the bedrock proposition of aesthetic motivations for re-viewing. This idea is clearly present in relation to foreign cinema, but it also pertains to other films that represent to these viewers difference within the Hollywood system. We can group these films loosely under the heading of "puzzle films."[36] Like chick flicks, puzzle films constitute a supergenre that associates films from otherwise different established genres through shared acts of taste. Science fiction, film noir, gangster, war, and other types of films can all fall under this heading. Puzzle films typically display several of the following characteristics: mature subject matter; a complex, atypical, multilayered narrative (that experiments with temporal order, for example); a confusion of objective and subjective realms; a visually dense style; an ending that depends on a reversal or surprise that makes viewers reevaluate their experience with the text; and the presence of an initially occult meaning that requires re-viewing to uncover the text's mysteries. Films frequently mentioned by students that fulfill some or all of these criteria include *The Matrix*, *Pulp Fiction*, *Out of Sight* (1998), *The Usual Suspects* (1995), *GoodFellas*, *Trainspotting* (1996), *Blue Velvet* (1986), *Apocalypse Now* (1979), and *2001: A Space Odyssey* (1968). Although the survey occurred before *The Sixth Sense* (1999) and *Memento* (2000) had worked their way into the audience's video consciousness, they too are prime candidates for this colloquial genre; the latter plays its narrative in reverse, and both mingle objective and subjective perspectives and feature revelatory endings that substantially alter their stories.

Students see their preference for these films as a demonstration of their unconventional tastes; the films repeated are not "normal," straightforward Hollywood fare but complicated and challenging thematically, narratively, and stylistically. In short, they require a labor of decoding to put together the pieces of the puzzle. Thus, respondents often wrote testimonials such as "*The Matrix* . . . I watch because it is so complicated. With each viewing, I discover something new," or "I re-watch *Pulp Fiction* because the way Tarantino manipulates Hollywood convention into something all his own is amazing. The out-of-sequence events along with different story lines that all tie flawlessly together are what make this movie so great. . . . Chances are I discover new hidden meanings about the story or uncover some type of important symbolic significance" (figure 17). The viewer becomes a detective who tries to find clues, missed in the first screening, that will reveal

Figure 17. Killed off in a previous sequence, Vincent Vega (John Travolta) reappears with Jules Winnfield (Samuel L. Jackson) from an earlier moment in the film, making anything possible in the time-scrambled world of Tarantino's *Pulp Fiction*.

the film's enigmas. Further, some of these viewers consider themselves "purists." Despite having seen these films before, they refuse to fast-forward, insisting on watching their favorites straight through with full attention.[37] In the world of the purist, this refusal to surrender to the remote control helps to preserve a film's aesthetic status and distinguishes the viewer as a discerning consumer of mass culture.

Films that have some cultural capital as a result of their apparent difference from the typical industry product, then, invite aesthetic assessment. However, aesthetic responses also strongly define the appreciation of more standard fare. Some students embrace traditional Hollywood entertainment films that have worked their way into the American consciousness, such as the *Indiana Jones* and original *Star Wars* series, with childhood fascinations paving the way for later appreciation of aesthetic variables. As a male student remarked, "I have been mesmerized by Spielberg movies since the age of six. He was the first director I ever heard of. At first, it was just the stories and the overall effect of little aliens and crazy adventurers. Now I see such beauty and design in these films." A female viewer noted further, "The *Star Wars* movies are more or less epic 'poems' of our culture. The icons, themes, and ideas in the films have been interwoven into our society."

While viewers may justify these choices through an awareness of the legendary place the works of Spielberg and Lucas occupy in American filmmaking and culture, less hallowed Hollywood films also elicited aesthetic re-

sponses. A journalism major who mainly rewatches contemporary comedies wrote that re-viewing "helps you memorize whole scenes and find
some subtle things you may miss. I have seen the *Naked Gun* [1988] many,
many times, but I still catch new jokes, funny lines, or something else new
each time." In addition, any film can achieve importance if it represents the
quintessence of its genre or exercises a steadfast appeal to this age group. So,
for example, viewers regard *Pretty Woman* as a "comedy classic" and *Dazed
and Confused* a "classic teen flick."

These examples feature a number of criteria at work in establishing aesthetic value. To attain some form of aesthetic status, films must be perceived
as artful, complex, culturally important, or emblematic in regard to generation or genre. The sense that upon each viewing, a film offers new insights
or, at the very least, something previously unnoticed is particularly important. As we have seen, the language of discovery is present in relation to
films that might fit more comfortably within a traditional modernist aesthetic (e.g., the puzzle film with its difficult or enigmatic structure that requires an explicit labor of decipherment) and films that an academic canon
might be loathe to recognize (e.g., *The Naked Gun*). Uncovering something
new in each encounter transforms any film into a multilayered, inex-
haustibly interesting entity, meaning that no text is immune from the process of discovery that lies at the heart of aesthetic enterprise. This pursuit
of film knowledge suggests that many repeat viewers are "close readers,"
searching a film for previously unseen elements to understand and enjoy it
better. Hence, if we grant that unofficial or disparaged tastes are just as important as critically sanctioned tastes for addressing how texts are socially
valued, then aesthetic pleasure, no matter what its origins or determinants,
can be grasped as a significant motivation for leisure activities and a telling
indicator of the dynamics involved in day-to-day textual experience.

Aesthetic motivations in the routine reappropriation of films become additionally important for the defensive function they serve. A one-time
viewing of a film is unlikely to necessitate elaborate justification; however,
indulgence in repeated screenings of the same film reflects on the viewer's
taste more extensively and thus requires a rationale. After all, the viewer
has chosen to spend his or her time and energy doing something that could
be construed as a nonproductive, frivolous activity that simply provides
more of the same. Worse, repeated viewing of the same title hints at an eccentric overinvestment in or obsession with the media. The language of discovery can be used to justify taste within the thorny context of anticipated
disapproval.

As scholars such as Ien Ang and Janice Radway have argued, aesthetic feelings, while deeply felt and fiercely held, often act to legitimate what fans know to be a devalued pastime.[38] When society negatively assesses the value of one's object of mass cultural desire, aesthetic rationales proliferate as a protection against disdain. This does not mean that fan aesthetics are simply defensive constructions; discovery is a genuine source of pleasure. But as they help to position the viewer as an astute observer who is able to catch nuances in a film, aesthetic exclamations strive to absolve repetition from negative, slothful connotations. In fact, repetition makes these nuances possible by allowing the viewer to behold previously unseen textual layers, converting what appears to be the same text into a new, more complex entity. Repetition's fortunes are thus reversed. No longer the signifier of passive or obsessive consumption, repetition empowers close readings that turn the viewer into a judge of value through the exercise of discrimination and taste.

The defensive foundations of the aesthetic rationale represent one means by which existing taste formations affected young adult re-viewers. Norms of taste drawn from the media industry and the peer group were also especially prominent. This is not to say that academic standards of taste were without influence. Although all of the students cited above were in introductory-level classes, not majors in the Department of Communication and Culture and hence not advanced in the academic study of film, they were still conscious of being in a film class. Academe thus may have shaped their responses, producing more aesthetic motivations than otherwise might have been the case. However, as we shall see, the educational setting did not prevent the expression of many nonaesthetic sentiments about re-viewing. Moreover, findings suggest that contexts outside of the ivory tower held more sway in the viewers' embrace of aesthetic impulses for watching films.

The film industry is well aware that films requiring relatively vigorous decoding, such as puzzle films, appeal to this generation. In fact, it designs some films for the theater and, especially, for the VHS and DVD market with this appeal in mind. Created with a surplus of information or narrative "tricks," the industry promotes such films as particularly re-viewable. As one student said of his puzzle film favorites: "Special attention to detail was made so that the viewer can catch new things every time they watch." In this vein, *Entertainment Weekly* has devoted articles to describing the pleasures of repeat viewing. In "Matrix Mania," an article that chronicles the extensive male repeat audience for *The Matrix*, the author quotes a twenty-six-year-old vice president of technology for an online company:

"The second time I saw *The Matrix* . . . I wanted to focus on everything outside the story—background characters, signs, and symbols. The third time, I picked up the subtleties. The more you see it, the more it rocks." The article's author provides an interpretive guide, writing, "God is in the details . . . the sci-fi thriller is a veritable 'Where's Waldo?' of religious symbolism. Here is everything you need to decode *The Matrix*."[39]

In another piece in the same magazine, this one on *The Phantom Menace*, the author asks, after pointing out that some viewers saw the film as many as seventy times at the box office, "How much of *The Phantom Menace* did any of us—obsessive or otherwise—*really* see? . . . That is why God—or was it George Lucas—invented video. In truth, *Star Wars* creator Lucas and his special effects team at Industrial Light and Magic crammed more detail into *Menace* than can be absorbed in a single or even sextuple theatrical viewings." But ancillary exhibition changes this frustrating situation: "Any fan with a VCR (or DVD player) can now search for what Coleman (the film's animation director) calls the movie's 'Easter eggs,' or nearly invisible details best savored with a pause button." As in the case of *The Matrix* (and other films such as *Toy Story* [1995]), the magazine provides a list of things to look for in playback.[40] In the VHS and DVD era, Andrew Sarris's edict from decades ago in *The American Cinema*—that film critics should look below the surface of genre films to locate their stylistic and thematic subtleties—has been internalized not only by academic and popular criticism but also by the media industry's production and exhibition strategies.[41]

This coverage assigns supreme mastery to filmmakers (hard to miss in the joking reference to George Lucas as God) and the pleasures they provide by producing movies that continually yield new insights and knowledge. This is particularly true of films with elaborate special effects. Because digital technologies are able to create complex layered spaces, filled with visual detail, any film with special effects is a candidate for puzzle film status. When media industries portray filmmakers as all-knowing and all-seeing manipulators of such detail, they define the viewer in a complementary fashion. As a savvy decoder of a text's mysteries, the viewer becomes something of an authority—an intrepid explorer who has discovered a terra incognita and mapped every path. As we have seen in other chapters, mastery is a steadfast component of home film reception in the digital era, given to different articulations by the discourses that seek to define domestic space as a special viewing territory. Here, the pleasure of repeat viewing lies in the viewer's ability to unearth visual details and layers of meaning that cannot be fully apprehended in initial screenings.

As in the cases of home theater and collecting, sources tend to target male audiences as subjects of technodiscourse. *Entertainment Weekly* explicitly addresses men as possessing the technical knowledge necessary for aesthetic expertise in today's film culture. In the survey too, male viewers were more likely than female viewers to discuss aesthetic appreciation as a prime motivation for repetition, with women citing other reasons for re-viewing as more compelling (such as therapy and nostalgia).[42] However, although some symmetry is evident between the gender-coded address of mainstream sources and the survey's findings, my study shows that so many travel across the gender divide in terms of motivations for re-viewing that gender tendencies must be regarded merely as trends within this group rather than as definitive markers of difference.

Since film knowledge is often displayed in social situations of viewing, peer considerations also permeate tastes. Participants' tastes attain a certain consistency because of both the alignment of preferences in their canon and an "outlaw" aesthetic that defines tastes as diverging from the mainstream or parent cultures. Puzzle films such as *The Matrix* and *Pulp Fiction* occupy a special place for this group because their violent worlds suggest a daring and a complexity that challenge the politesse of the parent culture. However, tastes are not simply homogeneous or without divisive effects. Even within the sample, different taste groups exist, from the "elite" cohort of puzzle film enthusiasts, who see their intricate decoding strategies as setting them apart from the perceived passive viewing habits of their peers, to the "potheads," who select certain films for re-viewing because they provide good accompaniments for smoking marijuana or drinking beer.

No matter what the specific subcommunity happens to be, viewers identify repeatable classics both to secure distinction (including infamy) within the broader peer culture and to display mass cultural prowess within their own group. Puzzle film viewers offer perhaps the clearest case of this dynamic in seeking prestige through preferences for work they regard as falling outside of Hollywood formulas. Being able to decode these films reflects directly on the viewer's powers of discernment, distinguishing him or her as "hip" and "in the know." Through a combination of knowledgeability and hipness, the viewer procures a share of what Thornton calls "subcultural capital," recognition by peers that he or she is a cognoscente (11). However, puzzle film viewers are not alone in using their favorite films to signal their expertise. Those whose primary motive for re-viewing is getting high emphasize how important their conversancy with "classic stoner films" (films that either depict drug use or are in some way fantastic or hallucinatory, from *Yellow Submarine* [1968] and *Easy Rider* [1969] to *Half Baked* [1998]) is to their place within the "stoner" subcommunity.[43] Knowing all the religious references in *The Matrix* or the funniest moments in a stoner classic provides a means of jockeying for or achieving authority with one's fellows. In this way, selections of repeatable films become a means of realizing and expressing stratifications within certain sectors of youth culture.

Survey participants' aesthetic choices and justifications allow us to reflect on the synergy between youth cultures and broader contexts—how individuals respond to judgments of merit from various contexts as they construct their own taste cultures. In anticipation of negative judgments, collegiate youth may marshal aesthetic reasons for their viewing habits so as not to appear as mindless consumers. They may embrace an "outlaw" aesthetic—long a means of self-identity for youth as well as a sales pitch deployed by commercial markets. Members of this group also incorporate aspects of aesthetic schema from academe, mainstream film criticism, industry promotions, and other centers of aesthetic discourse as they fashion generational and subcommunal worlds of value. These worlds are composed of multiple fragments of existing hierarchies and interpretive stances, so no individual act of taste is uniform or predictable. Yet, the shifting, recombinatory nature of acts of taste should not obscure the presence of significant taste formations developed from the reciprocal relation between viewers and public arenas of aesthetic discourse. The case of the puzzle film viewer, for example, suggests that not only do regions of taste from official and subcultural communities intersect; they also often serve to reinforce one another, creating an influential aesthetic that helps to constitute the landscape of contemporary taste.

However widespread, aesthetic rationales for re-viewing only begin to reveal the dynamics influencing the surveyed group's tastes in film. Other rationales continue to amplify the centrality of repetition to this group's domestic film experience and to the cultures of distinction maintained or generated from this encounter. Almost as dominant as aesthetic motivations for returning to a film, cinema's therapeutic potential drew students back to favorite titles. Although aesthetic reimmersion afforded deep satisfaction, those surveyed articulated their sense of "falling in love" with a film more dramatically in relation to its ability to function as a strong affective device.

Like any medium, film can arouse strong emotions and provide catharsis. The situation of household re-viewing transforms and strengthens this capacity in particularly telling ways. Like a CD played over and over again or a book reread until its pages fall out, the favorite film, once domesticated, is subject to the viewer's desire to harness and control its emotional effects. When a film's emotional profile is known, the viewer can screen it repeatedly to administer the kind of emotional "cure" sought. As this motivation sheds light on the personal, everyday use of cinema as a curative, it also helps to reveal connections to larger interests. Film's ability to be recycled in the privacy of the home has helped to nurture a mass cultural market in cinematic affect, wherein pop psychology embraces "must resee" cinema as a therapeutic tool.

Our Movies, Ourselves

As the exchange from *Dawson's Creek* intimates, revisiting favorite films can be a source of comfort, a means of shifting from life's problems to an imaginative landscape that temporarily relieves the stresses of the real world. According to those surveyed, this shifting serves diverse emotional functions. Viewers may return to certain titles to amplify or change moods, to insulate themselves from the world, to address or compensate for problems, or to learn inspirational life lessons. In each case, familiarity with a film's emotional effects allows the viewer to engage in a form of self-help through the administration of a predictable celluloid cure, lending a therapeutic dimension to cinema's impact.

As one might expect, the "feel-good" film occupies a prominent place in these desires for re-viewing. Students regard comedies and romances as genres that unfailingly raise spirits. As a female respondent wrote, "Many of my repeat movies are comedies. Jim Carrey, Adam Sandler, and Chris Farley always brighten your day by making you smile. The other movies I watch this way are sappy 'chick-flicks' that I can connect to." For another viewer, although *Father of the Bride* (1991), *My Best Friend's Wedding* (1997), and *Titanic* produce different types of affect, these films ultimately result in tactical catharsis: "I can pinpoint scenes that will make me cry at the drop of a hat, and it works every time. Even though they make me cry, I am in a better mood every time after watching."

Not all viewers, however, seek a feel-good experience. For many, cinema is attractive for its emotional versatility—its ability to produce an array of emotions. Different titles can thus be pressed into different kinds of emotional service. As one female student said, "I know that certain movies I watch repeatedly will put me in the kind of mood I want to be in. I equate certain films with certain emotions or moods. If I am scared or sad I will watch something light and funny. Sometimes I want to cry or be depressed so I watch a sad movie." A male student (whose film list includes *Annie*

Hall, The Godfather [1972], and *Pulp Fiction*) also types films according to affect: "The films I re-watch evoke unusual amounts of emotion—be it romantic or suspenseful, etc.—with exceptional effectiveness. Whenever I want to feel a certain emotion, I can find the right movie for the job. If I wish to feel a certain way, or momentarily view the world through a specific lens, I can count on my favorite films to deliver that feeling." Ultimately, viewers' ability to control cinema's emotional versatility, by choosing the right title for a particular affective job, strongly underwrites the therapeutic pleasures of re-viewing. Through film rentals or purchases, viewers strategically indulge in selected cinematic cures, exercising a sense of sovereignty over their own emotional worlds.

As the last respondent's comment indicates, it is not only women who equate cinema with feeling. Male students observed that they specifically seek out "tearjerkers" to achieve catharsis. Not as many of the men admitted this as women; however, several mentioned that they like to rewatch films that choke them up or make them cry, particularly *Braveheart* and *The Shawshank Redemption* but also titles such as *The English Patient* (1996), *Lone Star* (1996), and *The Sweet Hereafter* (1997) (figure 18). Each of the titles is an art film or a mainstream film with a weighty theme. While men watch comedies and lighter fare to raise their spirits as often as women do, and women are also attracted to art films for emotional reasons, male descriptions of the deeper emotional reaches that films can plumb tended to focus on more apparently serious films. This focus may allow men to balance aesthetics and therapy, rescuing them from a sense of indulgence in sheer emotion. At the same time, it seems more important to men that a profoundly affective experience be a solitary one. As one respondent explained, "I watch certain films alone. I don't feel at ease engaging in the presence of others. For instance, when depressed, I might watch *'Night Mother* [1986] or *The Haunting* [1999] as a ritual response to the depression." Although women suggested that they would rather view such films alone or with like-minded others, men made it especially clear that this is a governing condition of their encounter with the tearjerker. The male use of films to operate on mood thus includes some defensive maneuvers meant to offset peer criticism that might arise because of the social opprobrium often attached to the weeping or emotionally overwrought man.

Within emotional motivations, re-viewers may also deploy films to deal more overtly with or compensate for life's problems. As one woman wrote, "When I am in the middle of a breakup or having love problems, I watch *Waiting to Exhale* and *love jones*." As they deal with romantic entanglements, such African American chick flicks echo this African American stu-

Figure 18. *Braveheart* as male weepie: William Wallace (Mel Gibson) approaching his torture and execution at the film's end.

dent's own dilemmas. For her, the affirmative messages these films provide about women's ability to cope with or rise above difficult situations supply consolation and hope. Another female student pointed to the compensatory nature of film viewing: "Overall, there is something very comforting about these films. When I was lonely and unhappy in high school, a movie like *Point Break* [1991] or *Last of the Mohicans* [1992] was a nice escape." Action-adventure films provide a sense of relief to this viewer by showing her exotic worlds that provide solace through differences from, rather than similarities to, her life.

Such differences enable viewers to access intense emotions foreign to their experience. A series of comments from female students, who watch everything from comedies and chick flicks to art films and *Fight Club*, indicate that they return to these films because the films allow them to pretend to be the characters. The viewers want to "feel what [the characters] feel and do what they do," in the process traveling into an affective landscape that yields emotions they "can't feel in any other way." Because the films contain unfamiliar situations, they stimulate the viewers' imaginations, enabling acts of vicarious identification. As one said, "I get to laugh out loud or cry over someone else's problems or learn about people or even myself through character studies. I think mainstream film can give me a connection to the greater society which I don't otherwise get." Cinema's presentation of different characters and diverse worlds is, for many spectators, stimulating and mind altering, "like a drug"; it produces pleasure by revealing sights never seen, people never encountered, and feelings never before felt. For all its incessant formulas and other commonplaces, then, cinema—all kinds of cinema—has retained the capacity to represent the wondrous and the exotic, traits typically associated more with the medium's formative years or with contemporary special effects blockbusters than with ordinary movies.

In the balance between affirming and transforming one's emotions, between identifying and escaping, favorite films also provide life lessons that instruct and guide viewers, especially as they envision their futures. As one student stated, "I remember the dreams I used to have when watching the movies and get inspired to keep/start chasing those dreams again." Viewers believe that films offer hidden insightful comments on life and relationships relevant to their own lives. Of *Braveheart, The Shawshank Redemption,* and the basketball film *Hoosiers* (1986)—all films with male protagonists up against powerful forces—a male student wrote, "These films affect an emotional response that really touches the chords of my soul, whether it be through the score, storytelling, etc. Often, I watch the final scene and JUST the final scene of a movie that I have seen many times to tear up. They inspire me to believe that I can beat the odds and everything stacked against me, to succeed in all the ways one can succeed." Some female students similarly find *Rocky* (1976) and *G.I. Jane* (1997) inspiring for the images they furnish of heroism tested against apparently insurmountable obstacles. Some regard *G.I. Jane* as particularly compelling, because it pits a female Navy SEAL recruit against the military establishment, a confrontation charged with implications for gender equality. But love stories, too, can be inspirational. *Shakespeare in Love* (1998) and *My Best Friend's Wedding*—both stories of failed romances with strong female protagonists—remind one student of "the real meaning in life"; she explained, "They allow me to refocus my life on important things, while also reminding me to be hopeful of what love may come in the future." Lengthy testimonials on Web sites devoted to films such as *Braveheart* and *The Shawshank Redemption* underscore not only how emotionally moving and inspirational film experiences can be but also how life changing.[44] A film's impact is not necessarily limited to a momentary afterglow; supported by repeated screenings, it can last for years after a first encounter, potentially for life.

Although many of the emotions aroused by cinematic reencounters may not seem profound, the breadth and depth of affective transformations that occur in the process of re-viewing, coupled with the viewer's dexterity in administering cinematic cures, are notable for what they reveal about the dynamics of daily textual appropriation. As Nell remarks about the emotional motives behind reading for pleasure: "Using a book selected for the purpose from among countless others the . . . reader achieves the most startling changes of mood and consciousness—gloom explodes into delight, fear dissolves into power, and agitation becomes easy tranquillity. Indeed, little in the study of consciousness is as striking as the economy of means and precision of outcome with which skilled readers . . . operate on their own state of mind" (267). The familiar text is a strategic means to a therapeutic end, a key instrument in an active quest for affective metamorphosis. If, as Tan argues, "maintaining or regaining affective balance dominates reading behavior" (26), emotional imperatives involved in ordinary media consumption may make any text into an embodiment of a series of feelings (happiness, exhilaration, sadness, spiritual uplift, etc.). In the case of the repeated film, familiarity and the control afforded by home playback technologies enhance both the equation of film titles with certain feelings and the viewer's ability to use films as self-help remedies.

Cultural reformers have often conceived of the emotional influence of cinema and other mass media in terms of its negative effects on behavior. However, as survey examples suggest, cinema's everyday emotional impact can have far more felicitous results. In fact, in the broader social context, cinema's therapeutic potential may be one of its most visible qualities. From the clinical ranks of psychology to manifestations of pop psychology in mass culture, cinema's beneficial connection with affect is both widely recognized and extensively exploited.

Psychologists have increasingly adopted cinema as a means of helping clients deal with their problems, since, according to one therapist, people are "more inclined to experience intense feelings and garner psychological insights from the screen than elsewhere."[45] More than a few publications advocate the use of films in psychotherapy, including John W. Hesley's *Rent Two Movies and Let's Talk in the Morning* and Gary Solomon's *The Motion Picture Prescription: Watch This Movie and Call Me in the Morning*. Although mental health professionals have used art and fiction to help psychiatric patients since the 1930s and film since at least the 1950s, these authors link cinema's more pervasive presence in clinical practice to the rise of VHS.[46] Given the omnipresence and inexpensiveness of VHS and DVD, their association with entertainment, and their ability to be viewed in a private environment, "such prescriptions are easier to fill than an order of Prozac." Therapists also claim that movies result in faster breakthroughs for clients, since clients respond less resistantly and more reflectively to a therapist's recommendations "if they can focus on a similar story where fundamentally the same things are happening, but they're happening to someone else."[47] Thus, to a verbally abusive father, one counselor prescribed *The Great Santini* (1979), a film about a career Marine who rules his family with an iron hand. In an additional sign of cinema's acceptance by clinicians, psychology programs show films to train counselors in the arts of diagnosis and treatment. Films that deal directly with psychotherapy, such as *Girl, Interrupted* (1999) and *The Sixth Sense*, appear in such curriculums. Psychotherapy's use of movies has become so common that the profession employs the term *cinematherapy* to capture the intimate relationship between its practices and the medium.

At the same time, cinema occupies a steadfast place in contemporary American self-help culture, a culture characterized by massively successful publications (such as *Chicken Soup for the Soul* and *Men Are from Mars, Women Are from Venus*). The lay market in cinematherapy sells various programs and products under the self-help rubric, particularly to women. Thus, the cable network Women's Entertainment (WE), formerly known as Romance Classics, offers a show entitled *Cinematherapy*, hosted by its two "cinema psychoanalysts," girlfriends Nancy Peske and Beverly West. Peske and West are also authors of a number of books, including *Cinematherapy: The Girl's Guide to Movies for Every Mood*.[48] Their volumes discuss the therapeutic effects of feature films, organizing film rentals according to the emotions they arouse and the problems they address.

In their book *Cinematherapy*, the authors write that movies have the power to "shake us to the very core of our identity," helping "us to explore our unconscious drives even as we consciously work toward categorizing our everyday experience and infusing it with meaning" (232). Peske and West's identification of cinematherapy as a particularly feminine need makes the target audience clear: "As we women know, movies are more than entertainment: they're self-medication. A good flick is like a soothing tonic that, if administered properly, in combination with total inertia and something obscenely high in fat grams, can cure everything from an identity crisis to a bad-hair day to the I-hate-my-job blues. Of course, medicine is a precise science. You have to match the movie to the mood or the treatment won't work" (xi). Accordingly, the authors select movies that directly thematize female problems, from bad hair days and dysfunctional romances to conflicts with one's mother (ix–x). Thus, they classify *Mommie Dearest* (1981), an account of Hollywood star Joan Crawford's abusive relationship with her adopted daughter, as a "Mother-Issue Movie." Similarly, Peske and West place *Titanic* and *Clueless* under the category of "Men Behaving Well"—a category that reminds female viewers in despair about male behavior that chivalry and romantic commitment are not dead. Guides on Web sites with a female constituency, such as Ivillage.com, similarly deploy this "precise science" of coordinating movies with moods to provide the proper "treatment." In addition to a discussion board that asks users to name their "favorite 'chick flick'—be it a gal-pal movie, tearjerker or romance—why you love it and why other people should rent it," Ivillage.com hosts a chat room with Peske and West, providing another media platform for their advice.

The survey responses corroborate what cinema's presence in popular self-help venues suggests—that not only do marketers and consumers recognize the medium's ability to elicit "self-medicating" emotions, but also this ability forms the basis of a pervasive home film culture. Within this culture, films are regarded as remedies for what ails the viewer, particularly the contemporary female viewer. Meanwhile, the emotional classification of movies in self-help venues aims to define female subjectivity. The venues' rhetoric blends a kind of feminism "lite" with conventional notions of female needs and desires. For example, the book *Cinematherapy* suggests that girls and women can be liberated from constraints that typically define their film consumption by knowledgeably selecting titles at the video store, taking charge of the remote, and, ultimately, assuming control of their own emotions. To amplify the theme of female power, the book offers film categories, such as "I Am Woman, Hear Me Roar." Other categories (e.g., "Father-Issue Movies," "PMS Movies," "Bad-Hair Day Movies," and "Men Behaving Well") establish the importance of experiential terrains more typically characterized as feminine: the family, emotions, appearance, and relationships. *Cinematherapy* combines a strategic mix of pop feminism (which presumes female independence and "girl power") and stereotypes, then, as a primary method of appealing to female audiences. The dose of feminism prevents traditional ideas of gender from appearing outdated, while the familiarity of tradition offsets any potential disorderliness implied by the trappings of feminist discourse.

If we take this kind of pop feminism as nothing more than a thin veil for conventional notions of female desires and tastes, commercial cinematherapy appears to offer its audiences inherently conservative remedies. Since the contemporary chick flick is often imbued with a blend of feminism and traditional romance, any therapeutic effects the genre offers might similarly be understood as maintaining the status quo. In this view, the repetition of chick flicks by the survey's young women amounts to a kind of ritual anchoring of female subjectivity in normative standards of gender. The attraction to repetition in this film culture is seen to stem, then, from the viewer's desire, under the auspices of a faux feminism, to be comfortably repositioned within dominant expectations of women.

This view, however, provides only a partial view of possible effects. Fo-

Figure 19. Drawing from the iconography of Rapunzel, Vivian Ward (Julia Roberts) smiles down at Edward Lewis (Richard Gere), who, in *Pretty Woman*'s happy ending, is about to climb the fire escape of her apartment to propose marriage.

cusing for a moment on the chick flick most revered by survey participants, *Pretty Woman*, we can see that it synthesizes fairy tale romance (complete with the rescue of a damsel in distress) and popular feminism. Besides the general outline of its plot, in which a downtrodden Cinderella, a prostitute named Vivian (Julia Roberts), meets her Prince Charming, a Los Angeles corporate raider named Edward (Richard Gere), the film is full of references to fairy tales. When, for example, Edward asks Vivian what she wants from their relationship, she tells him the story of how, when she was a little girl, her mother locked her in the attic when she was bad. Vivian says, "I used to pretend I was a princess trapped in a tower by a wicked queen. Then suddenly this knight on a white horse . . . would come charging up. . . . I would wave and he would climb up the tower and rescue me." She tells him this while standing on a penthouse balcony, echoing the geography of the Rapunzel-like rescue in her fantasy—a motif repeated at the film's end, when Edward does indeed save her by climbing up her apartment's fire escape (figure 19). Although the patriarchal structure of the damsel's rescue is at the heart of the film, the fairy tale's traditional gender dynamics are somewhat altered. *Pretty Woman*'s closing lines suggest the thrust of the film's revisionism. Referring to Vivian's childhood story, Edward asks, "What happens after he climbs up the tower and rescues her?" Vivian answers, "She rescues him right back." These lines redress the brute fact of many fairy tales—that it is active men saving passive, victimized women—with Vivian's acknowledgment that she is also delivering Edward from an unsavory life (that of a heartless corporate raider). At the same time, Julia Roberts's star persona, coupled with her character's "spunk," conveys female independence to survey respondents, helping to further modify conventional portraits of the fairy tale maiden.

The hero transformed by love, the strong-willed heroine—these are familiar components of women's fiction, from the Gothic novel to the Harlequin romance.[49] Women readers and viewers have long found comfort in such narratives. Janice Radway, Tania Modleski, and other scholars have suggested that these stories are popular because they meet the otherwise unmet needs of their readers and viewers. By identifying with the heroine, "whom they believe is deeply appreciated and tenderly cared for by another," these readers "vicariously attend to their own requirements as independent individuals who require emotional sustenance and solicitude." The pleasure in reading lies both in identification with a character who is cherished and in the feeling of self-sufficiency achieved by choosing a text that will unfailingly raise spirits. By offering the opportunity to take charge of one's affective state, romance reading provides a "tool to help insure a woman's sense of emotional well-being" (Radway, 92–93). Similarly, for some college-aged women, chick flicks such as *Pretty Woman* provide them with shining examples of heroines who demonstrate how worthy women are of love and regard while also operating as "a security blanket you carry with you through the years"—a known quantity that furnishes satisfying and uplifting affect.

In her work on girls' comic books in Britain, Valerie Walkerdine offers a different perspective. Seeing a potent connection between coming-of-age stories and fairy tales in these comics, Walkerdine argues that the "happily ever after solutions in which the finding of the prince . . . comes to seem like a solution to a set of overwhelming desires and problems" poses heterosexuality as an answer to young women's dilemmas.[50] The rescue narrative represents a cultural form that reassures young women that they may resolve whatever challenges they face by finding the right man. The form thus becomes a template for feminine dreams of achievement. Since many mass media forms marketed to women in U.S. culture, including *Pretty Woman* and other chick flicks, define the female quest in terms of finding a mate, the repeated viewing of such titles serves to keep the rescue fantasy alive, maintaining its place within the viewer's imagination. In the case of chick flicks, their frequent rewatching by groups of friends as a form of female bonding enhances the status they have as bildungsromans or coming-of-age stories that model female subjectivity and desire as inextricably bound up with romance-and-rescue scenarios.

In these two opposing accounts of the impact of romance fictions on their consumers, a text's affective codes can lead either to self-affirmation and a utopian reimagining of self and the world or to the colonization of aspirations by focusing on romance as the antidote to female struggles. Certainly, remarks in the survey suggest that romance is at the center of dreams of achievement for some young women. As one student said of *Pretty Woman,* "Watching it over and over again makes me believe that something wonderful like that is bound to happen to me"—the something wonderful being a desirable man choosing an unlikely girl for his true love. The grip of heterosexual romance on the female imagination is also manifested in the success of wedding films among survey respondents. As one remarked, "*Father of the Bride*—I'm never bored with the storyline. I relate it to being a girl and hoping to get married someday. I enjoy watching the wedding planning process and the hijinks the characters experience."

Other results indicate that some viewers find heroines with a backbone more compelling. As a survey respondent commented, "*Pretty Woman, Steel Magnolias* [1989], *Fried Green Tomatoes* [1991]—many of these films are films I *relate to* or *fantasize about*—stories about strong, dynamic, troubled, but heroic women." This viewer's comfort in re-viewing arises from the possibilities of self-determination offered by visions of forceful femininity. In this regard, another viewer noted that her favorite titles, *Fried Green Tomatoes, When Night Is Falling* (1995), and *Bound* (1996), "deal with strong women in lesbian relationships that eventually break out of societal roles and get what they want, each other. These movies have personal applicable meaning in my life. I can see myself in the characters. I like to see that, yes, sometimes lesbian relationships (although strange in these movies) can work out." Despite narrative strategies that might compromise the chick flick's fledgling feminisms, such viewers embrace certain star personas, characters, and/or films that promote gender ideals less easy to square with status quo gender representations.

As the last viewer's comment suggests, although some may emerge thunderstruck from a life-changing screening, a film's alignment with and fulfillment of preexisting emotions and desires appear to matter most in its affective impact. Survey re-viewers looking for therapy interpreted films as relating directly to their lives and their own potentials. Key to the emotional impact clinicians and mass cultural marketers impute to cinema, relevance figures centrally in viewers' reactions. Although therapeutic practices may construct an overly mechanical association between a film's plot and a client's problem, the search for relevance and self-understanding informs emotionally based encounters with films, constituting a common dynamic within home film cultures devoted to repetition.

Ultimately, the way we regard cinematherapy—whether as a progressive or as a more conservative effect of re-viewing—cannot be determined solely by textual analysis or by isolating tendencies that materialize in the interactions between surveyed viewers and films. As Jacqueline Bobo's work on black women viewers of *The Color Purple* (1985) has demonstrated, an ideologically problematic work can be transformed into an empowering experience, depending on a viewer's personal and collective histories.[51] Assessment of textual meaning and affect depends heavily on the viewer's predisposition, understood as rooted in larger cultural frameworks. Hence, although various female viewers may be attracted to films for therapeutic reasons, cinematherapy's more specific ideological functions are potentially as diverse as the deeper social experiences (rooted in race, class, gender, and other categories of identity) that characterize their backgrounds.

It may seem that viewers looking for cinematic "cures" need to look no further than a replay-worthy chick flick to accomplish the task. However, cinematherapy is not the only important emotionally based motivation for repeating favorite titles. After aesthetics and therapy, respondents identified nostalgia as a major incentive for watching the same movie multiple times. Students re-view films for the express purpose of journeying back into the past to recapture aspects of their earlier years. Like cinematherapy, nostalgia can be curative; but as a substantially different dynamic in viewing, it merits consideration on its own terms.

The Time Machine

As defined by *Webster's* dictionary, *nostalgia* is "a wistful or excessively sentimental yearning for return to some past period or irrecoverable condition." We tend to associate nostalgia with middle and old age, but even the very young experience this longing for bygone years. Like reencountering popular songs, seeing a film again can trigger a flood of impressions that illuminate moments from one's history with unexpected vividness. In Proustian fashion, sensory impressions associated with the first time the film was seen rush in, recalling the milieu in which it was viewed and reminding the viewer of the person he or she once was. Re-viewed texts become highly personalized, providing viewers with a road map through their lives, autobiographical landmarks that represent points of orientation to the past as well as to the present.

As I mentioned in chapter 3, while some media companies are devoted to providing official memories of films, they cannot possibly exhaust cinema's potential as a memory catalyst. Research has shown that memory studies in media must consider the emotionally potent connection among visual media, recollection, and individual histories. Writing about her viewing of the British film *Mandy* (1953) in an academic context long after having seen the film as a child, Annette Kuhn argues that such reencounters are particularly revealing. By contemplating the confrontations of present and "half-forgotten" selves, of schooled and unschooled responses that occur within these reencounters, "memory work presents new possibilities for enriching our understanding not only of how films work as texts, but also of how we use films and other images and representations to make our selves, how we construct our own histories through memory, even how we position ourselves within wider, more public, histories."[52] Like other personal responses to films we have seen so far, the anecdotal evidence of individual memories activated by film helps to elucidate some basic conditions of media reception—how texts become meaningful within personal and social horizons. But perhaps more than other motivations, nostalgic impulses for re-viewing signal how individuals within a generation comprehend not only themselves and their peer group but also broader histories that define their social experience.

Survey participants seeking nostalgic pleasures mentioned often wishing to recapture their first experience of watching a film as a means of regaining their original emotions. Many expressed sentiments such as this: "Movies that I watch frequently tend to evoke some sort of emotion deep inside—it's an enjoyment hard to describe, but it seems to bring me back to my past. It's a feeling of nostalgia—a way to return to that moment of pure emotion when I first saw the film in the theater. These films make me feel happy. They're kind of like old memories." Although both genders cherish films that can take them back to their childhoods or younger teen years, the types of films they select for this purpose are different in what are by now familiar ways. Female viewers choose 1980s teen-oriented films or chick flicks for time travel, while male viewers gravitate toward the *Star Wars* trilogy or the *Indiana Jones* series as the most poignant reminders of their past. For both, films provide a particularly vivid, tangible means of returning to the past.

As one woman explained, "The John Hughes films (*Breakfast Club, Sixteen Candles*, and *Pretty in Pink* [1986]) are nostalgia films in that they've

Figure 20. Eighties icon Molly Ringwald as Claire Standish in the nostalgia film *The Breakfast Club.*

been with me since I was young. . . . It's as if I know the characters personally and I'm seeing a memory on screen. This is also true with *Stand by Me* [1986]. Those boys remind me of my childhood friends and adventures. That film touches me and makes me laugh. It's quite personal for me."[53] Another stated, "These movies are part of my past and my friends' pasts that we can identify with. I like the teen characters and the plots of the movies. In fact, I visited the northern Chicago suburbs to see where *Sixteen Candles* and *Breakfast Club* were filmed. It's like reliving a memory that happened to me personally." The era's films bring viewers back to their childhoods, for some "a happier time in life" (figure 20).

Male students described the importance of Lucas and Spielberg movies in similar terms. A student identifying himself as Native American wrote, "The *Star Wars* trilogy—my absolute favorite movies. I loved them as a kid and I've watched them almost too much. I still watch them the same way I did when I was seven or eight years old. It brings back good memories and takes you back to your innocence." Another participant commented, "*Star Wars* and *Indiana Jones* remind me of childhood vigor and imagination. They have a special visual feel that I like to remember. . . . *Jurassic Park*— I've always liked dinosaurs, so it brings me back to that childhood wonder." One fan also recalled fondly that, during a household renovation, he had his parents build pillars into his bedroom closet to mimic an Indiana Jones–style Temple of Doom.

As nostalgia involves an interplay between film narrative and the viewer's past, it ignites a chain of autobiographical associations, deeply affecting the process of comprehension. Using the familiar metaphor of a pebble striking a pond, Nell conceives of textual comprehension as a memory-enriched process; as the reader plunges into the text, "the first ripple taps aspects of the reader's episodic memory, with each successive ripple drawing on a wider circle of idiosyncratic associations dislodged from the reader's autobiography" (78). Comprehension is not, then, simply the act of understanding the flow of narrative events or the story's main theme. It lies, rather, in the connections set off while a text is being read or viewed. Repeated encounters with the same films over time amplify associative possibilities. Each successive viewing offers the opportunity to remember the time, place, and people involved in original or subsequent viewings, making the personal flashback a primary feature of reception. Of course, films are subject to autobiographical decoding on the big screen as well. But this dynamic is substantially enhanced when films and other media enter private space and become part of an intimate repertoire of domestic objects infused with personal meaning.

Of course, the autobiographical nature of the "ripple effect" guarantees that the process of comprehension is not completely uniform across film viewers. However, certain patterns in survey responses can be detected. Generally, those surveyed experienced therapeutic effects from film nostalgia as providing comfort in the form of a retreat from the additional responsibilities that come with age or the pressing concerns of everyday life. As women and men gravitate toward different films, film nostalgia helps to constitute and secure a common culture along gender lines. Films designed for young female or male audiences become shared frames of reference that contribute to a sense of group membership. For these respondents, to be an adolescent female or male in U.S. culture means, in part, to have experienced a certain communal cinematic past, constituted by genres with gender-specific appeal. As repeated films inspire autobiographical associations and help to shape gender distinctions, they also assume a quasi-historical value as documents of a certain era. The familiar film is not just a conveyor belt back into the past; it has itself attained the material status of a historical memory. As the comments about John Hughes's films indicate, a film's characters and world can appear as real, as "friends" that hearken back to the 1980s. Given that this decade is the era in which many of these college students first encountered cinema, it is not surprising that its films are most enshrined in remembrance.

In the previous chapter, I analyzed how the circulation of official nostalgia for classic Hollywood cinema via cable movie channels attempts to rewrite the past and present by defining cinema and, by inference, American society as reflecting progressive democratic principles (such as feminism and civil rights). Nostalgia typically has such an affirmative function. While official sources of nostalgia depict historical conflicts that could detract from a rosy picture of American life only in order to put them to rest, personal recollections recorded in the study do not appear to require this sanitation of unseemly elements. Instead, viewers appear unaware of or have chosen to ignore the crises that defined the times in which they first saw their favorite films. In fact, for some, it is the present that is complicated with "all its sex/drugs/alcohol crap." When a sense of dysfunction in the present empowers nostalgia, the past often represents an antidote to social complexity. Even if survey viewers didn't express condemnation of the present, they see the appeal of 1980s films as providing access to a period of open, uncompromised potential. Either way, movies become vehicles for celebrating the past's problem-free virtues.

What matters most to the study's re-viewers, then, is that these films take them back to their childhoods, a time when they were unaware of larger social contexts. Although they are now in a position to be informed of the political aspects of the 1980s, they prefer to remember less directly politicized aspects of these years. This attitude contrasts sharply with that of historians on the left, who would have difficulty remembering the Reagan and Bush administrations nostalgically. Further, academic critics have viewed *Star Wars* and *Raiders of the Lost Ark* as regressive fantasies that keep their audiences locked in a state of childhood and promote paternalistic and conservative views of women, sexuality, and race in the face of social upheavals around these issues.[54] From this perspective, the repeated nostalgic return to 1980s films masks their ideological operations and relationship to a conservative political era.

As the early years of the twenty-first century have seen a resurgence of the 1980s as fashionably "retro," even chic, among young adults, the eclipse of politics attains a significant place in public memories of the era.[55] Young adult feelings about 1980s films and other relics of the period are the frequent subject of nostalgia sites on the Web. Web testimonials suggest not only that nostalgia tends to be apolitical but also that it is bound inextricably to popular and consumer culture. Thus, the designer of one Web site writes, "I grew up at a most opportune time, when the country was being run by an obsolete actor named Ronald Reagan. I remember liking him for the sheer fact he seemed like a nice old man; I knew nothing about what he was doing to our economy or nation. I only saw his rosey cheeks and likable smile, and thought 'wow, he's gotta be nice.'" Another comments, "The '80s were a great time for me. I don't remember much other than pop culture material. But what I do remember is having a great time with great people and great friends." Those posting messages express a strong, enduring identification with the decade, frequently expressing sentiments such as this: "If there's anything you need to know about me, it's this: I am, forever, a Child of the '80s. I inevitably have to grow up, but I do not have to grow out. You can take the '80s away, but cannot take me away from the '80s. They were the foundation years of my life and made so many things possible." Love of the 1980s seems to be grounded in the ways in which the decade's personal relevance, located in its popular cultural look and feel, supersedes consideration of its social and political events.

Discussion boards cite numerous elements as composing the era's cultural zeitgeist, including Jordache jeans, Izod apparel, the video game Frogger, Pee Wee Herman, Molly Ringwald, and Valley girls, as well as certain music, TV shows, and films. Sites often pose questions about such icons to promote a sense of self-identification and community in relation to the period. In a site called "It Came from the 1980s," if users answer yes to a series of questions (e.g., "Have you ever seen a movie with Corey Feldman/Haim or Molly Ringwald? Have you stayed up all night playing the original Super Mario Brothers, Frogger, Pac-Man, or Space Invaders? Did you ever idolize Ferris Bueller and think that Matthew Broderick was just as cool?"), they "probably grew up in the greatest decade human existence has had to offer . . . the 80s!!!!!" and can consider themselves a bona fide part of this period.[56]

As for 1980s media, Web site directories provide year-by-year listings of the films, music, and television shows that played during the decade, as well as information on how to buy them. Films that long ago exhausted their theatrical runs, such as *The Breakfast Club* and *Ferris Bueller's Day Off*, have their own Web sites, and trivia contests on movie dialogue from the 1980s abound. As the 80's Film Preservation Society home page observes, "What can we say? No other decade has produced as many movies that define the attitudes, music, and culture of the time period in question. . . . The manifesto of this society is a simple one . . . these films should not be remembered only as programming fodder for [cable]. . . . They should be honored as the works of art they are, and viewed at the least on video tape sans commercial interruption." In addition to the above favorites, *Back to the Future* (1985), *Dirty Dancing, Fast Times at Ridgemont High* (1982), *Sixteen Candles, Raiders of the Lost Ark, Star Wars,* and *Goonies* (1985) help to compose the list of hit films on this site.[57]

There is a strong correlation between films mentioned in the survey and those celebrated on Web sites, signaling the widespread role nostalgia plays in appraising '80s films. Further, like other generations before them, "children of the '80s" feel that theirs was the defining American generation and use this feeling of privilege as a means of community building and self-identification. Like other forms of nostalgia, the yearning for yesterday inspired by 1980s movies can obscure awareness of politics or treat it as a colorful backdrop to more personal issues; what is important is the autobiographical trip the film allows its viewer to take. Although a film reencounter can possibly inspire a "bad trip" that arouses negative memories, the survey respondents indicated that for them films act mainly as vehicles to a fondly remembered youth.

Because of its inherent comparative dimension, however, time travel through films is not as stable as it might first appear. As one female viewer in the survey noted, "I can remember the person I was when I watched the film then and compare that to who I am today—how I can view the exact same movie and come away with different feelings. You always notice different things with each screening (as you grow older and change). The more you watch a movie, the reason why you watch it changes." For some, movies that once appeared believable to the childhood self (such as *Goonies*, for example) appear now as pure fantasy, creating a tension between the desire to reexperience the innocent viewing and the awareness that perceptions have changed. Between these two poles, the viewer may chart a course from his or her younger self to the present self as well as realize differences across a spectrum of topics, including the political and the historical. While movie nostalgia can promote a regressive self-awareness at the expense of sociopolitical consciousness, repetition allows viewers to reflect comparatively on then and now. Movie reencounters thus have the capacity to startle the viewer into recognizing contrasts—between younger and older selves, between social realities in the past and present—that are not subsumed by reverie or romanticism.

As Henry Jenkins and Lynn Spigel have argued, the goal of research on mass culture and popular memory "is not to obliterate the 'distorted' memories from the historical record, but to account for their construction of historical consciousness. By examining memories of past events, we might better understand the processes by which people shape their past and understand their present."[58] In this sense, nostalgia experienced by children of the '80s as they rewatch films suggests that the pleasures of "regression therapy" tend to overcome other realizations this experience may offer. Moreover, the films that viewers embrace as time machines help to consolidate generational, gender, and other bonds, broadly affirming this vision of the decade among certain groups. Yet, as nostalgia counterposes two or more eras, it represents the possibility of a critical reassessment of self and the world. Since movies can now be re-viewed throughout a lifetime, their capacity to evoke either response is endless.

The last major motivation for re-viewing I discuss is the memorization and recital of film dialogue. In comparison to other motivations I have considered, the viewer's desire to repeat films in order to master their dialogue seems more fleeting and less substantial in its implications for home film culture. However, dialogue mastery explicitly embodies a key aspect of domestic film viewing that more subtly informs other motivations for replay. Memorization and recital vividly realize the interactive and performative dimensions of home viewing.

Karaoke Cinema

The cover of the spring 2000 Special Collector's Edition of *Entertainment Weekly*, celebrating the magazine's tenth anniversary, is bordered by a procession of lines from songs, motion pictures, and TV shows that have become commonplace parts of American language. From *Seinfeld*, there is "Yada, yada, yada"; from *The Sixth Sense*, "I see dead people"; from a Ricky Martin song of the same title, "livin' la vida loca!"; and from *Austin Powers*, "Oh, behave!"; and so on. The cover signals one of the chief ways in which media texts achieve true popularity—by becoming the source of catchphrases that work themselves into everyday discourse.

Some high-profile catchphrases seem to storm the nation, but the use of films as raw material for quotables far exceeds these more visible examples. Those surveyed frequently explained that they re-view films in order to memorize lines so that they can quote them either when they see the film again or afterward in conversation with peers. A male student explained how *Dazed and Confused* was an important part of his high school experience: "We used to watch the film, quote the lines, and choose which characters were fictional representations of our friends and ourselves." This student, who also knows *Half-Baked* (a comedy about a group of potheads) by heart, continued, "Quoting lines from films is a part of my life and a bond within my group of friends. We constantly return to certain scenes because of their humor. I love being totally accurate when I quote a film. I like to know the lines, the delivery, the context, the visuals, everything. Watching a movie repeatedly helps me memorize." This function works in relation to specific subcommunities as well. For example, a student who is in a band reviews the rock mockumentary *This Is Spinal Tap* (1984) as a source of catch-phrases and inside jokes: "If you're in a band, you *must* know every line by heart."

As one older student remarked of movie quotation, "I see it as a tendency of mine more when I was younger (16–24), and having to do with social groups I was in—developing a shared language or an expertise over a body of culture." In this sense, quoting becomes part of what Eric Havelock calls a "tribal encyclopedia," a common idiom that helps to mark and unify a social group. The tribal functions of memorization extend into everyday life. Viewers repeatedly watch films to "steal the dialogue" so that they can employ it later in social interactions. Thus, friends may watch the Coen brothers' *The Big Lebowski* to use its lines "in conversations either as an allusion or because the dialogue strikes us as particularly relevant or effective in a situation." One viewer of *Kids* (1995) and *Dazed and Confused* had this to say: "The one-liners and humor—they remind me of my friends because we get a lot of our language from these movies. When the two movie lingos are mixed—it can make for some funny conversations."

In this way, dialogue memorization becomes yet another means of displaying mastery and proficiency within the group—a dynamic that can be seen in a film such as *Reality Bites* (1994), in which Gen X characters continually spout references to popular culture that, among other things, measure belonging and "coolness" (leading Michael [Ben Stiller] to be seen as a dolt for not knowing a quote from *Cool Hand Luke* [1967]). Similarly, students frequently remarked how much they enjoy being able to quote a scene word for word as a means of impressing their friends. By showing their conversancy with favorite texts and even possibly their superior skills at this game, they appear as film experts. Many times this expertise is based not just on a few lines but on the entire film's dialogue. Web sites with topics such as "Movies you know by heart or, at least, nearly word for word" imply that this more full-scale memorization is a part of broader teen and young adult patterns of film consumption. Fans posting on this site mention *Ferris Bueller's Day Off*, *The Breakfast Club*, *Goonies*, *The Princess Bride* (1987), *Star Wars*, and other titles familiar from the survey as part of a quotable canon.[59]

As testimonials suggest, line quotation is also a form of play and performance. At times, the performative dimension is literal. A student who watches Tom Cruise films such as *Top Gun* and comedies such as *Dumb and Dumber* with his friends wrote, "We know most of the lines so we will say them when they come up or after we're done watching the movie we will get into one scene and reenact the whole thing for fun." A social setting enhances the experience but is not necessary for those who enjoy solo quoting. A male re-viewer who bought a copy of Baz Luhrman's *Romeo and Juliet* commented, "Now that I own it I will have it on while I'm cleaning my room so I can quote the movie while cleaning." Viewers thus memorize and vocally reenact cinema's dialogue for various purposes. As with singing one's favorite song lyrics, part of the pleasure in repeating films lies in performance. Cinema thus becomes a karaoke-like experience.

Practiced in bars across the world, karaoke is the art of singing in the shower writ into public space. Invented in Japan in the 1970s and popularized in the United States and elsewhere in the 1980s, karaoke involves amateurs who sing a familiar song with recorded musical accompaniment in front of an audience. The performance is mediated by the karaoke machine, an apparatus that includes a microphone, a sound source (such as a CD), visual images to accompany the music, a system of distribution for sound and image, and additional components, such as echo chambers.[60] The equipment differs, but the analogy between musical karaoke and karaoke cinema rests on regular people's adoption of mass cultural texts in acts of performance that rely on the recitation of well-known lines. In "Movieoke," the only public manifestation of karaoke cinema to date, amateur would-be thespians (many from the same demographic as my survey participants) stand before a movie screen and reenact a scene in front of an audience.[61]

In films (such as *My Best Friend's Wedding* and *Lost in Translation* [2003]) and TV shows (such as the WB's *Angel* and MTV's *Say What? Karaoke*), musical karaoke has often been portrayed as intrinsically comic and somewhat embarrassing. This can be true even when it serves as the occasion for a preprofessional moment in the spotlight or for an especially revealing glimpse into the singer's soul. The comedy is produced by the substantial gap between the tone-deaf amateur and more professional versions of the song. However, although karaoke offers the humorousness of the underdog vocalist as an attraction, it is more than a laughable spectacle. It accentuates certain elements of the relationship between audiences and mass cultural texts that we have also seen as central to responses to cinema—namely, the interactivity of media experience, the use of media to consolidate identities and bestow status, and the personalization of texts. In this sense, karaoke is a model of the functions and pleasures of repetition.

Like cinematherapy and nostalgia, the inherently interactive karaoke cinema can cut both ways ideologically. On the one hand, this mode of film appropriation guarantees a place for the media text in the viewer's subjectivity. Viewers who recite movie lines internalize the film to such an extent that it becomes part of their language, social life, and self-identification. During this process, they may simply accept the movie's ideological meanings—for example, borrowing, as Ronald Reagan did during his presidency, Clint Eastwood's popular phrase "Make my day" in situations that draw upon the expression's American machismo and intransigence in the face of obstacles. On the other hand, this form of interactivity can result in the viewer "finding his or her self strengthened and enlarged by the experience." Trying on the identities of those who speak the lines can possibly help one to "discover new potentials in oneself, in the modes of expression, and in the response of . . . friends."[62] Along with leading to this discovery of new meanings and hidden potentials, line performance allows for any number of ironies and disjunctions in meaning (think, for example, of Sex Pistol Sid Vicious's cover of the Frank Sinatra standard "My Way"). Inserted into different contexts, film dialogue has unpredictable, situation-dependent meanings.

The kinds of lines individuals tend to memorize help further to flesh out the functions of karaoke cinema. Certain commonalities emerge, especially in the responses of young men in the survey and on the Web. Male viewers are often attracted to "tough guy" catchphrases (e.g., "Hasta la vista, baby" from *Terminator 2: Judgment Day* and "Zed's dead, baby" from *Pulp Fiction*); comic lines ("Why, it's just a flesh wound" from *Monty Python and the Holy Grail* [1975] and "He slimed me!" from *Ghostbusters* [1984]); and sarcastic or antiauthoritarian comebacks ("Does Barry Manilow know you raid his wardrobe?" from *The Breakfast Club* and "Pardon my French, but you're an asshole!" from *Ferris Bueller's Day Off*). Macho, zany, or antiauthoritarian dialogue offers these audience members images of masculinity—from the supercool to the laughably inept to the rebellious—that they can perform over and over again (figure 21).

Since those participating in the ritual of memorization are often in their formative years, karaoke cinema functions at least partly to rehearse different types of masculinity deemed attractive by young men. Although the survey does not provide conclusive information about this aspect of the ritual, comments suggest that this play with roles, rather than involving daring experimentation, involves vicarious shifts of identity that fall within norms of masculinity. Like other pleasures involved in the repetition of favorite films, inhabiting familiar cinematic characters and memorizing their dialogue tend to secure and maintain individual and community identities within this group of viewers. Keeping in mind that repetition can inspire the exploration of new identities, we can see that line memorization often confirms gender and generational ties. Further, most of the films that partici-

Figure 21. *Ghostbusters.* Dr. Peter Venkman (Bill Murray): "He slimed me!"

pants regard as quotable are U.S. products, meaning that this form of popular cultural literacy may subtly contribute to the maintenance of national
identity as well.

Whether quoters are male or female, as they recite the dialogue, the
contrast between amateur reenactment and professional performance preserves the character of both theft and homage that karaoke represents. The
amateur "steals" lines, taking them out of context, while affectionately de-
ifying the original text with a devoted rendition. Bolstered by the per-
former's impersonation of a star, the act of theft attains an aura of clever-
ness. At the same time, the reciter's knowledge of the film allows him or
her to achieve the status of expert—the person who knows *The Breakfast
Club* or *Back to the Future* by heart. Herein lies another source of subcultural capital. Quoters gain symbolic clout via their association with Hollywood, rendered in karaoke cinema by vocalized performances of popular
films. In turn, films that are frequently quoted become canonized through
citation in everyday exchanges, making audiences a linguistic offer they
can't refuse.

Because quotation is a literal reenactment of a film, it provides an especially visible instance of the medium's closeness to home viewers. Like other
motives for returning to favorite titles, the familiarity involved in karaoke
cinema makes film a part of the viewer's social routine. It allows viewers to
use certain films to articulate their identities as well as to express their hopes
and dreams. Unlike audience identifications at public screenings of *The
Rocky Horror Picture Show* (1975) or the rereleased sing-along version of
The Sound of Music in 2000 (in which audiences dress up as film characters,
chant lines, and act out parts), karaoke cinema is both more pervasive as a

phenomenon and less campy. It is not a case of spectacular fandom, and, although self-consciously pursued, it is not always done with a winking knowledge of its own excesses. Karaoke cinema is a routine criterion by which some viewers choose to see a film again on the basis of its performative value and ability to speak to their individual and group identities.

Personalized films thus become cult films. In the words of Umberto Eco, they "provide a completely furnished world so that . . . fans can quote characters and episodes as if they were aspects of the fan's private sectarian world, a world about which . . . the adepts of the sect recognize through each other a shared experience." Elaborating on the tribal implications of this practice, Eco remarks that those who recognize a quotation "feel as if they all belonged to the same little clique."[63] However, while Eco suggests that only internally "ramshackle," or somehow imperfect, films can qualify for this status, Timothy Corrigan argues that because of the video revolution "any movie today can become a cult movie." Revising Eco's text-centric definition, Corrigan contends that cult has less to do with textual properties than with how audiences act on movies. As films become "the property of any audience's private space," they are transformed into "furnishings or acquisitions within which any modern viewer temporarily inhabits and acts out different subjectivities." Cult films are not born but made. Moreover, cult appropriations no longer take place only among marginal groups; in the remote-control era, they are a general part of the audience's experience. In this "contemporary commercial cult," technology allows mass audiences to make a "personal paradise" out of any film.[64] In this way, movies are all about the performance of the spectator. This is true literally for the mimicking of film dialogue, but it applies equally to other pleasures of repetition, especially when they translate the text into a personal script.

Although Corrigan laments cinema's domestication—its subjection to fragmentary practices and personalization—Henry Jenkins sees media domestication as an opportunity for viewers to wrest power away from media producers and bring texts "more fully under their control."[65] Given these contrary viewpoints, what, ultimately, do survey results suggest about the powerful types of personalization favorite films undergo when watched repeatedly in the home?

Our Heart's Desire

Even for the most familiar texts, viewing in its everyday manifestations is a rich process, engaging viewers' imaginations and needs as they engage with cinema. Young adults who seek the pleasures of aesthetics, cine-matherapy, nostalgia, and memorization enter into an active, discriminating relationship with their favorite titles, creating value and regions of taste, while sustaining or testing identities. Through film as well as other forms of popular culture, those surveyed craft distinctions that represent both generational alliances (the creation of a teen canon) and the constitution and maintenance of subgroups (e.g., puzzle film viewers). While the performance of lines from films appears to be the most interactive of the reasons for re-viewing, each reason involves strategies of textual appropriation that rewrite films according to viewer desire. Once a film is consumed multiple times, the importance of narrative chronology can diminish; suspense is supplanted by foreknowledge and the comfort familiarity can bring. This alteration in priorities enables returning viewers to convert films into personal narratives (e.g., stories that therapeutically offer them life lessons or nostalgic views of their own pasts) and/or material embodiments of group identity (e.g., represented by the communal rewatching of chick flicks).

Some "purists" in the survey indicated that they rewatch films from start to finish without manipulation. However, repetition otherwise makes narratives highly frangible—especially likely to be fragmented or broken—because it inevitably transforms texts into well-known territories. Such frangibility is mediated by a shifting network of forces that help to foreground certain textual features over others.

The combination of genre and playback technologies alone begins to illustrate the selective practices of reception that define cultures of film repetition. Using the remote control, repeat viewers can focus on a film's "high points," which in turn often crystallize its generic identity. Many in the survey said they fast-forward to or replay the funniest jokes in a comedy, the most romantic scenes in a romance, the most apocalyptic turns in an action film, or the musical numbers in a musical, locating scenes that represent the essence of the film's genre. In this way, rewinding and fast-forwarding intervene in the consumption of films, particularly when, by dint of familiarity, audiences know what scenes to target as they re-view. Technology, generic competence, and familiarity are mutually reinforcing factors that inspire the bypassing of textual chronologies, providing immediate access to features that constitute a film's generic highlights or particular zones of pleasure. However, generic and other cinematic elements attain their captivating status because they are themselves situated within other frames of reference that enter into the relationship between film and viewer.

As we have seen, the puzzle film's narrative and visual characteristics gain their meaning and significance for the survey's participants from a cluster of forces, including industry discourses invested in the construction and circulation of aesthetic value and certain hierarchies in youth culture. Similarly, the chick flick attains particular resonance through associations with certain female stars, the legacy of the fairy tale, popular feminism, and self-help culture. The specificity of each viewer's response to these replay-worthy genres is shaped further by preexisting templates of identity created from yet other social and historical dynamics. Although individual response thus becomes a matter of an infinite regress of possibilities, we can observe the degree to which acts of viewing display traces of the clamoring discourses that surround film consumption in the home.

As Raymond Williams argues, such determinations set limits and exert pressures, "within which variable social practices are profoundly affected but never necessarily controlled."[66] Given the examples of personalized responses to popular texts in the survey, we can see that these texts are used within processes of socialization, just as we can see that possibilities for slippage and critique exist. Like music and novels, film and television can exercise substantial, even life-changing, effects on the way people see themselves and the world. Sometimes these effects materialize merely as small adjustments of identity within the mainstream (e.g., male viewers who feel emboldened by macho slogans such as "Make my day"). But they can also involve reassessments of identity.

In this respect, perhaps the most volatile social aspect of repetition lies in its diachronic dimension. The capacity for favorite films to accompany individuals through their lifetimes gives repetition contrasting potentials. Repeated experiences with the same film can operate normatively, continually reaffirming appropriate gender identities, for example. By the same token, favorite texts can continue to inspire feelings of liberation in women looking for strong role models (even in what appears to be a compromised genre such as the chick flick) or to offer hope to those struggling with nonnormative identities (such as the viewer who sees certain films as confirming the possibility of happiness for lesbians). As repetition forces viewers to recognize and negotiate continuities and differences between past and present selves, it may inspire nostalgia or elicit revisionist constructions of meaning. These kinds of instabilities exist in every motivation for repeat viewing. At a microlevel, repetition thus represents a means by which, over time, quotidian acts of film consumption in the home maintain the cultural status quo or, conversely, spark and sustain desires for change.

When, in this chapter's epigraph, John Cawelti describes how reading the same bedtime stories over and over again results in the world taking "on the shape of our heart's desire"—the sense of comfort and mastery that ensues from contact with the familiar—he deftly expresses the sublime pleasure that repetition can afford. At the same time, our heart's desire is never as personal as it appears to be, because it is the subject of massive appeals by media and social institutions as well as the continual negotiations that ensue between the self and the world.

Repeat Viewings of Films: Survey Questions

1. When you were a child (ages 3–12), do you remember watching the same films over and over again? If so, what are the titles of these films? If you're able to estimate, how many times do you think you watched each one?

2. Are there films that you've watched in your teens and 20s repeatedly (more than 5, 10, 20 times, etc.)? What are the titles, and how many times do you think you've watched each?

3. Now that you've listed the films you like to watch over and over again and how you like to watch them, say *why* you like to watch them. What brings you back to these films over and over again? What kind of enjoyment or pleasure do you get from watching a film multiple times?

4. Do favorite stars, directors, genres, or other things influence what films you like to watch again and again? That is, are there some characteristics or features your repeat movies tend to share?

5. When you watch these films repeatedly, do you view them from start to finish as you might in a movie theater or select particular scenes (through fast-forwarding or other devices) that you like to watch over again? Or is it more that you like to have these films on while you're doing other things? Please give some specific examples of how you like to watch your repeat movies.

6. Do you do most of your repeat viewings in movie theaters, on cable and/or satellite television, VHS, laser disc, DVD, or pay-per-view? Or a combination?

7. Do you usually wind up viewing your repeat movies by yourself or with friends—or both ways? Is there a reason you prefer alone or with friends?

8. Would you say that watching movies multiple times is a central part of your activities as a viewer (something you love to do and take time for), or is it more marginal than that or nonexistent as a desire?

9. Whether it's important, marginal, or nonexistent as a desire in relation to movies, are there other forms of media (television, music CDs, video or computer games, etc.) where repetition of the same episodes, same songs, or same games is a big part of your life? Describe.

5 To Infinity and Beyond
The Web Short, Parody, and Remediation

> No medium, it seems, can now function independently
> and establish its own separate and purified space of cultural
> meaning.
>
> **Jay David Bolter and Richard Grusin,** *Remediation,* 2000

As we have seen in previous chapters, television has proven to be a tube of plenty for cinema, providing millions of viewers with film content through numerous means, from cable broadcast to DVD playback. After nearly sixty years of marriage between the two, it is difficult to think of cinema without television, a medium that has become indispensable to the film experience. Recently, however, nontheatrical film exhibition has tapped into the potential of a different home screen: the computer monitor. Although its possibilities are far from being fully realized, the Internet is already a major mode of distributing films to Web-surfing home audiences. Via their computers, viewers can watch a vast assortment of films, from pirated Hollywood blockbusters to independent shorts, giving them another means of accessing movies beyond theatrical precincts.

Of course, Hollywood has heavily employed the Web to advertise its latest releases, creating sites to promote specific titles and stars. However, other kinds of Web sites are explicitly devoted to film screenings that enable viewers in homes, offices, and dormitories across the nation and around the world to watch entire films. After a hesitant start in the late 1990s with only a handful of Web sites showing films,[1] these sites numbered in the hundreds by 2003. As a result, tens of thousands of films are available legally and hundreds of thousands illegally on the Internet every day.[2]

My discussion will touch on the Internet exhibition of feature films, but I am primarily interested in a different variant of Web cinema—specifically, dot-coms that show original short films by amateur and professional film-makers. With its shift away from the home distribution of Hollywood features, this chapter represents a departure from previous case studies. Yet, as I will endeavor to show, examining Internet shorts provides an ideal springboard for a close examination of the synergies between cinema and the digital age in the realm of nontheatrical exhibition. Moreover, this examination, by providing a view of the media businesses, technologies, films, and viewing strategies involved in this new venue, contributes from a different angle to the book's running concerns.

Like cable television, DVD, and other developments, the Internet demonstrates the intricate relationships cinema has to ancillary exhibition technologies and media—in this case, allowing us to focus on the specific impact of the digital on cinema. Scholars have pondered this impact primarily in relation to the theatrical film, focusing either on the image (e.g., the changes in the ontology of the photographic image due to digitization) or on the industry (e.g., assessing Hollywood's alliances with new media companies).[3] Studying Internet film exhibition prompts investigation of how the so-called digital revolution has affected cinema on the small screen. More generally, studying the area of exhibition itself enables a particularly synthetic view of the interactions between cinema and the digital: the practice of exhibition is linked to other industry practices at the same time as it bears upon the aesthetics and reception of cinema. Because the Internet embodies an especially energetic and expansive union of past and emerging forms, it offers something else of importance to my study. Its polyglot nature presents a fitting opportunity to meditate more overtly than I have on how cinema's identity as a medium is influenced by the intermedia context that defines all types of home film exhibition.

Analyzing the short film accentuates and extends the implications of other issues I have addressed. The short film, like the chick flick and puzzle film, is a genre that has gained particular prominence in home film cultures. The live-action and animated shorts that serve as the chief source of content for short film dot-coms are pervasively present on the Internet and streamed by scores of users. However, unlike these other genres, the film short does not typically begin life on the silver screen; it has not appeared regularly in theatrical venues for decades. Now almost exclusively associated with the nontheatrical circuit, it is a true denizen of the alternate universe of film exhibition I have been describing. As the short vividly incarnates the nontheatrical film, it also represents a particularly material instance of viewer activity. The home theater enthusiast, the collector, and the repeat viewer are engaged in productions of various kinds—respectively, assembling an ideal system, organizing a personal archive, and selecting a canon of repeatable favorites. However, the fan who makes a film and circulates it on the Internet literally participates in film production and exhibition, more manifestly displaying the overlap between producing and consuming cultures.

Surprisingly, the short also brings us back to the persistence of Hollywood and its imperative of film recycling in exhibition. Although many short films are made by amateurs, individually financed or supported by small studios, and distributed through sites that define themselves as homes for independent filmmaking, the Web short is not as divorced from commercial cinema as it might at first appear. As in the case of other venues involved in the home delivery of films, the Web presents cinema through a matrix of discourses and standards of taste informed by the film industry. The Web short, for example, is indebted to various genres, such as animation, comedy, and horror, that have circulated endlessly on the big screen. Further, certain popular shorts on the Internet overtly depend on Hollywood's blockbusters and other films for their very existence. I speak here of the short film parody—a genre that fan filmmakers have made into a signature element of Web cinema and that also, as it sends up the industry's films, recycles them in the home in altered form. Analyzing the Web short thus subtly resurrects the issue of Hollywood's presence in the home and its impact on home film cultures.

I must add that, given the uncertainties of the Internet movie business, my discussion of Web cinema cannot be predictive. The same years that saw the first substantial surge in streaming video dot-coms (1999–2002) also witnessed the decline of a stock market previously energized by dot-com success and the increasing instability of the fortunes of companies venturing into the Internet business. The much-heralded merger of Time Warner Inc. and America Online in 2001 resulted in serious economic difficulties, particularly on the AOL side of the business, leading to questions about the feasibility of the media conglomerate composed by this kind of partnership. It is thus impossible to gauge with certainty the directions the movie dot-com business will take. Breaking technological developments add yet another dimension of changeability to Internet cinema. The quality of sound and image delivery is subject to continual improvement, assuring substantial alterations in current standards of transmission.

Rather than attempting to predict the future of Web cinema, then, I wish to capture a significant historical moment in the development of this exhibition venue for films. I focus primarily on the state of Web cinema as it existed from 1999 to 2002—a threshold period when streaming video sites gained real momentum and achieved cultural visibility. Like other dot-com enterprises, some of the companies I discuss are sure to disappear from the digital landscape; film sites rise and fall with ritual regularity. But their practices and the films they have screened mark a major turning point in film history that has considerable implications for understanding cinema's relationship to the information age.

I begin by discussing the short film, examining the factors that led to its proliferation on the Internet. I then turn to two case studies that help gauge the contexts in which short films appear to viewers. First, I profile one of the largest Web film companies specializing in the form—AtomFilms.com. This company commenced operations in 1998 at the threshold of the boom in online movie sites and, by 2002, was voted by Internet Video Magazine as one of the two top Web sites (along with Ifilm.com) providing access to shorts. With its pioneering status and success, AtomFilms provides a means of analyzing Internet business operations and exhibition strategies. Second, I analyze film parody. As inevitably tied to its source text, the parodic short graphically illustrates the complex relationship between fan films and commercial cinema, as well as the strategic interplay between production and consumption in fan filmmaking. Given their strong affiliation in different ways with Web culture and their spawning of substantial online parody industries during the period of my study, the takeoffs on *The Blair Witch Project* (1999) and *Star Wars—Episode I: The Phantom Menace* (1999) serve as my particular focus.

Ultimately, investigating the genesis of the online short, the operations of a Web film company, and the intricacies of film parody allows us to consider in detail the dynamics of the cinema-Internet relationship and major factors that have helped to define this recent and rapidly growing home film culture. This final set of case studies will also lead us to examine what the intermedia contexts characteristic of ancillary exhibition mean for cinema both in and beyond its appearances on the domestic front.

The Rise of the Web Film

We can define a Web film as one that has had sustained first-run exhibition on the Internet. Whether amateur or professional, a Web film is a production that either has been expressly designed for exhibition in this venue or has found its initial audiences there (outside of film festival competition). When screened in this new venue, Alfred Hitchcock's *The Lady Vanishes* (1938) would not be considered a Web film, while "405: The Movie," a short that premiered in 2000 on 405themovie.com and Ifilm.com, would classify.

Experimentation with Internet premieres of features has occurred,[4] but because of technical difficulties, anxieties about piracy, and other concerns, Hollywood has been reluctant thus far to embrace fully this new window as viable for first-run feature exhibition. As a result, most Web films appearing legally have been shorts, that is, according to the definition used by many film festivals, animated or live-action films lasting no longer than thirty minutes.

In 2000, observers estimated that more than three hundred thousand film shorts were made each year, and almost one hundred short film Web sites already existed (a select list of sites appears at the end of the chapter); in that year, one site alone—AtomFilms.com—received from five hundred to one thousand shorts per week to consider for exhibition. Such activity has caused short entertainment to be considered "one of the hottest businesses on the Web."[5] Even companies not previously in the streaming video business have embraced the short. BMW, for example, has produced a series of mininarrative films (under the umbrella title *The Hire*) to stream on its site BMWfilms.com as a means of attracting users to its home page and selling its products. In a particularly overt coupling of product placement and cinema, these films, directed by such well-known filmmakers as John Frankenheimer, Ang Lee, and Guy Ritchie, star Clive Owen as a driver of different kinds of BMWs in dramatic situations that show off the cars to great advantage.

Critics have greeted the appearance of Web films with a variety of nicknames meant to capture their unique circumstances of exhibition as well as their hybridity: for example, *cybercinema, microcinema, click flicks, the gigaplex,* and *e-cinema. Pocket cinema* and *cinema wear* have described movies designed "to go," that is, movies for viewing on devices such as PlayStation Portables (PSPs) and Pocket PCs. Another prominent coinage, *Webisode,* refers to Internet shows that, like TV series, have regular installments featuring the same characters in different narrative situations (such as Brilliant Digital Entertainment's *Xena, Warrior Princess,* adapted from the TV program of the same name). Since the *e-* prefix accords with the standard means of recognizing a fusion between an existing concern and the Internet (e.g., e-mail, e-trade, and e-book), *e-cinema* or *e-film* seem the most appropriate terms to use when referring to a Web film.

The proliferation of e-films has led critics to hail the Web as representing a new golden age of the short. From the moment cinema appeared (with the minute-long films of Lumiere and Edison), the short has been a steady part of the medium's identity. Avant-garde and independent films, newsreels, serials, comedies, educational films, animations, and documentaries have all been produced in short form. In terms of public visibility, the film short achieved its greatest prominence for decades as part of theatrical exhibition, often accompanying the feature in the program. However, the rise of the Hollywood blockbuster in the 1970s—a high-cost venture that required more daily screening of features to maximize profits and more trailers to draw audiences to upcoming blockbusters—helped to end the omnipresence of the theatrical short. Although television advertisements, cartoons, and music videos have maintained a place for this form in the commercial media universe, the film short as it was once known was displaced from theatrical exhibition by pressing economic considerations. Relegated to film festivals and annual nominations at the Academy Award ceremonies, it fell into obscurity.

The renaissance of the short on the Internet was tied initially to certain technological constraints. Before the end of the 1990s, users venturing onto the Internet to watch moving pictures would encounter a tiny, matchbook-sized image that, should they try to enlarge it, would become severely pixelated (broken up into mosaiclike tiles). In addition, viewers would experience lengthy waits for the transmission of an entire film, only to encounter images and sounds that flowed with an unsettling herky-jerky rhythm (a stop-and-start motion caused by pauses in the image and sound flow as more data were streamed). Such limitations help to explain why shorts became so quickly the sine qua non of this new venue; involving smaller files and thus easier and faster to stream, brief films were less of a nightmare to view than feature films. However, the more widespread growth of shorts on the Internet (as well as feature films and other moving-image forms) depended on a mix of technological, economic, and social factors that ameliorated or resolved these initial problems.

According to John Geirland and Eva Sonesh-Kedar, in 1999, more than "70 percent of the approximately 60 million users of the Web" looked for "some form of entertainment content—shows, entertainment information, music, sports, and games" when they went online.[6] The Web was no longer strictly synonymous with information; media-based programming had become a vital part of its offerings and allure. In this sense, the upcropping of film Web sites was part of a trend that defined cyberculture as devoted as much to amusement as to information. The appearance of faster computers and improved sound systems helped to improve the Internet's status as an appropriate place for audio-visual entertainment. However, the introduction of streaming video, improvements in broadband technologies and access, and the increased availability of DV equipment and movie-making computer software were especially important in fueling the return of the film short.

In the second half of the 1990s, Apple, RealNetworks, and Microsoft produced streaming video players entitled, respectively, QuickTime, RealVideo, and Windows Media Player, enabling moving images to materialize on individual computers almost simultaneously with their transmission. Following in the footsteps of compression technologies designed for music, such as RealAudio, streaming video players compressed and decompressed video information in real time, solving the troublesome issue of the interminable delivery of large data files. Viewers could watch video as it was being transmitted rather than having to wait for the completion of the entire process. Because of Microsoft's aggressive preinstallation of media players, they quickly became an indispensable accessory to personal computers. According to Media Metrix, Inc., by 2001 media players were installed on 99 percent of U.S. home PCs.

However, this advance did not sufficiently resolve other problems with the delivery of sound and image. Because capturing video and its rapidly changing images and sounds involves a large amount of digital information and thus consumes a great deal of bandwidth, standard analog dial-up modems result in inferior video and audio reproduction. When consumers go this route, they still find the image small, blurry, pixelated, and jerky. Because they provide greater speed and volume, broadband solutions, such as Digital Subscriber Line (DSL) and cable modems, result in faster and clearer transmission. With the high-speed Internet connection enabled by these and other technologies (such as satellite and fixed wireless), audio and video are largely free of interference, flowing clearly and smoothly. In addition, although the size of the window will vary depending on screen resolution and monitor settings, the film image can appear in a larger rectangle that surpasses its prior minuscule dimensions. While only 2.5 million broadband subscribers had taken advantage of these significant improvements by early 2000 and roughly 12 million by the end of 2001, a total of 22.5 million residences subscribed to cable and DSL Internet services in North America in mid-2003. EMarketer, an e-business research and analysis company, estimates that approximately 86 percent of the 50 million people going online at work in the United States have access to high-speed Internet connections.[7]

The penetration of streaming video players and broadband technologies into the consumer market has thus made watching movies and other streaming media on the Web not only increasingly feasible but also increasingly attractive. Because the short is still easier to stream and download than the feature film, these developments have helped to enhance its ubiquitousness on the Internet. Although some Web sites offer "high-definition" services, the movie experience in general still does not compare in quality to the theater or DVD. Nonetheless, viewers armed with a relatively powerful computer with speakers, a streaming video player, a high-speed Internet connection, and perhaps plug-ins, such as Macromedia Flash, can watch scores of shorts with relative ease, clarity, and VCR-like control that allows them to stop, rewind, or fast-forward at will.

Along with such technological advances, nontheatrical filmmaking itself has experienced changes that privilege the short. For one thing, access to production is simply broader. Bundled computer software designed for home moviemaking (including Apple's iMovie, Dell's Movie Studio, and Steven Spielberg's Movie Maker Set offered by Lego Studios) allows anyone with a computer to make a film. More formally, the growth of film schools has created expanded opportunities for students to enter the world of filmmaking. Offering a cheaper and less complicated alternative to celluloid, digital video and digital postproduction in schools and other settings have even further opened up this world. For another thing, the short has certain advantages over the feature film as well as a firmly established institutional role that make it either unavoidable or especially attractive to beginning filmmakers. Because of the short's brevity, its production and editing are more manageable and cost effective, making it a long-standing fixture in studio classes. In addition, the short is considered an indispensable training ground for the development of feature filmmaking skills, a preparation for the longer productions that may lie ahead. In this sense, the short often acts as a bridge between amateur status and professional. Many filmmakers begin their careers with short films (e.g., Martin Scorsese, Peter Greenaway, and Jane Campion), while an initial creative involvement in music videos or television ads has paved the way for others to helm their own feature-length projects (e.g., Michael Bay, McG, and Spike Jonze). The short, then, is a classic apprenticeship form.

The short's entry-level function does not mean that it lacks an aesthetic or occupies a place only at the threshold of theatrical cinema. Like the short story, the e-film is a compressed text that must operate efficiently to achieve its impact. As Eileen Elsey and Andrew Kelly argue in their work on short filmmaking in Britain, the short can be understood as a kind of "concise image-making" that amplifies or magnifies principles that structure forms of longer duration, such as the feature film or the novel. Under this kind of pressure, the short film's strengths and weaknesses clearly emerge. At their best, shorts offer "crystalline creations of precise, prismatic intensity"; at their worst, they are "desperately" banal, with "enough tedium to empty a graveyard."[8] Sublime or ridiculous, successful or failed, the e-film provides a highly focused means of experimenting with ideas in miniature. Among other motivations, the expressive potential of the short is one reason why directors long engaged in feature filmmaking return to or rediscover this form (such as Jim Jarmusch, who made "Int. Trailer Night" in 2002).

Whether the incentive to make shorts is institutionally mandated, economically motivated, and/or aesthetically inspired, the Internet provides an extensive new outlet for these films, serving as a complement or an alternative to competitive offline film festivals. In turn, Web sites gain something valuable from the films that fill their archives: free or inexpensive programming. A brief look at the offerings of a few sites reveals that, underneath obvious differences, similar programming principles apply. Alltrue.com shows reality videos, Charged.com specializes in films that are just sixty seconds long, and PlanetOut.com exhibits a combination of independent and Hollywood films with gay subject matter, either explicit or implicit (e.g., Laurel and Hardy films). The largest, most recognized Web film sites, such as AtomFilms.com and Ifilm.com, screen independent or studio-affiliated shorts. Other sites are characterized by more eclectic programming. For instance, BijouFlix (at BijouCafe.com) offers a selection of "B" films, especially cult horror films, along with its shorts, and MovieFlix.com screens a broad selection of genre films, silent cinema, African American features, and foreign titles. Like cable TV channels, these sites attempt to cultivate a distinct personality through programming choices. In addition, new venues urgently need cost-effective content to survive—content that can be ably provided by a range of recycled features, "B" movies, films in the public domain, reality videos, and shorts. If a film is in the public domain or has exhausted its theatrical run, it provides a cheap programming solution for Web outlets. Similarly, many shorts represent a source of free material, since Web companies often do not pay e-filmmakers to exhibit their work (the opportunity to have their films shown is supposed to be sufficient reward). As in the case of early television, cinema represents ready-made, inexpensive programming attractive to content-hungry media enterprises.

Aside from technological and economic considerations, the rise of the Internet short may also be due to a certain resonance with the contemporary social context. The e-film is well-suited to the rhythms of work, media, and information cultures. Some office employees, students, and other viewers with access to high-speed connections routinely surf the Web for these "tiny bursts of entertainment." The short allows viewers "quick fixes" of entertainment in the workplace when the boss goes to lunch or at some other tempting moment, also enabling a "movie-addicted generation to budget its entertainment time."[9] The online short thus supplies an expedient antidote to office or school routine, while fitting seamlessly into both the surfing mentality that defines media experience and the multitasking sensibility that pervades computer culture. In this sense, Elsey and Kelly regard the film short as indicative of the contemporary zeitgeist. Rather than relating its new visibility explicitly to postmodern fragmentation and information overload, these authors see the short more generally as an incarnation of society's "velocity." In cultures where there is "less time available," audiences are drawn to forms that both embody and accommodate this acceleration. Given its brevity, the e-film does not involve the kind of commitment of attention, time, and energy required by "longer and bulkier" artifacts.[10] Within such a social and media-rich whirl, the short's very leanness once again becomes a prime virtue.

In this discussion of factors that have led to the short's extensive Web presence, it is important to note the wide variance in the actual degree of exposure that e-films achieve. The enormous number of shorts, coupled with the transient nature of Web exhibition and the uncertain life span of a dot-com, plunges any filmmaker's work into a dispersed and competitive environment. This situation makes it all the more impressive when titles do manage to rise to the top and achieve great success with Internet audiences. For example, George Lucas's student venture at the University of Southern California, "Electronic Labyrinth: THX 1138 4EB," a science fiction short shot in 1967 that was the basis for his first commercial feature, *THX 1138* (1971), was streamed more than eighty-six thousand times after its debut on AtomFilms, making it the tenth most popular short on the Web in 2000. When it premiered in the same year, "405: The Movie," by Jeremy Hunt and Bruce Branit (professionals nominated for an Emmy Award for best visual effects on *Star Trek: Voyager*), had forty thousand hits in its first week and one hundred thousand during its first month. By mid-2003, the figure rose to more than 4.5 million. Showing a near collision between a car and a jet on a Los Angeles freeway (a visual feat accomplished by using Macintosh computers and "off the shelf software" to combine live-action and CGI footage; figure 22), "405" is still considered not only a must-see film by Web cognoscenti but also the Internet's most successful short.[11] Most films do not fare this well, but at times the Internet has proven to be a highly effective distributor and exhibitor of shorts.

To explore in more depth short film exhibition and its place in home film culture, I turn now to case studies of AtomFilms.com and the film parody. By investigating an e-cinema business and a definitive Web genre, I am not proposing a direct causal link between the spheres of economic and cultural production—that somehow economic considerations absolutely determine

Figure 22. E-film favorite "405: The Movie."

the nature of the forms that appear. Rather, the case studies work together to produce a sense of the inherently diverse intermedia and intertextual nature of e-cinema as a business, a technology, and an aesthetic form.

The Next Generation Entertainment Company

Founded in 1998 in Seattle, Washington, and launched online in 1999, AtomFilms.com appeared at an opportune moment, just as the short film business on the Internet was about to take off. The company's main office has since moved to San Francisco, with satellite offices in Los Angeles, New York, London, and Tokyo. Previously in the music business at both Sony and EMI and in the media and entertainment division of software company RealNetworks, Mika Salmi founded AtomFilms and acts as its CEO. The company's other executives, board members, and advisers come from similarly mixed backgrounds in the information, advertising, music, film, television, and publishing industries.

The company's mission is to make shorts into a "big-time form of entertainment" that will reveal a "diverse group of emerging and established artists to viewers who are enjoying the thrills of real choice, quality, and creative discovery." It all "adds up to a powerful alternative to traditional entertainment practices—and this time, creators and consumers are in control." AtomFilms depicts itself as creating a new industry, a "next generation entertainment company," that "values artistic vision and community participation over power lunches and opening-weekend box office." The company does not yet advertise upcoming Hollywood releases on its home page—a connection that competitor Ifilm has aggressively pursued.[12] Rather, AtomFilms.com provides news about film festivals, independent filmmakers, and other subjects associated with alternative cinema. But, as we shall see, like the status of many who bear the label "independent," AtomFilms' definition as such is a complicated affair.

To gain a sense of the site's scope, we can consider the size of its user base as well as the breadth of its archive. In 2000, before its 2001 merger with major multimedia gaming site Shockwave.com (making it AtomShockwave Corp.), AtomFilms boasted approximately 1.5 million "insiders" (that is, registered users), with 160,000 films watched per day and millions of monthly streams and downloads. The site maintained an archive of more than a thousand films and animations. Since the merger, combined resources consist of more than two thousand games, films, and animations, with forty-five million registered users and sixteen million unique users every month.[13] Along with top honors from Internet Video Magazine, Media Metrix has ranked AtomFilms.com as one of the best twenty entertainment sites; it has also won two Webby Awards for film and broadband and has been selected as the "Forbes Magazine Favorite" for short film Web sites.

AtomFilms operates at once as a producer, distributor, and exhibitor of live-action and animated shorts (as well as digital media and games). Since, at present, the site does not charge users or receive remuneration from filmmakers, questions about how its multiple roles are funded naturally arise. As Salmi matter-of-factly states, "We do a combination of whatever it takes."[14] Of course, screening films that have already been produced and financed by others is a cost-effective tactic, but the major support for initiatives comes from investments by other companies, advertising revenue, and sponsorships or partnerships with other businesses. Through its sources of support, AtomFilms allows us to see how the balancing act between a self-described independent concern and commercial interests has materialized on the Internet. In fact, *Premiere Magazine* has referred to AtomFilms as the "Miramax of microcinema," the "premiere arena for hip online flicks." Despite its reputation as a champion of critically lauded, arty ventures that might not otherwise get mainstream backing, Miramax is owned by media titan Disney. AtomFilms' relationship with Shockwave echoes this arrangement.[15] Although it defines itself as existing in a world opposed to power lunches, it is situated within a larger, more successful enterprise with a mass market. Further, it has received millions of dollars of financing from companies such as Chase Capital Entertainment Partners, Intel, and Warner Bros. and has earned advertising dollars from Skyy vodka, Volkswagen, Swatch, RealNetworks, the Sony Corporation, and other well-known businesses.[16]

Mainstream commercial sources of revenue are important, but Atom-Films supports its productions through alliances that run the gamut. The site engages in sponsorships and partnerships that represent a cross-section of companies, including film companies, seeking to expand into the digital market. For example, the Ford Motor Company approached AtomFilms about funding a number of shorts that would feature its automobiles, representing a case of product placement that has found a "digital marketing solution." Three of these films, including Jason Reitman's "Gulp," played on AtomFilms and also at the Sundance Film Festival. Similarly, the site partnered with the Paramount Television Group to produce *Forty and Shorty,* an "edgy and twisted" Flash-animated series. Among less mainstream businesses, AtomFilms cooperated with production houses Matador Pictures and Odyssey Film and TV and with film financier MBP to produce a series of ten-minute shorts on the subject of time (called *Ten Minutes Older*) by celebrated directors such as Bernardo Bertolucci, Jim Jarmusch, Jean-Luc Godard, and Wim Wenders. AtomFilms has also cooperated with Propaganda Films (which produced *Being John Malkovich* [1999]) to make shorts for worldwide distribution.[17]

Such relationships are at the heart of AtomFilms' activities as a cyberstudio, the means by which it gains backing for the production of original content. Different kinds of companies—including large, established nonmedia enterprises such as Ford, big studios such as Sony, and smaller independent film operations such as Propaganda—help to fund amateur work while also giving commercial filmmakers the opportunity to experiment with the short form and digital distribution. However, affiliations with independent producers do not suffice to keep the Web site afloat. Its economic health depends on a complex financial mix, in which rounds of financing from well-known players and cosponsorships with major concerns not only support specific productions but also help to attract additional financing.

Along with its role as cyberstudio, AtomFilms distributes and exhibits works submitted by independent filmmakers as well as those produced from partnerships and cosponsorships (titles from Propaganda Films' archive, for example). Viewers can, of course, access AtomFilms' site or watch its shorts through handheld devices by clicking on the "Mobile Movie Theater" menu. However, AtomFilms has also distributed its fare through numerous online channels during its history, including Internet portals such as Yahoo.com, Ifilm.com, and Google.com; media sites such as Blockbuster.com and NBC's Snap.com; technology company sites such as Intel and UPC/Chello (a European broadband Internet service); and corporation sites such as Volkswagen.[18]

Beyond gaining content for their streaming video operations, Web companies are attracted to e-films because of their advertising value. For businesses interested in new entertainment channels as additional venues for advertisements, the film short provides a subtle means of assisting their goals. Executives expect that shorts will "capture eyeballs" more successfully than direct advertising, keeping visitors at sites for longer times and thus gaining greater exposure for the company's products and services. In addition, these businesses benefit from the aura of hipness associated with e-cinema and independent film in general. Although now defunct, VW.com/films, for instance, presented an introductory graphic featuring a drive-in movie screen with various silhouettes of Volkswagens parked in front of it. On the screen a scrolling text appeared. It began with "We've got a pretty independent streak. We love music. We love art. We love people who use our cars as canvases of self-expression." The text then introduced AtomFilms' shorts as edgy, thought-provoking, or just plain "weird," commenting that each has a distinctive point of view, much like "a certain car company." Independent shorts thus help to advertise the VW as a unique automobile that attracts individuals with a distinct and aesthetically inclined sense of identity. Similarly, one's choice of car becomes a means of self-expression equivalent to painting or filmmaking. This collapsing of commodities and art, of consumerism and self-expression, is a standard feature of advertisement, particularly as it attempts to flatter potential upscale audiences with images of unconventional individualism, disguising the commodity's status as mass-produced. Here, independent cinema functions as a maverick art form that can elevate both the automobile and consumer to the aesthetic vanguard.

Aside from multiple Internet platforms, AtomFilms has exhibited its shorts, albeit in a more ad hoc fashion, in traditional offline outlets associated with the film industry. Like a studio, AtomFilms has shown its films in theaters and at film festivals; it has also released shorts on VHS and DVD and to cable television and the airlines. In 2000, to qualify for Academy

Award consideration, a selection of the site's films appeared before the feature films at the grand opening of the Century Theater's CineArts 6 multiplex in Evanston, Illinois, and at another Century theater in North Hollywood.[19] Filmmakers often circulate their wares between the Internet and film festival circuits; likewise, AtomFilms routinely screens shorts at festivals such as Cannes and Sundance. In addition, the company periodically sells shorts in thematic packages (such as "Definitely Not Hollywood" or "Women in Film") on VHS and DVD. The site also has licensing agreements with cable TV networks that regularly program shorts, such as the Sundance Channel, the Sci Fi Channel, and the European company Canal Plus. Further, AtomFilms has shown its shorts on various airlines, including United, Continental, and Singapore. Always searching for more outlets, the Web site has negotiated with shopping malls to show shorts on monitors "to catch shoppers' attention and hold it for advertising" and with Otis Elevator, on whose conveyances passengers will presumably have equally fleeting cinematic encounters.[20]

Thus, shorts appear to audiences in myriad locales and through diverse business arrangements—with traditional and emerging companies, large corporations and smaller concerns, and commercial and independent interests. AtomFilms' varied associations demonstrate how thoroughly involved new digital companies are with existing enterprises, just as these enterprises strive to have a presence in emerging markets. Although no established business model has arisen to structure this interaction more systematically, it is doubtful that this orgy of alliances is just a product of the newness of Internet cinema. Such alliances are entirely in keeping with a culture that has seen the merger of corporate giants such as Viacom and CBS or AOL and Time Warner create vast multimedia empires that stretch from print to the Internet. Making connections across different companies and products is at the heart of contemporary business practice. At the same time, although amateur filmmakers contribute most of the programming and the site promotes itself as dedicated to alternative fare, its economic structure depends to a large extent on the support of major businesses that fund operations, provide content, bankroll films, and act as distribution outlets. AtomFilms thus provides a good example of a cyber-studio associated with independent cinema that is simultaneously strongly affiliated with corporate interests. In this sense, the company and its offerings parallel developments in the film industry, which has seen increasing connections between Hollywood and independent productions, making it difficult, at times, to tell one from the other.

Intricate interrelations between the old and the new, between commercial and independent, are manifest as well in the site's presentation of films. Perhaps more than any other home exhibition forum I have discussed, the short film Web site provides an array of modes of classifying films, ranging from familiar generic categories to more loosely defined classifications. Like other Web sites, AtomFilms.com mixes traditional genres with more ad hoc categories. We find conventional labels such as *animation, comedy,* and *drama.* However, the site defines each of these genres through numerous subsets of films that demonstrate how traditions have changed. Its home-page shows that comedy is composed of groups of films labeled as spoofs, star power, and romantic, among other categories. Animation is divided up into stop motion, Flash, and comedy; and drama, into romance, suspense, and documentary. Other major headings, such as "extreme," have no place in genre history, resulting instead from the application of contemporary parlance (e.g., extreme sports) to film. This colloquial genre, too, is further subdivided into of-the-moment categories, including "sexual," "twisted," and "violent."

AtomFilms also groups shorts within thematic showcases. One such showcase is the "Official *Star Wars* Fan Film Network" (supported by the *Star Wars* Fan Network and Lucas Online, a division of Lucasfilm Ltd.). It accepts submissions of *Star Wars*–related films, including parodies, and sup-plies sound effects, music, and other aids to filmmakers wishing to pay hom-age to the series. It then hosts an annual contest to honor the best fan films produced. Drawing more explicitly on the specificity of digital media, an-other showcase features an interactive dimension. In conjunction with the Sony Corporation, the site has sponsored the making of "immersive" films, each shot with a special Sony camera that photographs in the round. One of these films, Amy Talkington's "New Arrival," apparently concerns the journey of a group of senior citizens to a retirement home; its surprise end-ing is a self-reflexive joke about outdated technologies, as the new arrival to the home is none other than a TV set. Interactivity resides in the viewer's ability to navigate this simulated 360-degree space with a mouse, theoreti-cally seeing a different film each time.

Whether films fall under conventional or unconventional designations, whether they imitate Hollywood epics or engage in cutting-edge experi-ments, the proliferation of genres and classifications on AtomFilms.com demonstrates how invested exhibition venues are in branding films as a condition of their circulation. The incessant nature of this branding reveals the capaciousness and unpredictability of generic designation on the Web (genres can be formed on almost any basis from subject matter to tech-nique) as well as the presentational strategies that accompany films into the home. Similarly, while AtomFilms and other Web film companies celebrate their mission to show films that might not otherwise gain exposure or that challenge commercial cinema, their films are preponderantly mini-examples of classic or more contemporary colloquial genres. Numerous shorts fall into categories of established genres such as documentary and romance; however, even if they seem unconventional in the context of recognized categories in genre theory and criticism, they are affiliated with contemporary generic cycles. For instance, with their graphic depictions of blood, exposed broken bones, and eviscerations played for laughs, Aardman Studio's *The Angry Kid* and other extreme series exhibited on AtomFilms dovetail with gross-out trends in today's comedy on television and in film (e.g., *South Park, Jackass,* and Farrelly brothers' movies). Known categories lend recognition to the short, mapping out familiar patterns of access for viewers; reciprocally, the short's economical form and the presence of new directors and new techniques can refresh genres or generic cycles, subjecting them to revision.

In offering a compendium of genres, the Web, like the video store, represents a significant phenomenon for genre studies. It defies the usual sense of a linear progression in a genre's history from classic to more revisionist and deconstructive phases. Because of new technologies of distribution and exhibition, there is an encyclopedic display of genres in which all manner of texts, from the most formulaic to the most iconoclastic, coexist and are simultaneously available to the public.

Perhaps nowhere on the Internet is the simultaneity of different phases of a genre better demonstrated than in the case of parody. Since the Web itself is a multimedia enterprise extraordinaire, it is not surprising that parody—a genre that relies completely on intertextuality for its effects—flourishes there, creating a virtual cottage industry in the form. As in the case of AtomFilms, cross-media alliances play an unavoidable role in film form on the Web, constituting a dialectical play between the newly arrived and the already here.

E-Cinema Genres: The Parody

Mimicking the content and/or style of an original work for comic and, at times, satiric effect, parody embodies the principle that all texts are constituted through the allusion to and revision of other texts. Parody depends absolutely on the imitation of previous works, representing a mode of intertextuality that foregrounds the inevitable interrelation of cultural practices. As the short telescopes and magnifies the principles of longer forms in acts of "concise image-making" in the words of Elsey and Kelly, the e-parody affords a particularly vivid view of intertextuality in action.

From adaptations and remakes to movie franchises, recycling old stories is standard Hollywood business. Less formally but just as pervasively, films are often sold to Hollywood as amalgams of past box office successes or otherwise notable films, making their indebtedness to the past one of their most prominent features. Thus, a film such as *Conspiracy Theory* (1997), starring Mel Gibson and Julia Roberts, features an unbalanced, taxi-driving, would-be assassin brainwashed by government forces, drawing from both *The Manchurian Candidate* (1962) and *Taxi Driver* (1976) for its premise. *Angel Eyes* (2001), starring Jennifer Lopez and Jim Caviezel, rehashes previous films dealing with the supernatural, particularly *City of Angels* (1998), *The Sixth Sense*, and *Frequency* (2000). These are "high-concept" films, pitched to producers and sold to the marketplace on the basis of the twists they provide to proven formulas.[21]

This kind of rehashing is related to, but distinct from, the impulses of parody. The narratives to which high-concept films refer are typically sympathetic with their mission; that is, there is a generic fit among all films concerned. High-concept films ultimately incorporate and subsume the originals while reverently trading off of their "magic." By contrast, parody is a more self-conscious form of intertextuality that brandishes its relation to the original as its raison d'être. Its visible commentary on previous forms contrasts with the more common practice of seamlessly referencing prior texts without comic intent—without the desire to send up the original's sincerity. Rather than trying to integrate all texts involved, parodists expose the presumptions of the original for humorous effect. However, as we shall see, parody is not entirely immune from the desire to recapture the mojo of a source. As the *Star Trek* parody in *Galaxy Quest* (1999) suggests, send-ups can display great affection for the original, eventually reaffirming its fundamental conceits (as when the film's has-been cast of a science fiction TV series really is able to save the day).

Parody's relationship to its sources ranges from such affectionate affirmation to more critical engagements that question, like Mikhail Bakhtin's notion of the carnivalesque, the hegemony and legitimacy of official worldviews. Within the same era, there are "multiple ways in which parody can invite the reader to examine, evaluate, and resituate the hypotextual material."[22] No matter what parody's critical function may be, caught between an homage to and rivalry with an original form, it occupies a complicated position in relation to cultural authority—a subject to which I shall return.

A wide variety of media and cultural phenomena serve as objects of Web parody. For example, "Black XXX-Mas" (Pieter Van Hees, AtomFilms) is a blaxploitation-style rewriting of the childhood fables "The Night Before Christmas" and "Little Red Riding Hood." With its black characters, urban setting, and explicit sex and violence, this short rewrites the lily-white milieu of the former text and amplifies the sexual and violent content of the latter. There are numerous takeoffs of television shows, such as the HBO series *The Sopranos* (e.g., "The Falsettos," David Morris, Ifilm.com). "Meat Clown" (Brooke Keesling, AtomFilms.com) and "New Testament" (Philip Pelletier and Verne Lindner, Swankytown.com) lampoon, respectively, the fast food and advertising industries. E-parodies also vary in terms of technological and stylistic sophistication, from low-tech shorts made with Legos or plastic figures and "found" soundtracks to films with polished CGI and aural effects.

As these examples suggest, e-filmmakers are especially fond of parodying legendary, commercially successful, or otherwise high-profile staples of mass culture. E-shorts dedicated to parodying films are no exception. At over 270,000 views and counting, the animated film "Titanic: The True Story" (Julien Reininger, Ifilm.com) shows that the ship was actually sunk by a group of penguins bent on avenging the death of a friend killed by the luxury liner. *Gladiator* has spawned animated parodies on AtomFilms.com such as "Gaydiator" (Martin Gardner) and "Minimus the Gladiator," which send up, respectively, the presumed heterosexuality of the ancient warrior and his physical stature. Tom Cruise and *Mission Impossible 2* (2000) have been parodied in "Admission Impossible 2" (Terrill Thomas, Atom Films.com), an animated short that depicts Cruise's misadventures after he is refused entry to a roller-coaster ride at an amusement park when he fails to meet the height requirement. Perhaps one of the best known spoofs of a major Hollywood film is "Saving Ryan's Privates" (Craig Moss, Atom Films.com), a scatological short that transposes the title of Steven Spielberg's World War II drama *Saving Private Ryan* (1998) while maintaining the original's sincere voice-over and dramatic music to realize its satiric effects. In the short's revision of the film, an army platoon searches not for Ryan himself but for his blown-off genitals. Each of these films lampoons the self-important seriousness of successful texts and also at times deflates the presumptions of machismo that support Hollywood event films.

The parodic urge is strong enough, though, that even more obscure celebrated films can serve as inspiration. The "Revenge of the Red Balloon" (Gregg Rossen, AtomFilms.com) hearkens back to the French fantasy film *The Red Balloon* (1956), in which a young boy bonds with a balloon that follows him everywhere. In the parody, as the AtomFilms.com blurb says, the balloon returns to track down and kill the "nasty little garçons who popped him 40 years ago." The balloon's methods of murdering its attackers, now middle-aged men, include strangling one with its string and putting processed cheese on the toast of another who, being a Frenchman unaccustomed to such a culinary affront, falls off a balcony in shock. At the end of the short, the red balloon seeks the company of the one boy who befriended him, only to have the now-grown man pop him with his cigar. In perhaps the ultimate act of self-reflexivity, popular Web films themselves can draw parodic fire.[23] The much-viewed, award-winning "405" spawned a low-tech takeoff entitled "405 Too" (Scott Martin, Undergroundfilms.com), in which the viewer sees a man in a car but only hears of the mishap with the plane on the sound track. The point is that if a film has visibility of any kind, it can serve as grist for parody's mill.

Acknowledging the diversity of Internet parodies, I want to concentrate on a particularly prominent variation of the genre in this venue: the hybrid parody. This variation sends up more than one source, often involving quite disparate texts. Wordplay in the hybrid's title signals the bridging of texts that are incongruous in genre, narrative, and tone. Thus, borrowing a page from *Superstar: The Karen Carpenter Story* (1987), which is Todd Haynes's reenactment of the singer's life using Barbie and Ken dolls, "The Barbiecist" (Jim Hollander, Ifilm.com) provides a shot-by-shot re-creation of *The Exorcist's* (1973) closing exorcism scene, with a Barbie doll playing Linda Blair's possessed character and Ken dolls playing Catholic priests. Anthony Scarpa mixes *Being John Malkovich*, Spike Jonze's surreal comedy about a puppeteer who discovers a portal into the mind of actor John Malkovich, with the TV game show *Who Wants to Be a Millionaire?*, hosted by Regis Philbin, to produce "Being Regis Philbin" (Bijou Cafe.com). Similarly, in "Being Erin Brockovich" (Stephen Croke, Ifilm.com), Jonze's film is grafted onto *Erin Brockovich* (2000), Steven Soderbergh's story of a divorced mother's successful crusade against corrupt industry. *American Pie*, a teen comedy that details the sexual exploits of four male high school seniors, also figures in an assortment of e-films. Robert Ritger's "Pies Wide Shut" (Ifilm.com), for example, takes a signature element from *American Pie*—the attempt by one of the teens to couple with a warm apple pie—to reread Stanley Kubrick's last film *Eyes Wide Shut* (1999). Here, the Kubrick couple's sexual estrangement and obsessions are redefined around an erotic desire for pastries. Hence, anything goes in the world of hybrid parodies; a Kubrick film can indeed wind up "in bed" with a raunchy teen comedy.

Because the hybrid is such a dramatic case of parody's self-reflexive and intertextual play, it provides a clear view of the genre's capabilities. Since hybridity itself is a widespread aesthetic, it also helps to reveal the significance of the reflexive, metafictional impulses that more generally characterize contemporary cultural production. From the high-concept film's references to *The Simpsons* send-ups, crafting new works often depends on the particular alchemy achieved by deploying notable established texts within new, sometimes incompatible, contexts. E-film hybrids, then, not only shed light on the Internet's impact on home viewing; as a formulaic part of media practice, they also have implications for understanding the broader social functions of intertextuality and textual recycling.

My discussion of hybrids is devoted primarily to takeoffs of very different films: on one hand, *The Blair Witch Project*, and on the other, the films of the *Star Wars* franchise, particularly *The Phantom Menace*. As one of the first films to demonstrate the Internet's ability to create a media sensation around a low-budget film made by fledgling filmmakers with unknown actors, *The Blair Witch Project* occupies a special place in Web history. The faux-documentary features of its Web site (including journal entries and police reports) attracted millions of viewers, helping to secure its extraordinary box office success (made for $35,000, it went on to gross nearly $150 million in 1999).[24] By contrast, the *Star Wars* sagas constitute a quintessential blockbuster phenomenon that has elicited one of the most substantial and sustained fan communities on the Web. Lucasfilm Ltd. claims that the home page of its official site, www.starwars.com, alone is linked to more than eleven thousand other sites.[25] Given the dissimilar modes of production they represent, *The Blair Witch Project* and *The Phantom Menace* illustrate how films of various origins can attain great visibility online. Each film has forged especially close associations with the Web and attracted sizable online followings, spawning an impressive number of short film homages and parodies.[26]

Spoofs of *The Blair Witch Project* and the *Star Wars* series are often done by fans who have taken camera in hand to "talk back" to the original's producers while expressing their own conversancy with mass culture. The hybrid parody presents a special display of mass cultural competence, because the maker shows his or her own prowess not merely by imitation but also by forging clever intertextual alliances between different sources. In its relationship to invested viewers, the hybrid parody offers yet another instance of the importance of demonstrations of mastery to the fan community. In this case, such demonstrations result in the production and circulation of artifacts that compete with the originals in the Internet's vast marketplace of ideas.

Bambi Meets Godzilla

Along with the fan networks of TheForce.net and other sites, both Atom-Films and Ifilm have special channels devoted to *Star Wars* spin-offs. Many fan films, like fan fictions, are homages that create alternative dramatic texts out of the originals (such as "Duality" [Mark Thomas and Dave Macomber, Ifilm.com] and "The Bounty Trail" [Justin Dix, Ifilm.com]). In contrast, parodies may in part pay homage, but they create their alternative textual universes through less earnest means than those of such dramas.

Blending *Star Wars*, a massively popular work of science fiction aimed at younger audiences, and *Shakespeare in Love*, an Academy Award–winning Elizabethan-era comedy/drama produced by Miramax for more "sophisticated" audiences, "George Lucas in Love" (Mediatrip.com; figures 23–26) is a notable hybrid parody. Directed by Joe Nussbaum and set in 1967 at Lucas's alma mater, the University of Southern California, the short depicts Lucas (played by Martin Hynes) struggling to find the inspiration necessary to write the script that will one day become *Star Wars*. He finds it in the form of a Princess Leia–like coed muse (complete with hair-muffin coif). Throughout "George Lucas in Love," things in Lucas's daily life find their way into his script (such as a huge car mechanic who shakes a wrench above his head making incoherent sounds à la Chewbacca). The short looks forward to one of the major plot twists of the *Star Wars* series (i.e., that Luke and Leia are siblings) by ending with the discovery that Lucas and his muse are in fact brother and sister. Thus, structuring components of *Shakespeare in Love*—a fictionalized saga about Shakespeare's writer's block and his search for a muse that is answered by a female love interest—are incorporated into another fictionalized saga of an author's struggle to create memorable characters and a work of importance. The fusion forces connections between two very different source texts, comically transforming each in the process.

Other hybrids include: "Episode One: The Qui-Jon Show" (Jason Wishnow, AtomFilms.com), which marries *The Phantom Menace* to *The Truman Show* (1998), as Qui-Jon finds out his life is a Hollywood sham and he is just a digital figure; "American Jedi" (Adam Schwartz, Ifilm.com), which combines the Lucas saga with *American Pie* to produce a scenario in which Yoda instructs Luke that the final step to becoming a Jedi knight is to "get laid"; and "Park Wars: The Little Menace" (Ayaz A. Asif, TheNewVenue.com), which recasts *The Phantom Menace* with characters from the TV series *South Park*. Such are the possibilities of colliding narratives in parodies of the Lucas films that viewers can find shorts running the spectrum of high and low culture in their fusions; *Star Wars* is coupled with everything from *Beowulf* and *Macbeth* to *Titanic*, gangsta rap, and *Celebrity Deathmatch* (an animated TV show already premised on incongruous face-offs).

"The *Bewitched* Project" (Howie Nicoll, Ifilm.com) and "The Oz Witch Project" (Michael Rotman, Ifilm.com) are among numerous send-ups of *The Blair Witch Project*. The former parody translates the independent horror film through *Bewitched*, a TV sitcom about witches in suburbia that ran from the 1960s to the early 1970s. The latter casts the central characters from *The Wizard of Oz* (1939) as travelers through a spooky wood who become terrified after wandering off the yellow brick road. Other shorts include "The Blair Muppet Project" (Kurt Roylance, Ifilm.com), which finds three Muppets searching the forest for Jim Henson's ghost, and "The Penny Marshall Project" (Greg Pak, AtomFilms.com), in which directors Penny Marshall, Francis Ford Coppola, and Akira Kurosawa, despite their different aesthetics, try to create a collective independent film project in the woods.

Filmmakers have also merged *The Phantom Menace* and *The Blair Witch Project*. In "The Phantom Menace Project" (Scott Martin, Undergroundfilm.com), an actor playing a scared George Lucas is lost somewhere in the woods behind his Skywalker Ranch. He stares into the camera in extreme close-up, mimicking the sequence toward the end of *The Blair Witch Project*, in which Heather Donahue's character apologizes to family and friends for her costly lapses in judgment. Here "Lucas" expresses regret to audiences and critics for having made *The Phantom Menace*. In another short, "The Truth" (ContagiousPictures.com), young filmmakers go into the forest to discover the truth about the Blair witch, only to learn that the real monster is none other than Jar Jar Binks, a character from *The Phantom Menace*.

These titles begin to suggest some of the defining characteristics of this kind of e-film. To examine these characteristics in more detail, we need to consider the e-parody's form and use of hybridity, as well as its relationship to the original's authority. These considerations will inevitably return us to questions of parody's cultural politics and status as critique and, ultimately, of the genre's functions for viewers and fans.

Of film parody's form, Wes Gehring writes, "To maximize the comic dismantling of a given film or films, the parodist must know and showcase all the fundamental properties of [the] target."[27] Parody works by identifying distinctive aspects of the original and rewriting them into a new narrative context through exaggeration. *The Blair Witch Project* parodies operate like well-oiled machines in this regard. Most shorts send up the same core components of the story: several filmmakers (or adventurers) search for an

Figures 23–25. The resemblance at the heart of parody: Martin Hynes as the young George Lucas in the beginning of "George Lucas in Love"; the young George Lucas himself during the filming of "Electronic Labyrinth"; and Joseph Fiennes as Will Shakespeare in the beginning of *Shakespeare in Love.*

Figure 26. The Princess Leia look-alike coed in "George Lucas in Love."

unknown entity in the wilds, recording their experience with a handheld camera; when they get lost, they descend into chaos and are harassed by unseen forces, losing one of their party; finally, they are never heard from again. Within this framework, several elements from the target text have proven especially prone to revision: the characters; the nature of the quest and the "monster"; the loss of the map; the searchers' bickering; the stick figures found in the woods; the tent scenes with something or someone making noise outside; and, more than any other single moment, the Heather Donahue character's apologies in extreme close-up toward the film's end (figures 27 and 28).

Instead of Heather, Mike, and Josh (the three filmmakers in *The Blair Witch Project*), "The Oz Witch Project" features Dorothy, the Tin Man, the Scarecrow, and the Cowardly Lion as those who disappear while filming in the woods. Their quest is to find the Oz-Blair witch. Dorothy and the others maintain their polite Hollywood fantasy voices and attitudes for a while, even after they lose the map (Dorothy says, "Begging your pardon, but I don't have the map"). When the descent into chaos takes over, however, characters start to utter such phrases as "Where the fuck is the yellow brick road?" Similarly, when Dorothy prepares to sing "Over the Rainbow," the song made famous by Judy Garland in the original film, one of the other characters yells, "Don't you even fucking start!" Along the way, the characters find frightening lollipop sculptures rather than the stick figures of *The Blair Witch Project* (figures 29 and 30). Instead of children's laughter

Figures 27 and 28. Two central iconographic images from *The Blair Witch Project:* the stick figures and Heather Donahue's confession in extreme close-up.

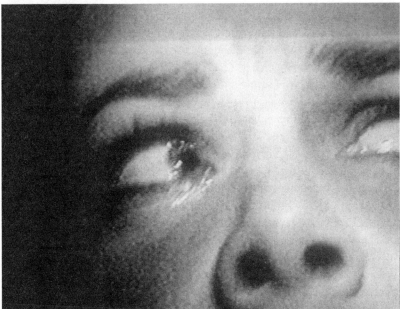

Figures 29 and 30. "The Oz Witch Project": Lollipops in the woods instead of stick figures and a confession from Dorothy shot in extreme close-up parody familiar elements from *The Blair Witch Project.*

disturbing their sleep, these characters hear Munchkin voices singing "We represent the Lullaby League," one of the melodies from *The Wizard of Oz*. The film ends with three of the characters in an abandoned house and Dorothy clicking the heels of her red shoes together in a futile attempt to return to reality. The short's parodic thrust thus relies on a staged meeting of fantasy and horror and the conversion of G-rated into R-rated fare.

In "The *Bewitched* Project," three drag queens from L.A.—an African American, a Latina, and a Caucasian (invoking yet another source, *To Wong Foo, Thanks for Everything! Julie Newmar* [1995])—disappear while sight-seeing in Beverly Hills. They set out with a star map but are warned to "stay away from number 13," because a bad witch named Endora, "like from *Bewitched*," lives there. But, of course, this is exactly the house they try to find. En route they discuss the TV series, alleging that Agnes Moorehead, who played Endora on the sitcom, was a lesbian as well as a real witch. As one says, "Just imagine being in that double closet." Used as toilet paper by a member of the group, the map can no longer guide them, and they get lost; eventually one goes missing. With growing hysteria, they find stick sculptures in the form of tic-tac-toe diagrams. This short contains a version of Donahue's apology scene, where a character expresses regret to Ricky Martin "for not being able to experience my vida loca." Donahue's relatively modest nasal mucous in the original film becomes here (as well as in other parodies) a long visible strand. Finally, after having transformed *The Blair Witch Project* and *Bewitched* through gay rereadings, the two remaining characters disappear in terror in number 13 (figure 31).

"The Phantom Menace Project" is composed solely of the confession scene, making it the chief icon from the original. The Lucas stand-in apologizes to his actors' moms for making the actors star in the film and to critics and fans for having introduced Jar Jar Binks (who was criticized for his racially based buffoonery and for being generally annoying). Because of what critics and audiences might say, "Lucas" is scared to death—scared to make another movie and scared not to. Thus, the horrors of the unknown that haunted the characters in *The Blair Witch Project* are translated here into the horrors of filmmaking gaffes and negative public response.

The question of why these particular elements from the source text have become so prominent on the Internet is difficult to answer with certainty. Some components, such as the search for a mysterious and threatening entity, represent the source's most fundamental narrative aspects. In addition, the adventures of amateur filmmakers and their handheld cameras no doubt appeal to growing legions of beginning auteurs. The recurrence of some other elements can be linked to the circulation of discourses about *The*

Figure 31. "The *Bewitched* Project": After the third member of their party disappears, two of the protagonists remain lost in the woods before their demise in number 13, at the hands of Endora.

Blair Witch Project. For example, the film's promotional campaigns made extensive use of the stick figure images and Donahue's confessional close-up. In part, then, e-directors draw from an orthodoxy, a series of icons that media industries deem important, to inform their send-ups. However, the hybrid parody is also unpredictable, depending on what other text(s) are brought into play to transform the original. Settings, characters, and dialogue change to reflect the influence of the companion text(s), making possibilities for revisionism potentially endless.

To clarify the relation between form and hybridity further, we can look to a popular 1969 animated short made well before the Internet existed. Set in a pastoral locale, with pleasant music playing on the soundtrack, Marv Newland's "Bambi Meets Godzilla" finds Bambi grazing peacefully until a monstrous foot crashes down from above, annihilating him (figures 32 and 33). Bambi has met Godzilla—end of movie. Representing the hybrid parody's essential spirit, the short gains momentum from the incongruity of texts and genres forced together as well as from the reductive impact of its

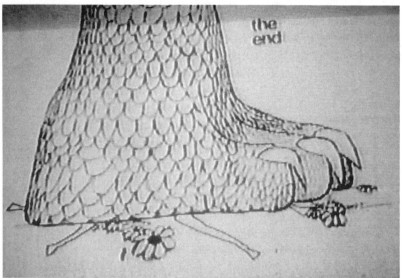

Figures 32 and 33. "Bambi Meets Godzilla."

primitive animation. Bambi, a diminutive figure that hails from Disney's animated fantasy, meets Godzilla, a behemoth star of low-budget Japanese horror films, born as a response to the nuclear devastations of Hiroshima and Nagasaki. The parody's spare technique decontextualizes and recontextualizes the characters, making the juxtaposition of Bambi's innocent unawareness and Godzilla's towering menace especially pointed. The Internet short, "Son of Bambi Meets Godzilla" (Eric Fernandes, Ifilm.com), capitalizes on these incongruities while reversing the outcome of the former film. Using a machine gun, Bambi's descendant gets revenge on Godzilla, evening the score from thirty years ago.

As Jim Collins argues, the "film x meets film y" phenomenon is a commonplace feature of contemporary narratives induced by patterns of intensive circulation and exchange that have characterized popular culture since the advent of such technologies as cable television and the VCR.[28] The sheer increase in the volume of images necessary to fill time slots and answer proliferating programming demands has caused an "accumulated past of pop culture," a "suspended simultaneity" in which potentially all cultural productions can exist at once, serving as intertextual fodder for new works. Such "x meets y" films handle their sampling in different ways. They may aim for a "new sincerity" that strives to recover "some sort of missing harmony, where everything works in unison" (as in *Angel Eyes*), or they may be radically eclectic, "founded on dissonance" with elements that "very obviously don't belong together" (Collins, 127). E-cinema parodies fall into this latter mode of hybridization, foregrounding the artifice of the forced juxtaposition of divergent genres and characters for a laugh and/or for the purposes of critique. However, as the examples of "Bambi Meets Godzilla" and earlier films such as *Abbott and Costello Meet Frankenstein* (1948) (which capitalized on the asymmetries between comedy and classic horror) suggest, combining dissonant genres for parodic effect is nothing new. E-film hybrids are just as much a part of parody traditions that predate the VCR era as they are a result of the increased hyperconsciousness that defines the contemporary media landscape.

Whether or not they feature the "meets" characteristic in their titles, most e-parodies feed off the effects produced by clashing codes. Clearly, "The Barbiecist" relies on the comedy of terrors produced by showing the chaste figure of Barbie inhabited by Satan, while "Saving Ryan's Privates" sends up the war film via the imagery and conventions of the gross-out comedy. Similarly, as the high-tech animated "Womb Wars" (Tom E. Newby, AtomFilms.com) redefines the final assault on the Death Star as an act of conception with sperm-ships, science fiction encounters the sex education film. In fact, e-film parodies often cite more than two source texts or genres in performing their acts of sabotage. For instance, as it mixes *Being John Malkovich* and *Who Wants to Be a Millionaire?*, "Being Regis Philbin" also cites the world of rap music: Philbin's mind is inhabited by an African American member of a struggling rap group on a quest for success.

The tendency to marshal conflicting sources could conceivably lead to uncontrollable entropy in these films; however, sufficient congruities between texts ward off this possibility. "The Oz Witch Project," for example, fuses two plot structures already concerned with small groups of characters searching in unknown woods for mystical personas. In addition, the generic complementarity of each source comes to the fore: there is a blend of horror and fantasy in both *The Wizard of Oz* (with its wicked witch, flying monkeys, and singing Munchkins) and *The Blair Witch Project* (with its legendary murderous witch, terrorized characters, and fanciful faux documentary). In the process of fusing two or more texts, filmmakers not only exploit clashing codes, making hybridity ultravisible, but also utilize points of agreement that lay a foundation for the intermarriage of texts. This is "strange bedfellows" humor, created out of a choreography of affinities and dissimilarities between texts that seeks to mine the comic possibilities of dissonance. At the same time, no matter how shrill the dissonance, the parody gains its visibility and momentum from the status of the text it imitates, raising the issue of the nature of the relationship between e-parody and the original's cultural authority.

Parody's subsidiary position often elicits the image of a parasite that must feed off a host to sustain its existence. If the parasitic metaphor were to hold sway, parodies would always be subordinate texts, poor relations in the realm of cultural production. However, this metaphor fails to capture the more complex associations parodies have to their "parents." Because parody emphasizes the inevitable intertextuality that marks cultural production, there is a certain "chicken and egg" circularity to the issue of origins. That is, no parent text is free of the substantial influence of other texts; the source is itself deeply connected to previous works. A *Star Wars* takeoff, "Beowulf in Space" (D. Shaffer, Ifilm.com) borrows from the tenth-century epic poem *Beowulf* and the Lucas film. *Beowulf* is itself born from a mixture of Scandinavian history, pagan mythology, and Christian imagery, and *Star Wars* is indebted to old Hollywood serials, Akira Kurosawa's *The Hidden Fortress* (1958), and Joseph Campbell's writings on myth. The imitative impulses that animate all texts thus confuse the picture when trying to portray a clear "host-parasite" relation among textual phenomena.

The circular kinship between parodies and their sources is emphasized additionally by the send-up's inherent ambivalence. As Simon Dentith argues, the "paradox of parody" is that the form "preserves as much as it destroys—or rather, it preserves in the moment that it destroys—and thus the parasite becomes the occasion for itself to act as host" (189). The parodic text is simultaneously an archive and a disassembler of tradition. As parodies of *The Blair Witch Project* deface its original structure, tone, and intent, they perpetuate its reputation and underscore its legendary status as a box office wonder. These defacements are necessary not only to produce laughter but also because parody is a form of competitive display, vying for a place in the limelight through its distinctive riffs on the original.[29] Although it maintains the source text's presence in the public eye, parody creates a new utterance, advancing its own claims to visibility and importance.

Beyond avoiding the reductive derivativeness of the host/parasite model, the paradox of parody affords a more complex sense of the genre's cultural role. Like all parodies, these e-films engage in different degrees of homage and critique with respect to their sources. "George Lucas in Love" is clearly devoted to the principle of affectionate appropriation. In one scene, "George" leaves his room and meets Aaron, a wheezing, asthmatic neighbor. In sinister tones, Aaron tells George that his own script is complete, adding, "Soon I will rule the industry, and you'll still be writing line one of whatever it's called." George replies, "3XR-259.7." This moment comically renders a confrontation with a character who resembles master adversary Darth Vader through the lens of a competitive graduate school relationship, which is in turn informed by the authorial rivalry we witness between Shakespeare and Christopher Marlowe in *Shakespeare in Love*. In addition, George's reply gently pokes fun at the penchant the director displayed for arcane film titles in his USC short "Electronic Labyrinth: THX 1138 4EB" and in his feature-length follow-up, *THX 1138*. "George Lucas in Love" invests in this kind of knowing humor with an utter lack of malice. In fact, allusions to the Shakespeare narrative playfully romanticize Lucas and his creative efforts, just as references to *Star Wars* humorously bring high art into contact with mass culture.

"Park Wars: The Little Menace," a low-tech animated hybrid, is far less committed to homage, in part because of the stark contrast between its sources. *South Park* is an animated TV series known for self-reflexivity as well as rude audacity and irreverence, while the Lucas film is associated with moral earnestness and sincerity. Perhaps the least respected of Lucas's films, *The Phantom Menace* has proven to be especially susceptible to parodic revision (or, in the case of the unauthorized *The Phantom Edit*, to an outright reediting to excise those parts fans found most objectionable). "Park Wars" opens with the THX logo, proclaiming that the film has been "digitally mastered for mediocre video and sound." Instead of the 20th Century Fox logo, the studio name "2 Much Time" appears, and a scrolling opening typical of the *Star Wars* films reads, "A long time ago in a quiet little podunk red-neck galaxy far, far away . . ." The first half of the short replays, scene for scene, the dialogue and John Williams score from the opening of *The Phantom Menace,* substituting *South Park* characters for some of the film's actors. A character then interrupts the faithful rendition of the sound track, saying, "Don't you know by using the audio from *The Phantom Menace,* you're violating copyright? George Lucas will beat your balls into carbonite." A compilation of scenes follows from the latter parts of *The Phantom Menace,* including a fight between Kenny from *South Park* and Darth Maul. Remaking the film in the image of *South Park,* the short translates the original into an amateurish, low-tech play on Lucas's obsession with technological quality, on ownership and copyright, and on the grand epic purpose of the *Star Wars* series. Against the backdrop of debates about copyright, media piracy, and Lucasfilm Ltd.'s reputation for policing fan activities, "Park Wars" literally and figuratively champions "the little guys"—the diminutive characters against the fearsome villains of the Lucas film, the amateur filmmaker against the corporate film industry.

"The *Bewitched* Project" represents another extreme rewriting of sources. In addition to its comic deflations of the original's foreboding setting, props, and dangerous mission, the short is full of intertextual references to popular culture. The characters frequently discuss *Bewitched,* outing actresses and actors on the show as gay. They also discuss the music cable channel VH1, the TV show *Unsolved Mysteries* (as one character remarks about the show's host, "Robert Stack—he can interrogate me anytime"), and Ricky Martin. The parody uses *The Blair Witch Project* as a pretext with which to uncover gay subtexts in *Bewitched* and to demonstrate the prowess of gay readings of mass culture in general. With three transvestites taking the place of the white, desexualized trio of the original film, a multiracial, gay text pervades the dialogue.

These examples suggest that parodists can support or undermine the source's authority, strive for the invisible Hollywood style or call attention to its fabrication, and embrace or confront the original's assumptions about gender and sexuality. The attack on normative depictions of gender in "The *Bewitched* Project," "Gaydiator," "Admission Impossible 2," and other shorts suggests that this is an e-parody formula. Toppling towering images of stoic, macho heroes or heterosexual norms is a major means of puncturing Hollywood myths and a special sport for parodists.

At first glance, we can see that the more iconoclastic parodies engage in self-reflexive play to challenge the original. In so doing, they question the right and the ability of institutions to control meaning—in these cases, to dictate how a mainstream film will circulate and acquire significance for viewers. This questioning has carnivalesque dimensions insofar as it mobilizes utterances from the lower ranks to expose official seriousness as sham (e.g., "Admission Impossible 2" deflates the visual strategies used to make Cruise appear as a formidable physical presence in his films). Forcing awareness of the existence of other languages, of other ways of considering the world, the very presence of such expressions challenges the dominance of a single language. In this way, some e-films can be considered as critical responses to the empire of corporate capitalism and the media mythos that supports it.

However, even the most irreverent work displays a core affection, fascination, or grudging admiration for the original. Parodies may refuse to allow an official voice to dominate absolutely, may deny, as Jim Collins argues, "cultural *sovereignty* to any institution, as it counters one sort of authority with another," but this refusal to let the original have the last word does not negate cultural authority (93). A source's attraction of numerous auxiliary forms, from sequels and merchandise tie-ins to fan parodies and straight homages, magnifies its cultural range and power. The wild popularity of the *Star Wars* sagas and *The Blair Witch Project* on the Internet is manifested in their ability to attract diverse voices with varying intentions toward the originals. Although unanimity of response (particularly if it is negative) can influence attitudes toward a text, it is not necessary for turning a text into a cultural icon. Ultimately, the sheer volume of commentary matters most, including the dissonant postings on message boards, the different visions of fan fiction, and the varied appropriations of e-cinema parodies. In their heterogeneity, such discourses help to canonize the text and sustain its presence in the public eye.

The instability of parody's thrust is compounded by the critique's uncertain social dimensions. "Being Erin Brockovich," for example, uses sex to comment on Jonze's and Soderbergh's films. The short's main joke is that the "tourists" inhabiting Erin Brockovich see the world not through her eyes but from the point of view of her breasts. This change makes a much discussed aspect of the Soderbergh film—Julia Roberts's cleavage—excessively explicit, mocking the American obsession with breasts. At the same time, this emphasis draws from the genre of the teen sex film, where such fixations function to display the female body's "ogling" value for characters and viewers alike. Since this genre figures so prominently in hybrid parodies and in e-shorts in general and targets the substantial demographic of teenage boys using the Web, its presence is not negligible. The "generic stew" that makes up the hybrid short thus conveys mixed motives. In "The *Bewitched* Project," too, we might consider whether translating the hysteria present in *The Blair Witch Project* into the over-the-top behavior of the short's three characters radically rewrites the original film only to inadvertently endorse stereotypes of transvestites and gays as comically and excessively neurotic. It is important to note that the e-film is not exceptional in its mixed messages; it demonstrates the ambiguity, ambivalence, and contradiction that generally characterize media forms.

The economic and cultural contexts in which these films circulate factor further into a consideration of their politics. As I have mentioned, e-filmmakers tend to be amateurs, film school students, or professionals from a variety of backgrounds who are attracted to the Web as a new venue for their work. Because the Internet is characterized by a prolific amount of information and a heterogeneous population of users, film exhibition here has a Darwinian aspect—a sense of the survival of the fittest for filmmakers and dot-coms alike. For e-filmmakers, survival is often based on visibility, on the eyeball-catching potential of their work. Evoking a famous film in a short's title gives the short an automatic prominence that, unless a well-known director or actor is attached to the project, is otherwise hard to attain. A film with an intertextual ring to it has less chance of getting lost in the shuffle. Hybrid parodies simply double these stakes, making the viewer curious as to how different media texts are combined. The parody thus capitalizes on the original text's authority for the purposes of self-promotion; it appears "with it" as it takes aim at contemporary high-profile fare. Fame by association may mean more hits on the Web for the e-filmmaker's short and thus more attention for the Web site itself. This state of affairs is so commonplace that it has led some filmmakers and critics to lament the "get-discovered-quick mentality of many digital newcomers and the spoof-obsessed sites courting them."[30]

Parody today can be controversial, notably in cases in which outraged authors, media companies, or estates bring legal action against parodists for libel or copyright violations (e.g., rap music sampling or novels such as Alice Randall's *The Wind Done Gone*, a rewriting of Margaret Mitchell's *Gone with the Wind* from a slave's perspective). Oftentimes, however, legal hardship and the notoriety that ensues can redound to the parodist's fame and fortune, suggesting once again that the genre's foundations in imitation can translate into economic gain and cultural capital.[31] Whether or not celebrity ensues from contested instances of parody, parody's success as a polemic might be measured by the effectiveness of its intervention in the circulation of meaning. That is, it becomes such a part of the swirl of information surrounding a person or a text that audiences have difficulty thinking of the source without accompanying parodic lacerations (e.g., William Randolph Hearst without Orson Welles's *Citizen Kane*, presidents without their imitators). An e-film parody can similarly drive a wedge between a formerly obeisant viewer and a blockbuster, making its own silliness unforgettable in the encounter between the two.

As always, though, we must consider the genre's inherent ambivalence, its dual urges to destroy and preserve. Where once parody could conceivably turn public opinion against major public figures, today politicians and others have "become increasingly savvy about the rhetorical power of self-deprecation, which has led them to embrace their own caricatures." Caricatures have become a kind of "perverse Mount Rushmore," lessening the chances of a truly effective "graphic assassination" of the powers-that-be. Parody can signify and magnify the social importance of its object.[32] Moreover, the public has become accustomed to the form. The rise in college-educated people since the 1960s and a population exposed to endless media recycling have created audiences conversant with aesthetic conventions and thus primed for parody. This mode of imitation has become a steadfast component of cultural lingoes today.[33]

Ultimately, given its formal ambivalence and the economic and cultural conditions that define its presentation, e-parody cannot easily be privileged as truly interventionist. Perhaps we can identify the genre's most significant contribution to cultural critique, then, as lying in its most obvious feature: its routine activation of multiple, conflicting meanings for texts. Parody may not constitute a specialized type of discourse as much as a particularly pointed embodiment of a standard aspect of culture. As Dentith writes, parodies represent the "inevitable manoeuvres in the to-and-fro of language, in the competition between genres, and in the unceasing struggle over meanings and values that make up any social order" (188). Because parody's essence lies in imitative takeoffs on originals, the genre crystallizes the conflicts over meaning that materialize in society as heterogeneous voices address and debate central issues.

Thus, we can consider the e-parody as an arresting form of rebuttal, mounted in the main by amateurs with mixed motives who refuse to let the media industry have the last word. By refusing, they inevitably inspire a play of meaning that demonstrates the vulnerability of texts to irreverent treatment from any quarter, testifying to the susceptibility of all utterances to commentary "from below." In this way, e-film parodies effect constant reorientation to master texts, while maintaining those texts as valuable objects. As a semiotic act, this reorientation constitutes aesthetic work that is an intimate part of mass culture, as well as mass cultural competence.

E-cinema's relationship to audiences and fan filmmakers is as complex and multifaceted as its cultural politics. At the most fundamental level, parody's effectiveness relies on timely references: parodies usually refer to recent sources or sources that have maintained currency through other means, such as canonization. For e-cinema, timeliness is an especially important ingredient. Allusions to recent blockbusters or otherwise popular films help to win audiences on the congested Net as well as the attention of industry personnel. At the same time, the imperative of timeliness ultimately makes films in the genre transitory. With the exception of phenomena that have had an impressive shelf life in popular culture, such as the *Star Wars* films, what is "hot" and ripe for parody one day is destined soon to become yesterday's news. Even if it is able to stand on its own as comedy, a dated parody will lose some of its impact if audiences cannot recognize its allusions.

Recognition of allusions is key to the experience and pleasurable consumption of the genre.[34] In fact, even if users deplore the technological quality or sophomoric humor of an e-cinema short, they might still enjoy their own ability to decipher the parodic recodings of the original. That is to say, no matter what the viewer's degree of engrossment, he or she obtains some pleasure in the very act of recognition, in "getting" the parody's references. In this sense, parody is a mirror held up to viewers in which they see their own capabilities as interpreters of popular culture.

As we discovered in chapter 4, quoting and exchanging lines from films serve as a marker of community and cultural literacy for some university students. E-parody allusions test and reward this group's knowledge of cinema, television shows, and music. In this sense, the short parody provides another example of the constitution of taste groups that result from repurposing; as it replays a source, parody is a mode of recycling. However, demonstrations of taste materialize here not just in the form of consumption (as viewers recognize allusions) but also in the form of production (as fans astutely remake movies). Further, fan filmmakers themselves embody a complex interplay between production and consumption: the act of remaking the original depends on a strong conversancy gained from multiple viewings and related investments. While it is not always possible to determine an e-filmmaker's race, young white men are among the major producers of short film parodies on the Internet. Some in this group are "film nuts," devotees of filmmaking, who represent a variation of the gadgeteers we have encountered in previous chapters. Granting that the Web is a forum for many different kinds of filmmakers, short film parodies are strongly associated with white men whose avid fandom continues to enter influentially into the world of cinema and new technologies on the home front.

As these fans parody *The Blair Witch Project* and the *Star Wars* films, they fulfill a prime condition of mass media fandom: they express their knowledge of cinema and other media, signaling their status as experts. This status is enhanced by their creation of material commentary on the original. By remodeling the source text, they prove their facility with its textual universe. In hybrids, filmmakers who successfully manipulate the convergences and divergences between different narratives show command of a range of media texts: they know what the defining features are and how to combine them imaginatively. Just as in fan fiction and other forms of amateur production, fan filmmakers rearrange the original's priorities and characteristics to their own ends, deriving pleasure, as Henry Jenkins argues, from "watching familiar images wrenched free from their previous contexts and assigned alternative meanings."[35] Parodies perform this act of liberation in particularly vivid terms, since they often manhandle what for some may be a sacred text.

Because of their pointed send-ups of revered originals, films in the genre forge a conspiratorial alliance between e-filmmaker and viewer; they produce a "feeling that the artist and viewer are in complicity, exposing themselves to some social risk."[36] Parody is an enshrinement of the right of individuals to rejoin official culture, a generative principle of fan culture even in its most adulatory modes. It is also an invitation to viewers to take part in an apparently clandestine activity, in which those knowledgeable in mass culture meet to practice and savor their special status as fans, acting without the consent of the media industries.

The sense of parodists and their audiences as renegades is an important self-defining feature of fan communities, fueled periodically by stories of industry behemoths such as Lucasfilm legally pursuing fans who infringe on copyright. However, rather than accepting the opposition between fan and industry, we may best see this opposition as a mutually beneficial construction that obscures the continuum existing between them.[37] On the one hand, portraits of Hollywood as monolithically oppressive enhance the credibility and importance of dissenting fan response. On the other hand, when Hollywood does accommodate fans, such gestures show its flexibility and interest in audiences (as well as a potential desire to commandeer them, a desire that then reignites its imperialistic image). Because the reputed antagonism between fan and industry is capable of serving a felicitous function for each, strong points of confederation exist, belying the sense of antithesis. In the case of e-cinema, what we can refer to as the rhetoric of discovery is particularly indicative of the deeper dynamics informing the relationship of Hollywood and fan filmmaking.

Newspapers, magazines, and dot-coms often chronicle the breakthroughs of e-directors, portraying them at once as fresh, creative individuals laboring outside of the mainstream and as "wannabe" professionals who have struck it rich by landing jobs in some sector of the industry. While the short film dot-com promotes famous and fledgling auteurs alike, the most pervasive discussions of Web filmmaking are steeped in the concept of apprenticeship, regarding the Internet as a preliminary step toward commercial feature filmmaking. Like independent features designed for big-screen exhibition, e-films often surface in news coverage if they have found a large audience or if their exhibition has led to some measure of commercial success for their makers (e.g., distribution deals and/or studio contracts). This kind of success story is familiar from press coverage of major film festivals such as Sundance and Cannes, which have helped to make the reputations of many unknowns, including Steven Soderbergh and Quentin Tarantino. The most recognized Web directors are similarly those who have parlayed their Web cinema ventures into a future that either is or seems destined to be connected to a Hollywood career.

There is, of course, *The Blair Witch Project*, a film launched with great success via its Web site before it was released to movie theaters, transforming directors Eduardo Sanchez and Daniel Myrich into wunderkinder of Internet promotion. The initial fame of numerous other directors has also been associated with the Web, among them, Darren Aronofsky and Joe Nussbaum. Aronofsky's mind-tripping *PI* (1998) gained notoriety from its award-winning festival run and exhibition on SightSound.com and other Web sites. *PI* was given a limited theatrical release and then distributed on VHS and DVD. Aronofsky went on to make *Requiem for a Dream* (2000), a bigger-budget feature concerning the degradations of drug addiction that was produced and distributed by a number of companies, including Artisan Entertainment. Meanwhile, MediaTrip offered Nussbaum and producer Joseph Levy, of "George Lucas in Love," a distribution arrangement with Amazon.com that resulted in healthy sales online and in stores. The filmmakers also sold broadcast rights to the Sci Fi Channel in the United States and to other media concerns abroad, ultimately attracting the attention of movie executives. According to reports, Levy took a job heading the digital division at Bandeira Entertainment. Eventually, Nussbaum was hired by MGM to direct the tweener picture *Sleepover* (2004).

Encompassing very different kinds of films and filmmakers, these success stories demonstrate the potential for the hit e-film to find broad nontheatrical distribution and pave the way for further career opportunities. Such stories encourage the view that the Internet is a mighty distributor and exhibitor of movies made by beginners—an apprentice's dream. As Marion Hart of the *New York Times* writes, "The Internet has the power to vault the best shorts and their directors out of film festival obscurity and onto your computer—and the computers of talent scouts searching for the next big thing."[38] Thus, the "next Spielberg" may be a "kid out there" who is using the Web to "crack open" Hollywood.[39] In the mainstream press as well as in many of the Web sites showing e-films, the rhetoric of discovery is omnipresent. Project Greenlight, for example, was overtly crafted from the idea that the Internet can make filmmaking dreams come true. Writers and filmmakers whose proposals were given the green light by users voting in an annual contest hosted by Matt Damon and Ben Affleck's Web site, Live Planet.com, were awarded one million dollars to make their movies. Once the films were completed, Miramax put them into limited theatrical release, followed by an HBO series about the making of the film and ancillary release on VHS and DVD.[40]

A closer look at Project Greenlight reveals the importance of the figure of the apprentice. Only amateurs with no Hollywood connections were invited to apply; further, the best scripts were chosen by Internet users. The project thus seemed to embrace the Internet as a haven for novices, while employing the kinds of democratic and interactive potentials associated with digital forums. At the same time, the project was underwritten by the powerful Hollywood fable of discovery that parallels the organizers' rags-to-riches story. Just as Damon and Affleck came from virtually nowhere to win the Academy Award for their screenplay for *Good Will Hunting* (1997), other struggling beginners are given the chance to ascend into the Hollywood limelight. This chance is presented through a vision of Hollywood as a land of open opportunity that one can enter with the requisite amount of hard work. As in other discussions of amateur Internet filmmaking, there is an implicit assumption that the Web is part of a new system of apprenticeship in which a natural, commonsense passage from amateur to commercial professional takes place.

As we have seen, the Internet can function effectively as a film distributor and exhibitor. However, the overwhelming amount of information and streaming video tempers the kinds of enthusiastic claims about discovery that so routinely appear. Further, such claims tend to be overblown, even misleading (for example, although Project Greenlight has been picked up by

Bravo, HBO withdrew its support from what many consider to be a failed experiment, and five years after *The Blair Witch Project* exploded onto the scene, its directors have yet to get another film project off the ground). Rather than genuinely indicating an ascending career trajectory, the rhetoric of discovery more often functions to promote the continuing viability and desirability of the dream of mainstream success. Still, this rhetoric is central to understanding how new technologies are introduced to the public through familiar formulas and also bears significantly on the activities of fans and amateur filmmakers.

Because e-parodies so visibly imitate and court the blockbuster, they can appear to be particularly opportunistic in their upwardly mobile desires. Sometimes, as we have seen, e-films do lead their directors to studio contracts. As Sara Jones has argued, when commercial success is actually achieved, as it was in the case of Kevin Rubio, amateur director of the *Star Wars* spoof "Troops," who was later hired as a director by Lucasfilm, the boundaries between fan and producer, between illicit appropriator and official owner, are blurred. Such a continuum suggests that sustaining the binary oppositions that typically form those boundaries is a matter of discursive manipulation rather than an accurate depiction of the relations between fans and producers.[41]

Although cases in which fans are transformed into members of the professional family are fascinating for their implications for fan theory, I am more interested here in the function of the rhetoric of discovery irrespective of the success or failure of aspiring amateurs. Indeed, especially given the rarity of "making it," the importance of this rhetoric lies less in any real promise it holds and more in how it helps to "discipline" creative aspirations in a new forum for filmmaking. To be sure, critics and artists often hail Web cinema as a place where new voices defying normative categories can be heard. Nonetheless, the dream of mainstream success puts pressure on this venue and its contributors to conceive of their creations as "calling cards" to Hollywood. According to Patty Zimmermann, this kind of pressure has historically characterized how amateur filmmaking is publicly constructed and understood, influencing the ambitions of those who pick up cameras.[42] Phenomena such as the *Star Wars* fan sites on AtomFilms.com and Ifilm.com and accompanying contests to determine the best e-film knock-offs make this discursive pressure explicit. Such sites attempt to channel amateur practices within a Hollywood ethos by offering beginning filmmakers advice, resources, and distribution outlets for their films, thereby also encouraging them to pay homage to or parody the series.

In this sense, the film parody embodies imitation as the sincerest form of flattery; newcomers hope that their clever understanding of the original will be duly noted by media professionals. Armed with various new technologies that allow the fledgling filmmaker to approximate more easily the characteristics of Hollywood cinema, fan parodists take their position within the apprenticeship ranks, not simply by showing command of the narrative and visual language of mainstream film, but by trumping this language through a winking knowledge of its conceits and assumptions. Although Jenkins argues that this new brand of amateur filmmaking is "neither fully commercial nor fully alternative, existing as a grass-roots dialogue with mass culture," it is worth reflecting on the degree to which this dialogue is infused with visions of a blockbuster-sized future.[43]

The prevalence of the rhetoric of discovery in various sources suggests that Hollywood success is at once, then, the gold standard and the object of the artistic quest. E-parody's play with the blockbuster, its ability to produce multiple, conflicting meanings, and its constitution of fan filmmakers and their audiences as culturally literate are linked to the persistent dream of Hollywood. This dream inspires views of the amateur as a preprofessional, a member of Hollywood's independent "farm team" who is waiting in the wings to make it in the big time. It also sets standards of cultural literacy, wherein those who can manipulate original texts with the most aplomb or adroitly decipher parodic allusions show superior knowledge of mainstream fictions. Meanwhile, the industry trades off the e-filmmaker's status as outsider and heterogeneous fan reactions to maintain an image of itself as a vital, artistic enterprise ultimately at the center of everything.

The Web has unquestionably acted as a crucial point of circulation for fan activity, from message boards and fan fiction to e-cinema. It has, in addition, made the participatory culture of fans a definitive part of the media experience. Only part of the diaspora of taste cultures that define the Web, e-cinema suggests that this new development in home film exhibition has a vital relationship with existing conditions of production and consumption. The parodist's knowing manipulation of codes and defiance of the powers-that-be, as well as the viewer's pleasurable recognition of this manipulation and shared sense of risk, are part of cultural custom. As they participate in the intertextual sphere of relations defining the original text, parodies help the original to gain or maintain a toehold in mass cultural canons, just as they help to indicate what constitutes mass cultural legitimacy. Their tactics may differ, but as an ensemble they signal what is worthy of extended commentary and what is not. They operate to harness an excess of information, gravitating toward the most successful titles to make their mark. In this way, e-parodists carve out a territory of taste that continues to make the

234 / CHAPTER 5

popular text into a cause célèbre at the same time as it bestows distinction on the filmmaker and his or her audience as able to orchestrate and appreciate the most self-conscious confrontations with authoritative originals. The paradox of parody—the genre's ambivalence—is not only its most essential trait but also a larger dynamic within the fandom and home film culture surrounding e-cinema.

Cinema and Remediation

E-parodies perform extensive semiotic labor, mingling incongruous conventions, characters, and codes to create a rollicking festival of slights. They are subject to the Darwinian economies of Hollywood and the Web, searching for discovery through their takeoffs on proven titles. As they undertake this labor, they mix multiple media and rely on streaming video technologies and other digital-era delivery mechanisms of the Internet. The e-short's polyglot nature provides particularly rich territory for exploring the intricate technological, economic, and formal alliances between cinema and other media, leading ultimately to a closer understanding of the multifaceted relationship cinema has to exhibition venues in the home.

The e-film's picture and sound are delivered through an amalgam of technologies that include computer hardware and software and DSL or cable modems. Further, e-films themselves are materially diverse. Shorts may originate on 16mm film, analog video, digital video, or computer; no matter what the point of origin, all formats are compressed into a digital file for exhibition on a site. This situation is not so different from theatrical cinema, in which films originate on celluloid or digital video, are edited digitally, and eventually converted to other formats for home exhibition. Business models deployed by Web film sites are equally heterogeneous in terms of intermedia relationships. For instance, pay-per-view or monthly-pay sites (such as SightSound.com) use precedents established by video outlets and cable television, asking their users to rent films for a short period of time or subscribe to the service for more continuous access. As we have seen, some Web companies, such as AtomFilms, are designed in the likeness of a film studio or production company, signing and promoting talent, distributing and exhibiting films, and making ancillary exhibition deals. An important source of financing comes in the form of partnerships with technology, entertainment, or other corporate interests to produce original programming. Whether sites launch innovative independent films or show more standard fare, their operations call upon established businesses and practices.

E-cinema also showcases familiar programming types, including genres of all kinds. But the aesthetic play among media is more complex than mere genre interdependency would suggest. For example, *Xena, Warrior Princess*, a Webisode designed exclusively for Internet exhibition, is owned by Brilliant Digital Entertainment, which champions digital experimentation with streaming video—hence, the Webisode's 3-D veneer and interactive path component. The series' graphics are drawn from computer games, and its 3-D imagery further associates its visuals with 1950s cinema and more recent experiments with image dimensionality. Because of its path component, the Webisode is narratively indebted to computer games. Its structure as a series points to TV. In addition, the original cable series has roots in forms as diverse as *Wonder Woman* (both the comic book and TV series) and Greek and Roman mythology. This brief genealogy demonstrates that cutting-edge digital experiments in Internet imagery are pervasively indebted to previous forms. This kind of aesthetic back-and-forth is only enhanced by the involvement of film and television directors and stars in Web productions. In the meantime, success in this new industry is often measured by a familiar formula—making it in Hollywood. The fluid circulation of personnel across media guarantees a degree of cross-fertilization among art forms while the presence of commercial standards of success helps to define aspirations—what can and should be done within the new medium.

Across these and other frontiers, e-cinema continually demonstrates links to other media and media concerns. With the intersection of cinema and the Web still in its emergent phase, indebtedness to other media is to be expected. But if e-cinema is like other media before it, continuities, rather than ruptures, will shape its later manifestations. As Jay Bolter and Richard Grusin contend, new media cannot simply eradicate older media or achieve an aesthetic removed from commerce with preexisting forms. Through the concept of remediation (not to be confused with the term's usual meaning of instruction aimed at improving competence), the authors depict media as fundamentally engaged in mutual and ongoing "strategies of incorporation," in which they constantly comment upon, embody, or otherwise refashion one another. Rejecting visions of new technologies as revolutionary, the authors offer instead a "genealogy of affiliations" in which media interact in a vital, reciprocal manner throughout their histories; newer forms borrow from older for the sake of familiarity and credibility, and older borrow from newer to maintain currency and legitimacy. What is novel is the ways in which new media "refashion older media and the ways in which older media refashion themselves to answer the challenges of new media."[44] Identifying the constellation of intermedia alliances that define a recently introduced technology helps us to understand its impact—how and to what effect it has entered into the existing order of things.

Some critics, artists, and entrepreneurs tend to minimize the impact of the existing order of things on new developments, depicting culture as something over which technology can triumph. Hence, with its potential emphasis on interactivity over passive engagement, process over completed works, discontinuity over continuity (via such features as hyperlinks), and questioning of authenticity (due to the loss of the indexicality of the sign), digital language is seen by some as bringing an end to the era of cohesive, linear narratives, creating radically new artistic endeavors and states of mind. However, as Brian Winston argues, histories of communications technologies have shown that it is not the invention itself but the social sphere that has primacy in "conditioning and determining technological developments," often operating to limit their potential "to radically disrupt pre-existing social formations."[45] Innovations are met by standard patterns of assimilation, even in the overloaded and overcoded information age. On this point, Jim Collins observes that "as the rate of technological innovation accelerates, so does the rate of cultural mediation, technologies of innovation being matched, virtually stride for stride, by technologies of absorption and domestication" (5–6).

Remediation and cultural assimilation describe the status of cinema in general on the small screen. Since it appears through the auspices of digital and earlier entertainment technologies and media, cinema is necessarily tied to and experienced through these venues. In addition to other functions, new venues become portals for cinema and other established media, creating a definitive bond between existing and emerging forms, between existing and emerging modes of viewing. But intermedia alliances do not apply solely to nontheatrical cinema. Just as intricately, theatrical cinema exists within a multicorporate, intermedia, and intertextual environment in which no medium is an island. From the horizontal integration of multinational corporations, which guarantees extensive media crossovers, to the digitization of Hollywood, which has affected the business, production, and marketing of cinema, big-screen films are indebted to a similar intimate congress among media. In fact, from its earliest years, cinema has been constitutionally interrelated at every level with other media and forms of entertainment. The conditions in which films are screened nontheatrically simply display this state of affairs in unmistakable terms.

Part of the challenge of thinking about film in this way is to acknowledge its alliances with other media as constitutive of, in André Bazin's terms, its ontology and epistemology—of what it is inherently as a medium as well as how it is perceived and understood. For some scholars in the field, this view jeopardizes the autonomy and uniqueness of cinema.[46] The digital era aggravates these anxieties, for it promises to displace celluloid as the foundation of cinema. Can film still be film if it relies on a digital technology that renders celluloid obsolete and redefines projection as a matter of transmitting digital files? Such a question registers the anxiety that marks the transformation in elements that have defined film for more than a century. But this all-or-nothing proposition obscures the fact that cinema has always assimilated other media, just as other media have assimilated cinema.[47] It is not that film won't change; it already has, through such developments as the incorporation of CGI and the use of digital video cameras to shoot major productions. But this change will be negotiated by cultural forces, consistent with the principles of incorporation and diffusion that have long defined film. E-cinema is an example of the way that film has traditionally expanded its fortunes as it is redefined for a contemporary context. This process cannot be understood apart from the coalitions formed between cinema and other media concerns. These coalitions establish the very basis on which films are generated and appear on multiple and continually multiplying screens.

In seeking to grasp the economic, formal, and cultural particularities of cinema as it enters into associations with fellow media, film aestheticians and cultural analysts need to push the recognition of these articulations further. The specificity of cinema lies in its apparent lack of identity—in the way it alludes to, incorporates, and forges confederations across entertainment forms, guaranteeing its own survival while taking part in a robust media culture dedicated to the principle of the interface.

Selected Short Film Web Sites (1999–2002)

All sites have the suffix ".com" unless otherwise indicated. Sites that invite submissions from filmmakers are marked with an asterisk.

AFIonline	Bitscreen*	ContagiousPictures*
Alltrue*	Blockbuster	Coppernob
Alwaysi	Brilliantdigital	Countingdown
Anewmovie	Broadcast.yahoo	Dfilm*
Anteye*	Charged*	Dreamspan* (linked
Atom-bomb	Cinemaelectric	with ShortSpan)
AtomFilms*	Cinemanow*	Endependent*
BigFilmShorts	Cinemapop	Entertaindom
BijouCafe*	Clipcrap	(Warnerbros.com)

Eveo*
Filmfilm*
TheForce.net*
Heavy
Hypnotic* (formerly
 Reelshort)
Icebox*
Ifctv
Ifilm
Ilive*
Indie.hollywood
Inetfilm*
Level13.net
Liketelevision*
Mediatrip
MeTV

Movieflix*
NewVenue*
Nibblebox*
PlanetOut
Pop
Rampt
Reelplay
Scour
Screen47*
Sho
Shockwave
ShortSpan*
ShortTV*
SightSound
SixMinuteCinema*
Snap

Sputnik*
Stanlee.net
Station
Studentfilms*
Swankytown
Sundanceonlinefilm
 festival.org
TheSync*
3btv*
Triggerstreet*
UKscreen
Undergroundfilm*
Videoseeker
Wirebreak
Zeroonefilms*
Zoiefilms*

Conclusion

Of Fortresses and Film Cultures

In 2003, ancillary forms of cinema once again figured centrally in a controversy surrounding the Academy Awards. This time, the debate did not focus on what constitutes genuine cinema and legitimate viewing conditions for the medium. Rather, it concerned the difficulty of controlling the circulation of the VHS and DVD copies of films routinely sent to the Academy's nearly six thousand members to facilitate their determination of the year's potential Oscar nominees. Specifically, in September 2003, the Motion Picture Association of America, which represents the major movie studios, mounted an effort to ban these "screeners" altogether. The organization presented the "no-screeners" policy as a safeguard against the piracy that has occurred once copies of contending films are sent to members. The MPAA alleged that, because Academy members have given screeners freely to others, copies have appeared illegally online or in the black market. With more than an estimated three billion dollars lost annually by the U.S. film industry to piracy, not counting losses accrued from illicit Internet exhibition, film theft has become a prime concern of the MPAA and a hot-button industry issue. To add insult to injury, certain studies have suggested that the lion's share of unauthorized movies appearing online have come from industry insiders.[1] Although screeners account for only part of the problem, their highly visible insider status coupled with their function as emissaries of the year's most important films has made addressing their unlawful circulation particularly pressing.

However, shortly after then chief executive of the MPAA, Jack Valenti, made the no-screeners announcement, the policy elicited outcry from art house and independent studios and filmmakers as well as from critics and critics' organizations. These groups argued that, while piracy was a serious issue, the ban on screeners had another agenda. They saw Valenti's action as an attempt by major motion picture studios to give Hollywood's big moneymaking films an unfair advantage over smaller pictures at the Academy Awards, especially since smaller pictures had seen increasing success at the ceremony. Because the shorter and more selective distribution patterns of art-house and independent films made them traditionally more difficult for Academy members to view theatrically, mainstream studio fare would have greater representation in a voting process that proceeded without the aid of screeners. Additionally, since low-budget films often depended on the laureates bestowed by Oscar nominations and awards for exposure and financial success, their makers would have the most to lose. By the end of the year, after a series of negotiations between Valenti and the protestors and a court ruling that found in favor of independent filmmakers, the uproar appeared to be resolved. The ban was lifted, and studios big and small hurriedly began sending out screeners, albeit with restrictions prescribed by the MPAA.[2]

Together with the post–Academy Awards contretemps in 1999, this more recent incident demonstrates that the sheer existence of cinema in ancillary forms can bedevil contemporary Hollywood. It is no accident that such melodramas, pitting celluloid against VHS and DVD, theatrical against home viewing, and legal against illegal exhibition, are enacted in relation to Hollywood's crowning moment of self-definition and promotion. The Academy Awards have legendarily honored works and artists that epitomize cinematic achievement and thus represent the state of the film industry itself. As the interests of independent art and major studios collide, issues of quality often exist in an uneasy relationship with issues of power and money. Hence, this high-stakes competition can breed intense, broadly publicized battles that foreground the industry's economic and aesthetic anxieties in the form of controversial policy changes and disputes. Screeners provide ripe territory for such reactions for several reasons. For one thing, they are "other" within the traditional celluloid and theatrical hierarchies that define cinema in this context; their material composition and the situations in which they are viewed depart from conditions associated with "real" cinema. For another, screeners embody the matter-of-fact iterability of cinema in surrogate forms, so they produce, for some, unwanted instabilities in exhibition that can lead not only to judgments of value outside of customary aesthetics but also to promiscuous acts of distribution.

Given this state of affairs, screeners came to represent the possible destabilization of significant industry verities pertaining to quality and financial control. As such, they serve as small, but symbolically charged, reminders of the degree to which Hollywood can be unsettled in relation to new media venues involved in the distribution of its products, even after the profit potential of these venues has been vividly realized and exploited. Despite the magnificent financial gains the film industry has seen from cable television, VHS, and DVD, cinema's ability to be so easily reproduced for nontheatrical exhibition still manages to introduce the specter of chaos, a looming circumvention of tradition and regulation that can arouse Hollywood's protective reaction.

Nonetheless, the alarm about the unruliness of the nontheatrical circulation of films in this and other situations needs to be weighed against the industrial, social, and historical conditions that affect film viewing outside of theatrical precincts. In fact, in equating ancillary exhibition with disorder, such alarms draw our attention away from the rich cultivation of these alternative sites for viewing. Although film scholars have long studied the film industry's efforts to define moviegoing in relation to first-run features on the big screen, there has been comparatively little systematic analysis of how these efforts materialize in relation to nontheatrical situations of viewing and the recycled films that circulate so prolifically therein. For decades the most significant economic site for nontheatrical film exhibition in the United States, the home has naturally attracted the interest of Hollywood studios, along with myriad other entertainment businesses and industries, from the manufacturers of home theater equipment to Internet movie dot-coms. Moreover, as a crossroads for all manner of cultural discourses, the home emerges further as an intricate space of film consumption that requires substantial unpacking.

My book has examined multiple forces involved in the contemporary presentation and reception of Hollywood movies in the home. While my subject matter could be addressed through a number of different approaches, I have focused on the concept of home film cultures as a useful way of apprehending domestic space as an exhibition environment for cinema. The definition of public film cultures as entailing "an intermingling of ideas and institutions into recognisable formations" has provided a framework for identifying networks of industrial, cultural, aesthetic, historical, and personal discourses that have been influential in creating and maintaining a series of home film cultures.[3] In deploying this concept in relation to a private setting, I have tried to provide a sense of the meaningful circulation of films far from the madding cineplex crowd. Given the indispensable role that new media and technologies have played in the home, the film cultures I discuss are associated with developments that have helped to make the contemporary home into the most profitable and, arguably, the most experientially important sector of film exhibition.

Since each case study presents a distinct profile of a home film culture, I would like to consider points of symmetry that have emerged across the ensemble, especially to reckon with the orientation that the concept of film culture affords regarding the home's impact on movie exhibition and reception. Once mobilized in relation to the domestic sphere, film culture presupposes an intense process of social mediation at the heart of what might otherwise be considered a private encounter between viewer and film. Moreover, because film cultures are customarily concerned with the celebration of certain movies as well as with specific modes of interpretation, we can envisage the home as an important site for the constitution and exercise of taste, the canonization of particular genres and films, and interventions in narrative flow and textual meaning. Film cultures are often thought of as rarefied provinces, inhabited by elite communities of specialists or fiery devotees of one kind or another. My case studies, however, have illuminated the routine, bountiful presence of film cultures in everyday viewing. The home is a veritable factory of film cultures, making the formations of taste and value and accompanying strategies of textual appropriation into definitive features of ordinary fandom and media viewing.

As we have seen, neither the home nor its film cultures are sequestered from outside influences; rather, boundaries are permeable, allowing a reciprocal flow of discourses between public and private spheres. Hence, references to the home as a fortress in various sources reveal more about the cultural and ideological construction of the contemporary home than they do about the attainment of any actual sanctuary. That is, by depicting the home as a walled-off stronghold against the dangers of contemporary life, from terrorist acts to threatening microbes, industries attempt to create a siege mentality on the part of the homeowner. This mentality helps to expand markets in consumables designed to give the home a sense of insularity and/or security, from entertainment technologies to surveillance devices.[4] Within this circular logic, home theater is but one example of what we might call a fortress technology. It provides a domestic version of the public movie theater that saves the individual from the trouble, if not the risk, of going out; it thus depends on importing the newest and best products from the outside in order to generate a vision of a self-sufficient, inviolable interior space. Within the late twentieth and early twenty-first centuries, the figure of the fortress operates as a consumer label that opens the home to an array of products that appear to lock it down while enhancing its customary status as an alternative to the public sphere.

Although fortress imagery is not as explicitly deployed in relation to home film cultures unaffiliated with home theater, these cultures nonetheless demonstrate the importance of considering private acts of consumption in relation to the "ideas and institutions" that animate the encounters between viewers and films. Repeated consumption of the chick flick on the home front, for example, involves a constellation of discourses. Chick flicks and their home viewers meet in a highly charged environment—charged by industry promotions and film criticism that have accompanied the theatrical and ancillary debuts of the films; the sedimented significations that stars such as Julia Roberts have accumulated through other roles, interviews, and so on; teen canons created through repeat screenings by female viewers and their communities; romance genre conventions; contemporary understandings of feminism; the cultural trends of "cinematherapy" and 1980s nostalgia; and the individual viewer's socialization. Each of the other home film cultures I have discussed—home theater, high-tech film collecting, the cable recycling of Hollywood classics, and Internet short filmmaking—is similarly articulated through densely interwoven discursive networks.

Along with the notion of social mediation, I have stressed the extensive evaluative and interpretive dimensions of home film exhibition and reception. In home film cultures, these dimensions are most evident in relation to technologies with digital affiliations, such as home theater and DVD. An engagement with the digital world of cinema confers, to paraphrase Bourdieu, titles of cultural nobility on those viewers most immersed in this world. In this respect, home theater owners, "techie" film collectors, and other gadgeteers qualify as royalty in home film cultures. However, a sense of refined connoisseurship is also part of film cultures not always or as explicitly associated with the apparent perfections of digital technology. Puzzle film enthusiasts, for example, appear to display superior media competence through their ability to unlock the many secrets of quasi-modernist films. At the same time, cable TV's christening and celebration of older Hollywood films as American classics provide another means of elevating cinema and its viewers. However, the "high-toned" aspects of some domestic film cultures should not obscure the fact that taste is not always exercised within the framework of upwardly mobile class and/or aesthetic discourses. Given the culturally devalued nature of some preferences, coupled with a relative lack of affiliation with either sophisticated technological achievement or revered texts, some home viewers—ardent consumers of chick flicks or "pothead" films come to mind—inhabit a lower stratum in taste hierarchies.

Yet, this differential between high and low tastes is not primarily important for whatever discussion of culture wars in the home it might generate. Such differences simply confirm that the home is not a homogeneous

arena of exhibition; it is a fully fluid environment of reception, characterized by multiple taste formations that may collude, collide, or otherwise coexist in the everyday household consumption of texts. Further, the existence
of the varied tastes that cover the spectrum from high to low points to a fundamental characteristic of home film cultures: no matter whether the act of
cinematic taste is construed as refined or debased, it functions to bestow distinction on the viewer, if not in the eyes of society, then in the eyes of like-
minded peers. A family's elaborate home theater system may radiate the father's knowing management of the latest technologies, making him into
neighborhood nobility; however, the band member who can recite every
line from *Spinal Tap* likewise accedes to a princely domain among peers
similarly invested in a kind of cult literacy. Households are sites of profuse
qualitative distinctions about media, distinctions circulated by media industries and viewers intent on creating an aura of hipness and/or belonging through acts of taste.

As we have seen, some discourses within ancillary exhibition are expressly devoted to creating a sense of distinction. Discourses of mastery and
of the industry insider are particularly prominent in the industry address
of certain audiences as well as in the self-conception of some viewers themselves: home theater aficionados, discerning film collectors, puzzle film de-
coders, avid dialogue quoters, and clever parodists of Hollywood blockbusters. Through the proliferation of specialized communities devoted to
certain entertainment technologies and/or films, home film cultures attain
the sort of insular, privileged status associated with subcultures. That is,
home film cultures give rise to a sense of distinctiveness and difference born
out of a special knowledge, unique behavior, and/or cultural style that seem
to set one apart from the mainstream. A young woman's extensive ac-
quaintance with a particular chick flick represents a preference that is
shared by some and rejected by others, drawing boundaries between members of the taste group and indifferent or disapproving "outsiders." This
taste formation provides one example of how, despite their popular, mainstream status, home film cultures are infused with a sense of marginality
that in turn creates identities through media consumption.

Most of the home film cultures I have discussed would not qualify as
subcultures under accepted definitions of the term; indeed, they lack the
aura of danger and cultural effrontery associated with spectacular subcultures such as punk. They demonstrate, though, what Sarah Thornton refers
to as "subcultural capital," a display of being in the know that bestows status on certain individuals within a social group. As they are constituted and
expressed through acts of taste, home film cultures reveal how exceedingly

common the trade in this kind of capital is between cultural producers and consumers and within the consuming ranks themselves. Indeed, the opportunity to be in the know is as much a general form of address by mass cultural enterprises as it is an intimate form of self-understanding on the part of media viewers and fans. It is thus pivotal to the nature of the relationships among new entertainment technologies, media texts, and home viewers.

This mode of address also reveals how personal and social identities are routinely performed in the domestic exhibition environment. In the home film cultures I have analyzed, industry and other representations of who gets to be in the know are strongly marked by considerations of gender, race, and age. Here, white women and older demographics figure into the mix. But it is especially the cadres of white male "-philes" and young male viewers who attain a level of visibility that forges an implicit relationship between certain social identities and cinema technologies. Celebrations of fandom or the new freedoms enabled by technological developments must reckon more squarely with the strategies of inclusion and exclusion that pervade discourses of home media exhibition and reception. Whether in relation to male demographics or other groups of viewers, such strategies provide insight into the role that representations of media savvy and mastery play in generating and circulating notions of identity and difference.

Within the value-laden terrain of the home, certain genres and texts, some already successful at the box office, rise to prominence and are canonized. In this respect, we can recognize how extensively home film cultures amplify the blockbuster's cultural presence. As we have seen, the theatrical event film's sophisticated sound tracks and displays of CGI have found their counterpart in home theater and DVD. Because home theater and DVD represent technological excellence, films that realize the optimum operations of the machines involved are most suitable for a high-tech aesthetic. Genres heavy with dazzling visuals, special effects, and sound effects, such as action/adventure movies or science fiction films, assume a significant presence in the canons of home viewers fascinated with new advances in entertainment technologies.[5]

Blockbusters circulate through home film cultures in other ways as well. In the process of home replay, contemporary epics such as *The Matrix* attain a following on the basis of their complex visual style and "mind-bending" narratives, responding to a system of value as preoccupied with technology as it is with a modernist aesthetic. In addition, constantly recycled and repeatedly viewed, the event films of yore (e.g., the *Star Wars* and *Indiana Jones* series) maintain contemporary relevance for some viewers as nostalgic markers of childhood. Because of their sheer presence and popularity, blockbusters also serve as a ready source of catchphrases for those wishing to make cinematic lingo a part of their daily life or as eye-catching material for short film parodists to send up. Less directly, blockbusters represent standards of technological achievement that hover over the judgment of classic films when they are reissued in digitally remastered form or otherwise rejuvenated. Will these "old" films go the way of Woody Allen's earlier popular features on their rerelease, dismally failing to pass the rigorous test of technological relevance? Or will they, digitally "spruced up" and boasting extensive extra features, succeed in the digitally fixated market of images and sounds? As an embodiment of entertainment and its technologies, the blockbuster serves as fodder for diverse kinds of household appropriations, signaling its status as both a central principle of contemporary viewing and a model that informs the prerogatives of particular film cultures and desires.

Of course, the blockbuster does not monopolize the world of popular home film genres. Other types of films find new or renewed life in a domestic context. The Internet provides a cornucopia of popular genres, including parody, and mixes conventional with unconventional or local genres. Transitory colloquial genres are, in fact, a hallmark of ancillary markets. Puzzle films, such as *The Matrix*, can be blockbusters, but the criteria that matter most to this supergenre have less to do with technological pyrotechnics than with the film's ability to play "mind games" through an assembly of narrative and visual traits that demonstrate artistry, complexity, and surprise. Already a major theatrical category, the chick flick embraces numerous genres, as long as they feature a spunky female protagonist on a quest for self-identity that proceeds through a maze of relationship conflicts. As classic Hollywood films make up their own genre in ancillary markets, they too experience the effects of new generic markers; although individual films may exhibit the traits of films noir or Westerns, they unite across generic borders by signifying pastness and the presumption of quality that accompanies age and the legendary status of Hollywood studios, directors, and stars.

Beyond showing the home's influence in the posttheatrical life of a film, such examples highlight how central repurposing is to comprehending the phenomenon of genre, the activity of textual interpretation, and the specificity of audiences. Films and genres emerge not as stable entities but as texts and groupings of texts that gain their meaning and significance within processes of exhibition and reception. These processes may be informal and transient, but they tangibly demonstrate how audiences appropriate the films in their midst and how, in turn, recycled films are subject to shifting meanings. Whether domesticated films attract expected audiences (e.g., chick flicks and women) or unexpected audiences (e.g., Brian De Palma's *Scarface* [1983] and gangsta rappers), they provide the opportunity to weigh, beyond theatrical provinces, the connections between media consumption and subjectivity, the manner in which people deploy media to shore up, transform, or otherwise operate on individual and collective identities.

Home exhibition has also affected film narrative; in fact, the home represents an extraordinary forum for manipulating and reconfiguring narrative. The remote control alone offers the continuous potential for muscular intervention in the orderly procession of filmic events. It is conceivable that the viewer might use the remote's fast-forward, pause, rewind, scene selection, and other functions to career willy-nilly through a film—the cinematic equivalent of a joy ride. Indeed, the remote is often considered an emblem of viewer freedom. My study suggests, however, that remote functions tend to be deployed in a more organized manner. Specifically, the remote enables viewers to target moments that embody the crux of a film's generic appeal (e.g., action scenes in an action/adventure film or musical numbers in a musical), allowing considerations of genre to trump narrative chronology and drive the viewer's pleasurable engagement. Genre and the viewer's competency—that is, the ability to recognize the genre's definitive moments—help to choreograph the remote control's intervention in the narrative flow. In contrast, some viewers refuse to interrupt the narrative, shunning the remote as a device that compromises film aesthetics. Considering themselves purists, these individuals attempt to reproduce the standards of the motion picture theater in the home, watching films from start to finish in a darkened environment that encourages this continuous rapport. Despite their refusal of narrative surfing, purists' use of the remote nonetheless suggests the influence of factors associated with the public circulation of films—at the very least, the theatrical situation itself as it has become a model for home viewing.

Other viewing strategies and practices function in different ways either to displace or to embrace narrative. The home theater and DVD hardware aesthetic displaces narrative by prizing digital images and sounds over considerations of story and acting. Short film parodies, such as those sending up *The Blair Witch Project* and *The Phantom Menace*, invest more heavily in narrative, reworking or foregrounding story elements as a signature component of their appropriation. A similar kind of foregrounding occurs in less material practices of interpretation. In re-viewing, textual appropriations focus on elements that realize the viewer's aesthetic, emotional, nostalgic, or imitative interests. Each of these processes personalizes a film through repeated use, interacting differently with the narrative. For instance, while the aesthetically inclined viewer may scour the narrative for multilayered meanings or for clues that help to signal and explain the surprise ending, the viewer trolling for emotional satisfaction may watch just the final scene from a male weepie to immerse himself in its tragic and/or heroic conclusion. Similarly, audience members regarding a film as a performance they can imitate in daily life may select certain scenes or lines of dialogue that best represent their individual or group identities, and those seeking a nostalgic fix may experience the narrative as a series of signposts to the past. These modes of re-viewing are by no means mutually exclusive—indeed, their pleasures can mingle during the same screening. Taken alone, each simply indicates the degree to which narrative is subject to graphically different reimaginings within the frames of particular film cultures.

As the example of teen nostalgia suggests, the remotivation of narrative also prompts us to consider the effects that repurposing has on the relationship between film and history. When older films reappear on classic cable television, VHS, and DVD, they are greeted with inevitable processes of historical revisionism—inevitable because texts are made accessible or relevant to new audiences by updating or otherwise operating on their previous historical identities. This adaptive reuse occurs through different kinds of presentism: the technological presentism of the hardware aesthetic, in which older films must approximate contemporary visual and aural standards to attain value in a contemporary market; and a subtler type of presentism, in which the histories of classical Hollywood films are redefined within a progressive, nationalistic narrative that visualizes the past as marching toward a just and egalitarian contemporary time. Although remembrances of classic films sometimes involve the depiction of a better past, teen nostalgia invests more systematically in this vision to achieve its emotional effects, comparing a less-than-perfect present with a more desirable past. This vision helps to identify the 1980s as a repository of poignant, sentimental reminders of a simpler childhood in contrast with a more turbulent today.

In either case, cinematic variables—stars, narratives, mise-en-scènes, cinematography, and/or sound—provide the materials for a wrestling match between the past and present in which the older artifact becomes a vehicle for expressing the concerns of contemporary society. Thus, in the process of restoring a film such as *Vertigo* for commercial rerelease, claims of fidelity to the director's original vision are realized through a digital update of image and sound that not only foregrounds film style but also promotes the technical superiority of the men who remake the movies in an era when U.S. global power is both asserted and contested. Similarly, *Ferris Bueller's Day Off*—not a nostalgia film when it was first released—has become a cult exemplar of the travails of 1980s teen life for university students who privilege the mass cultural fun of the 1980s over its more dystopian elements.

These remotivations of narrative neither sweep other historical claims from the playing field nor prevent other versions of the past from coexisting in dialectical tension. The rescripting of history that occurs through home forums most pointedly offers evidence of the historical stakes involved in media recycling. Repurposing does not return a film to us in some historically innocent form; the film is resuscitated through a host of contemporary interests. Each of the film cultures I have discussed thus represents a mode of interpretation that offers, at the same time, a particular way of historicizing the past that must find its way among numerous competing accounts of what came before.

Like other dynamics in home film cultures, the phenomenon of rehistoricization invites us to untangle the discourses that inform the presentation and consumption of recycled movies in the household. While home exhibition and reception are reciprocally related to theatrical practices economically, aesthetically, and experientially, the home, as I have endeavored to show, is animated by specific forces that help to define the cultural relations surrounding moviegoing in an alternative sphere.

Once the notion of social mediation assumes a central place in a theory of reception, the possibility of countermainstream or radical film readings becomes more complicated. By focusing on the home as a "signal" system for cinema, I have not intended to deny this possibility. Nor have I meant to discredit or demonize ways of watching films that fail to generate against-the-grain readings. Rather, by exploring the depth and breadth of the discursive elements involved in home film cultures, I have aimed to develop an account of ordinary viewing that addresses the politics of interpretation. Instead of considering the ordinary as though it is opposed to resistant political modes of viewing, I see it as involving what scholars would consider both mainstream and counterhegemonic readings. Resistant readings, including fan appropriations, are not an exception to the rule; they are an intimate, indispensable part of everyday decodings of mass cultural texts. Further, no act of viewing is "pure"; each is multilayered, intricate, immersed in sometimes contradictory social and discursive worlds. Recalling karaoke cinema practitioners for a moment, one sees that they poach from the Hollywood preserve for their materials, "stealing" from the industry for their own purposes. These purposes may include a performance of masculine identity that simultaneously foregrounds the artifice of gender and negotiates a kinship with dominant ideas of masculinity and nationalism. By suggesting the everydayness of resistant textual appropriations and their implication in deeper social circuits that may result in contradiction, I want to entertain the idea that resistance is at once a more common and more knotty affair than we might have thought. Throughout my book I have argued that ordinary viewing always involves the potential for critique at the same time as it displays the tense harmonies that exist between critique and other discourses flowing through the encounters between viewers and films.

Granting that the real effects of cultural domination are, as Stuart Hall has argued, "neither all-powerful nor all-inclusive," it remains important to grasp how they materialize at street level—or, in this case, at the threshold of the home as a site of movie consumption.[6] This perspective allows us to uncover the cultural processes that negotiate ways of viewing films introduced by new entertainment technologies. As home theater and DVD have taken home entertainment by storm, suggesting a revolution in the domestic film experience, evidence shows that their promotion and use have often been inscribed within traditional associations of men and machines, white masculinity and technology. Contemporary discourses may tweak these associations in various ways, but they have thus far tended to maintain a privileged status for certain viewers and cultural identities. The persistence of powerful ideologies in new phenomena is seen in a different way in the case of Internet film parodists. These parodists lampoon the conceits of Hollywood epics, yet their interventions are caught up in the paradoxes of the form in which original sources are both revered and deposed. These paradoxes are amplified by an Internet filmmaking ethos that considers amateur acts of sabotage as rites of passage to Hollywood success.

While all acts of reception need to be understood within discursive contexts, my case studies have profiled film cultures that demonstrate vivid continuities between producing and consuming cultures. However, as I have argued, any film culture is volatile. Comprising numerous discursive flows and subject to historical change, a film culture mixes "progressive elements and stone age elements" and thus is always potentially unstable and unpredictable ideologically.[7] Further, each of the home film cultures I have discussed is multifaceted; clearly, different kinds of home theater owners, film collectors, classic Hollywood buffs, repeat viewers, and e-filmmakers dwell in the home. The existence of other new technologies and media involved in film exhibition—for example, satellite television, HDTV, pay-per-view, TiVo—only emphasizes the immense scope of this terrain, its status as a bountiful locale for diverse investigations of the "ideas and institutions" at play in the household consumption of movies. Equally important, as Charlotte Brunsdon has maintained, the relationship between viewers and media technologies is characterized by fluctuating identifications that shift according to situation and other variables. We should thus be "cautious about ascribing essential qualities to technologies and technological use." That said, we must continue to be "alert to the patternings of power in specific historical divisions of labour, use, and attitude."[8]

Like other nontheatrical exhibition sites in film history, from the street carnival to the airplane, the home is at once a cultural institution, a material space, a habitat for individuals and their interactions, a sphere of entertainment, and a register of social and historical dynamics and developments. Although it would be impossible to map comprehensively the implications of any nontheatrical venue for the study of film exhibition and reception, such venues suggest the clamorous presence of a cinema of everywhere stretching intimately into myriad precincts of everyday life.

Notes

Introduction. What Is Cinema Today?

1. Quoted in Bernard Weinraub, "A Movie Mogul in Love . . . with Winning," *New York Times*, March 23, 1999, sec. B, 1, 7.

2. For representative discussions of cinema's alteration in the home, see Douglas Gomery, *Shared Pleasures: A History of Movie Presentation in the United States* (Madison: University of Wisconsin Press, 1992), 257–62; and Kerry Segrave, *Movies at Home: How Hollywood Came to Television* (Jefferson, NC: McFarland, 1999), 123–58.

3. Susan Sontag, "The Decay of Cinema," *New York Times Magazine*, February 25, 1996, 60.

4. Roy Rosenzweig, "From Rum Shop to Rialto: Workers and Movies," in *Moviegoing in America*, ed. Gregory A. Waller (Oxford: Blackwell Publishers, 2002), 32–33; and Janet Staiger, "Writing the History of American Film Reception," in *Hollywood Spectatorship: Changing Perceptions of Cinema Audiences*, ed. Melvyn Stokes and Richard Maltby (London: British Film Institute Publishing, 2001), 20–26. Haidee Wasson's *Museum Movies: The Museum of Modern Art and the Birth of Art Cinema* (Berkeley: University of California Press, 2004) suggests that reverent modes of watching movies are not a natural consequence of the darkened motion picture theater; they are, rather, institutionally mandated and enforced.

5. Uma Dinsmore-Tuli, "The Pleasures of 'Home Cinema,' or Watching Movies on Telly: An Audience Study of Cinephiliac VCR Use," *Screen* 41, no. 3 (2000): 315–27.

6. Excellent work on nontheatrical cinema ranges from Gregory Waller's exploration of prenickelodeon movie exhibition in *Main Street Amusements: Movies and Commercial Entertainment in a Southern City, 1896–1930* (Washington, DC: Smithsonian Institution Press, 1995) to Ann Gray's empirical study of VCR use in U.K. households in *Video Playtime: The Gendering of a Leisure Technology* (London: Routledge, 1992).

7. Janet Wasko, *Hollywood in the Information Age: Beyond the Silver Screen* (Austin: University of Texas Press, 1994), 3.

8. Toby Miller et al., *Global Hollywood* (London: British Film Institute Publishing, 2001), 8.

9. Ethnographic approaches to audiences have been a particular mainstay in television and new media studies. See, for example, David Morley, *The "Nationwide" Audience: Structure and Decoding* (London: British Film Institute Publishing, 1980); Roger Silverstone and Eric Hirsch, *Consuming Technologies: Media and Information in Domestic Spaces* (London: Routledge, 1992); and Ellen Seiter, *Television and New Media* (Oxford: Clarendon Press, 1999).

10. Ben Singer, "Early Home Cinema and the Edison Home Projecting Kinetoscope," *Film History* 2 (1988): 37–38.

11. Moya Luckett, "'Filming the Family': Home Movie Systems and the Domestication of Spectatorship," *Velvet Light Trap* 36 (1995): 21–32.

12. Patrick R. Parsons and Robert M. Friedan, *The Cable and Satellite Television Industries* (Needham Heights, MA: Allyn and Bacon, 1998), 199.

13. Ibid., 244.

14. Umberto Eco, *Travels in Hyperreality*, trans. William Weaver (New York: Harcourt, Brace, and Company, 1986), 3–6.

15. David Morley, *Home Territories: Media, Mobility, and Identity* (London: Routledge, 2000), especially 16–30 and 86–104.

16. Roger Silverstone, *Television and Everyday Life* (London: Routledge, 1994), 98–99.

17. Tom Ryall, *Alfred Hitchcock and the British Cinema* (Urbana: University of Illinois Press, 1986), 2.

18. Shaun Moores, *Satellite Television and Everyday Life* (Luton, UK: University of Luton Press, 1996), 57–60.

19. Henry Jenkins wrote the foundational text for this view of fans: *Textual Poachers: Television Fans and Participatory Culture* (London: Routledge, 1992).

20. Hazel Carby, "The Multicultural Wars," in *Black Popular Culture*, ed. Gina Dent (Seattle: Bay Press, 1992), 193; and Richard Dyer, *White* (London: Routledge, 1997), 2.

1. The New Media Aristocrats

1. S. C. Gilfillan, "The Future of Home Theater," *Independent* 17 (October 1912): 886, 887.

2. Peter Kramer, "The Lure of the Big Picture: Film, Television, and Hollywood," in *Big Picture, Small Screen: Relations between Film and Television*, ed. John Hill and Martin McLoone (Luton, UK: University of Luton Press, 1996), 15.

3. Lynn Spigel, *Make Room for Television: Television and the Family Ideal in Postwar America* (Chicago: University of Chicago Press, 1992), 99–135.

4. André Bazin, *What Is Cinema?*, vol. 1, trans. Hugh Gray (Berkeley: University of California Press, 1967), 21.

5. Sabra Chartrand, "Patents," *New York Times*, April 23, 2001, sec. C, 2.

6. Raymond Williams, *The Sociology of Culture* (New York: Schocken Books, 1982), 130–31.

7. Pierre Bourdieu, *Distinction: A Social Critique of the Judgement of Taste*, trans. Richard Nice (Cambridge, MA: Harvard University Press, 1984), 23–24. Hereafter, this work is cited parenthetically in the text.

8. For a discussion of the similar marketing of radio as superior to existing media, see Roland Marchand, *Advertising and the American Dream: Making Way for Modernity, 1920–1940* (Berkeley: University of California Press, 1985), 140–46.

9. Eric Hirsch, "New Technologies and Domestic Consumption," in *The Television Studies Book*, ed. Christine Geraghty and David Lusted (London: Arnold, 1998), 159, 160.

10. Joel Brinkley, "After 15 Years, the Music CD Faces an Upscale Competitor," *New York Times*, July 28, 1997, sec. C, 6; *Billboard*, November 25, 2000: 58; Consumer Electronics Association, "Home Theater Advances 2003–2004," www.ce.org/publications/books_references/digital_america/home_theater/default.asp (accessed on May 1, 2005).

11. *Billboard*, November 25, 2000, 58.

12. Lawrence B. Johnson, "After Sonic Saturation, a Quiet Return to Hi-Fi Values," *New York Times*, September 8, 1996, 38.

13. Lawrence B. Johnson, "DVD Hype Gives Way to DVD," *New York Times*, April 13, 1997, 37; and Katie Hafner, "Drawn to the Hearth's Electronic Glow," *New York Times*, January 24, 2002, sec. D, 1. Hereafter, the latter work is cited parenthetically in the text.

14. *Billboard*, December 15, 2001, 42.

15. Advertisement for Macintosh Laboratory, Inc., *Home Theater Technology Buyer's Guide* (1995), 63; and advertisement for Sound by Singer, *Audio Visual Interiors* (December 1995): 104.

16. Advertisement for Parasound Products, Inc., *Widescreen Review* (May/June 1995): 91.

17. J. D. Biersdorfer, "For Stay-at-Home Film Buffs with a Taste for the Opulent," *New York Times*, February 27, 2003, sec. E, 3; and Stephen G. Henderson, "Home Movies," www.sunspot.net/features/home, August 24, 2003.

18. Advertisement for Professional Audio/Video Retailers Association, *Audio Video Interiors* (December 1995): 44.

19. Advertisement for Kenwood USA, Ltd., *Home Theater Technology* (September 1995): 1–2.

20. Advertisements for Runco International and Marantz America, Inc., *Home Theater* (November 1998): 31, 35.

21. William Boddy, "Archaeologies of Electronic Vision and the Gendered Spectator," *Screen* 35, no. 2 (1994): 107.

22. Douglas Gomery, *Shared Pleasures: A History of Movie Presentation in the United States* (Madison: University of Wisconsin Press, 1992), 103–4; and Rick Lyman, "A Partly Cloudy Forecast for Theater Owners," *New York Times*, March 12, 2001, sec. C, 12.

23. On theater owners' difficulties, see Lyman, "A Partly Cloudy Forecast," sec. C, 12; and Geraldine Fabrikant, "Ticket Sales Cool in August, but a Strong

Year Is Seen," *New York Times,* September 2, 2002, sec. C, 4. As these writers observe, by the end of 2000, it appeared that theater owners had been too enthusiastic in their plans for expansion. Overbuilding caused eleven theater chains (including Carmike, Regal, and Loews) to file for bankruptcy, close theaters, and reorganize.

24. See Brett Anderson et al., *Theo Kalomirakis' Private Theaters* (Malibu, CA: Home Theater Magazine, 1997); and Steven Castle et al., *Great Escapes: New Designs for Home Theaters by Theo Kalomirakis* (New York: Harry N. Abrams, 2003).

25. Advertisement for Zenith Electronics Incorporation, *Home Theater* (January 2002): 31.

26. Advertisement for Sanus Systems, *Home Theater Buyer's Guide 2001,* 93.

27. Advertisement for Radia Series, *Home Theater Technology* (July 1995): 139.

28. Advertisement for AudioEase, *Home Theater* (June 1997): 161.

29. Advertisement for Stereostone, Inc., *Home Theater Technology* (July 1995): 111.

30. Amy Goldwasser, "Where to Put a TV So Big That It's On When It's Off," *New York Times,* January 31, 2002, sec. B, 10.

31. Spigel, 49; Charlotte Brunsdon, *Screen Tastes: Soap Opera to Satellite Dishes* (London: Routledge, 1997), 148–64.

32. Quoted phrase from David Morley, "Television: Not So Much a Visual Medium, More a Visible Object," in *Visual Culture,* ed. Chris Jenks (London: Routledge, 1995), 181.

33. On this point, see Gomery, *Shared Pleasures,* 47–56.

34. Advertisement for Meridian Audio, *Home Theater* (June 1997): 55.

35. Marchand, *Advertising and the American Dream,* 140–46.

36. Julie V. Iovine, "Families Realign for Sunday 'Guilt' TV," *New York Times,* September 22, 2002, 2.

37. Advertisement for the Professional Audio/Video Retailers Association, *Audio Video Interiors* (December 1995): 44; and advertisement for Zenith Electronics Corporation, *Home Theater* (February 1999), 107.

38. Rebecca Day, "LightStyles," *Audio Video Interiors* (December 1995): 28.

39. Steve Kempster, "Snacks, Wine, Videotape," *Home Theater Technology* (June 1995): 54–55.

40. "Libations," *Home Theater* (November 1998): 111; and *Home Theater* (January 2002): 115.

41. Roy Rosenzweig, "From Rum Shop to Rialto: Workers and Movies," *Moviegoing in America,* ed. Gregory A. Waller (Oxford, UK: Blackwell Publishers, 2002), 34; and Gomery, *Shared Pleasures,* 79.

42. "What to Watch," *Entertainment Weekly,* August 22, 1997, 64.

43. See, for example, Marchand, *Advertising and the American Dream;* Don LeDuc, *Cable Television and the FCC: A Crisis in Media Control* (Philadelphia: Temple University Press, 1973); and Boddy, "Archaeologies of Electronic Vision and the Gendered Spectator."

44. James Naremore, "Authorship," in *A Companion to Film Theory*, ed. Toby Miller and Robert Stam (Oxford: Blackwell Publishers, 1999), 21.

45. Advertisement for *Home Theater Technology*, *Home Theater Technology* (July 1995): 105.

46. Advertisement for Pioneer Special Editions, *Home Theater Technology* (July 1995): 125.

47. Advertisement for Vidikron, *Home Theater* (November 1998): 77.

48. Advertisement for AV Architecture, *Home Theater Buyer's Guide 1995*, 111.

49. Advertisement for Toshiba DVD, *Home Theater* (June 1997): 37.

50. Advertisement for Martin Logan Ltd., *Audio Video Interiors* (December 1995): 21.

51. Advertisement for Parasound Products, Inc., *Audio Video Interiors* (December 1995): 6–7; and advertisement for Energy Speaker Systems, *Home Theater Buyer's Guide 1995*, 77.

52. Bill Wolfe, "Are You Experienced?" *Video* (July/August 1995): 6.

53. Jean Baudrillard, *Simulations*, trans. Paul Foss et al. (New York: Semiotext[e], 1983), 4.

54. Martha Rossler, "Image Simulations, Computer Manipulations: Some Considerations," *Afterimage* 17, no. 4 (1989): 7–11.

55. Advertisement for Universal Remote Control, Inc., *Home Theater Buyer's Guide 1997*, 33.

56. Advertisement for Loewe, *Home Theater* (November 1998): 25–27.

57. William L. Hamilton, "The Stylish Seek Stars, but TV Seating Draws Crowds," *New York Times*, May 22, 2003, sec. D, 7.

58. Ibid.

59. For a discussion of the father's place in the home in 1950s television, see Spigel, *Make Room for Television*, 60–65.

60. Anne-Jorunn Berg has written on the masculine nature of the smart home's promotion in Europe in "A Gendered Socio-Technical Construction: The Smart House," in *Bringing Technology Home: Gender and Technology in a Changing Europe*, ed. Cynthia Cockburn and Ruza Furst Dilic (Buckingham, UK: Open University Press, 1994), 165–80.

61. Quoted phrase from Shaun Moores, *Satellite Television and Everyday Life: Articulating Technology* (Luton, UK: University of Luton, 1996), 57.

62. Ann Gray, *Video Playtime: The Gendering of a Leisure Technology* (London: Routledge, 1992).

63. Stuart Ewen, *Captains of Consciousness: Advertising and the Social Roots of Consumer Culture* (New York: McGraw-Hill, 1976), 94.

64. Gray, *Video Playtime*, 252. Besides Gray's book and Cockburn and Furst's edited volume, other works that reflect on technology's relationship to gender in the home include David Morley, *Family Television: Cultural Power and Domestic Leisure* (London: Routledge, 1988), and Stevi Jackson and Shaun Moores, eds., *The Politics of Domestic Consumption* (London: Prentice-Hall, 1995). For a study that considers multiple new technologies and media in rela-

tion to the home and questions of the public and private sphere, see David Morley, *Television, Audiences & Cultural Studies* (London: Routledge, 1992), especially 221–69.

65. Gianluca Sergi usefully suggests that, while bigger budgets can finance extravagant soundtracks as well as complex, multilayered sound environments, no definitive line occurs between "average" Hollywood productions and blockbusters in terms of sound. In its emphasis on digital surround sound, home theater may help muddy these waters even further, giving every film the chance to realize superior sound. See Sergi, "Blockbusting Sound: The Case of *The Fugitive*," in *Movie Blockbusters*, ed. Julian Stringer (London: Routledge, 2003), 150–51.

66. John Ellis, *Visible Fictions: Cinema, Television, Video* (London: Routledge, 1992), 38–61.

67. John Thornton Caldwell, *Televisuality: Style, Crisis, and Authority in American Television* (New Brunswick, NJ: Rutgers University Press, 1995).

68. Rick Altman, "Television/Sound," in *Studies in Entertainment: Critical Approaches to Mass Culture*, ed. Tania Modleski (Bloomington: Indiana University Press, 1986), 46.

69. Elaine Tyler May, *Homeward Bound: American Families in the Cold War Era* (New York: Basic Books, 1988), 16–20.

70. On disaster movies and the millennium, see Diane Negra, "*Titanic*, Survivalism, and the Millennial Myth," in *Titanic: Anatomy of a Blockbuster*, ed. Kevin S. Sandler and Gaylyn Studlar (New Brunswick, NJ: Rutgers University Press, 1999), 220–38.

71. Morley, "Not So Much a Visual Medium," 170–71.

2. The Contemporary Cinephile

1. Christian Metz, *The Imaginary Signifier: Psychoanalysis and the Cinema*, trans. Celia Britton et al. (Bloomington: Indiana University Press, 1977), 74–75 and 79.

2. Roland Barthes, "Upon Leaving the Movie Theater," trans. Bertrand Augst and Susan White, in *Cinematographic Apparatus: Selected Writings*, ed. Theresa Hak Kyung Cha (New York: Tanam Press, 1980), 2.

3. Shaun Moores, *Satellite Television and Everyday Life: Articulating Technology* (Luton, UK: University of Luton, 1996), 58.

4. Anthony Slide, *Before Video: A History of the Non-Theatrical Film* (Westport, CT: Greenwood Press, 1992), 116–17.

5. Haidee Wasson has written on an earlier moment of home film collecting in "The Film of the Month Club: 16mm, the Home Film Library, and Educated Viewing in the 1920s," paper presented at the Cinema and Everyday Life conference, University College, London, June 2003. On the activities of noted collectors and organizations to archive and preserve films, see Anthony Slide, *Nitrate Won't Wait: Film Preservation in the United States* (Jefferson, NC: McFarland, 1992), especially 45–60.

6. Timothy Corrigan, *A Cinema without Walls: Movies and Culture after Vietnam* (New Brunswick, NJ: Rutgers University Press, 1991), 81.

7. Rick Lyman, "Revolt in the Den: DVD Has the VCR Headed to the Attic," *New York Times*, August 26, 2002, sec. A, 1, 13; David D. Kirkpatrick, "Action-Hungry DVD Fans Sway Hollywood," *New York Times*, August 17, 2003, 1; Laurie J. Flynn, "One Man's 2 Challenges," *New York Times*, June 3, 2002, sec. C, 4; William L. Hamilton, "For Home Theaters, Chairs Are a Blockbuster," *New York Times*, May 22, 2003, sec. D, 7; Jon Gertner, "Box Office in a Box," *New York Times Magazine*, November 14, 2004, 107; and Digital Entertainment Group, "Industry Boosted by $21.2 Billion in Annual DVD Sales and Rentals," www.dvdinformation.com/News/press/CESO/0605.htm (accessed January 6, 2005).

8. Peter M. Nichols, "Land of the Cineplex, Home of the Cassette," *New York Times*, July 13, 1997, sec. 2, 1.

9. Robert C. Allen, "Home Alone Together: Hollywood and the 'Family Film,'" in *Identifying Hollywood Audiences*, ed. Melvyn Stokes and Richard Maltby (London: British Film Institute Publishing, 1999), 113.

10. Bruce Austin has written on early pricing structures in the video market in "Home Video: The Second-Run 'Theater' of the 1990s," in *Hollywood in the Age of Television*, ed. Tino Balio (Cambridge, MA: Unwin Hyman, 1990), 319–49.

11. Megumi Komiya and Barry Litman, "The Economics of the Prerecorded Videocassette Industry," in *Social and Cultural Aspects of VCR Use*, ed. Julia R. Dobrow (Hillsdale, NJ: Lawrence Erlbaum Associates, 1990), 41.

12. Allen, "Home Alone Together," 118.

13. Lyman, "Revolt in the Den," 1; Peter M. Nichols, "Video Revenue Is Still Rising," *New York Times*, July 25, 2003, sec. B, 26.

14. Wilson Rothman, "I Don't Rent. I Own," *New York Times*, February 26, 2004, sec. E, 1; and Digital Entertainment Group, "Industry Boosted by $21.2 Billion in Annual DVD Sales and Rentals."

15. A new film costs vendors approximately eighteen dollars on DVD and thirty-five dollars on VHS. With obvious benefits for consumers, lower wholesale rates for DVD also mean that vendors need fewer rentals to make a profit. Further, while videos degenerate and get dirty through multiple rentals and are thus less useful when it comes time to sell overstocks, the more durable DVDs can be more easily sold after a few weeks of rental. See Peter M. Nichols, "DVD Has Begun to Take Over," *New York Times*, June 28, 2002, sec. B, 25.

16. Peter M. Nichols, "DVD Struggles with Success," *New York Times*, January 19, 2001, sec. B, 33.

17. Advertisement, *Entertainment Weekly*, November 7, 1997, 17.

18. Advertisement, *Entertainment Weekly*, October 31, 1997, 21.

19. Allen, "Home Alone Together," 118. His study provides a history of family video use.

20. On the subject of "low-end" media audiences, see Jeffrey Sconce, "'Trashing' the Academy: Taste, Excess, and the Emerging Politics of Cinematic

Style," *Screen* 36, no. 4 (1995): 371–93; and Joan Hawkins, *Cutting Edge: Art Horror and the Horrific Avant-Garde* (Minneapolis: University of Minnesota Press, 2000), 41–49.

21. Advertisement, *Video Magazine* (July 1995): 25.

22. Peter M. Nichols, "DVD and VCR: Ménage à Deux," *New York Times,* April 20, 2001, sec. B, 26.

23. In terms of male tastes in genre, Guzzlefish.com, a site with fourteen thousand subscriber-collectors, reflects the proclivity toward action and special-effects films among its members. In 2004, it ranked the top four collected titles on DVD among its constituency, in order of popularity, as *The Lord of the Rings: The Fellowship of the Ring* (2001), *The Lord of the Rings: The Two Towers* (2002), *The Matrix,* and *Fight Club* (1999), with action-film stars Samuel Jackson, Robert De Niro, and Chow Yun-Fat as the most "collected" actors.

24. Kirkpatrick, "Action-Hungry DVD Fans," 1, 15.

25. Ibid.; Peter M. Nichols, "Older Viewers Turn to DVD," *New York Times,* March 28, 2003, sec. E, 34.

26. Walter Benjamin, "Unpacking My Library," in *Illuminations,* trans. Harry Zohn (New York: Schocken Books, 1969), 60, 67.

27. James Clifford, "On Collecting Art and Culture," in *The Cultural Studies Reader,* ed. Simon During (London: Routledge, 1993), 52–53. On this subject as it relates to film, see Uma Dinsmore, "Chaos, Order, and Plastic Boxes: The Significance of Videotapes for the People Who Collect Them," in *The Television Studies Book,* ed. Christine Geraghty and David Lusted (London: Arnold, 1998), 317–26. Dinsmore finds that, while many collectors have elaborate organization systems, some libraries exist in apparent disorder, wherein the collector's intimate knowledge of a film's whereabouts allows him or her to locate it. Just the same, recognizing that their collections will grow, these individuals realize the need for a more efficient system.

28. "Laser Disc Collector for Windows," from "The Obsessive Collector," *Laser Disc Newsletter* (February 1997): 17. The title of the *Laser Disc Newsletter* was changed in 1999 to the *DVD–Laser Disc Newsletter* to reflect the growth of the DVD market and subsequent dwindling of laser disc as the digital format of choice for home exhibition. Online sites that catalog collections for collectors according to title, director, actor, and so forth, include Guzzlefish.com.

29. Advertisement for Goldwyn Classics Eddie Cantor Series, *Home Theater Technology* (July 1995): 119.

30. Advertisement for Pioneer Entertainment's "Star Trek: The Movie Voyages," *Home Theater Technology Buyer's Guide* (1995), 29.

31. Charles Tashiro, "The Contradictions of Video Collecting," *Film Quarterly* 50 (Winter 1996/97): 15. See also *Laser Disc Newsletter* (February 1997): 13–17.

32. On the vote, see *Laser Disc Newsletter* (February 1997): 1, 10–11.

33. Peter M. Nichols, "Home Video: From Directors, a Word, or Two," *New York Times,* September 6, 2002, sec. E, 26.

34. Henry Jenkins, *Textual Poachers: Television Fans and Participatory Culture* (New York: Routledge, 1992), 87.

35. Scholars differ on how to assess the fan's relation to media knowledge. Some, such as Jenkins, see the fan's intimate knowledge of and ability to produce criticism of TV shows as an empowering development. Others, such as Bernard Sharratt, regard the popular cultural experts' status as a "semifantasy" maintained to compensate for their lack of power within larger political and social systems ("The Politics of the Popular? From Melodrama to Television," in *Performance and Politics in Popular Drama*, ed. David Bradby et al. [Cambridge: Cambridge University Press, 1980], 283).

36. Tashiro, "The Contradictions of Video Collecting," 11, 15–16.

37. Ibid., 16, 13.

38. Kirkpatrick, "Action-Hungry DVD Fans," 1.

39. Dinsmore, "Chaos, Order, and Plastic Boxes," 324. In her report of interviews with two film collectors in Britain, Dinsmore shows that technophilia is present in video collecting while also pointing out that technophobes (especially those interested in older films) focus on other priorities in their selection process, such as stars, studios, and the periods in which films were produced.

40. Advertisement, *Home Theater* (June 1997): 9; and advertisement, *Widescreen Review* (May/June 1995): 9.

41. Review of *Last Man Standing*, by Walter Hill, *Laser Disc Newsletter* (July 1997): 1–2.

42. Review of *Annie Hall*, by Woody Allen, *Total DVD* (September 2000): 44.

43. Ibid.

44. Doug Brod et al., "The 50 Essential DVDs," *Entertainment Weekly*, January 19, 2001, 22–43.

45. Ibid., 24.

46. Review of *Sanjuro*, by Akira Kurosawa, *Widescreen Review* (May/June 1995): 129.

47. Review of *The Fly*, by Kurt Neumann, *Widescreen Review* (May 1997): 156.

48. Review of *The Pirate*, by Vincente Minnelli, *Video Magazine* (July/August 1995): 70.

49. Review of *The Sound of Music*, by Robert Wise, *Ultimate Widescreen DVD Movie Guide* 1, no. 1 (2001): 176–77.

50. Review of *Forrest Gump*, by Robert Zemeckis, *Video Magazine* (July/August 1995): 69.

51. "*Platoon:* Oliver Stone's Epic Vietnam War Masterpiece," *Widescreen Review* (May/June 1995): 110.

52. Internet newsgroup alt.video.laserdisc, June 24, 1997.

53. Ibid.

54. Susan Stewart, *On Longing: Narratives of the Miniature, the Gigantic, the Souvenir, the Collection* (Durham, NC: Duke University Press, 1993),

151–54; Rheims quoted by Jean Baudrillard, *The System of Objects,* trans. James Benedict (London: Verso, 1996), 95; and for Baudrillard's direct quote, 95. Despite my view of the importance of presentism, clearly the issue of time is a complex subject that bears further scrutiny in relation to contemporary film collecting.

55. Stewart, *On Longing,* 158, 162, 159. This displacement of the material conditions of production to serve consumer fantasies recalls Theodor Adorno's discussion of commodity fetishism in mass culture in "On the Fetish Character in Music and the Regression of Listening," in *The Essential Frankfurt School Reader,* ed. Andrew Arato and Eike Gebhardt (New York: Urizen Books, 1978), 270–99.

56. Many who study collecting see it as an instance of narcissism and regression, also components of Metz's argument about cinephilia. See, for example, Werner Muensterberger, *Collecting: An Unruly Passion* (New York: Harcourt, Brace, 1994).

3. Remembrance of Films Past

1. For example, Lynn Spigel and Henry Jenkins have written on personal media recollections in "Same Bat Channel, Different Bat Times: Mass Culture and Popular Memory," in *The Many Lives of Batman: Critical Approaches to a Superhero and His Media,* ed. Roberta E. Pearson and William Uricchio (New York: Routledge, 1991), 117–48. For work on film texts and memory, see, for example, Miriam Bratu Hansen, "*Schindler's List* Is Not *Shoah:* The Second Commandment, Popular Modernism, and Public Memory," *Critical Inquiry* 22, no. 2 (1996): 292–312.

2. Stephen Henderson, "Teaching New Generations the Joys of Old Movies," *New York Times,* June 8, 1997, 29–30.

3. Les Luchter, "AMC, Bravo Uphold Cable's Original Promise, Sapan Says," *Multichannel News,* November 16, 1987, 11; Ron Alexander, "AMC, Where the Movie Never Ends," *New York Times,* November 12, 1991, 52.

4. Michael Bommes and Patrick Wright, "'Charms of Residence': The Public and the Past," in *Making Histories: Studies in History Writing and Politics,* ed. Richard Johnson et al. (Minneapolis: University of Minnesota Press, 1982), 264. Hereafter, this work is cited parenthetically in the text.

5. Thomas F. Gieryn has written about the contested nature of commemorations in "Balancing Acts: Science, *Enola Gay,* and History Wars at the Smithsonian," in *The Politics of Display: Museums, Science, and Culture,* ed. Sharon MacDonald (London: Routledge, 1998), 197–228.

6. Janet Wasko, *Hollywood in the Information Age: Beyond the Silver Screen* (Austin: University of Texas Press, 1994), 87. For more on AMC's origins and history, see Douglas Gomery, "American Movie Classics," in *The Cable Networks Handbook,* ed. Robert G. Picard (Riverside, CA: Carpelan Publishing, 1993), 8–14.

7. Patrick R. Parsons and Robert M. Frieden, *The Cable and Satellite Television Industries* (Needham Heights, MA: Allyn and Bacon, 1998), 123.

8. *Channels Field Guide '85* (December 1984): 62; and Richard Katz, "Reaching Classic Heights," *Channels,* December 17, 1990, 16–18, 22.

9. *Broadcasting Yearbook 1991* (Washington, DC: Broadcasting Publications, 1991), D-3; National Cable Television Association, *Cable Television Developments* (Fall 1996): 16–17; Richard Campbell, *Media and Culture: An Introduction to Mass Communication* (New York: St. Martin's Press, 1998), 164; "About AMC," www.amctv.com (accessed on October 10, 2004); and Gomery, "American Movie Classics," 8.

10. "AMC Reaches Agreement with 5 MSOs," *Cablevision,* December 9, 1985, 28; and Gomery, "American Movie Classics," 9–10.

11. "About AMC," www.amctv.com (accessed on January 6, 2003).

12. As one executive remarks, "TV viewers over the age of 45 are especially underserved because of cable programmers' preoccupation with pleasing advertisers. This also damages cable systems . . . because this age group dominates the cable-resister category that systems should be trying to reach." Les Luchter, "AMC, Bravo Uphold Cable's Original Promise, Sapan Says," *Multichannel News,* November 16, 1987, 11. See also Katz, "Reaching Classic Heights," 16–17; and Gomery, "American Movie Classics," 11. For academic studies on elderly media audiences, see John Tulloch, "Approaching the Audience: The Elderly," in *Remote Control: Television, Audiences, and Cultural Power,* ed. Ellen Seiter et al. (New York: Routledge, 1989), 180–203; and Nancy Wood Bliese, "Media in the Rocking Chair: Media Uses and Functions among the Elderly," in *Inter/Media: Interpersonal Communication in a Media World,* ed. Gary Gumpert and Robert Cathcart (New York: Oxford University Press, 1986), 573–82.

13. Katz, "Reaching Classic Heights," 22.

14. Advertisement, *American Movie Classics Magazine* (October 1996): 23.

15. Pierre Bourdieu, *The Field of Cultural Production: Essays on Art and Literature* (New York: Columbia University Press, 1993), 120–21. Hereafter, this work is cited parenthetically in the text.

16. Gerald Peary, "A Singular Voice: Bing Crosby's Style Changed the Sound of Popular Music Forever," *American Movie Classics Magazine* (December 1994): 4; and Eve Golden, "The Complete Cary: It Takes Five Modern Leading Men to Make One Classic Grant," *American Movie Classics Magazine* (August 1996): 7–8.

17. Joseph Varsalona, "Battle of the Big Bands: A Salute to the Finest Films of the Swing Era," *American Movie Classics Magazine* (February 1992): 4–6; and Ann McGuire, "America's Movie Palace Memories," *American Movie Classics Magazine* (April 1993): 3, 6–7.

18. On nostalgia's reactionary nature, see Michael Kammen, *Mystic Chords of Memory: The Transformation of Tradition in American Culture* (New York: Vintage Books, 1993). Hereafter, this work is cited parenthetically in the text.

19. Fredric Jameson, *The Geopolitical Aesthetic: Cinema and Space in the World System* (Bloomington: Indiana University Press, 1992), 120–21.

20. AMC brochure, *Second Annual Film Preservation Festival.*

21. "Shots Seen 'round the World," *American Movie Classics Magazine* (November 1993): 8.

22. Nat Segaloff, "An American Legend: A Memorial Day Tribute to the Man Who Came to Define the American Persona," *American Movie Classics Magazine* (May 1992): 8–9.

23. www.members.aol.com/fortscott/ and www.jwplace.com/patriot.html (accessed on February 20, 2003). A Google search on John Wayne turns up approximately five million results. Even with the repetition built into these searches, along with incidental inclusions (such as John Wayne Gacy and John Wayne Airport), this is still an impressive return, indicating Wayne's continuing place in the celebrity firmament.

24. Gerard Peary, "American Hero," *American Movie Classics Magazine* (July 1995): 4–7. The Fonda festival is called "Fireworks and Fonda: An All-American Tribute to a National Icon."

25. Steven Cohan, "Judy on the Net: Judy Garland Fandom and 'the Gay Thing' Revisited," in *Keyframes: Popular Cinema and Cultural Studies,* ed. Matthew Tinkcom and Amy Vallarejo (London: Routledge, 2001), 119–36.

26. Ann McGuire, "The Great Kate: She Has a Style All Her Own," *American Movie Classics Magazine* (July 1992): 8–9.

27. Alicia Potter, "Rosalind Russell: The Original Working Girl," *American Movie Classics Magazine* (September 1996): 11.

28. McGuire, "The Great Kate," 9.

29. Ed Hazell, "Classic Debut: Mr. Bojangles," *American Movie Classics Magazine* (December 1991): 7; Nick Clooney, "Ellington Onscreen: A Word from Duke's Biographer," *American Movie Classics Magazine* (April 1999): 7.

30. Hazell, "Classic Debut," 7.

31. Clooney, "Ellington," 7.

32. Thomas Doherty, "Black and White Hollywood," *American Movie Classics Magazine* (February 1994): 6–7.

33. Although popularizing the Hollywood past involves social inclusiveness to respond to contemporary developments, we should ask whether this inclusiveness disturbs existing hierarchies or ultimately functions to reassert white dominance over the now included social "others." For example, in the 1980s and 1990s, African American stars (such as Lena Horne and Sidney Poitier) appear on the cover of *American Movie Classics Magazine* primarily in relation to Black History Month. However, these February covers tend to feature more white than black stars. This suggests that African American stars are compartmentalized within a designated area of commemoration and that, even within this area, the memory of white stars can appear as a more commercially viable gateway to the past.

34. Thomas Cripps has chronicled Hollywood's compromised attempts to produce more liberal racial fare in *Making Movies Black: The Hollywood Mes-*

sage Movie from World War II to the Civil Rights Movement (New York: Oxford University Press, 1993).

35. Numerous histories gauge the impact of the Reagan and Bush (George H. W.) years on minorities. See, for example, Robert R. Detlefsen, *Civil Rights under Reagan* (San Francisco: Institute for Contemporary Studies, 1991); and Steven A. Shull, *A Kindler, Gentler Racism? The Reagan-Bush Civil Rights Legacy* (Armonk, NY: M. E. Sharpe, 1993). Shull argues that, although this period saw some improvements, women and African Americans continued to be overrepresented in lower-level jobs. Further, the latter group experienced increased unemployment, a rise in segregated schooling and housing, and, generally, a poorer standard of living.

36. Michael Wallace "Mickey Mouse History: Portraying the Past at Disney World," *Radical History Review* 32 (1985): 52.

37. Dipesh Chakrabarty, "The Death of History? Historical Consciousness and the Culture of Late Capitalism," *Public Culture* 4, no. 2 (1992): 63.

38. For example, in *Time Passages: Collective Memory and American Popular Culture* (Minneapolis: University of Minnesota Press, 1990), 39–75, George Lipsitz focuses on the inability of early network television to shoulder completely the ideological burden resulting from the clashing juxtaposition of ethnic, working-class communities rooted in pre–World War II traditions and the new suburban consumer order in the post–World War II era. Tensions and contradictions arose, questioning the implicit rightness of capitalist progress and threatening the smooth operation of the hegemonic enterprise.

39. Michael Wallace, "Ronald Reagan and the Politics of History," *Tikkun* 2, no. 1 (1987): 16–18.

40. The meanings of the terms *preservation, restoration,* and *digital reconstruction* can vary depending on context; further, they are not necessarily mutually exclusive. That said, preservation generally refers to the repair and/or safe storage of original celluloid; restoration returns a film negative to a form congruent with its original release condition and/or artistic intentions; and, without physically altering the celluloid version, digital reconstruction repairs defects of a degenerated negative to simulate original quality. For more on these distinctions, see Mark-Paul Meyer, "Work in Progress: Ethics of Film Restoration and New Technologies," http://evora.omega.it/~demos/faol/digital/digital.htm#1 (accessed on February 17, 2004).

41. Steve Bryant discusses the extensive neglect of old TV shows as well as events that led to a greater archival sensibility in Britain, in *The Television Heritage: Television Archiving Now and in an Uncertain Future* (London: British Film Institute Publishing, 1989). On the recycling of TV shows in Britain, see Tim O'Sullivan, "Nostalgia, Revelation, and Intimacy: Tendencies in the Flow of Modern Popular Television," in *The Television Studies Book,* ed. Christine Geraghty and David Lusted (London: Arnold, 1998), especially 201–4. For more on the subject of television heritage in a U.S. context, see Derek Kompare, *Rerun Nation: How Repeats Invented American Television* (New York: Routledge, 2005), especially 101–68.

42. Michael Wallace has written on the subject of the relationship of capitalism and conservation, in "Reflections on the History of Historic Preservation," in *Presenting the Past: Essays on History and the Public,* ed. Susan Porter Benson et al. (Philadelphia: Temple University Press, 1986), 165–99. Hereafter, this work is cited parenthetically in the text. The *Stanford Humanities Review*'s special issue on film preservation (Winter 2000) details the relationship of studios and archivists.

43. In *American Movie Classics Magazine:* "The Wang Center" (December 1991): 2; see also "The Stanley Performing Arts Center" (February 1992): 2; "The Kentucky Theater" (May 1992): 2; "The Circle Theater" (September 1992): 2; "The Orpheum Theater" (June 1992): 2; and "The Paramount Theater" (August 1992): 2. All of these articles were written by Ann McGuire.

44. Philip Rosen has written on the tension among preservation, restoration, and nationalism in architecture, in *Change Mummified: Cinema, Historicity, Theory* (Minneapolis: University of Minnesota Press, 2001), especially 44–78.

45. Bill Desowitz, "Only the Good Die and Return," *Los Angeles Times,* May 18, 1997, 21.

46. On *Vertigo*'s restoration, see also Royal S. Brown, "Back from among the Dead: The Restoration of Alfred Hitchcock's *Vertigo,*" *Cineaste* 23, no. 1 (1997): 4–9.

47. Liner notes for the 1996 widescreen video edition of *Vertigo.*

48. James Katz and Robert Harris, quoted in *Obsessed with "Vertigo"* and in the liner notes for the 1996 widescreen video edition of *Vertigo.*

49. Paul Grainge discusses politicized attempts to reconcile the issue of authenticity with the impact of new technologies in "Reclaiming Heritage: Colourization, Culture Wars, and the Politics of Nostalgia," *Cultural Studies* 13, no. 4 (1999): 621–38.

50. For more on organizations devoted to film preservation, see online sites such as the National Film Preservation Board of the Library of Congress (www.loc.gov/film/); the National Film Registry (www.loc.gov/film/titles .html); the National Film Preservation Foundation (www.filmpreservation .org/); the Association of Moving Image Archivists (www.amianet.org/); and the American Film Institute National Center For Film and Video Preservation (www.afi.com/about/preservation/preservation.aspx).

51. See *American Movie Classics Magazine,* issues for March 1993, October 1994, October 1995, and July 1996, for coverage of the first four preservation festivals.

52. For more on these findings, see www.filmpreservation.org or www.loc .gov/film/.

53. www.filmpreservation.org; Robert Moses, "Film Preservation: Making History, by Saving It," *American Movie Classics Magazine* (March 1993): 4–6; and *American Movie Classics Magazine* (October 1994): 8.

54. *National Film Preservation Act of 1988,* Public Law 100-446, 100th Cong., 2nd sess. (September 27, 1988). The complete text for each preservation

act is available in LexisNexis Congressional (www.lexisnexis.com/academic/
universe/congress/).

55. Ibid.

56. Although the board's membership changes, some additional members
include the Department of Theatre, Film and Television, UCLA; the Depart-
ment of Cinema Studies, NYU; the University Film and Video Association; the
Motion Picture Association of America; The Association of Motion Picture
and Television Producers; the Screen Actors Guild of America; the National
Society of Film Critics; the National Association of Theater Owners; the
American Society of Cinematographers; and the International Photographers
Guild.

57. The films honored by the registry since 1989 are listed on www.loc.gov/
film/titles.html. In an effort to promote a grass-roots awareness of film preservation, a selection of the registry films periodically tours the nation.

58. *National Film Preservation Act of 1992*, Public Law 102-307, 102nd
Cong., 2nd sess. (June 26, 1992).

59. For information on these findings, see the National Film Preservation
Foundation's Web site, www.filmpreservation.org, or that of the National Film
Preservation Board, www.loc.gov/film/.

60. *National Film Preservation Act of 1996*, Public Law 104-285, 104th
Cong., 2nd sess. (October 11, 1996), HR 1734.

61. The site www.filmpreservation.org offers a complete description of the
National Film Preservation Foundation; it also lists orphan films already preserved through the foundation's auspices. Further, in cooperation with the National Film Preservation Foundation, collections of rare films have been released
on video and DVD.

62. For factors influencing the growth of the U.S. conservation movement,
see the Library of Congress's conservation site, http://memory.loc.gov/
ammem/amrvhtml/conspref.html.

63. Albert Rains et al., *With Heritage So Rich* (New York: Random House,
1966).

64. See, for example, Laurence Zuckerman, "As Media Influence Grows for
a Handful, Can That Be a Good Thing?" *New York Times*, January 13, 2000, sec.
C, 6.

65. U.S. Congress, House, Committee on Energy and Commerce, *Globalization of the Media: Hearing before the Subcommittee on Telecommunications and Finance*, 101st Cong., 1st sess., November 15, 1989, 8. Hereafter, this
work is cited parenthetically in the text.

66. David Morley and Kevin Robins, *Spaces of Identity: Global Media, Electronic Landscapes, and Cultural Boundaries* (London: Routledge, 1995),
147–73.

67. Wasko, *Hollywood in the Information Age*, 67–68.

68. Steve Wilson, "On-Line Piracy Turns from Music to Movies," *New York
Times*, July 29, 1999, sec. D, 1, 6.

69. Steve Lohr, "Welcome to the Internet, the First Global Colony," *New York Times*, January 9, 2000, sec. 4, 1, 4.

70. For a discussion of both positions on globalization, see Robert J. Holton, *Globalization and the Nation State* (London: Macmillan Press, 1998); and Ian Clark, *Globalization and Fragmentation: International Relations in the Twentieth Century* (New York: Oxford University Press, 1997).

71. Holton, *Globalization and the Nation State*, 106.

72. Wilson, "On-Line Piracy Turns from Music to Movies," sec. D, 6.

73. On this point, see Robert Hewison, quoted in David Harvey, *The Condition of Postmodernity: An Enquiry into the Origins of Cultural Change* (Oxford: Basil Blackwell, 1989), 86.

74. Homi K. Bhabha, ed., *Nation and Narration* (London: Routledge, 1990), 1.

75. Annette Kuhn, *Family Secrets: Acts of Memory and Imagination* (London: Verso, 1995); Kuhn, *Dreaming of Fred and Ginger: Cinema and Cultural Memory* (Washington Square, NY: New York University Press, 2002); and Jackie Stacey, *Star Gazing: Hollywood Cinema and Female Spectatorship* (London: Routledge, 1994).

76. Lipsitz, *Time Passages*, 67, 213.

77. Marita Sturken, *Tangled Memories: The Vietnam War, the AIDS Epidemic, and the Politics of Remembering* (Berkeley: University of California Press, 1997), 94–97; and the Popular Memory Group, "Popular Memory: Theory, Politics, Method," in *Making Histories*, ed. Johnson et al., 211.

78. The Popular Memory Group, "Popular Memory," 211, 207.

4. Once Is Not Enough

1. Melanie Nash and Martti Lahti, "'Almost Ashamed to Say I Am One of Those Girls': *Titanic*, Leonardo DiCaprio, and the Paradoxes of Girls' Fandom," in *Titanic: Anatomy of a Blockbuster*, ed. Kevin S. Sandler and Gaylyn Studlar (New Brunswick, NJ: Rutgers University Press, 1999), 64.

2. David Ansen, "Our *Titanic* Love Affair," *Newsweek*, February 23, 1998, 61; and Bernard Weintraub, "Who's Lining Up at the Box Office? Lots and Lots of Girls," *New York Times*, February 23, 1998, sec. E, 1, 4.

3. Phil Williams, "Feeding Off the Past: The Evolution of the Television Rerun," *Journal of Popular Film and Television* 21, no. 4 (1994): 163. See also Derek Kompare's *Rerun Nation: How Repeats Invented American Television* (New York: Routledge, 2005), which came out when this book was in press.

4. On the prevalence of film re-viewing on video, see Uma Dinsmore-Tuli, "The Pleasures of 'Home Cinema,' or Watching Movies on Telly: An Audience Study of Cinephiliac VCR Use," *Screen* 41, no. 3 (2000): 315–27; Julia R. Dobrow, "The Re-Run Ritual: Using VCRs to Re-View," in *Social and Cultural Aspects of VCR Use*, ed. Julia R. Dobrow (Hillsdale, NJ: Lawrence Erlbaum Associates, 1990), 181–93; Valerie Walkerdine, "Video Replay: Families, Films, and Fantasy," in *Formations of Fantasy*, ed. Victor Burgin et al. (London: Methuen,

1986), 167–99; and Ann Gray, *Video Playtime: The Gendering of a Leisure Technology* (London: Routledge, 1992), 204–14.

5. Dinsmore-Tuli, "The Pleasures of 'Home Cinema,'" 327.

6. On the relationship of children and re-viewing, see Emily Yoffe, "Play It Again, Mom (Again and Again . . .)," *New York Times*, July 13, 2003, 9. Walkerdine, Dobrow, and Gray point out how common re-viewing is among families, and Jenkins's *Textual Poachers* (London: Routledge, 1992) discusses the intimate relation between adult TV fans and repeat viewing.

7. The survey was conducted in seven classes (five were media classes; two were nonmedia classes). Introductory courses included in the survey were Introduction to Media, Public Speaking, Hollywood, and World Media. I also surveyed more advanced students in courses on Women Directors and Stanley Kubrick. I taught Introduction to Media. Other classes were taught by faculty or graduate students. I included two freshmen speech classes to see if students enrolled in nonmedia classes and relatively uninitiated in the university answered differently from those in media classes. They did not, suggesting that this generation's already established viewing cultures and tastes may be more important than media education in deciding what films will be watched repeatedly and why.

8. The good response rate may be due to the administration of the questionnaires during class time. Since participation was voluntary and unrelated to course credit, it might also indicate enthusiasm for the topic.

9. Seventy-seven majors responded. In declining order of response, the number of nonmajor participants is as follows: business, 43; telecommunications, 41; exploratory/unknown, 32; English, 28; journalism, 15; history, 11; physical education, 10; theater and drama, 10; political science, 9; education, 7; psychology, 7; sociology, 7; art, 4; computer science, 4; criminal justice, 4; environmental science, 4; biology, 3; comparative literature, 3; general studies, 3; interior design, 3. Other nonmajors represented with either one or two responses include Afro-American studies, American studies, anthropology, apparel merchandising, chemistry, cognitive science, dental hygiene, French and Italian, geology, Germanic studies, Jewish studies, music, nursing, physics, and Spanish.

10. The low number of students of color in the survey hinders reliable statements about race. This issue is further complicated by many students' having left the racial identification line blank. My desire is not to exclude race as a factor in re-viewing but to base findings on elements more securely indicated by the survey (such as gender). Still, the group's whiteness delimits my study. For discussion of the problem of the domination of white experience and audiences in feminist thought as well as in empirical audience work, see Jacqueline Bobo and Ellen Seiter, "Black Feminism and Media Criticism: *The Women of Brewster Place*," *Screen* 32, no. 3 (1991): 286–302.

11. Studies have found that the most frequent moviegoers are young and college educated; see, for example, Garth Jowett and J. M. Linton, *Movies as Mass Communication* (Beverly Hills: Sage, 1980); and "Gallup Looks at the Movies," *Gallup Report*, no. 195 (1981). Students have also served as research

subjects for surveys on theatrical moviegoing motivations. See Bruce A. Austin, "Film Attendance: Why College Students Chose to See Their Most Recent Film," *Journal of Popular Film and Television* 9 (1981): 43–49, and Austin, "Motivations for Movie Attendance," *Communication Quarterly* 34 (Spring 1986): 115–26. This research focuses on quantifiable data regarding why and how often this audience attends films. My study concentrates, rather, on the aesthetic and cultural implications of the viewing habits of youth.

12. David Morley's *The "Nationwide" Audience: Structure and Decoding* (London: British Film Institute Publishing, 1980) is a canonical example of audience research that shows how shifts in identity result in different interpretations of a TV show. Research by scholars such as Jacqueline Bobo (*Black Women as Cultural Readers* [New York: Columbia University Press, 1995]) has vividly demonstrated how race matters in the decoding of media texts.

13. Herman Gray has discussed the pervasive significance of a black youth culture in the United States in *Watching Race: Television and the Struggle for "Blackness"* (Minneapolis: University of Minnesota Press, 1995), 147–61. Hardly monolithic, youth culture is composed of a multiplicity of youth cultures, shaped, at the very least, by the social identities of participants.

14. For instance, Dobrow investigated the re-viewing motivations of a demographically diverse audience of two hundred in the Boston area. She found that they were attracted to film repetition for a number of reasons, including the desire for education (to see more in a film than a single viewing will allow), the pleasures of nostalgia (elicited by reexperiencing an old film), and a sense of group solidarity (produced from rewatching together). Additional motivations for regular moviegoing, such as aesthetic experience, mood change, self-understanding, and understanding of the world are present in other research covering a range of audiences, including Philip Palmgreen et al., "The Motivational Framework of Moviegoing: Uses and Avoidances of Theatrical Films," *Current Research in Film: Audiences, Economics, and Law*, vol. 4, ed. Bruce A. Austin (Norwood, NJ: Ablex Publishing Corporation, 1988), 1–23; and K. E. Kristian Moller and Pirjo Karppinen, "Role of Motives and Attributes in Consumer Motion Picture Choice," *Journal of Economic Psychology* 4 (1983): 239–62.

15. Roger Silverstone, *Television and Everyday Life* (London: Routledge, 1994), 98.

16. Ellen Seiter, *Sold Separately: Parents & Children in Consumer Culture* (New Brunswick, NJ: Rutgers University Press, 1995), 37–50.

17. Silverstone, *Television and Everyday Life*, 153–54.

18. If used alone as a method of inquiry or for statistical purposes, the survey format relies on "self-reporting" and thus the self-understanding of the respondents, potentially failing to address deeper motivations. Framed questionnaires, on which participants merely mark "yes" or "no" or respond to fixed questions, are particularly problematic because they direct and control answers. These problems can be mitigated by designing more open-ended questions and by situating participants' reactions within social and ideological contexts, as I at-

tempt to do in my research. But the questionnaire remains a method of inquiry that, while examining actual responses, cannot exhaust their implications.

19. Numerous texts discuss the complexities of and contrasts between ethnographic approaches to the media, especially in television and new media studies. Among overviews of ethnographic methodologies are Shaun Moores, *Interpreting Audiences: The Ethnography of Media Consumption* (London: Sage Publications, 1993); Christine Geraghty, "Audiences and 'Ethnography': Questions of Practice," in *The Television Studies Book,* ed. Christine Geraghty and David Lusted (London: Arnold, 1998), 141–57; and Ellen Seiter, *Television and New Media Audiences* (Oxford: Clarendon Press, 1999), 1–33.

20. S. Elizabeth Bird, *The Audience in Everyday Life: Living in a Media World* (New York: Routledge, 2003), 7.

21. Sarah Thornton, *Club Cultures: Music, Media and Subcultural Capital* (Cambridge: Polity Press, 1995), 7–8. Hereafter, this work is cited parenthetically in the text.

22. James Naremore, *More Than Night: Film Noir in Its Contexts* (Berkeley: University of California Press, 1998), 9–39. On the concept of genre and taste distinctions, see also Mark Jancovich, "Genre and the Audience: Genre Classifications and Cultural Distinctions in the Mediation of *The Silence of the Lambs,*" in *Hollywood Spectatorship: Changing Perceptions of Cinema Audiences,* ed. Melvyn Stokes and Richard Maltby (London: British Film Institute Publishing, 2001), 33–45.

23. Other findings suggest that horror films have occupied a much larger place in youth home viewing habits. See Julian Wood's study of the tastes of working-class teenage boys in Britain in "Repeatable Pleasures: Notes on Young People's Use of Video," in *Reading Audiences: Young People and the Media,* ed. David Buckingham (Manchester: Manchester University Press, 1993), 184–201.

24. Terry McMillan's success with *Waiting to Exhale* has inspired chick lit to become a major publication area for black women authors, relieving the genre of its typical association with white female protagonists and desires. See Lola Ogunnaike, "Black Writers Seize Glamorous Ground around 'Chick Lit,'" *New York Times,* May 31, 2004, sec. A, 1, 15.

25. On the issue of the disparagement of young female tastes in relation to the media, see Nash and Lahti, "'Almost Ashamed to Say I Am One of Those Girls,'" 64–88; and Seiter, *Sold Separately,* 145–71.

26. Any film can have "watch-alongs"—those who will rewatch a film just because their partner or friend wants to see it. In light of this, I made estimations of gender preferences not only on the basis of film lists but also by looking at commentary elsewhere in survey responses.

27. Since it is estimated that teenagers spent $160 billion in 2000—a 60 percent increase over 1997—the economy, including the entertainment market, is in hot pursuit of this group. See "American Graffiti: Behind the Wheel and Driving the Nation's Culture," *New York Times,* September 17, 2000, sec. 4, 1, 6.

28. Thomas Doherty, *Teenagers and Teenpics: The Juvenilization of American Movies in the 1950s* (Boston: Unwin Hyman, 1988), 46.

29. Ava Preacher Collins, "Loose Canons: Constructing Cultural Traditions inside and outside the Academy," in *Film Theory Goes to the Movies*, ed. Jim Collins et al. (New York: Routledge, 1993), 86–102. On the importance of entertaining revisionist notions of the canon in relation to contemporary Hollywood, see Richard Maltby, "'Nobody Knows Everything': Post-Classical Historiographies and Consolidated Entertainment," in *Contemporary Hollywood Cinema*, ed. Steve Neale and Murray Smith (London: Routledge, 1998), 39–40.

30. Mike Budd, "The Moments of Caligari," in *The Cabinet of Dr. Caligari: Texts, Contexts, Histories*, ed. Mike Budd (New Brunswick, NJ: Rutgers University Press, 1990), 41; and Matei Calinescu, *Rereading* (New Haven, CT: Yale University Press, 1993), 95, 139.

31. Theodor W. Adorno, "On the Fetish Character in Music and the Regression of Listening," in *The Essential Frankfurt School Reader*, ed. Andrew Arato and Eike Gebhardt (New York: Urizen Books, 1978), 290, 271.

32. Calinescu, *Rereading*, 159, 191.

33. Ed S. Tan, *Emotion and the Structure of Narrative Film: Film as an Emotion Machine*, trans. Barbara Fasting (Mahwah, NJ: Lawrence Erlbaum Associates, 1996), 22. Hereafter, this work is cited parenthetically in the text.

34. Victor Nell, *Lost in a Book: The Psychology of Reading for Pleasure* (New Haven: Yale University Press, 1988), 26–27. Hereafter, this work is cited parenthetically in the text.

35. Roland Barthes, *S/Z*, trans. Richard Miller (New York: Hill and Wang, 1974), 16.

36. David Bordwell has written about the prevalence of the puzzle film in contemporary production and its precedents in film history in *The Way Hollywood Tells It: Story and Style in Modern Movies* (Berkeley: University of California Press, 2006).

37. In Dinsmore-Tuli's analysis of video cinephiles, she refutes assumptions that home viewers always watch films piecemeal ("The Pleasures of 'Home Cinema'").

38. Janice Radway, *Reading the Romance: Women, Patriarchy, and Popular Literature* (Chapel Hill: University of North Carolina Press, 1984), 107. Hereafter, this work is cited parenthetically in the text. And Ien Ang, *Watching Dallas: Soap Opera and the Melodramatic Imagination*, trans. Della Couling (New York: Methuen, 1985), 86–116.

39. Andrew Essex, "Matrix Mania," *Entertainment Weekly*, May 14, 1999, 40–41.

40. *EW* staff, "Phantom Secrets Revealed," *Entertainment Weekly*, April 21, 2000, 34–35; and Steve Daly, "Deconstructing Woody," *Entertainment Weekly*, December 10, 1999, 12–13.

41. Andrew Sarris, *The American Cinema: Directors and Directions, 1929–1968* (1968; New York: Octagon Books, 1982), 19–37.

42. Although the survey sample is not large enough to draw conclusions about equivalences between gender and viewing motivations, one hundred male and sixty female participants mentioned aesthetics as a consideration in choos-

ing which films to rewatch. Ninety women and fifty-five men found therapy the most compelling reason. Although members of both genders could be equally passionate about aesthetics and therapy, women tended to use films more to seek comfort than for aesthetic gratification.

43. A number of commercial film guides, such as John Hulme and Michael Wexler's *Baked Potatoes: A Pot Smoker's Guide to Film and Video*, suggest that a readership for "reefer" aesthetics exists. This guide establishes a film hierarchy based on enjoyment when under the influence (ranked by number of marijuana leaves).

44. For example, www.geocities.com/Hollywood/Hills/6760/home.htm and home.bip.net/pascal/shawshank/feedback.htm were discussion boards for, respectively, *Braveheart* and *The Shawshank Redemption*. That the films affected both men and women was clear in the testimonials available in 2000 on these now-defunct sites.

45. Alison Aproberts, "Calling Dr. Video," *Herald-Times* (Bloomington, IN), sec. D, 1.

46. John W. Hesley, *Rent Two Movies and Let's Talk in the Morning* (New York: John Wiley and Sons, 1998); and Dr. Gary Solomon, *The Motion Picture Prescription: Watch This Movie and Call Me in the Morning* (New York: Aslan Publishing, 1995). For one of the earliest works on the subject of movies and mental health, see Adolf Nichtenhauser, MD, et al., *Films in Psychiatry, Psychology, and Mental Health* (New York: Health Education Council, 1953).

47. Aproberts, "Calling Dr. Video," 1.

48. Nancy Peske and Beverly West, *Cinematherapy: The Girl's Guide to Movies for Every Mood* (New York: Dell Publishing, 1999); Peske and West, *Advanced Cinematherapy: The Girl's Guide to Finding Happiness One Movie at a Time* (New York: Dell Publishing, 2002); and Peske and West, *Cinematherapy for Lovers: The Girl's Guide to Finding True Love One Movie at a Time* (New York: Bantam Dell, 2003). Hereafter, the first work is cited parenthetically in the text.

49. See Tania Modleski's work on the female Gothic and the Harlequin romance in *Loving with a Vengeance: Mass-Produced Fantasies for Women* (New York: Methuen, 1984).

50. Valerie Walkerdine, "Some Day My Prince Will Come: Young Girls and the Preparation for Adolescent Sexuality," in *Gender and Generation*, ed. Angela McRobbie and Mica Nava (London: Macmillan Publishers, 1984), 163.

51. Bobo, *Black Women as Cultural Readers*, 91–132.

52. Annette Kuhn, *Family Secrets: Acts of Memory and Imagination* (London: Verso, 1995), 39.

53. Web sites on the films of John Hughes featuring similar commentary about the films include "John Hughes files," www.riverblue.com; "Save Ferris!" www.80s.com/saveferris/intro.html; and The Breakfast Club, www.fortune city.com/meltingpot/regent/827/tbc.html.

54. For example, Robin Wood, *Hollywood from Vietnam to Reagan* (New York: Columbia University Press, 1986), 162–74.

55. On the resurgence of the 1980s as fashionable, see Michiko Kakutani, "Get Out Your Shoulder Pads: The 80's Are Here," *New York Times*, April 25, 2001, sec. B, 1; and Simon Reynolds, "The 70's Are So 90's. The 80's Are the Thing Now," *New York Times*, May 5, 2002, sec. 2, 1, 48. Also, Fox airs *That '80s Show*.

56. "ChildrenOfThe80s?" www.80s.com/ChildrenoftheEighties/; "It Came from the 80's!," www.geocities.com/SunsetStrip/Mezzanine/4480/; "The '80s Server," www.80s.com (all accessed on June 20, 2002).

57. The 80's Film Preservation Society, www.geocities.com/Hollywood/ Boulevard/1221; "Welcome to the 'Daily 100,' Our Very Own Tribute to the Great Lines That Came Out of '80s Films," www.80s.com/Entertainment/ Movies/Daily 100/; and "Welcome to the '80s Movie Gateway," www.fast rewind.com/main.htm (all accessed on June 20, 2002).

58. Lynn Spigel and Henry Jenkins, "Same Bat Channel, Different Bat Times: Mass Culture and Popular Memory," in *The Many Lives of The Batman: Critical Approaches to a Superhero and His Media*, ed. Roberta E. Pearson and William Uricchio (New York: Routledge, 1991), 131.

59. Talk.dvdtalk.com/ubb/Forum3/html (accessed on September 25, 2000). See also Useless Movie Quotes, www.uselessmoviequotes.com/ (accessed on June 20, 2002); and "Greatest Film or Movie Quotes of All Time," www .filmsite.org/greatfilmquotes.html (accessed on April 28, 2005).

60. Toru Mitsui and Shuhei Hosokawa, eds., *Karaoke around the World: Global Technology, Local Singing* (London: Routledge, 1998), 8.

61. Reuters, "Karaoke's Offspring, Movieoke, Hits NYC," February 12, 2004, www.msnbc.msn.com/id/4252908.

62. Johan Fornäs, "Filling Voids along the Byway: Identification and Interpretation in the Swedish Forms of Karaoke," in *Karaoke around the World*, ed. Mitsui and Hosokawa, 130–31.

63. Umberto Eco, "Casablanca: Cult Movies and Intertextual Collage," in *Travels in Hyperreality*, trans. William Weaver (New York: Harcourt, Brace, 1990), 198.

64. Timothy Corrigan, *A Cinema without Walls: Movies and Culture after Vietnam* (New Brunswick, NJ: Rutgers University Press, 1991), 81–82, 91.

65. Jenkins, *Textual Poachers*, 68–69.

66. Raymond Williams, *Television: Technology and Cultural Form* (New York: Schocken Books, 1974), 130.

5. To Infinity and Beyond

1. Rick Lyman, "Lights, Camera, Streaming Video," *New York Times*, June 9, 2000, sec. C, 1.

2. Jason Bellini, "Studios Hope to Prevent a Movie 'Napster' from Taking Hold," www.CNN.com, February 20, 2001.

3. See, for example, Janet Wasko's work on the film industry's relation to new technologies in *Hollywood in the Information Age: Beyond the Silver Screen* (Austin: University of Texas Press, 1994) and Scott Bukatman's study of

the impact of the digital on the visual image and subjectivity in *Terminal Identity: The Virtual Subject in Postmodern Science Fiction* (Durham, NC: Duke University Press, 1993).

4. The Internet has occasionally functioned as a first-run or "split-run" forum for features. For example, in March 2000, before its theatrical appearance in April, Mike Figgis's experiment with digital filmmaking and storytelling, *Time Code*, premiered on the Internet. One of the first films to open on a split-run basis (that is, with simultaneous Internet and theatrical screenings) was Ed Vilga's 1999 noir *Dead Broke*, which was streamed on www.Ifilm.net (now Ifilm.com).

5. Jamie Allen, "The Golden Age of the Short: Shorts Move from Film-Class Project to Big Time on the Web," www.CNN.com, May 15, 2000.

6. John Geirland and Eva Sonesh-Kedar, *Digital Babylon: How the Geeks, the Suits, and the Ponytails Tried to Bring Hollywood to the Internet* (New York: Arcade Publishing, 1999), 254–55.

7. Eric Brown, "Broadband Portals Get a Boost," www.PCWorld.com, April 20, 2000; and Legg, Mason, Wood, Walker, Inc., "Coming Down the Pipe," www.CableDatacomNews.com, April 2000.

8. Eileen Elsey and Andrew Kelly, *In Short: A Guide to Short Film-Making in the Digital Age* (London: British Film Institute Publishing, 2002), x–xi.

9. Peter M. Nichols, "Now Playing, Short Stories at a Web Theater Near You," *New York Times*, December 30, 2000, sec. A, 28.

10. Elsey and Kelly, *In Short*, x–xi.

11. *The Ifilm Internet Movie Guide*, ed. Lew Harris (Hollywood, CA: Lone Eagle Publishing Company, 2002), ranks *405* number one among fifty best Web films.

12. "About Atom," www.AtomFilms.com, January 2001; press release cited in "About Atom," www.AtomFilms.com, June 7, 2000. On Ifilm's relation to the film industry, see Laura Rich, "News Flash: Hollywood Has Already Gone Dotcom," www.TheStandard.com, June 26, 2000; and Robert La Franco and K. N. Cukier, www.Redherring.com, May 23, 2000.

13. "Press," www.AtomFilms.com, July 10, 2000; www.AdLink.net.

14. Eugene Hernandez and Anthony Kaufman, "Future 4: Mika Salmi, AtomFilms," www.IndieWire.com, January 17, 2001.

15. In this merger, Shockwave acquired 70 percent of AtomFilms. With twelve million viewers in 2001, Shockwave represented a hefty constituency and a more solid business footing for the periodically shaky AtomFilms. Hernandez and Kaufman report that the combined company "has a likely online audience larger than the viewership of many cable networks" ("Future 4").

16. Corporations sponsor Web film sites today not simply because they represent another venue in which to advertise. This corporate "outreach" is also a response to the development of technologies, such as TiVo, that allow consumers to ignore commercials on television. It is hoped that ads on new platforms, such as broadband and interactive TV, will offset a possible eclipse of the thirty-second TV spot.

17. Hernandez and Kaufman, "Future 4"; and www.AtomFilms.com, March 22, 2000, May 2, 2000, May 16, 2000, July 19, 2000, and September 14, 2000.

18. Car companies have traditionally sought tie-ins with the film industry to showcase their products. In addition to BMWfilms.com's and AtomFilms' alliances with Ford and Volkswagen, Warner Bros. Online has used its site's shorts to advertise the Chevy Venture WB edition, a vehicle equipped with an entertainment center complete with TV monitor, VCR (or DVD player), and earphones.

19. "Press," www.AtomFilms.com, November 13, 2000.

20. Frank Houston, "Hollywood Flirts with Short Films on the Web," *New York Times*, June 15, 2000, sec. D, 13.

21. Justin Wyatt, *High Concept: Movies and Marketing in Hollywood* (Austin: University of Texas Press, 1994), 1–22.

22. Simon Dentith, *Parody* (New York: Routledge, 2000), 15. Hereafter, this work is cited parenthetically in the text.

23. Films that demonstrate further that parody has become a subject in its own right, even an obsession on the Web, include "Spoof! An Insider's Guide to Short Film Success" (William Sherak and Jason Shuman, Ifilm.com), which laments the tendency for everyone who has access to a camera to use it to create a spoof, and "Screw Da Blair Witch" (Christopher McCullough et al., Ifilm.com), which involves a man who goes crazy at the thought of doing another spoof of *The Blair Witch Project*.

24. For an article that discusses the impact that the successful Web promotion of *The Blair Witch Project* had on Hollywood, see David Ansen and Corie Brown, "A Hex upon Hollywood," *Newsweek*, August 16, 1999, 51.

25. Joe Hutsko, "Behind the Scenes via Movie Web Sites," *New York Times*, July 10, 2003, sec. E, 3.

26. For more information on the explosion of *Star Wars* homages and parodies on the Internet, see Glenn Gaslin, "'Star' Turns," *Entertainment Weekly*, June 1, 2001, 92. Also, *Star Wars* was given to parody long before the existence of the Internet in feature films such as Mel Brooks's *Spaceballs* (1987) and in other shorts such as Ernie Fosselius's "Hardware Wars" (1977).

27. Wes D. Gehring, *Parody as Film Genre* (Westport, CT: Greenwood Press, 1999), 197. Gehring uses the terms *compound genre* and *compound parody* to describe the way films display the characteristics of two or more genres (13).

28. Jim Collins, *Architectures of Excess: Cultural Life in the Information Age* (New York: Routledge, 1995), 128–35. Hereafter, this work is cited parenthetically in the text.

29. John Brooks, *Showing Off in America: From Conspicuous Consumption to Parody Display* (Boston: Little, Brown, 1981), 228.

30. Marion Hart, "A Comeback for Short Films Is Linked to the Web," *New York Times*, January 14, 2001, 31.

31. For example, after the Margaret Mitchell estate contested the publication of *The Wind Done Gone*, eBay sold the novel as an "unauthorized parody" for an astronomical amount. Author Alice Randall gained celebrity status as a

test case of First Amendment rights and as an African American writer daring to revise an American classic radically. When the court decided to allow publication, Randall's novel became a best seller. Thus, as often happens, the controversy surrounding a parody contributed to its success.

32. Steven Heller, "A President Can Never Be Accused of a Lack of Caricature," *New York Times*, June 17, 2001, 16.

33. A typical position toward parody in the postmodern era, forwarded by Fredric Jameson and others, is that it has been supplanted by pastiche, a form of imitation bereft of parody's traditional critical sting. In pastiche, forms constantly allude to one another in an unending cycle of production that marches in lockstep with the demands of late capitalism and a ceaseless circulation of consumer goods. In this way pastiche signifies the eclipse of the historical, an embrace of false spectacles and events that substitutes an array of images for history. As Jim Collins rightly points out in *Architectures of Excess*, this position has become a truism about cultural production in the postmodern era that "doesn't tell us much at all about the particularity of different forms of rearticulation . . . [their] circuit of exchange, institutional arena, or animating motivation" (92). Redefining parody as pastiche leaves us with an all-encompassing term to describe the prolific nature of imitation in cultural production, begging important aesthetic, social, and historical questions that continue to characterize contemporary practices of imitation. Different kinds of textual practices based on imitation and allusion perform different kinds of social and ideological work. In this sense, parody survives as a particular mode of imitation that can tell us a great deal about the media industry, the circulation of cultural meaning, and reception.

34. Gehring, *Parody as Film Genre*, 2–3.

35. Henry Jenkins, *Textual Poachers: Television Fans and Participatory Culture* (London: Routledge, 1992), 227.

36. Donald Crafton, "The View from Termite Terrace: Caricature and Parody in Warner Bros. Animation," in *Reading the Rabbit: Explorations in Warner Bros. Animation*, ed. Kevin Sandler (New Brunswick, NJ: Rutgers University Press, 1998), 103.

37. Henry Jenkins argues that rather than entertain this binary at all, we might consider the relationship between fans and the industry as multifaceted, characterized at times by conflict, critique, collaboration, recruitment, and so on. See Jenkins's "*Quentin Tarantino's Star Wars?* Digital Cinema, Media Convergence, and Participatory Culture," in *Rethinking Media Change: The Aesthetics of Transition*, ed. David Thorburn and Henry Jenkins (Cambridge, MA: MIT Press, 2003), 292. In *Fan Cultures* (London: Routledge, 2002), Matt Hills offers a more radical approach in arguing that fans live out the "inescapable contradiction" between "'resisting' norms of capitalist society and its rapid turnover of novel commodities" and being "implicated in these very economic and cultural processes" (29). Theories of fandom thus must be able to recognize and "*tolerate* contradiction without seeking to close it down prematurely." While each reformulation of the binary provides a productive way out of the static either/or logic that often governs discussion of the fan-industry relationship, my

goal in this chapter is to consider how the binary, although theoretically insufficient as an account of this relationship, supervises the public and self-definition of fan filmmakers.

38. Hart, "A Comeback for Short Films Is Linked to the Web," 31.

39. Rick Lyman, "Internet Strategy to Help Others Make Films," *New York Times*, November 29, 2000, sec. B, 1.

40. In 2002 Pete Jones won for his script for *Stolen Summer*, and in 2003 writer Erica Beeney and directors Kyle Rankin and Efram Potelle won for *The Battle of Shaker Heights*.

41. Sara Gwenllian Jones, "Phantom Menace: Killer Fans, Consumer Activism, and Digital Filmmakers," in *Underground U.S.A.: Filmmaking beyond the Hollywood Canon*, ed. Xavier Mendik and Steven Jay Schneider (London: Wallflower Press, 2002), 169–79. Other revisionist work on fandom includes Mark Jancovich, "Cult Fictions: Cult Movies, Subcultural Capital and the Production of Cultural Distinctions," *Cultural Studies* 16, no. 2 (2002): 306–22.

42. Patricia Zimmermann, *Reel Families: A Social History of the Amateur Film* (Bloomington: Indiana University Press, 1995).

43. Jenkins, "*Quentin Tarantino's Star Wars?*," 308–9.

44. Jay David Bolter and Richard Grusin, *Remediation: Understanding New Media* (Cambridge, MA: MIT Press, 2000), 48, 55, 15.

45. Brian Winston, *Media Technology and Society: A History: From the Telegraph to the Internet* (London: Routledge, 1998), 2, 11.

46. Several scholars have addressed the fallacies underpinning film studies' "repression" of or alarm about cinema's intermedia affiliations. For example, see Douglas Gomery, "New Media Economics," in *Post-Theory: Reconstructing Film Studies*, ed. David Bordwell and Noel Carroll (Madison: University of Wisconsin Press, 1996), 407–18; and Laura Kipnis, "Film and Changing Technologies," in *World Cinema: Critical Approaches*, ed. John Hill and Pamela Church Gibson (Oxford: Oxford University Press, 2000), 211–20.

47. For example, in a key discussion of cinema's first novelty phase, Charles Musser shows how indebted early cinema was in subject matter, style, and exhibition to other forms, particularly magic lantern shows. See his "The Early Cinema of Edwin Porter," *Cinema Journal* 19, no. 1 (Fall 1979): 3–37. As cinema moved out of its novelty phase, models more conducive to smoother narrative construction and cinematic visual style came to the fore. On the influence of the short story and other forms on the development of classical Hollywood style, see Kristin Thompson, "The Formulation of the Classical Style, 1909–28," in *The Classical Hollywood Cinema: Film Style & Mode of Production to 1960*, ed. David Bordwell, Janet Staiger, and Kristin Thompson (New York: Columbia University Press, 1985), 157–73.

Conclusion. Of Fortresses and Film Cultures

1. While figures pertaining to piracy are always a matter of debate and the sources for piracy are multifaceted and complex, a study published by AT&T

Labs in 2003 found that almost 80 percent of three hundred copies of feature films appearing on online file-sharing sites had come from industry insiders. For more on this study, see John Schwartz, "Is Legal Action against File Swappers Good Business? Hollywood Is Facing Online Piracy, but It Looks Like an Inside Job," *New York Times*, September 15, 2003, 1, 3. For more on the phenomenon and extent of film piracy worldwide, see the MPAA's official Web site, www.mpaa.org.

2. In terms of restrictions, voting members had to sign a pledge vowing not to circulate their copies (or face the consequence of expulsion from the MPAA). Screeners themselves were encoded so that, in case of piracy, illegal copies could be traced back to the offending Academy member. In a sign of an intent to enforce MPAA regulations that remained after the judicial decision lifting the screener ban, the FBI apprehended an Illinois man early in 2004 for pirating screener copies of Oscar contenders and distributing them on the Internet. The MPAA member who had allegedly given him the screeners, Carmine Caridi, was expelled from the organization. See "An Arrest in a 'Screener' Case," *New York Times*, January 24, 2004, sec. A, 26; and Steven Rosen, "Raiders of the Art House: Is Piracy a Threat to Indie Film?" www.Indiewire.com/biz, March 11, 2004.

3. The phrase, again, is Siegfried Kracauer's, as quoted in Ryall, *Alfred Hitchcock and the British Cinema*, 2.

4. A recent article entitled "Fortress Home: Welcome Mat Bites" commented that in "a nation of households [that] imagines itself under siege . . . for every domestic fear . . . a new product is coming to the rescue" (Bradford McKee, *New York Times*, January 22, 2004, sec. D, 1, 4).

5. Now that most home viewers have moved into DVD, it would be interesting to weigh the preferences of family viewers, a traditionally important clientele for home video purchase and rental, against the primarily male-oriented hardware aesthetic that characterizes home theater and DVD—that is, interesting to see how and if issues of technology and digital quality factor into family choices.

6. Stuart Hall, "Notes on Deconstructing the Popular," in *People's History and Socialist Theory*, ed. Raphael Samuel (London: Routledge and Kegan Paul, 1981), 233.

7. Stuart Hall, quoted in Henry Jenkins, *Textual Poachers: Television Fans and Participatory Culture* (London: Routledge, 1992), 34.

8. Charlotte Brunsdon, *Screen Tastes: Soap Operas to Satellite Dishes* (London: Routledge, 1997), 157. Here Brunsdon reflects on Shaun Moores's work on identification and new technologies.

Selected Bibliography

Adorno, Theodor. "On the Fetish Character in Music and the Regression of Listening." In *The Essential Frankfurt School Reader,* ed. Andrew Arato and Eike Gebhardt, 270–99. New York: Urizen Books, 1978.

Allen, Robert C. "Home Alone Together: Hollywood and the 'Family Film.'" In *Identifying Hollywood Audiences,* ed. Melvyn Stokes and Richard Maltby, 109–31. London: British Film Institute Publishing, 1999.

Altman, Rick. "Television/Sound." In *Studies in Entertainment: Critical Approaches to Mass Culture,* ed. Tania Modleski, 39–54. Bloomington: Indiana University Press, 1986.

Ang, Ien. *Watching Dallas: Soap Opera and the Melodramatic Imagination.* Translated by Della Couling. New York: Methuen, 1985.

Austin, Bruce A. "Home Video: The Second Run 'Theater' of the 1990s." In *Hollywood in the Age of Television,* ed. Tino Balio, 319–49. Cambridge, MA: Unwin Hyman, 1990.

Barthes, Roland. *S/Z.* Translated by Richard Miller. New York: Hill and Wang, 1974.

———. "Upon Leaving the Movie Theater." Translated by Bertrand Augst and Susan White. In *Cinematographic Apparatus: Selected Writings,* ed. Theresa Hak Kyung Cha, 1–4. New York: Tanam Press, 1980.

Baudrillard, Jean. *The System of Objects.* Translated by James Benedict. London: Verso, 1996.

Bazin, André. *What Is Cinema?* Vol. 1. Translated by Hugh Gray. Berkeley: University of California Press, 1967.

Benjamin, Walter. "Unpacking My Library." In *Illuminations,* 59–67. Translated by Harry Zohn. New York: Schocken Books, 1969.

Bhabha, Homi K., ed. *Nation and Narration.* London: Routledge, 1990.

Bird, S. Elizabeth. *The Audience in Everyday Life: Living in a Media World.* New York: Routledge, 2003.

Bobo, Jacqueline. *Black Women as Cultural Readers.* New York: Columbia University Press, 1995.

Boddy, William. "Archaeologies of Electronic Vision and the Gendered Spectator." *Screen* 35, no. 2 (1994): 105–22.

Bolter, Jay David, and Richard Grusin. *Remediation: Understanding New Media.* Cambridge, MA: MIT Press, 2000.

Bommes, Michael, and Patrick Wright. "'Charms of Residence': The Public and the Past." In *Making Histories: Studies in History Writing and Politics,* ed. Richard Johnson et al., 253–310. Minneapolis: University of Minnesota Press, 1982.

Bourdieu, Pierre. *Distinction: A Social Critique of the Judgement of Taste.* Translated by Richard Nice. Cambridge, MA: Harvard University Press, 1984.

———. *The Field of Cultural Production: Essays on Art and Literature.* New York: Columbia University Press, 1993.

Brooks, John. *Showing Off in America: From Conspicuous Consumption to Parody Display.* Boston: Little, Brown, 1981.

Brunsdon, Charlotte. *Screen Tastes: Soap Opera to Satellite Dishes.* London: Routledge, 1997.

Budd, Mike. "The Moments of Caligari." In *The Cabinet of Dr. Caligari: Texts, Contexts, Histories,* ed. Mike Budd, 7–119. New Brunswick, NJ: Rutgers University Press, 1990.

Caldwell, John Thornton. *Televisuality: Style, Crisis, and Authority in American Television.* New Brunswick, NJ: Rutgers University Press, 1995.

Calinescu, Matei. *Rereading.* New Haven, CT: Yale University Press, 1993.

Carby, Hazel. "The Multicultural Wars." In *Black Popular Culture,* ed. Gina Dent, 187–99. Seattle: Bay Press, 1992.

Chakrabarty, Dipesh. "The Death of History? Historical Consciousness and the Culture of Late Capitalism." *Public Culture* 4, no. 2 (1992): 47–65.

Clark, Ian. *Globalization and Fragmentation: International Relations in the Twentieth Century.* New York: Oxford University Press, 1997.

Clifford, James. "On Collecting Art and Culture." In *The Cultural Studies Reader,* ed. Simon During, 49–73. London: Routledge, 1993.

Cohan, Steven. "Judy on the Net: Judy Garland Fandom and the 'Gay Thing' Revisited." In *Keyframes: Popular Cinema and Cultural Studies,* ed. Matthew Tinkcom and Amy Vallarejo, 119–36. London: Routledge, 2001.

Collins, Ava Preacher. "Loose Canons: Constructing Cultural Traditions Inside and Outside the Academy." In *Film Theory Goes to the Movies,* ed. Jim Collins et al., 86–102. New York: Routledge, 1993.

Collins, Jim. *Architectures of Excess: Cultural Life in the Information Age.* New York: Routledge, 1995.

Corrigan, Timothy. *A Cinema without Walls: Movies and Culture after Vietnam.* New Brunswick, NJ: Rutgers University Press, 1991.

Crafton, Donald. "The View from Termite Terrace: Caricature and Parody in Warner Bros. Animation." In *Reading the Rabbit: Explorations in Warner Bros. Animation,* ed. Kevin Sandler, 101–20. New Brunswick, NJ: Rutgers University Press, 1998.

Cubitt, Sean. *Time-Shift: On Video Culture*. London: Routledge, 1991.

Dentith, Simon. *Parody*. New York: Routledge, 2000.

Dinsmore, Uma. "Chaos, Order, and Plastic Boxes: The Significance of Videotapes for People Who Collect Them." In *The Television Studies Book*, ed. Christine Geraghty and David Lusted, 315–26. London: Arnold, 1998.

Dinsmore-Tuli, Uma. "The Pleasures of 'Home Cinema,' or Watching Movies on Telly: An Audience Study of Cinephiliac VCR Use." *Screen* 41, no. 3 (2000): 315–27.

Dobrow, Julia. "The Re-run Ritual: Using VCRs to Re-view." In *Social and Cultural Aspects of VCR Use*, ed. Julia Dobrow, 181–93. Hillsdale, NJ: Lawrence Erlbaum Associates, 1990.

Doherty, Thomas. *Teenagers and Teenpics: The Juvenalization of American Movies in the 1950s*. Boston: Unwin Hyman, 1988.

Dyer, Richard. *White*. London: Routledge, 1997.

Eco, Umberto. *Travels in Hyperreality*. Translated by William Weaver. New York: Harcourt, Brace, 1986.

Ellis, John. *Visible Fictions: Cinema, Television, Video*. London: Routledge, 1992.

Elsey, Eileen, and Andrew Kelly. *In Short: A Guide to Short Film-Making in the Digital Age*. London: British Film Institute Publishing, 2002.

Ewen, Stuart. *Captains of Consciousness: Advertising and the Social Roots of Consumer Culture*. New York: McGraw-Hill, 1976.

Gehring, Wes. *Parody as Film Genre*. Westport, CT: Greenwood Press, 1999.

Geirland, John, and Eva Sonesh-Kedar. *Digital Babylon: How the Geeks, the Suits, and the Ponytails Tried to Bring Hollywood to the Internet*. New York: Arcade Publishing, 1999.

Gomery, Douglas. *Shared Pleasures: A History of Movie Presentation in the United States*. Madison: University of Wisconsin Press, 1992.

Grainge, Paul. "Reclaiming Heritage: Colourization, Culture Wars, and the Politics of Nostalgia." *Cultural Studies* 13, no. 4 (1999): 621–38.

Gray, Ann. *Video Playtime: The Gendering of a Leisure Technology*. London: Routledge, 1992.

Hall, Stuart. "Notes on Deconstructing the Popular." In *People's History and Socialist Theory*, ed. Raphael Samuel, 227–40. London: Routledge and Kegan Paul, 1981.

Hirsch, Eric. "New Technologies and Domestic Consumption." In *The Television Studies Book*, ed. Christine Geraghty and David Lusted, 158–74. London: Arnold, 1998.

Holton, Robert J. *Globalization and the Nation State*. London: Macmillan Press, 1998.

Jameson, Fredric. *The Geopolitical Aesthetic: Cinema and Space in the World System*. Bloomington: Indiana University Press, 1992.

Jancovich, Mark. "Cult Fictions: Cult Movies, Subcultural Capital, and the Production of Cultural Distinctions." *Cultural Studies* 16, no. 2 (2002): 306–22.

Jenkins, Henry. "*Quentin Tarantino's Star Wars?* Digital Cinema, Media Convergence, and Participatory Culture." In *Rethinking Media Change: The Aesthetics of Transition,* ed. David Thorburn and Henry Jenkins, 281–312. Cambridge, MA: MIT Press, 2003.

———. *Textual Poachers: Television Fans and Participatory Culture.* London: Routledge, 1992.

Jones, Sara Gwenllian. "Phantom Menace: Killer Fans, Consumer Activism, and Digital Filmmakers." In *Underground U.S.A.: Filmmaking beyond the Hollywood Canon,* ed. Xavier Mendik and Steven Jay Schneider, 169–79. London: Wallflower Press, 2002.

Kammen, Michael. *Mystic Chords of Memory: The Transformation of Tradition in American Culture.* New York: Vintage Books, 1993.

Komiya, Megumi, and Barry Litman. "The Economics of the Prerecorded Videocassette Industry." In *Social and Cultural Aspects of VCR Use,* ed. Julia R. Dobrow, 25–44. Hillsdale, NJ: Lawrence Erlbaum Associates, 1990.

Kramer, Peter. "The Lure of the Big Picture: Film, Television, and Hollywood." In *Big Picture, Small Screen: Relations between Film and Television,* ed. John Hill and Martin McLoone, 9–46. Luton, UK: University of Luton Press, 1996.

Kuhn, Annette. *Family Secrets: Acts of Memory and Imagination.* London: Verso, 1995.

Lipsitz, George. *Time Passages: Collective Memory and American Popular Culture.* Minneapolis: University of Minnesota Press, 1990.

Luckett, Moya. "'Filming the Family': Home Movie Systems and the Domestication of Spectatorship." *Velvet Light Trap* 36 (1995): 21–32.

Marchand, Roland. *Advertising and the American Dream: Making Way for Modernity 1920–1940.* Berkeley: University of California Press, 1985.

Metz, Christian. *The Imaginary Signifier: Psychoanalysis and the Cinema.* Translated by Celia Britton et al. Bloomington: Indiana University Press, 1977.

Miller, Toby, Nitin Govil, John McMurria, and Richard Maxwell. *Global Hollywood.* London: British Film Institute Publishing, 2001.

Mitsui, Toru, and Shuhei Hosokawa, eds. *Karaoke around the World: Global Technology, Local Singing.* London: Routledge, 1998.

Modleski, Tania. *Loving with a Vengeance: Mass-Produced Fantasies for Women.* New York: Methuen, 1984.

Moores, Shaun. *Satellite Television and Everyday Life.* Luton, UK: University of Luton Press, 1996.

Morley, David. *Home Territories: Media, Mobility, and Identity.* London: Routledge, 2000.

———. "Television: Not So Much a Visual Medium, More a Visible Object." In *Visual Culture,* ed. Chris Jenks, 170–89. London: Routledge, 1995.

———. *Television, Audiences & Cultural Studies.* London: Routledge, 1992.

Morley, David, and Kevin Robins, *Spaces of Identity: Global Media, Electronic Landscapes, and Cultural Boundaries.* London: Routledge, 1995.

Naremore, James. "Authorship." In *A Companion to Film Theory,* ed. Toby Miller and Robert Stam, 9–24. Oxford: Blackwell Publishers, 1999.

————. *More Than Night: Film Noir in Its Contexts.* Berkeley: University of California Press, 1998.

Nash, Melanie, and Martti Lahti, "'Almost Ashamed to Say I Am One of Those Girls': *Titanic*, Leonardo DiCaprio, and the Paradoxes of Girls' Fandom." In *Titanic: Anatomy of a Blockbuster*, ed. Kevin S. Sandler and Gaylyn Studlar, 64–88. New Brunswick, NJ: Rutgers University Press, 1999.

Negra, Diane. "*Titanic*, Survivalism, and the Millennial Myth." In *Titanic: Anatomy of a Blockbuster*, ed. Kevin S. Sandler and Gaylyn Studlar, 220–38. New Brunswick, NJ: Rutgers University Press, 1999.

Nell, Victor. *Lost in a Book: The Psychology of Reading for Pleasure.* New Haven, CT: Yale University Press, 1988.

Parsons, Patrick R., and Robert M. Friedan. *The Cable and Satellite Television Industries.* Needham Heights, MA: Allyn and Bacon, 1998.

Popular Memory Group. "Popular Memory: Theory, Politics, Method." In *Making Histories: Studies in History Writing and Politics*, ed. Richard Johnson et al., 205–52. Minneapolis: University of Minnesota Press, 1982.

Radway, Janice. *Reading the Romance: Women, Patriarchy, and Popular Literature.* Chapel Hill: University of North Carolina Press, 1984.

Rosenzweig, Roy. "From Rum Shop to Rialto: Workers and Movies." In *Moviegoing in America*, ed. Gregory Waller, 27–45. Oxford: Blackwell Publishers, 2002.

Rossler, Martha. "Image Simulations, Computer Manipulations: Some Considerations." *Afterimage* 17, no. 4 (1989): 7–11.

Ryall, Tom. *Alfred Hitchcock and the British Cinema.* Urbana: University of Illinois Press, 1986.

Segrave, Kerry. *Movies at Home: How Hollywood Came to Television.* Jefferson, NC: McFarland, 1999.

Seiter, Ellen. *Sold Separately: Parents & Children in Consumer Culture.* New Brunswick, NJ: Rutgers University Press, 1995.

Sergi, Gianluca. "Blockbusting Sound: The Case of *The Fugitive*." In *Movie Blockbusters*, ed. Julian Stringer, 141–52. London: Routledge, 2003.

Silverstone, Roger. *Television and Everyday Life.* London: Routledge, 1994.

Silverstone, Roger, and Eric Hirsch. *Consuming Technologies: Media and Information in Domestic Spaces.* London: Routledge, 1992.

Singer, Ben. "Early Home Cinema and the Edison Projecting Kinetoscope." *Film History* 2, no. 1 (1988): 37–70.

Slide, Anthony. *Before Video: A History of the Non-Theatrical Film.* Westport, CT: Greenwood Press, 1992.

————. *Nitrate Won't Wait: Film Preservation in the United States.* Jefferson, NC: McFarland, 1992.

Sontag, Susan. "The Decay of Cinema." *New York Times Magazine*, February 25, 1996, 60–61.

Spigel, Lynn. *Make Room for Television: Television and the Family Ideal in Postwar America.* Chicago: University of Chicago Press, 1992.

Spigel, Lynn, and Henry Jenkins. "Same Bat Channel, Different Bat Times: Mass Culture and Popular Memory." In *The Many Lives of Batman: Critical Approaches to a Superhero and His Media*, ed. Roberta E. Pearson and William Uricchio, 117–48. New York: Routledge, 1991.

Staiger, Janet. "Writing the History of American Film Reception." In *Hollywood Spectatorship: Changing Perceptions of Cinema Audiences*, ed. Melvyn Stokes and Richard Maltby, 117–48. London: British Film Institute Publishing, 2001.

Stewart, Susan. *On Longing: Narratives of the Miniature, the Gigantic, the Souvenir, the Collection*. Durham, NC: Duke University Press, 1993.

Sturken, Marita. *Tangled Memories: The Vietnam War, the AIDS Epidemic, and the Politics of Remembering*. Berkeley: University of California Press, 1997.

Tan, Ed S. *Emotion and the Structure of Narrative Film: Film as an Emotion Machine*. Translated by Barbara Fasting. Mahwah, NJ: Lawrence Erlbaum Associates, 1996.

Tashiro, Charles. "The Contradictions of Video Collecting." *Film Quarterly* 50 (1996–97): 11–18.

Thornton, Sarah. *Club Cultures: Music, Media, and Subcultural Capital*. Cambridge: Polity Press, 1995.

Tyler-May, Elaine. *Homeward Bound: American Families in the Cold War Era*. New York: Basic Books, 1988.

Walkerdine, Valerie. "Some Day My Prince Will Come: Young Girls and the Preparation for Adolescent Sexuality." In *Gender and Generation*, ed. Angela McRobbie and Mica Nava, 162–84. London: Macmillan Publishers, 1984.

———. "Video Replay: Families, Films, and Fantasy." In *Formations of Fantasy*, ed. Victor Burgin et al., 167–99. London: Methuen, 1986.

Wallace, Michael. "Mickey Mouse History: Portraying the Past at Disney World." *Radical History Review* 32 (1985): 33–57.

———. "Reflections on the History of Historic Preservation." In *Presenting the Past: Essays on History and the Public*, ed. Susan Porter Benson et al., 165–99. Philadelphia: Temple University Press, 1986.

———. "Ronald Reagan and the Politics of History." *Tikkun* 2, no. 1 (1987): 14–21.

Waller, Gregory. *Main Street Amusements: Movies and Commercial Entertainment in a Southern City, 1896–1930*. Washington: Smithsonian Institution Press, 1995.

Wasko, Janet. *Hollywood in the Information Age: Beyond the Silver Screen*. Austin: University of Texas Press, 1994.

Williams, Phil. "Feeding Off the Past: The Evolution of the Television Rerun." *Journal of Popular Film and Television* 21, no. 4 (1994): 52–73.

Williams, Raymond. *The Sociology of Culture*. New York: Schocken Books, 1982.

———. *Television: Technology and Cultural Form*. New York: Schocken Books, 1974.

Winston, Brian. *Media Technology and Society: A History: From the Telegraph to the Internet.* London: Routledge, 1998.

Wood, Julian. "Repeatable Pleasures: Notes on Young People's Use of Video." In *Reading Audiences: Young People and the Media,* ed. David Buckingham, 184–201. Manchester: Manchester University Press, 1993.

Wyatt, Justin. *High Concept: Movies and Marketing in Hollywood.* Austin: University of Texas Press, 1994.

Zimmermann, Patricia. *Reel Families: A Social History of the Amateur Film.* Bloomington: Indiana University Press, 1995.

Index

Italicized page numbers refer to illustrations and tables.

-philes, 245; and film collecting, 54–56, 61, 63–64, 68, 85, 88, 90, 261n30, 262n56; and home theater, 22, 45, 47; and repeat viewing, 272n37
phonograph, 6, 17–18
PI (1998), 230
"Pies Wide Shut," 210
Ping, Yuen Wo, 61
Pioneer Entertainment, 39, 43, 66, 83
piracy, 5, 129–30, 191, 195, 224, 239–40, 278–79n1, 279n2
Piranha (1978), 36
The Pirate (1948), 81
Pixar, 78–79, 79
PlanetOut.com, 199
plasma TV, 26, 44
Platoon (1986), 83–84
playback technologies: and film collecting, 55–56, 60, 63, 76, 83–84; and repeat viewing, 136, 138, 187. *See also* hardware aesthetic
PlayStation, 10, 21
PlayStation Portables (PSPs), 195
pocket cinema, 195
Pocket PCs, 195
Point Break (1991), 166
Poitier, Sidney, 112, 264n33
Polk Audio, 76
Pollack, Sydney, 123
pop feminism, 170–71, 173, 188
popular canons, 6, 8, 143–51, 146–47, 159
popular culture. *See* mass culture
Popular Memory Group, 133
postmodernism, 33, 200, 227, 277n33
"post-9/11 cocooning," 25
Potelle, Efram, 278n40
pothead films. *See* stoner classics
Premiere Magazine, 202
premium cable movie channels, 8
presentism, 75, 87–88, 248, 261–62n54
preservation. *See* film preservation
Press, Terry, 2
prestige factor, 99–100, 162
Pretty in Pink (1986), 146, 175
Pretty Woman (1990), 144, 146, 159, 171–73, 171

The Princess Bride (1987), 146, 182
private. *See* public and private
privilege, sense of, 34, 47
producing cultures, 10, 13, 250; and film collecting, 85–86, 89; and film shorts, 15, 193. *See also* consuming cultures
progressive narratives, 121–22
Project Greenlight, 231–32
projection systems, 21, 26, 26, 27, 38
promotions. *See* advertising; marketing campaigns
Propaganda Films, 203
prosthetics, 69, 70
protectionism, 129
Protestant ethic, 155–56
Proust, Marcel, 134, 174
public and private: and film collecting, 57–58, 88–89; and home film cultures, 8–13, 242–43; and memory, 132–34; in motion picture theaters vs. home theaters, 17–21, 23, 29
Pulp Fiction (1994), 144–45, 147, 149, 154, 157, 158, 162, 165, 184
puppet masters, 73
purists, 158, 187, 247
puzzle films, 157–60, 158, 161–63, 187, 188, 243–44, 272nn36–37
puzzle solving, 70, 71, 73

Quaid, Dennis, 97
QuickTime, 197

The Race to Save 100 Years (documentary), 116
racial identity, 13–14; and classic Hollywood films, 94, 101, 109, 111–14, 113, 115, 264n33, 264–65n34, 265n35; and film collecting, 63–64; and home theater, 20, 46–47, 52; and repeat viewing, 137–38, 145, 150, 174, 269n10, 270nn12–13, 271n24
radio, 7, 9, 18, 33, 38, 92
Radio City Music Hall, 128
Radway, Janice, 160, 172
Rainbow Media Holdings, Inc., 95–96
Randall, Alice, 226, 276–77n31

Text: 10/13 Aldus
Display: Franklin Gothic
Compositor: Binghamton Valley Composition, LLC
Printer and Binder: Maple-Vail Manufacturing Group